Collected Works of Professor B.R. Grover
Vol. II

Medieval Punjab : Perspectives on Historiography and Polity

Collected Works of
Professor B.R. Grover
Vol. II

Medieval Punjab : Perspectives on Historiography and Polity

Edited by
Amrita Grover
Dr. Anju Grover Chaudhary
Dr. J C Dua

Originals
(an imprint of Low Price Publications)
Delhi-110052

Distributed by
D.K. Publishers Distributors (P) Ltd.
4834/24, Ansari Road, Darya Ganj,
New Delhi-110002
Phones: 41562573, 41562575, 41562578
e-mail: dkpd@del3.vsnl.net.in
visit us at: www.dkpd.com

First Published 2006

ISBN 81-88629-34-0 (Vol. 2)

Published by
Originals
(an imprint of Low Price Publications)
A-6, Nimri Commercial Centre,
Near Ashok Vihar Phase-IV, Delhi-110052
Phones: 27302453
e-mail: lpp@nde.vsnl.net.in
visit us at: www.lppindia.com

Printed at
D K Fine Art Press P Ltd.
Delhi-110052

PRINTED IN INDIA

Dedicated to the Memory of my
Esteemed Brother
Professor B.R. Grover

Amrita Grover

About the Author

(b. 1923- d. 2001)

Professor B.R. Grover, former Chairman of the Indian Council of Historical Research, with an academic and administrative career spanning more than 55 years, has left an indelible mark as one of India's most eminent and dedicated historians. He has left behind a massive wealth of historical research based on original Persian, Urdu, Ottoman Turkish, Punjabi and English sources. Known for doing intensive research in the archives and libraries of India, several European countries and the United States of America, Professor Grover had carved out a distinct position for himself as a moving encyclopaedia of source material on agrarian history of the Mughals, especially the land revenue administration.

Upon his death on May 10, 2001, the then Prime Minister Atal Behari Vajpayee paid him a rich tribute, stating: "He would always be remembered for his formidable legacy of excellence, erudition, and dedication to historical research and academic administration." Dr. Murli Manohar Joshi, then Minister of Human Resources and Scientific Research, paid him a personal homage and called him a real "Karma Yogi". He said, "He lived like a Yogi and died like a Yogi." Former Vice President of India, Justice Hidayatullah, had also applauded him for his research. His colleagues described him as "a man of sterling qualities of head and heart"; and "a dynamic and objective head of country's premier historical Institute who has left a rich legacy of his outstanding achievements in the world of historical research," among other things.

Born on February 10, 1923, Professor Grover started his career in teaching in 1946 in Lahore and later taught at the University of Punjab and various universities in Delhi until 1974, including Delhi University, Jawahar Lal Nehru University and Jamia Milia Islamia, where he also served as head of the Department of Indian History and Culture. In 1974, he was called upon to join as Director cum Member-Secretary of the newly established Indian Council of Historical Research (ICHR), a premier historical research Institute, where he served from 1974 to 1985 as Director and was later appointed as Chairman in 1999. For his long association with ICHR, his colleague, Prof. A.R. Khan, wrote in his obituary: "On account of his long association with the Council and the services rendered by him to it, Professor Grover became an institution by himself and he and the Council became a synonymy, as the latter came to be identified, both in India and abroad, with Professor Grover, even when he was not holding any office in the Council."

Initially having received training at Paris under the auspices of UNESCO for the promotion of history as a means of international understanding, Professor Grover wrote and published books in British history. Later, because of his deep interest in the study of original sources and his proficiency in Persian language, his research interests shifted to the medieval period of Indian history. His interest later widened to the study and research in regard to the social, cultural and economic impact of the Indian immigrants in West Asia and East European countries. As an avid researcher, Professor Grover wrote and published copiously on various aspects of the Mughal Agrarian System, Patterns of Rural Trade, The Concept of Village Community and a host of other topics. His writings, mostly published in prestigious journals, like the journals of the Delhi School of Economics and the proceedings of various conferences, became nodal points for the scholars of his generation. His published writings in *The Indian Economic and Social History Review, Proceedings of the Indian Historical Records Commission, Indian Archives, Proceedings of the Punjab History Conference, Punjab Past and Present* and *The Proceedings of the Indian History Congress,* among others, brought him national and international recognition. At an early stage of Professor Grover's career, Prof. M.M. Pearson of Pennsylvania University, U.S.A., wrote about his Mughal Agrarian writings as "...an impressive start...brilliant, which makes fundamental contribution in this area." Prof. C.A. Bailey of Cambridge University, complimented him for "comprehensive listing of materials" and "excellent bibliographies."

Because of his expertise in historical manuscripts/documents and objects, Professor Grover was nominated by the Government of India for several honorary positions such as member of the Indian Historical Records Commission, member of the Historical Documents Purchase Committee of the National Archives of India, member of the Committee on Preservation and Development of Cultural Heritage of Delhi, and an expert member of the Verification Committee of National Museum, India. Professor Grover was also a member of the Publication Committee of the "Comprehensive History of India". For the Indian History Congress, he served intermittently as a Joint Secretary, a Treasurer and Sectional President (Medieval India). Professor Grover also edited the well-known Time Capsule in 1978, and advised the Government to display it in the National Museum instead of inserting it again underground. He also served on the Editorial Board constituted by the Government of India for the production of documentaries on "Freedom Struggle for India's Independence, 1984-2001." Under this scheme, more than 75 documentaries were published by the Films Division, Ministry of Information and Broadcasting.

Professor Grover represented India at several international organizations, including UNESCO in 1951; Indian delegate to West Germany, 1957; delegate to the International Conference in History, Bucharest, 1980; delegate to the International Conference on the Bulgarian Studies, Sofia, 1986; and delegate to the World Archaeological Congress, Croatia, 1998, among others. Besides participating in numerous Indo-European cultural exchange programmes, presiding over innumerable regional/national/international seminars and conferences and contributing papers to various national/ international seminars and conferences, he also lectured widely in West Germany (1957), Bulgaria (1986), Zagreb (1998), UK (1998), Holland (1998), and United States (1998 and 2000).

Professor Grover received several honours and awards for his historical research. For his writings on Georgi Dimitrov, the "Role of the Indian Immigrants in the Culture and Economy of the West Asian and East European Countries During the Medieval Age," and "The Social, Religious and Agrarian Aspects in East Europe, especially Bulgaria under the Ottoman-Turkish Rule (14th-19th centuries)," he was awarded Georgi Dimitrov Gold Medal by the Peoples Republic of Bulgaria. For his work on Punjab History, Professor Grover was awarded Saropa Roll of Honour by the Punjabi University, Patiala, in 1996. A life-long scholar of medieval and Islamic India, Professor Grover again came in limelight in 2001 when (upon the demolition of Buddhist statues at Bamiyan by the Taliban government), his expert opinion was sought by the Indian media to determine whether there was any parallel between Bamiyan and Ayodhya.

As a distinguished historian and a scholar with an integrated and scientific approach to the analysis of the historical process, Professor Grover, being a liberal thinker, was a great believer in the social cohesion and national integration in India and made an immense contribution in this regard.

Introduction

Professor B.R. Grover, doyen of Punjab history, was a veteran scholar of medieval Punjab. He had been Director and subsequently Chairman of the Indian Council of Historical Research, New Delhi. He was one of the builders of Punjab History Conference, Punjabi University, Patiala, and has been attending it regularly. Whenever he came to attend the Punjab History Conference, he always consulted Persian works or other records, in the Punjab Archives, Patiala. He was so much devoted to history records that he could lay his hands on research material wherever he attended a seminar or conference. In 1948, I was his student of M.A. History in the East Punjab Camp College, New Delhi. Later on we became friends and fellow travellers on the path of Punjab history research. I am grateful to Ms. Amrita Grover, his sister, who has asked me to write an Introduction to his research papers to be published in the book form.

About half of the papers in this anthology deal with historiography of medieval Punjab. It has been argued that we should follow the method of comparative study in dealing with or study of administration of Turkish rulers. It is essential to know how Turkish institutions worked in Afghanistan and with what limitations. The nature of Turkish rule in Central Asia has to be understood. Besides that it is essential to know what were the conditions in India before the Turkish rule was established.

In 'Some Problems of Indian Historiography with a special reference to Punjab', Professor Grover has quoted C.A. Bayly's discussion on the cause for the decline of Mughal Empire and had come to the conclusion rightly that the religious policy of Aurangzeb was, by and large, the main cause of disintegration of the Mughal Empire.

The connotation of the word "culture" has been discussed and made clear. It is not synonymous with religion. We cannot appreciate the culture of people without going into details of various aspects of social-economic pattern in an integrated manner. It has been stated that 'for clear understanding of the 13th -16th centuries of Turkish and Afghan rule in the Punjab, one has to understand not only their religion but the institutions they had known before the establishment of their rule and the extent to which they were enforced, their limitations and evolution in practice. One has to equally understand the prehistoric Indian socio-economic and political institutions which continued in operation subject to the limitation imposed by Turkish rule'. For instance, Panchayat in the villages continued to work as before despite several changes in the power structure in the central government.

Regarding Regional history, it has been rightly stated:

"Regional history is a very fruitful exercise as it affords full opportunities for the exploitation of regional source material of multifarious nature. All the same, an objective approach and disciplined methodology of historical research may caution against parochialism and chauvinism."

The paper entitled "Analysis of the Contemporary Durrani Revenue Documents and Correspondence pertaining to Patiala Chieftainship" is a very interesting one. It has translated the two original Persian documents relating to Baba Ala Singh, the founder of the Patiala Kingdom.

In the paper, "Agrarian System of the Punjab during the 18th century," Professor Grover has brought out a very realistic picture of the times: "The 18th century is a crucial period in the Agrarian history of the Punjab. The socio-political forces had shaken the foundations of the Mughal Empire to the point of dismemberment. This had great impact on the regional polity and agrarian set-up with mutual reaction. A comparison of the dominant zamindari clans as known from the *Ain-i-Akbari* (late 16th century) with the dominant clannish order noticeable from the 18th century sources shows considerable change and reshuffling in the dominant and suppressed clannish order in respect of the enjoyment of the surplus produce and land rights. At the same time, the emergence of the Sikh misls, based on traditional territorial zamindari pattern with landed hierarchy, the suppression of the other landed castes into *khud-kashta*, *riaya* and *muzarian* for the realisation of the revenues and extraction of the surplus produce, the inter-misl rivalry and mutual warfare, is a continuous feature till the emergence of the Lahore Kingdom under Ranjit Singh by the end of the 18th and early 19th century."

Professor Grover was one of the historians not committed to any ideology of preconceived notions. Like a true scholar, he would delve deep into sources, especially Persian ones.

This anthology of research papers provides a mine of information relating to medieval Punjab, its historiography and source material. Eighteenth century history of Punjab had been his special field of study. Professor Grover's research papers would be more beneficial to the non-Persian knowing scholars of medieval Punjab history.

The intensive effort made by the editors Amrita Grover, Anju Grover Chaudhary & J C Dua in collecting all these valuable scattered research papers of Professor B R Grover is highly commendable.

I hope that the students of history and public in general will be greatly benefitted by the publication of his research papers.

KIRPAL SINGH
Former Professor and Head
Punjab Historical Studies Department,
Punjabi University,
Patiala

New Delhi
9 May, 2005

Preface

Professor Grover believed that Regional history is the 'key to history' and its study and analysis "is a very fruitful exercise as it affords full opportunity for the exploitation of regional source material of multifarious nature," which has essentially to be linked with a larger landscape at all India level. The Punjab under Maharaja Ranjit Singh and his successors attracted a great deal of attention on the part of the British and the Indian historians, and whereas a number of writers have laid emphasis on the political and religious aspects of the Punjab, not much attention was paid to the agrarian aspects and historiographical study about eighteenth century Punjab. This neglected area was covered by Professor Grover through his critical study and analysis about the nature of relationship that existed between the Durrani chiefs and the Sikh Sardars, and between the Punjab Hill Chiefs and the Mughals, the Afghans and the Lahore Darbar and other important aspects bearing on social and economic life of the people in both rural and urban areas.

This second volume of **The Collected Works of Professor B.R. Grover** presents a collection of Professor Grover's articles mainly on $18^{th}-19^{th}$ century Punjab history including its agrarian aspects—another forte of his expertise.

Professor Grover, being well-versed in Persian, Urdu, Punjabi, and English and with an insatiable hunger for more and more knowledge about the history of Punjab, not only unearthed the hitherto untapped sources but also interpreted them and presented them in the form of several articles and research papers. Being the founder-member of Punjab History Conference, most of the articles included in the present volume are the ones presented there as a delegate, as Sectional President (Medieval Punjab), as General President, and Guest of Honour, and published in the *Proceedings* of the Conference or in *Punjab—Past and Present*. The other articles included in this volume were presented by him in some national and international seminars. For example the article on 'The Emergence of *Nanak Panth*—A Hindu Sect and its Evolution unto Khalsa from the Sixteenth to Nineteenth Centuries. (Based on the Contemporary

Persian and Gurumukhi (Punjabi) Source-Material' was presented at *The XXXVI International Congress of Asian and North-African Studies,* Montreal (Canada) 27th August–2nd September 2000, and 'Political and Social Situation of Punjab after Ranjit Singh Era' was presented as *Maharaja Ranjit Singh Memorial Lecture,* organized by the Punjabi Academy, Delhi, on 9th October, 1992.

Some of the articles presented by Professor Grover at various conferences were, for instance, 'Relationship between the Sovereign State (the Mughals and Afghans) and Punjab Hill Chiefs during the 17th and 18th centuries (A Case Study of Chamba Chieftainship based on Bhuri Singh Museum, Chamba Documents)', 'Relationship between the Lahore Darbar and Punjab Hill Chief during the first half of the 19th century till 1846', 'Relationship between the Sirmur Chieftainship and the Mughal State based on the Sirmur Family Mughal Documents (second half of 17th and early 18th centuries)', 'The Importance of *Nuskha-i-Insha-i-Majma al Qawanin* of Ganesh Das Badehra *(Munshiat-i-Ganesh Das)* for the late 18th and early 19th centuries history of the Punjab', 'An Analysis of the Contemporary Durrani Revenue Documents and Correspondence Pertaining to the Patiala Chieftainship (Zamindari) during the later half of the 19th century'.

Professor Grover's research on various aspects of Punjab history shows that during the 18th century, the socio-economic forces shook the foundations of the Mughal Empire to the point of dismemberment. This had great impact on the regional polity and agrarian set up. There was a considerable change and reshuffling in the dominant and suppressed clannish order in respect of enjoyment of surplus produce and land rights. At the same time, the emergence of Sikh *misls* based on traditional territorial *zamindari* pattern with landed hierarchy led to the suppression of the other landed castes into *khudkashta-riaya* and *muzarian* for the realization of the revenues and exaction of the surplus produce. "The Sikh Sardars... were as much interested in the territorial superior *zamindari* claims and suzerainty over the cis-Sutlej territories, Sutlej-Jamuna regions *(subha* Delhi), territories to the north and around Delhi itself and even Rajasthan as other powers of the times *viz.,* the Marathas, the Rohilas, and the Jats"; "It is rather significant to note that the chronicles of the Sikh period ordinarily do not refer to the *peshkash* and use other general terms denoting the revenues to be paid by... (the) chiefs"; and "A close examination of *Nuskha-i-Insha-i-Majma al Qawanin* reveals striking elements of continuity in the local revenue administration from the Mughal age to the Durrani phase as well as that of the Sikh (Khalsa) Sardars and Muslim and Hindu zamindars who assumed the role of Chiefs, even though on fragmented scale in the West Punjab before the establishment of Kingdom of Maharaja Ranjit Singh."

The 18th century Punjab politics assumed triangular character with three main contestants: viz, the Mughals, the Sikh *Misls,* and the Durranis of Kabul. During the first half of the 18th century, the Mughal government had its hold over the administrative pattern and agrarian landed classes. But during the second half of the century, the Mughal sovereign rights over the Punjab territories had practically vanished and the Durrani rule of Kabul was reestablished. Apart from the occupation of Kashmir and Multan, the Durranis claimed political sovereignty over the Punjab territories and realized *peshkash* more or less on the Mughal pattern. However, the Durrani rule was rather intermittent and the Sikh *misls* always tried to assert as a *de-facto* power whereas the Durranis continued to claim only *de-jure* political rights.

Since Professor Grover found that "no adequate scientific analysis has been done in respect of relationship covering the economic aspects involved between the local chiefs and the sovereign power", and "there are a number of issues which have still to be gone into based on functional analysis rather than merely on theoretical basis," he felt that it was necessary to provide a scientific as well as functional analysis, and as such, gave a detailed description of many aspects on which the chronicles are either silent or make a cursory reference. He strongly believed that a scholar has to "deliberately adopt the method of following a historical process step by step which according to annalistic method is blended with the mode of fitting the facts within a well-defined frame of institutions", and he put this to practice as his writings reflect a methodical scientific as well as functional analysis of issues within well-defined frame of institutions. For example, regarding the issue of "whether the India polity was feudal in character or whether the chieftainships within a big state were autonomous in character or the territories of the chieftains in a larger state by themselves were segmented states," he analyzed these against "the nature of the political power as well as demographic and tribal background of the people settled in different parts of India."

Based on sound methodical analysis tailored to the issues of the relationship between the sovereign State and Punjab Hill Chiefs; relationship between the Sirmur Chieftainship and the Mughal State; Relationship between the Lahore Darbar and the Punjab Hill Chiefs during the first half of the 19th century, etc. some of the conclusions offered by Professor Grover in the articles being published in this volume are: "The (Chamba) documents . . . make it absolutely clear that the zamindari pattern of the Chamba chieftainship was based on the hierarchical pattern of the landed intermediaries (zamindars) who acted as malguzars (revenue peers) to the Raja of Chamba who was regarded as superior (*bazurg*) zamindar-cum-jagirdar in respect of this pargana".

Apart from making an extensive study of the various aspects of 18th-19th centuries Punjab history, Professor Grover also made a critical analysis of the philosophy of Guru Nanak. He has opined that "Though basically devoted to the Bhakti school of thought, he (Guru Nanak) evolved a fresh socio-economic philosophy and code of conduct to be pursued by the elite and the common people." "The gradual transformation of the socio-religious character of the *Nanak-Panth* into socio-religious cum political aspect of the Sikh community comprising followers from various clans *(aqwam)* and castes (jatis) during the course of the 17th and 18th centuries is a significant feature of the social change."

The editors are confident that this collection of articles written by Professor Grover would not only give a significant insight into the various aspects of the history of Punjab but would also prove a valuable source material for the students of Punjab history. As most of these chapters consist of papers presented at various conferences on similar topics, there may be some repetition. The editors did not consider it desirable to make any changes since this is a collection of Professor Grover's original writings.

The editors are grateful to Professor Kirpal Singh, former Professor of History and Head, Punjab Historical Studies Department, Punjabi University, Patiala, for sparing his valuable time and being kind enough to write an Introduction to this volume.

The editors are deeply indebted to Dr. Surinder Singh, an expert in the study and a collector of coins for supplying the missing write-up on the obverse of the Nanak Shah coin mentioned in Chapter 12 on Maharaja Ranjit Singh's administration.

The editors also express their sincere thanks to Originals (an imprint of Low Price Publications), for undertaking this publication with usual scrupulous care.

Ms. Amrita Grover
Dr. Anju Grover Chaudhary
Dr. J. C. Dua

Table of Contents

Chapter 1

Approach and Methodology to the Study of Medieval Punjab*

Madam President, Mr. Minister, Madam Vice-Chancellor, distinguished Scholars, Ladies and Gentlemen:

I have no words to express my gratitude to the organisers of the Punjab History Conference for inviting me to preside over the Medieval Section of the present session of the Conference. More than anybody else, I am quite aware of my own limitations in comparison to the distinguished historians who have held this chair in the past. It is only my long association with the Conference and the affection of my colleagues over here which has given me the honour and privilege of presiding over this section of the Conference.

A great challenge which faces the Indian history today is the reconstruction of Indian history. From the British times, especially the days of James Mill, we have inherited the popular division of the Indian history into Hindu, Muslim and British periods. As this division is extremely illogical and arbitrary, we have discarded this concept. An attempt has been made to recast the periodisation of Indian history on European model, *viz.*, ancient, medieval and modern. Though the centuries and the factors governing the medieval and the modern phases of western history are quite different from the history of India, we may accept this division of periodisation into ancient, medieval and modern. However, in this respect, the first question that faces us is as to when the medieval phase starts in the history of India. Hitherto, the popular version adopted so far in the Indian historiography is the religious factor. It is commonly assumed that with the Muslim in-roads and the establishment of the Turkish rule in North India towards

---

* Presidential Address (Medieval Section), Proceedings of the Punjab History Conference, Tenth Session, February 28-29 1976. Punjabi University, Patiala.

the close of the 12th and early 13th centuries, India entered the medieval phase and that it lasted till the emergence of the British power in India in the 18th century. Such a view is not acceptable. In fact, the beginning and the end of a phase of a civilization of any country cannot be characterised by an single historical date or single factor like religion, however significant it may be. The medieval concept of Indian culture comprises the ages from the 7th -8th century to the late 18th and beginning of the 19th century. Where the phase of modern industrialisation and mode of thought emerges, we end with the medieval ages.

The land of five rivers, i.e., Punjab, is a territorial concept and during course of the medieval ages, especially before the Mughal age, it was denoted by either different chieftainships or different administrative units. The Arab accounts refer to Sindh and Hind. Multan formed part of Hind and so did the other territories of the Punjab under different chieftains. During the Sultanate period, the territories of the land of five rivers were divided into various *Shiqqs*. According to the 14th century Arab account of Shihab al Dinal-Umari's *Masalik al-absarfi-mamalik al-amsar,* there were *bilads* (extensive provinces) or *shiqqs,* i.e., Lahore, Multan, Kalanaur, Sarsuti, Kuhram, Hansi and Samana. Delhi was a different *shiqq*. The *Ain-i-Akbari* and most of the other Mughal chronicles as well as the accounts of the foreigners mention *Subah* Lahore as one of the provinces of the Mughal Empire. Multan was a separate *Subah*. According to *Ain-i-Akbari,* the *Subah* of Lahore had 5 *Doabs* sub-divided into 234 *Parganas*. This was bounded on the East by Sirhind, on the North by Kashmir, on the South by Bikaner and Ajmer, and on the West by Multan. The author of *Munshiat-wa-Ruqat-i-Mamkin* (17th century), while describing the administrative re-organisation of the *Parganas* and *Sarkars* into *Chaklas* under Akbar, incidently does refer to *Sarkar* Punjab. The letters of Muheeb Ali (Ms. State Archives, Patiala) refer to *Mulk-i-Punjab,* i.e., the territories of the Punjab. It seems in the context that here Punjab is synonymous with the *Subah* of Lahore. During the Mughal age, for administrative purposes, even some of the *Parganas* of the cis-Sutlej region formed a part of *Sarkar* Sirhind of *Subah* Delhi. There was reshuffling in the Punjab territories carried out by the British Government after 1858 and some portions were transferred to N.W.F.P. Even though in the course of the centuries during the medieval ages the administrative units of the Punjab have been fluctuating, the cultural impact of the movement in the Punjab on the people of the neighbouring region otherwise a part of *Subah* Delhi was tremendous. Thus, from the cultural view point, it becomes well-nigh impossible to separate the people of this region from the other people of the *Doabs* of the Punjab.

Moreover, the regions of the Punjab have always occupied strategic position bounded by the Himalayas in the North-West and lying between Central Asia and the valley of the Ganges of Hindustan. It has been a meeting ground of various tribes and cultures. This gives distinctiveness to the cultural history of the Punjab.

Another important fact to be borne in mind is that the vastness of the Indian sub-continent offers regional variations because of the diversity in the geographical situation and the habits of the tribal people settled in different regions. In the medieval period, the socio-economic and the political phases affected the growth of various regions differently. The scattered source-material is equally unproportionate in relation to time and areas. For some regions, ample source-material is forthcoming which shortens the time gap for gathering consecutive information, while for others the data is sufficiently time gapped and still others for which practically no source-material exists. The abundance or the paucity of the available source-materials, with regard to time and areas, is bound to affect the methodology in the techniques so as to avoid sweeping generalisation. As a precaution, it is wroth-while to note that though we have to be fully conversant with the methodology of historical research in Europe, we cannot transplant it en-block in the Indian history. Though certain rough parallelisms may be drawn, the problems and the methods of study of the socio-economic and the political history of India *vis-a-vis* Europe of the pre-industrial era are quite different. Thus, both because of the difference in the degrees of the available contemporary source-material as well as variation in the stages of the socio-economic developments, the source material of the European societies for the parallel centuries (in Europe from the closing of the 15th century, modern age starts), is very vast. With the development of the latest research techniques and the computation of data on a countrywise or regional scale, it is possible to attempt generalisation about the socio-economic problems. But in India, our generalisation is based on different factors and theorisation is still impossible. Above all, we have to be equally cautious against the use of European terminology in the Indian context.

Thus, regional variation is an important factor in the socio-economic and political analysis of the Indian society. Social and political ideas as well as their institutional set-up has to be worked out. Apart from the trends of the historiography in the medieval times, emphasis as well has to be laid on the historical languages, literature, speculative ideas, thought, art, architecture, music, science, technology and medicine. Notwithstanding the continuation of work on the traditional line of political history, a beginning has as well been made in the social history of medieval Punjab. All the same, we are to concentrate more on the rural society, the agrarian set up, the role of caste, landed intermediaries, the condition of the peasantry, the concept of the village community, rural trade, handicrafts and industries in the rural and the urban society. Even though we have ample source-material in Arabic, Persian and regional languages supplemented by epigraphic source, we have mostly carried on the tradition from the British times to bank mostly on the Persian chronicles, which is an extremely inadequate methodology. Unless we exploit the full range of source-material available to us, we can never reconstruct a proper perspective of the social development of people during the medieval ages. We have to study both at the regional and the all-India level. The varying and the unifying factors of the Indian culture have to be underlined.

As the medieval factor emerges in the 7th and the 8th centuries, the early medieval phase of the Punjab history lasts till the Turkish conquest by the end of the 12th century. Sindh was occupied by the Arabs in the beginning of the 8th century and it remained attached to the Umayyad and the Abbassid Caliphs of Baghdad. However, with the decline of the Abbassid Caliphs, the kingdom of Multan and Mansurah lost link with Baghdad and continued to remain independent local states, side by side with the other Rajput kingdoms in the Punjab. The Arab occupation of Sindh and southern portion of the Punjab is not a mere episode in the history of India. In the 8th and the 9th centuries, there is the impact of the Arab culture and the Arabic languages on the people of these regions. Many educational centres were set up in Sindh and Multan. It seems that it was from these regions that the Sanskrit Pandits went to the Arab countries and translated Sanskrit books into Arabic.

As a consequence of Mahmud of Ghazni's raids, Punjab was annexed to the Ghaznwid Empire. Mahmud wrested Multan from Qaramitah Muslim rulers of Shia sect and attached it to the Punjab Province but his occuption of Sindh remained incomplete. A few years after Mahmud's death, Multan again became independent and occupied even greater part of upper Sindh. A local converted tribe of Sumra established its rule in the lower part of the Sindh with capital at Debal. The Ghaznwid Empire was ended by the Seljuqs and the rulers took refuge in the Punjab which henceforth remained their sole possession. During the 12th century, the south-east frontiers of the Punjab remained quite unstable and the Rajput rulers made steady intrusions. The fact that Multan and Sindh were separated from the Caliphate of Baghdad and came to be ruled by the local converted Muslim tribes suggests that the indigenous notions of socio-economic order must have continued to predominate. The Ghaznwid occupation of the Punjab was mostly a military occupation. All this points towards the continuance of the early medieval village communities based on clannish order though it can be well imagined that for the purposes of land revenue collection, the officialdom, in line with the Arab and the Turkish institutions of revenue machinery, must have been imposed upon the local landed intermediaries in Sindh, Multan and the Punjab.

For a clear understanding of the 13th-16th centuries of the Turkish and the Afghan rule in the Punjab, one has to understand not only their religion but the institutions they had known before the establishment of their rule, the extent to which they were enforced, their limitations and evolution in practice. One has to equally understand the pre-Turkish Indian socio-economic and political institutions which continued in operation subject to the limitations imposed by the Turkish rule or working independently of Turkish concept of governance. For a clear understanding of the nature of the Turkish elite, one may sift not only the Indian chronicles but also the detailed records left behind by the Arabic and Persian chroniclers of Iran and Afghanistan from the 10th century onwards. Just as for the history of Persia and Afghanistan, it is essential to co-ordinate their chronicles with the Chinese sources for Central Asia, for the Punjab history, it is imperative to understand the nature of the Turkish rule in Central Asia, Persia and Afghanistan from their chronicles, geographical accounts and documents. At this stage, a few problems must be posed :

(i) Did the Samanid, Ghaznwids and the Seljuqs follow the *Shari* Islamic practices and canons of administration? How far were the Islamic ideas tampered by the indigenous Persian practices and expediency and as to what is the element of flexibility in the operation of the Islamic Law?

(ii) Did the administrative concept, evolved by the Turkish elite in South Asian Muslim countries, leave any measure of autonomy in law and custom to the economical productive sections of the population?

(iii) As to the study of socio-economic structure of the people of these territories, can any parallelism be drawn with the pre-Turkish Indian Society? If so, on what historical and geographical factors?

In fact, these questions are very much related to the nature of the Turkish rule in India and our analysis of the Punjabi society during the Sultanate's period would depend on their answers. Even though a few scholars have tried to examine the 13th-16th centuries Indian history against the background of Turkish rule in the South-Asian Muslim countries, their approach has been too theoretically wedded to the concept of Islam and they have not taken into consideration any of the problems posed above. In this respect, attention may be drawn to the vast list of *Kharoshthi* documents discovered by M.A. Stein and now preserved in collections outside India. The classified data relates to the dates furnished by the documents, society, economic conditions, administration, cultural life and important topographical names.

Our methodology is essentially related to our purpose of research for discerning the historical and evolutionary analysis. A scholar has to deliberately adopt the mode of following a historical process step by step which, according to the annalistic method, is blended with the mode of fitting the facts within a well-defined frame of institutions. Thus, the emphasis on institutions rather than merely on dynasties would clearly underline the element of continuity from the pre-Turkish socio-economic pattern to the Turkish period in India. For this purpose, it is necessary to have a detailed analysis of the socio-economic and political structure of the Hindu society in the pre-Turkish period. The impact of the Hun invasions, the nature of the rule of Gurjra-Pratiharas, the Rajput dynasties require a detailed study. The Rajput clans (7th or 8th century-12th century) ruled over the last Hindu states which fell before the Turkish onslaught. The imposition and the reimposition of the intermediary rights of the conquering clans is a recurrent phenomena which persisted throughout the mediaval ages. The nature of the Hindu State, the ethnic settlement in the rural areas, and the relationship of the clannish landed interests with the caste ridden villages during the early medieval age cover much of explanation of the study of society during the Turkish rule.

The concept of the medieval chroniclers was essentially conditioned by the contemporary social life. The historians of the Sultanate period did introduce a deliberate mode of cultural expression in the form of historiography with conscious attempt for narration of the past, specially of Hindustan. From the 13th to the 15th century, it was more of limitation of the mode and manner of the Arabic and Persian historians who mostly recorded the adventures and activities of the military chiefs and Sultans. Their model was either general history, especially that of the Muslim community in West Asia and India or prose eulogy or artistic form of writing or a didactic historical approach. The historical works generally refer to the history of Islam and the Muslim rulers of India.Their emphasis is on the Muslim conquest of India and the activities of the Muslim rulers. They saw in Indian history a constant conflict between Islam and the non-Muslim people of different regions of India. The underlying ideas for writing the history, the form and content of the compilation of the data may differ from one historian to another.

Ziauddin Barani in *Tarikh-i-Firuzshahi* (1357) looks upon history as panorama of human activities as the retrospect of the past and which had a definite role to play in rectifying the present. What leads to the rise and fall of the dynasties is illustrated by the process of historical change. History is man's insight into human affairs and helps in distinguishing between good and evil and makes him realistic in outlook as he learns from the experience of others. All the same, with Barani too, the centre of emphasis remains with the rulers as history enables the rulers in the light of the past to face difficulties and to treat the various ailments of the body politic of the present day. Barani emphasises "truthfulness" as the foundation of history. His understanding of history is conditioned both by pragmatic and religious considerations. Barani does realise the concept of change in society, but it is only secondary to the description of the careers and activities of the Sultans who dominate the scene. Thus, Barani's description of administration, economic life, as well as assessment about the luminaries of the Muslim culture, set a stage for the main theme.

Thus, the historian during this age is more of a scribe than a researcher. His historiography is not an independent intellectual discipline but subordinate to the Muslim intellectual life. However, this concept changes considerably with Abul Fazl in *Akbar Nama* (end of 16th century) who is highly critical of the previous concept of history. He thought that past experience and achievements of man, recorded in history books, were positive source of enlightenment and wisdom. History recorded the knowledge of wisdom of the sages and philosophers and transmitted them to posterity. The study of history was a source of strength to reason and realization of truth which was the ultimate end of man's life. Abul Fazl attached great importance to a rational approach to history and was inclined to establish a close relationship between history and philosophy. He tried to record facts after careful enquiry and investigation and his history was source-oriented. Unlike the previous historians, history was not simply intended to enlighten and warn the 'believers' only. Nor was it the conflict between the people of Islam and the people of other faiths in India. The tone of writing is secular rather than religious. Apart from political and military history, Abul Fazl describes the conditions of the people as well as the policies of the government. He equally recalls the wisdoms of the sages and learning of the scholars. Abul Fazl's history embodies the change that takes place in the society. Badauni's *Muntakhab-ul-Tawarikh* (late 16th-early 17th century) is an intensely subjective reflection of his age.

Abul Fazl's school of historical thought did influence the writings of history in the 17th century. Sujan Rai Bhandari of Batala (Punjab) wrote *Khulāsat-ut-Tawarikh* at the fag end of the 17th century (1695-96). It gives a fairly good account of geography, social and economic life of the people of the Punjab. The concept of social change in the course of the century is clearly marked. However, it must be stated that along with the new trends in historiography from Abul Fazl to Sujan Rai Bhandari, the old school of thought which looked upon history as a collection of examples from which one may learn lessons for a successful and virtuous life and recording of moral, political and military events does persist down to the 18th century. This is well illustrated by the author of *Mirat-i-Aftab Nama,* who represented the spirit of most of the medieval historians from 13th to 18th century. Thus, both the schools of thought co-exist during the 17th and the 18th centuries. Apparently, from Abul Fazl onwards, the compass of some of the historians is larger. The connotation of social change is clearly underlined. Lot of source-oriented historical literature is produced on many socio-economic and administrative aspects of state and society during the 18th century covering Punjab as well.

In the annals of medieval Indian history, Sufism has left indelible impact on the social and cultural history of the Punjab. The concept of Sufism as a social order came to India from the West Asian Islamic culture. Having passed through various phases, it had developed into a potent socio-religious order by the 12th & 13th centuries. In its initial stages, it had emerged as a reaction against the worldly ambitions of the dominant political and military sections of the society within the ambit of an Islamic state and had endeavoured to establish itself on the true underlying principles of Islam. It stressed the fear of God and later emphasised the inner development of man, purification of mind through prayers and love of God. When the Islamic society faced fissiparous tendencies, Sufism stood for the acquisition of knowledge through *Shariat* and the true path of life (*Tariqat*) as the two aspects were by no means incompatible. Sufism could be practised within the bounds of the *Shariat* and *Sunaah*. The true path of life lay in the inner qualities of man: prayers, patience, charity, love of man and God. It also meant direct personal relationship between man and God. By the 12th-13th centuries, Sufism reached the culmination point in the social life of the Muslim community. Even though all Sufis searched for truth, in the soul's eternal yearnings to have direct experience of the Ultimate Reality, one Sufi may differ from another in thought and action. The *tariqah* covered a wide range of thought and feeling and emphasis on its one aspect or another depended upon the comprehension of the Sufi. The importance of the prayer and fast varied in degree with an individual Sufi. The canvas of the Sufi thought is very large. It dealt as much with metaphysical speculation and the philosophical idea as with the social concept. The ideas of Sufism were equally influenced by the contemporary socio-economic order and political set-up.

The Sufi mind rebelled against the formalism, hair-splitting Islamic theology, and the rigidity of the interpretation of the Muslim jurisprudence. A Sufi had a passion for direct experience with the Supreme Being and the religious truth. Above all, the Sufi experience rebelled against the injustice of the social order which accepted the difference between the theory and practice of the Islamic ideas and principles. It is this trait of Sufism which has been essentially coeval with social concern which needs emphasis. The resentment against the social structure, based on marked division between the privileged governing classes and the poor people, becomes more pronounced and is a marked feature of Sufism from the 12th-13th centuries onwards. The view expressed hitherto that the political conquest of Islam brought in its wake an egalitarian concept of socio-economic order in the conquered territories cannot be accepted on the basis of the available contemporary evidence. Islam was a unifying force for a new civilization of the Muslim world. Islam offered the mass of people release from the condition of social inferiority. If Islam offered to influence the social and economic institutions, in its own the Islamic theory was modified by the prevalent pre-Islamic social concept and customs of the conquered territories. The pre-Islamic social order in Persia, Afghanistan and India attached sanctity to family ties, private property and landed estates. There was a marked distinction between the different classes of society. Each class had its own assigned place in the social order. Islam itself recognized the concept of private property and materially affected the development of landed property and landed-tenure. In practice, the pre-Islamic landed hierarchy was maintained. The social class division was not only recognized but further accentuated by the taxation and administrative policy of the Turkish rulers. The concept of ownership of land subject to the payment of *Kharaj* by the land owing class constituting the *rais*, the *iqta* and the *muqta* system for the collection of revenues, created marked cleavage in the social classes in respect of privilege and financial mainstay. Except for the imposition of *Jizya* upon the non-Muslims, it is very doubtful if the Turkish rule brought about any fundamental changes in the existing pre-Muslim agrarian administration. In the initial stages, the Muslim *emigres* to India largely belonged to the professional classes and did not involve any economic and social displacement of the agrarian population. The caste distinction was applicable as much to the Hindu as to the converted Muslim society. So, the social class division was confirmed by the Turkish rulers. The Sufi mind revolted against the prevalent social disparities in the life of man and essentially viewed the poorer sections of the society with sympathy and consideration. The Sufi mind took up the challenge and questioned the very basis and purpose of human life and culture. There is considerable identity of ideas of Khwaja Fariduddin Attar and Maulana Jalal-ud-din Rumi (ob.1273), the great Sufi poets of Persia and the Sufi saints of India. In the Sufi *Jamat Khanna,* no discrimination is made between man and man on any ground whatsoever as in its eyes all human beings are equal. The *Jamat Khanna* and the *Khanqah* life is free from all social complexes, caste and creed inhibitions. The rich and the poor, the old and young, the officials and the non-officials, the Muslims and the non-Muslims, the *faqirs* and the *jogis*, the foreigners and the natives find equal treatment in every respect, *viz.*, food, accommodation and dignity. Every person being a creature of God has his own worldly dignity, which must be respected on an equal basis.

It is to the credit of Punjab that the first systematic treatise on Sufism in Persian, the *Kashf-ul-Mahjoob* by Shaikh Abdul Hasan Al-Hujwiri, popularly known as Data Ganj Bakhsh was written here and served as a guide to the later Sufis. Another Sufi luminary who has left great impact on the cultural life of the medieval Punjab is Shaikh Fariduddin Masud Ganj-i-Shakar, popularly known as Baba Farid, the third in succession in the Chistia *Silsilah* in India. The incorporation of Farid's Sufi thought in poetical Multani dialect of the Punjabi language (*slokas*), entitled *Sloke Baba Farid Ke,* in the *Adi Granth* is the highest tribute that Guru Nanak could pay to Farid, the exponent of human truth. Both Farid and Guru Nanak stood for the regeneration and spiritual elevation of man at times when worldly ambitions and political vicissitudes had victimised the common man in the caste-ridden social order. Both have left an important legacy to the people of Punjab and India as a whole. The Suhrawardi Sufi thought flourished in Multan of which Bahauddin Zakaria was a great exponent.

The medieval Indian mystics (*siddhas*) and the saint-poets, i.e., *bhaktas*, *naths* and other ascetics (*yogins*) have played a considerable role in the religious history of medieval India. Though many *siddhas* and Sufis are associated with north-western part of the Punjab, except for Guru Nanak, none of the well-known saints-poets belongs to the Punjab. An important work on the spiritual concept and cultural impact of the *siddhas* and *bhakts* has already been done. Guru Nanak belonged to the *bhakti* tradition. All the same, Guru Nanak's inheritance from the previous Sufi and other socio-religious sects needs further emphasis. Guru Nanak's impact on the cultural life of the people of Punjab was of a revolutionary character. It is not for me here to run into detail about the social concept and religious views of the Nanak *Panth*, as in the presence of this distinguished scholarly audience, it would be like showing light to the sun. With proper connotation and understanding of the vocabulary of 15th and 16th centuries, Punjabi and Persian language, reading in between the slokas of the *Adi Granth* would reveal in Guru Nanak a great social revolutionary. Apart from his emphasis on the spiritual attainment on man's part, Guru Nanak made a severe attack on the social injustice and political corruption of the times. He indicted as much the Afghan regime as the first phase of the Mughal Empire. It needs further probing of the fact whether Guru Nanak's *Panth* was sheer religious entity or whether it equally stood for a new socio-political order which later on brought the *Panth*; the internal institutional organization of the *Panth* can be well worked out in detail from the contemporary Sikh literature.

In the course of the 17th century, the *Panth* grew quite popular amongst the rural population—both agricultural and non-agricultural—of the Punjab and some territory of *Suba* Delhi. The distinct development in the cult of *Panth* leadership was underlined by Guru Har Gobind who combined in him both spiritual and military leadership. In the recent years, considerable literature on Sikhism has been produced in the wake of the Guru Nanak, Guru Gobind Singh and Guru Teg Bahadur's centenary celebrations. It seems very difficult for me to add more to it except to point out the methodology for the co-ordination of the Sikh literature and the other source material available in the shape of chronicles and documents.

In India, we are very sensitive on religious problems and are very much gullible by the traditional viewpoint of history. We ordinarily refuse to see the obverse side of the medal. Three popular instances as case studies, *i.e.*, the interference in the succession matter to *Gaddi* of the Guru, execution of Guru Teg Bahadur and Guru Gobind Singh's conflict with the sub-Himalayan chiefs and the Mughal state, may be cited. On the death of Guru Har Rai, Har Kishan became the Guru but the *Gaddi* was contested by Ram Rai. This gave excuse to Aurangzeb to interfere into the internal Sikh affairs for succession to gurudom. It may be observed that in matters of succession of the Rajput Principalities, Mughal empire had always enjoyed the prerogative of confirming a newly ascended chief or even forcing a candidate of its own choice on the *Gaddi*. This concerned the temporal affairs of the state but could the Mughal state interfere into the internal affairs of the religious organizations? Akbar had interfered in the internal disputes of *Dargah* of Hazrat Khwaja Moinuddin Chisti of Ajmer. On account of constant conflict between *Khadims* (holy servants and the custodians) and Shaikh Hussain, the *sajjadanashin*, the latter was deposed and exiled. Hitherto, the office of the *mutawalli* of the *Dargah* was combined with the *sajjadanashin,* which was hereditary in character. But Akbar segregated the two offices and appointed a *mutawalli* as the government officer. Later on in 1600 A.D., Shaikh Husain was reinstated to his hereditary post of the *sajjadanashin* but the practice of appointing a separate government *mutawalli* as the administrator of the *Dargah* continued throughout the Mughal age. The interference on the part of the state was justified by the fact that the state gave *waqf* (revenue free) grants and insisted on the proper administration of the finances. Though the Sikh missionary centres also enjoyed *waqf* and *madad-i-maash* grants since Akbar's time, the Guru mostly lived on private contributions and offerings of the donators. Hitherto, no Mughal king had interfered in the internal succession matters of the Sikh Gurudom. Under the Mughal law, the *waqf* and a *maafi* grant had to be renewed at the accession of every monarch and were subject to periodical inspection. Ordinarily they were renewed but legally, the renewal rested on the discretion of the monarch. It is in this capacity that the Mughal king asserted his claim for arbitration to the disputed *Gaddi*. Guru Har Kishan was summoned to Delhi but no amicable settlement could be effected between him and Ram Rai. Aurangzeb, however, consoled Ram Rai by making a fresh *rnaafi* grant at Dehradun.

Guru Har Kishan's period was short-lived. His successor Guru Tegh Bahadur possessed an ascetic bent of mind and finding hostile attitude by the Sikh *masands* established his headquarters in the Himalayan foot hills at Anandpur (abode of bliss) at some distance to the north of Kiratpur. As he did not find cooperation from his relations, he left Punjab and came to Delhi. Here, through the intrigues of Ram Rai, the Guru was declared an imposter and imprisoned. Later on, he was released through the intervention of Mirza Raja Jai Singh. After his tour of Assam, the Guru came back to the Punjab. In 1675, the Guru was tried on the charge of treason and was sentenced to death by the chief *qazi* of Delhi. On the basis of cross examination method, it may be maintained that *Siyar-ul-Mutakherin* of Ghulam Hussian Khan gives a much later 18th century version. As against this, Khwafi Khan, the author of *Muntkhib-ul Lubab*, who had otherwise exploited the 17th century source material for the reign of Aurangzeb, maintains that the Guru took a stand against the destruction of the temples, the suppression of the Sikhs, and the expulsion of the Sikh *masands* from the cities. This accounted for his conflict with the state. However, nearest to the event is the version of Guru Gobind Singh, who in *Bachittar Natak* refers to his father's martyrdom for the protection of the Brahmin who wore 'caste marks and sacred thread and for the sake of his faith'. It seems in the context that Guru Teg Bahadur's execution was an act of religious persecution though it is difficult to prove Aurangzeb's personal hand in the matter.

As regards Guru Gobind Singh's conflict with the Mughal state, four-fold contemporary sources, Guru Gobind Singh's *Atam Katha* forming a part of *Bachittar Natak*, *Gursobha* of Sainapat and a few scattered news bulletins of news writers (*waqainavis*) to the Mughal court (known as *Akhbarat-i-Darbar-i-Mualla*), and *Tarikh-i-Bahadur Shahi,* though a little later source dealing with the last phase of Guru's life may be examined. It is difficult to say whether the well-known letter *Zafar Nama* of the Guru was written by him or by somebody on his behalf. It needs further investigation. For the issues involved between Guru Gobind Singh and the Mughal state, it is necessary to bear in mind the evolution of Sikhism and the emergence of the *Khalsa* under Guru Gobind Singh, the institutional set-up and relationship between the hill chiefs (zamindars) and the Mughal state and lastly, Aurangzeb's own concept of polity. In *Bachittar Natak,* Guru Gobind Singh himself is very clear about the nature and scope of conflict against the Hill Zamindars based on social and political differences and against the Mughal state guided by religio-political considerations. On a socio-religious plane, the Guru was deadly against the idolatory. It is clear from the *Akhbarat* that the Guru's camp at Anandpur was suspected by the Mughal state as a military camp with religious backing. At the same time, Guru Gobind Singh's involvement in the *zamindari* revolt on the part of the Hill Zamindars was taken as political act. Guru's refusal for payment of revenue for the territory under his occupation was an equal affront to the economic and political policy of the Mughal state. Whether the Guru had any political and military designs or not, it was on this plea that the Hill Chiefs—being zamindars of the Mughal state—appealed to the latter for protection. For all the issues involved, one has to understand the contemporary *zamindari* set-up, the underlying principles which governed the political and economic relationship between the Mughal state and the Chief Zamindars (*zamindaran-i-umda*), the technique of warfare for pillage of the revenue-paying villages of the adversary which could strike at the economic root, and resources of the opponent. For the Guru's mission, one has still to scrutinize the *Hukam Namas* and the correspondence that he had with the *mahants* of Kurukshetra and other holy places.

The source material for the Mughal age and the later phase of the 18th century Punjab is vast indeed. A political history can be well constructed on the basis of chronicles and the well-known autobiographies of Babur and Jahangir. But for the detailed account of administration and socio-economic life of Punjab, we have to bank on number of other sources as well. Of course, *Ain-i-Akbari,* though a supplementary volume to the *Akbarnama,* supplies extremely useful material for the *Subah* Lahore as for other provinces. Chandar Bhan Brahman's writings make a definite contribution both in the *insha* and historical literature. His *Munshaat-i-Brahaman* throws light on the activities of the historical personages. The *Guldasta-i-quwid-ul-Saltanat* and *Chahar Chaman* serve as an important source for our knowledge of the working of the Mughal administration and the geographical details of the Mughal *Subahs*. Sujan Rai Bhandari's *Khulāsat-ut-Tawarikh* is a general history of India and covers Aurangzeb's reign till A.D. 1695-96. It is very significant in its account of the Mughal *Subahs* and, at times, supplies more useful information on the topography and socio-economic life of the various regions than the *Ain-i-Akbari*. Of the *Insha* literature, the letters of Shaikh Jalal Hissari and Balkrishan Brahaman included in a manuscript entitled *Muktubat-i-Muzaffar Khan Wa Gawaliar Namah* (Shah Jahan's reign), *Mahzar-i-Shah Jahani* by Yusuf Mirah, 1634 A.D., (a recently discovered manuscript and published in Karachi, Pakistan) covering the Indus valley and a portion of *Subah* Multan, *Maktubat-i-Alamgiri* (Aurangzeb's letters) and *Nigar Nama-i-Munshi* by Malik Zada, 1684 A.D., throw considerable light on the administrative and economic condition of the times.

During the 18th century, considerable progress was made in historical literature. *Bahadur Shah Namah* is an official history of Bahadur Shah's first two years. Iradat Khan's *Tarikh-i-Iradat Khan* (A.D. 1714) is a good biography covering the period of seven years (A.D. 1707-14). Muhammad Hadi's *Haft Gulshan* is a province-wise general history of India till A.D. 1719. Khafi Khan's *Muntakhab-ul-Lubab* covers Mughal history from Babur's times to A.D. 1713. Khafi Khan drew heavily upon Muhammad Sadiq and Abu'l Fazl Mamuri's histories. However, his work is very significant for the early 18th century politics and the problems of the land revenue administration. Some of the *Insha* literature of this period is quite informative. The letters of Muheeb Ali (Ms. State Archieves, Patiala) gave a detailed account of the local *Zamindari* and *Jagir* problems of the Punjab. Anand Ram Mukhlis's *Mirat-ul-Islam,* an excellent dictionary of Persian problems, explains the administrative and revenue terminology with apt historical illustrations. *Tadhkirah-i-Anand Ram Mukhlis* records the war history of Muhammad Shah with Nadir Shah. *Safar Namah-i-Anand Ram Mukhlis* (A.D. 1739) throws considerable light on the socio-economic and political activities of the times. Chataraman Kayastha Saksena's *Chahar Gulshan* (or *Akbar-ul-nawadir*) is a general history of India till A.D. 1759-60 and it gives a detailed topographical account of the *Subahs*. Shah Nawaz Khan's *Maathir-ul-Umara* gives full biographical sketches of the Mughal dignitaries. Kanwar Prem

Kishor Firaqi's *Waqai Alam Shahi* (A.D. 1784) reveals excellent insight into the late 18th century North Indian politics and its impact on the socio-economic life. Ghulam Ali Khan's *Muqaddama-i-Shah Alam Namah* and Tabatabai Ghulam Hussain's *Siyar-ul-Mutakherin* give a detailed history of the Mughals from Aurangzeb's death (A.D. 1707) to A.D. 1754 and 1781 respectively. Lachmi Marayan Shafiq's *Haqiqathai-Hindustan* (A.D. 1789-90) contains an excellent historical and topographical account of India. It also contains a detailed statement of the revenues of India.

The archival source-material in Persian which enriches our knowledge of the socio-economic life of the Punjab, especially from the 16th to the 18th centuries, is tremendous. Though the Mughal *farmans, sanads* and *madad-i-maash* (charitable land grants) documents are available at numerous places, the bulk of this valuable collection has been concentrated in the State Archives, Bikaner and National Archives of India, New Delhi. But many of them lie scattered at the State Archives, Patiala, and other family depositories in the states of East Punjab, Haryana, Himachal Pradesh and West Punjab. The Rajasthan Archieves, Bikaner, comprises various Mughal *farmans, sanads,* news bulletins of the Mughal court (*Kaghadhat-Akhbarat-i-Darbari-i-Mualla*), pargana *atsatta* documents, miscellaneous correspondence of the provincial and pargana officials (*Khutut-i-Ahlkaran, Mutafarriq Kaghadhat-i-Ahlkaran* and reports of the *wakils* of the Maharajas. These documents relate to a number of *subahas* of North India during the Mughal age and many of them relate to the *Subah* of Lahore. Importance of the *Dastur-ul-amls* (Administration Manuals) of the 17th and the 18th centuries can by no means be underestimated for the administration of *Subah* Lahore. The National Archives, in its oriental collection, has also preserved the *Akhbarat* (news bulletins) sent by the *Waqai-i-nawis* of the English East India Company to the Governor General in Council. These documents cover the late 18th and early 19th centuries. They are extremely useful in understanding the socio-economic and political trends of the times.

The underlying purpose of the narration of the above mentioned source-materials is to draw attention to the fact that where a large number of manuscripts are available, we have essentially to resort to the method of cross-examination. The comparative evaluation and annotation of the published texts or the available manuscripts is rather imperative. The comparative evaluation of the same fact from different sources-Persian or non-Persian (where available)—is highly desirable.

Some of the manuscripts offer the simplified or abridged version of the chronicles. They give an important clue to the understanding of the highly technical terminology used in earlier chronicles. The sources in regional languages offer rich material wherein for the 17th and the 18th centuries, the influence of Persian and Mughal terminology on the Rajasthani and Punjabi is rather marked. Where incidently documents in the same region are available, a comparison of the 17th and the 18th centuries and their statistical analysis is always worthwhile. The original documents and the *Insha* literature help us considerably in understanding the otherwise general description available in the chronicles and enable us equally to interpret the administrative manuals. They equally help us to bridge the gulf in the analysis of the situation which is otherwise time-gapped.

The accounts of the foreign travellers are extremely useful for the analysis of the socio-economic life during the 17th and 18th centuries. But they, too, have their own limitations, motives and complexes. The statements about the economic life cannot be accepted at the face value unless authenticated by the contemporary documentary or literary evidence. The description available about the social life has to be equally compared with the picture available in the regional Punjabi literature. However, the detailed description available from the accounts of the foreign travellers of the 18th century, especially for the urban centres and commercial life, can be well compared with the pithy description available from the chronicles and the geographical *Subah* accounts. This also helps us to have more of general understanding and imagination from working on the Persian chronicles and the archival sources. The historical portions of the earliest district gazetteers, assessment and settlement reports of the early British period are only descriptive snd cannot be taken as part of authentic history. However, the physical, geographical and ethnic descriptions are more useful and the nature of the ethnic settlements and the revenue practices can be well understood in collaboration with *dastur-ul-amls* and chronicles of the 17th and 18th centuries. There may be continuity in various spheres. The element of continuity and surmises can be framed but it is too risky to accept the 18th and early 19th century description of the people and their habits for the back centuries unless fully supported by the contemporary evidence. It is an intellectual exercise which has to be handled very carefully by a professional historian. In all this, the principle of importance of the selection of source-material must be kept in view.

The various accounts of the revenue documents of the 17th and 18th centuries throw considerable light on the concept of ownership of land, nature of land holding on the part of various catrgories of the *Zamindari, mucadami, rais* and *puzarian* families. Some of the village documents give details of the units of the holdings, the castes of the cultivators and even the agricultural population of the village. The *Ain-i-Akbari* and the contemporary revenue literature also throw light on the nature of the land rights of the tribes and the clans settled in different parts of the Punjab. Similarly, description is available for *Subah* Lahore from the 18th century source. The composition of an agricultural population and the nature of land tenures may vary from one group of villages to another or, at times, from one village to another. During the medieval ages under review, in the course of the historical development, the peoples belonging to various tribes, clans and castes imposed and super-imposed their *Zamindari* rights in the settled villages and many a new village were developed by the various cultivating clans and castes in different regions of the Punjab. Under the Mughal rule, the rights of the revenue paying land owning *Zamindari, riaya,* the ordinary peasant proprietor, *riays,* the *muzarian* settled in the villages—whether belonging to the same clan or different cultivating clans and castes—were confirmed acquiring an element of stability. All the same, a comparison of the clans and castes with *Zamindari* rights in the 17th century Punjab and later half of the 18th century Punjab would show that tremendous changes had occurred in the *Zamindari* title to the ownership of the land in the villages. Thus, the social picture on an ethnic plane in the agrarian society is by no means static. The practice of communal *vesh,* traceable in many villages in the western Punjab during the second half of the 19th century, involved periodical redistribution of the land amongst various branches of the clan on inter-village basis or the redistribution and readjustment of the land within a single village or periodical exchange of certain ancestral land within a single family. The ethnology and economic study of these tribes suggests how the joint family proprietary notions of the medieval age descended from the communal rights of the tribes. It is not intended to suggest that this communal order of land ownership has existed in these villages throughout the medieval age, for this region had been the scene of political vicistitudes and clannish domination in the 18th century which may have brought about this practice into existence. There were no communal land owned by the 'village community'. So far as the 16th and 17th century documents reveal, it is difficult to trace such a concept. In matters relating to the agricultural life, their revenue administration and social behaviour, a village society was never a complete socio-economic entity. It was essentially an integral part of larger territorial and clannish settlement. The obligation of the maintenance of the irrigation and channels drawn from the lakes, canals, streams and river beds was basically a territorial and clannish concept being the joint of the Zamindars and the *riaya* even though it ultimately devolved on the village agricultural *riaya*. During the 18th century, in many a region of the Punjab, the nature of *pattidari* and *bhaichara* land tenures are traceable. The entire concept of the village community in the Punjab has to be recast on the basis of the contemporary documentary evidence available from the 16th to the 18th centuries.

Based on the chronicles and the contemporary documents, it can be well maintained that in the Punjab, the Mughal Government was keenly interested in the extension of the irrigation facilities to the cultivators for the development of agricultural economy. Though the chronicles attach importance to the construction of a few canals like those in East Punjab, *i.e.,* West Jamna, the Lahore, *i.e.,* Upper Bari, the Delhi canal entitled *Nahr-i-Bihisht,* scattered regional contemporary sources point towards the existence of many a perennial small canals in either parched areas or at places where even constant water was available from the streams, and the *nalas*. A number of such canals were constructed both by the Mughal state and the Mughal Zamindars for stepping up the agricultural and horlicultural production. There were no private canals during the Mughal age. Even when some of the Mughal nobles got a few canals repaired or excavated at their own initiative for the irrigation of their gardens or assigned Jagir lands, they could not claim these canals as their private property. In fact, the real basis of irrigation administration was cooperation between the Government and the cultivators. The headworks of the canals, the main lines and branches, the distributaries were all constructed and maintained by the state administration but the water-source and the field channels were constructed and invariably maintained by the *riaya*. In regions close to the main rivers or streams, the construction of the canals, the water-course and the *bunds* was the joint responsibility of the state and the *riaya*. In this respect, the *riaya* met a part of the maintenance charges on collective basis. Though the British Government improved and extended the perennial irrigation system in the Punjab, it has yet to be established whether the apparent addition to the irrigated area by the large scale Government canals was a net addition to the effectively irrigated acreage. This is because of the fact that the new canals often replaced the older inundation canals and the problem of water logging and salinity resulted from the neglect or proper drainage system. The problem has also to be viewed against the demographic factor.

On the basis of the source material of the various categories mentioned above, it can be well established that there was an intergrated pattern of commercial life during the 16th–18th centuries. In the developed regions, the concept of village self-sufficiency can no longer be maintained. The regional sources point towards the inter-dependence of groups of adjacent villages on the local *mandis* both for commercial crops and non-agricultural product. Within a *pargana* or a larger territory, a few commercial centres served as links between the villages and the *qasbas*. The *qasba,* apart from serving as the administrative head-quarters of the pargana, was also the main commercial centre of the rural areas. However, it is hard to lay a strict line of demarcation between the rural and the urban areas in the medieval Punjab society; a *qasba* with its jurisdiction over *tappahs,* mandis and villages was more a part of the rural society than an urban centre. The names of the 17 century peddling castes with specialisation in certain merchandise commodities as well as the pastoral and animal breeding tribes are available for the Punjab. The internal trade, the local agricultural and industrial products, the export commodities, the river-system for transportation, the inland road transportation, organisations with *Hundi* system, the revenues from the commercial items, the commercial organisation in the urban centres, the inter-provincial and foreign trade and the role of the trading castes can be well constructed from the above sources. A clear picture of the inland trade routes and external routes connecting with the other provinces and the neighbouring West and Central Asian countries can be well drawn. Because of the turbulent conditions of the 18th century, a change occured in the commercial set-up which equally affected the trade routes.

In the end, I must say that with an objective approach and disciplined methodology of research, we can construct a fairly accurate and dependable picture of the social and economic life of people of the medieval Punjab.

I thank you all for the indulgence and the patience shown to me during the course of my address.

Chapter 2

Some Problems of Indian Historiography with Special Reference to the Punjab*

Mr. Vice-Chancellor, Prof. Sarkar, Presidents of the three sections, Ladies and Gentlemen:

It was only a few days back that I was asked to inaugrate the 28th Session of the Punjab History Conference. I feel honoured but constraints of time allow me only to express a few stray thoughts, especially in current experiences that the nation is going through. Today, we will reflect on some problems of Indian historiography with special reference to the Punjab.

Every age brings with it some new ideas about the historical thinking on the part of the people in respect of their past life. The writing and interpretation of history has been going on from one period to another, not only because new facts and data have been discovered but because life and culture of the people has to be looked at from new aspects than done in the past.

In the recent time, the canvas and scope of history has been sufficiently widened so as to cover the culture of the people with its multidimensional aspects and phases of life. The methodology of historical research demands not only coordination with the other social scientists for analysing the cultural and institutional aspects of the people but to develop scientific and objective approach for the mitigation of historical biases and distortions which have crept in it from time to time. Notwithstanding these well cherished ideals, it is most unfortunate that in the recent times, the Indian historiography has developed a serious crisis and is passing through a very crucial stage. The present day democratic and social structure based on the

---

* Inaugural Address of the 28th Session of Punjab History Conference, March, 1996, Punjabi University, Patiala.

concept of 'secularism' has considerably affected the historical thinking. However, it is a pity that for many an issue inspired more by ideological thinking, far from having frank and fearless viewpoint based on historical facts and removing the paid distortions in Indian history, attempt is being made to create more distortions rather than to rectify them. The analysis of the past events has been, unfortunately, linked up even with the false concept of secularism and political electoral vote bank. In the present address, I propose to take up some gaps and distortions in historiography for ancient, medieval and modern phases of Indian history.

(1) It is well accepted that by the end of the 4th millennium and early 3rd millennium, the Indus Valley people had established contacts with Mesopotamia and Egypt. For the historical period prior to Alexander's Indian campaign (326 B.C.), the early classical Greek geographers and writers did not have a very clear perception about the exact position and extent of the Indian sub-continent. Herodotus (484-431 B.C.) considered India as "the remotest provinces of the Persian Empire towards the East" and could not visualise its territorial extent and the position of the Indian Ocean around its western and eastern coasts. In fact, he speaks of a part of India as the twentieth satrapy of the Emperor Darius. He speaks of presence of the Indian continent in the army of Xerxes clad in cotton garments and armed with canebows and iron tipped cane arrows.

Herodotus' testimony about the settlement of Indians, i.e., the Medes, Kurks/Kers, etc., in the Mediterranean region and the East European countries is of crucial importance. The writings of Diodorus (100 B.C.-A.D.11), Sterabo (60 B.C.-A.D.19), Plutarch (A.D. 46-120), Arraian (A.D.200) and Pliny (A.D. 200), deal with not only the military campaigns of Alexander but provide adequate description about the people belonging to different tribes and communities settled in North West, Punjab and Sindh. As such, these writers cover various tribes i.e., the *Malli, Mand/Min, Sogdi/Sodrae/Sambesta-/Musicani, Arabi/ Arabitae/Hendians, Xarthi* (*Ksatris* of Punjab) in the accounts left by them. They have spelled out not only their respective geographical territorial jurisdictions but have also dilated upon their characteristics, especially with regard to the inland warring and sea-faring activities.

Alexander's Indian campaign left mutual cultural impact, both on West Asia, North Western India as well as the Western Society under the then Hellenic domination. So far, by and large, only one side of the coin relating to the Greek influence on the Indian socio-economic and political life has been highlighted. Nearchus and the later Greek writers mention the fact of the establishement of a new city in Sindh at the conflux of the Akesines (Chenab) with the Indus which was put under the territorial jurisdiction of Philip's satrapy along with all the Thracians and the other troops needed for the defence of the Province. Even though no archaeological remains of the city founded by Alexander are traceable, the fact about the presence of a large number of Thracians in Alexander's army and their settlement in the territories of West Punjab and Sindh, (covered by Philip's satrapy) is rather significant as it was bound to have cultural interaction with the local Indian population. At the same time, considerable stress has already been laid on the Greek influence on the Indian art and sculpture in the wake of the short-lived Greek occupation of the Indian territories both under Alexander the Great and his generals, Eudamus and Seleucus Nicator. However, on the contrary, excepting the maritime commercial linkage, the effects of the other aspects of the Indian culture on the West have not been underscored.

In the Indian art of warfare, the deployment of the elephants played a crucial role. In his battle against Porus on the bank of the river Hydaspes (Jhelum), Alexander had noticed the frightening utility of the war elephants against the cavalry at certain junctures. So, after his victorious battles against Porus and other Indian Chiefs in West Punjab and Sindh, Alexander captured a large number of elephants which he utilised not only in his campaigns against the Indian Chiefs but also planned to transport them along with heavy luggage to the Euphrates, Babylon and finally to Macedonia. Nearchus states that while Alexander was preparing for his return voyage, he dispatched Craterus as the head of two divisions of the Macedonian forces along with the elephants and with clear instructions to follow the course by an inland route to Karmania, and join the main army in that province. Later on, when Seleucus Nicator was defeated by Chandragupta Maurya (about 375 B.C.), even though, as per the Treaty, he was obliged to surrender to the latter parts of the territories, now called Afghanistan. He received in exchange five hundred elephants. Of course, Seleucus took them back to his Syrian satrapy and to Macedonia.

It may be well appreciated that the maintenance of the war-elephants and their transportation entailed the deployment of a large number of Indian personnel for serving as *mohawats*, trained coaches, guards and other staff required for feeding the elephants as well as for looking after the elephant stables. As such, thousands of Indians from Punjab and Sindh who accompanied the elephants in the entourage of Alexander the Great and Seleucus Nicator emigrated to Euphrates, Babylon, Syria, in West Asia and then to Macedonia and the Thracian territories in East Europe. Apart from the elephant staff, Alexander took several prisoners of war who were, otherwise, professionals well-versed in different aspects of the art of warfare.

Plutarch bears testimony to the fact that, in addition to the above categories, Alaxender also took in his retinue a number of civilians whom he had taken in his service. He also mentions the settlement of the Indian civilians in Athens, some of whom joined the retinue of Augustus Caesar. The Indian immigrants kept up their traditional customs and religious rites. On death, they were cremated on a funeral pyre in the traditional Hindu style, even though for important state functionaries, a *samadi* (so-called tomb) would also be built for veneration. At the same time, it is also contended that in the aftermath of Alexander's Indian campaign, more so with the accelerated commercial intercourse with the Greek and the Roma Empires, some sections of the Indian people emigrated to the West Asian and East European countries.

(2) The Supreme Court's Judgement (11.12.1995) on Hindu/ Hindutva does not, in any way, hold religion and culture synonymous and is very clear that culture has much wider content with multi-dimensional aspects than proper religion. The apex court held that in the words 'Hindutva' of Hinduism were not confined to mere religion, popularly known today as Hindu religion but they connoted a way of life. In fact, the entire code of conduct of life (*dharma*) incorporated values of life, i.e., spirit of tolerance, respect for all religions and adherence to secularism. In fact, the terms cover every sphere of human activity, which is well comprised by the culture and *dharma* of the people inherited from the ancient times. As such, these days, in the political sphere or during the electoral process, any appeal made in the name of Hindutva does not tantamount to making an appeal on ground of religion and, therefore, is not a corrupt practice.

There is no denying the fact that the word 'Hindu' seems to be of foreign origin but it cannot be maintained that it was not at all reflected in the ancient Indian literature.

The name India is derived from the 5th Century B.C. Greek word 'Indi' which was a corrupt form of the 6th century B.C. Iranian word 'Hindu' (used for the people of this sub-continent). This shows continous philological relationship amongst the words 'Hindu', 'Indi' and India.

Both the terms, Hindu and Indi (Indian) are of foreign origin, the former used by the Iranian and the West Asian Arabs (6th century B.C. onwards) and the latter used by the Greeks (5th century B.C. onwards). Initially, the Arabs called the land of the Hindus as Hind, which later on was termed as Hindustan. However, in the course of history, the connotation of the territorial extent of Hind/Hindustan continued to change. Initially, the term 'Hind' stood for Northern India from the east of river Indus to West of Bengal, and thereafter the word 'Hind' also put as Hindustan, covered the whole of North India and distinct from Deccan and Southern India and finally by the 16-17the centuries, invariably it covered the whole of India.

During the ancient period, the term Hindu was basically geographical and cultural in connotation. This name was given by the ancient Iranians for the people of this sub-continent to the east of the river, Sindh. According to the Achaemeind inscriptions, the Iranian monarch Darius I (C. 522-486 B.C.), during the 6th and 5th century B.C., extended his empire not only towards a part of Central Asia inhabited by the Skuthai (Scythians) including the people named Sakas but towards the east as well comprising this sub-continent's territories of North West, Western Punjab as well as Sindh, to the West of the river Sindh. Even the Greek writer Herodotus (484-451 B.C.) speaks of this part or Indi (India) being "the remotest provinces of the Persian Empire towards the East" which constituted the twentieth satrapy of the Emperor Darius. As the Iranians pronounced the Vowel 'S' as 'H' they called the people of Sindh and beyond as the Hindus. As such, during the ancient period as well as early medieval and pre-Islamic era, a person from this sub-continent (Indi/India) belonging to any tribal social order or any other religious sect, i.e., Brahmanical, Buddhism, Jainism, Shaivite and Vaishnavite etc., was termed as Hindu. Apart from it, during the ancient and early medieval periods, many a tribe viz., Jats (Zotts), Meds, Gujars and Rajputs, etc., along with their branches from Sindh, Punjab and Western India migrated to the Arab countries; they were all named 'Zotts' and described as Hindus. By the early Christian era, even the Sanskrit language was termed as *Hindwani*. It also seems that the Sanskrit literature had also picked up the term Hindu as a Sanskrit manuscript quoted by the later Arab/ Persian sources stated, "By the Arab the Hindus are called Zatt". Interestingly, during the medieval age, in due course of time, even after conversion to Islam, these immigrants continued to be named as Zatt/Hindus.

As such, during the ancient period, the Hindu culture comprised all faiths, viz., the Brahmanical, Buddhism, Jainism, Vashnavite and Shaivite, etc., and all their literature affords information for an analysis of the ancient Indian society. Even during the medieval age and pre-colonial era (8th-18th centuries), the term 'Hindu' was never used in the strict religious sense. As a matter of fact, right from the 8th century onwards, the Muslim writers used the term Hindu (*Hanud*) in India in contrast to the followers of Islam (*Musalmeen*). In the early medieval age, even though Buddhism was well established in Sind, Multan and other parts of the west Punjab, despite social tension between the Buddhists and the Brahmans, the Arab accounts insist on covering both as a part of the Hindu society. From 13th century onwards, the Persian sources maintain this concept of Hindu which was outside the Islamic religion and its people (*musalmeen*) as the Hindu people (*Hanud*), though, of course, both were divided into various clannish social groups (*firqas*).

Even the well-known Indo (till 1947)-Pakistani historian, I.H. Qureshi ('A Short History of Pakistan', Karachi, 1967) concedes that in ancient period, the name 'Hindu' stood for the traditions of culture of the people of the Indian sub-continent, though he takes credit that 'the roots of this culture lay in West Pakistan, the land of river Sind, the 'Indus' of the Greeks. He states that as connotation of the term 'Hindu' changed at a much later stage, it came to be associated, even though wrongly, with the religious invocations. He further comments that the "society gave a final direction to many of the trends which led to the growth of modern Hinduism and developed a spirit that led to classicism".

It was only during the British Raj, especially in the 19th and 20th centuries, that the term 'Hinduism' was coined. It was made co-terminous simply with the religion of the Brahamins, Vivasaivya, Lingayats, Brahmo, Prarthana and Arya Samaj, etc. It was rendered distinct from the religious faiths and tenets of the Buddhists, Jains and the Sikhs.

According to the professed liberal and secular school of Indian thought, the medieval Indian history had been communalised as the epigraphic and the Sanskrit literary sources depict the conflict as between the invading Turks and the Indian Chiefs rather than between the Muslims and the Hindus. It is contended that the term *Turushkhadanda,* which implied tax levied on the people for defence against the onslaught of the Turushkas, shows that the defence was organised by the Indian Chiefs against the foreign Turks rather than against the Muslims as the word Muslim does not occur in the available textual Sanskrit description.

For understanding the nature of the Turkish campaigns during the 11th and 12th centuries, the Arabic and the Persian contemporary sources bring out the real nature of the conflict with the Hindu Chiefs of North India. In this regard, to quote only a few authorities, Al Biruni's *Kitabal-Hind,* Al Utbi's *Tarikh-i-Yamini* and Minhaj-ud-dinb, Sirajud-din's *Tabqat-i-Nasiri* and Ziaud Din Barn's *Tarikhi-Firoz Shahi* clearly bring out the motives of the Turkish campaigns against India. These sources narrate not only the Turkish designs for the territorial conquest but equally emphasise the motives for pillage and plunder of wealth as well as the destruction of the Hindu temples, thereby signalling the triumph of Islam over the heathnic ways of worship and idolatry customs and manners of the Hindus (*ahl-i-Hinud*).

In this regard, it is not out of place to refer to the Pakistani historians who equally claim to be scientific and objective in their approach to the study of medieval history of the Indian sub-continent (what they call Indo-Pakistan sub-continent). They, too, point out various distortions in medieval history created by the western or the Indian scholarship. Most interestingly, for the medieval age, they bank on the same Arabic and Persian sources as we do. All the same, based on these sources, they often use the terminologies like 'Muslim invadors'; 'History of Muslim India; 'Indo-Muslim historiography'; Muslim Empire in India'; 'Muslim conquest of India'; 'Muslim Rule', or 'Muslim Empire in Sind'; 'Muslim Bengal; 'Victories of Muslims over large Hindu hords'; 'Ary of Islam', 'Consolidation of Muslim India', Hindustan as 'Cital of Islam', 'Muslim historians', 'Hindu sources' and 'Hindu inscriptions', etc. Some historians consider even the Arab conquest by Muhammad Bin Qasim (712 A.D.) as the 'triumph of Islam' and for Mahmud of Ghazni's campaigns in early eleventh century ascribe the motives of not only conquest, pillage and plunder of wealth but even iconoclasm, spread of Islam (*tabligh*) and mitigation of the Indian culture based on Brahamanism. For such historiography, only a few well known Pakistani historians like S. M. Ikram, I. H. Qureshi, K. K. Aziz, Mian Abdul Rashid, Muhammad Munawwar, Manzoor Ahmed Manzoor and Rafi Ullah Shehab may be mentioned. We may not agree with various terms used by them but in the face of the contemporary or near contemporary evidence for the motives and nature of the Turkish (Muslim) conquest of India, as already stated above, it is not essential to disagree with them.

Innumerable examples can be cited from medieval Indian history where the most sacred temples of the Hindus were destroyed and in many a case, mosques were also constructed thereupon. The discipline of history demands that along with political and economic factors, one may equally discern and underline the role that religion played in the medieval times. It is the examination of the totality of the then thinking and action which should determine the scientific approach to history.

After the establishment of Muslim rule in North India, many venerated Hindu temples, which served as great pilgrimage centres, were desecrated and devastated. In this regard, the first Hindu temple to fall victim was the well-known Devalaya temple in Sindh, about 75 km. situated east of Karachi, in the early 8th century to Mohammed Bin Qasim (712 A.D.). The latest archaeological evidence published in Pakistan and the ruins discovered at the site confirm the classical Arab accounts that the Jama-i-Masjid in the region of Debal/Banhore was constructed at the exact site of the Devalaya temple after its demolition. Similarly, many Buddhist monastries in Sindh were devastated by Mohammad Bin Qasim and the Arab generals of Sindh during the period of Umavyed Caliphs. A few centuries later, the famous Sun Temple at Multan met the same fate, but it was reconstructed and continued to be a Hindu pilgrimage centre. All these are now in the present day Pakistan.

Destruction of Golden Temple by Abdali

In the Punjab, during the 15th-16th centuries, Guru Nanak Dev founded the Nanak Panth, which later on in due course of time came to be known as Sikhism. The initial headquarters of the first three succeeding Gurus to the *Gadi,* was at Goindwal Sahib in District Amritsar, which became a pilgrimage centre of the followers of *Nanak Panth.* Later on, the fourth and the fifth Gurus of the *Panth,* Guru Ram Das and Guru Angad Dev, shifted the centre of the *Gadi* to Amritsar after having built 'Guru ke Mehal', Guru Ram Das selected a site with a water pond considered sacred by the Hindus since the Purana age and which is supposed to have been visited by Guru Nanak Dev. On this site, Guru Ram Das and Guru Arjun Dev built the

Harmandir, which became a centre of pilgrimage for the Hindus/Sikhs from all over India. The sixth Guru Hargobind also added a secular place named *Akal Takht* for the sports and cultural activities of the followers of the *Panth*. Whereas Harmandir continued to be the most sacred place of worship of Guru Granth Sahib, for lakhs of pilgrims from the Punjab and other places, the *Akal Takht* developed into the centre for political and military activities of the Sikhs fighting against the injustice and tyranny of the Mughals as well as the Abdalis, especially during the 18th century.

In the later Mughal period, the sacrilege of Harmandir Sahib was done by the *Faujdar* of the region, who converted it into a dance-hall for the *mujras* performed over there. Later on, the Afghan invader, Ahmed Shah Abdali exploded the entire structure of the Harmandir and filled the holy tank with dirty earth (1762). However, it was recaptured by the Sikh Sardar, Sardar Jassa Singh Ahluwalia, who later on became the first ruler of the Kapurthala state, with the help of Bhai Des Raj got the Harmandir Sahib rebuilt (1764) on the original late 16th century model along with all the artistic traits prevalent in the 18th century. The construction of the *bungas* around it and *Katras* as residential-cum-commercial markets led to the planned development of the Amritsar town. During the regime of Maharaja Ranjit Singh (1799-1839), the ceilings and the roofs of the Harmandir were got gold plated by the Maharaja himself, whereas the upper storeys of *Akal Takht* were got built by Diwan Sawan Mal, the Governor of Multan. During the 19th-20th centuries, the Harmandir Sahib (The golden temple) at Amritsar has developed as one of the biggest pilgrimage places of the Sikhs as well as the Hindus.

(3) In the Kangra Valley (Himachal Pradesh), there were numerous sacred temples visited by thousands of devotees but ever since the ancient period, of these, the tribe temple complex comprising Jawalamukhi, Vrijeshwari Devi and Mahadev Mandir, Bujnath, has been of great religious significance for the Hindus from all over India. These temples had also rich collection of books on the varying aspects of the Hindu culture in their respective libraries. They equally fell victims to the sacrilege and vandalism on the part of Mahmud Ghazni (1018) as well as Firuz Tughluk (1351). Of course, after having seized numerous sacred books of the Hindus from the library of the Jawalamukhi temple, Firuz Tughluk got a few of these books on natural sciences and music translated from Sanskrit to Persian and with due acknowledgement in the preface, named the titles after his own name.

(4) In the recent times, a few Pakistani historians have revived the well-trodden concept about "the so-called Bhakti Movement" resulting from interaction of Islam and Hinduism. To them, Guru Nanak, Kabir, and Dadu were the founders of the syncretic sects for the reform of the Hindu society which, according to them, was essentially due to the impact of Islam which changed the character of the Hindu society. Even though most of the ideas of Shankara, Ramanuja and Ramananda could be traced to ancient Indian thought, in their totality and characteristic emphasis in medieval India, appear to indicate Muslim influence. Many a scholar in India, based on the original ancient Sanskrit texts, have already done away with this traditional Indo-Pakistan viewpoint.

Most recently, another Pakistani scholar, Manzoor Ahmed Manzoor, has viewed the ideas and thoughts of Guru Nanak Dev and the emerging Sikh movement with consideration and sympathy. He considers Nanak's movement as a peaceful silent revolution. Nanak's rejection of idolatory, caste destructions, religious asceticism or renunciation was to upgrade the Hindus in beliefs and practices to face the onslaught of Muslim rule. He compares the Hindu position of Guru Nanak Dev with that of Sir Sayyid Ahmed Khan of 'Muslim India' of later days, who wanted to upgrade Muslims in view of their backwardness with reference to the better culture offered by the English. Such a comparison is rather odious in character as Guru Nanak, far from being a mere reformer, founded the Nanak Panth which ultimately commanded the mass support of the people in the Punjab. All the same, Manzoor Ahmed pays tribute to the high intellectual calibre of Nanak's followers and the succeeding Gurus. He further comments that the martyrdom of Guru Arjun Dev proved an impetus for further development and that "if birth or emergence of Nanak may be termed the origin, then right from the second half of the 15th century (Nanak born 1469) to 1800 i.e., the rise of Ranjeet Singh, this variation of Hindus continued to produce leaders of high calibre. This cannot be an accident or chance in the history of our land. Nothing but the tyrannies of the age on the people of the land was fueling the process of history which produced these men." He further comments that Nanak's movement, its character and outward form changed as it progressed and ended up in the formation of Sikh power in the Punjab. It was a people's movement and it threw up men of character from amongst the common folk. "The Hindus of the Punjab dared to think, did not accept Muslim supermacy, updated themselves, even taking ideas from their oppressors and continued the struggle. The time came when imperialism weakened and the revolt triumphed."

(5) Of the Pakistani writers, Faqir's book titled, 'The Real Ranjit Singh' portrays the personality, religious toleration and the achievements of Ranjit Singh in most lauding terms. On the other hand, Ikram Ali ('The History of Punjab', 1799-1947, Lahore) considers that even though Ranjit Singh utilised to the fullest extent the fervour of the Khalsa against Moslems in general and the Afghans in particular, he was opposed to ruthless persecution and that neither he was a bigot nor a vein religious dreamer. He also tried to keep in check the fanatical tendencies of the Akalis, and entrusted some of the most responsible positions in his government to Mohammedans. However, Ikram Ali accuses Ranjit Singh for the deliberate damage and desecration of the Muslim monuments. In this regard, he cites the main cases of the Badshah's Masjid, Sunhari Masjid, and Jahangir's masoleum in Lahore and provides details of the destruction of some portions of these monuments or using them for the storage of gun-powder. However, Akram Ali himself concedes that some of the mounments were used for stroage of war-armaments during the disturbed periods.

The concept of secularism in India in the modern sense is a recent development since the late 19th and 20th centuries. In the medieval polity, religious tolerance, equity in taxation and co-existence of different religious communities may constitute the hallmark of a liberal state. But the state may deviate partially in one respect or another; it may still consider itself to be broad-minded and tolerant. Notwithstanding the socio-political background of the Durrani regime in the Punjab, Ranjit Singh established a liberal and just state, though of course to some extent, within the limitations imposed by the contemporary social atmosphere. He stopped the practice of cow-slaughter (*gau kushi*) and as a symbol of ascendancy of the *Khalsa,* he forbade public calls for prayers (*azan*) at certain significant mosques in some cities. Even though it is conceded that because of certain social inhibitions of the age, Maharaja Ranjit Singh's rule in Kashmir was not completely secular in the modern sense of the word, it was liberal enough to foster peaceful co-existence amongst different religious communities. The Shia-Muslim community had often been the target of repression and intermittent persecution during the Afghan rule and even earlier during the later Mughal times in the 18th century. In Ranjit Singh's period, there was only one unfortunate communal

Shia-Sunni riot during the Governship of Bhamman Singh Ardli (1830-31 A.D.) which was crushed with an iron hand by the administration. With all its limitations, Maharaja Ranjit Singh gave a stable government to his kingdom which it had not known since the times of the great Mughals. In all these respects, the broad-minded state policy was continued by his successors.

Ordinarily, the medieval chronicles deal mostly with the political history and aspects of the social life of the people have to be gleaned from their accounts. However, Mufti Ali-ud-din, a resident of Lahore, in his *Ibrat Nama* (1854), has dealt with the social life of the common people during the reign of Maharaja Ranjit Singh and thereafter in a comprehensive manner. According to him, the society comprised three major groups of people, i.e., the Muslims, the Hindus and the Sikhs. The Muslims formed nearly two third of the entire population. They were soft-spoken, courteous and brave with great fondness for sports like horse-riding and fighting. They were very much averse for riding in a palanquin which was considered rather womanish. They were equally fond of keeping guns, swords, spears, daggers and nachakhs. They also exhibited fondness for recreations and enjoying picnic in the gardens. Even though they did not neglect education, there was a lot of economic backwardness, social segregation and stagnation. The author does not blame the Sikh government for their economic weakness as it did not make any discrimination against the Muslims on account of their faith. He rather ascribes it to their own extreme laziness and lack of initiative for accumulation of capital. Ordinarily, they did not take to trade and business as their vocation. They equally lacked originality in arts and crafts. Despite education, they showed fanatic attachment to the Laws of *Shariat*. Even though the Quran accorded fairly equitable treatment to women, the Muslims never gave up their claims for the plurality of wives in spite of lack of financial resources. They were fond of back-biting, and were rather treacherous. It was their fanaticism which was responsbile for their hatred of the Sikhs and utter disregard of the *faqirs* and saints of other denominations and sects. Their fanaticism was equally matched by the Akalis and the *Nihangs* among the Sikhs. They would never eat food cooked by a Sikh. All such traits were responsible for their segregation from the general social life and their economic backwardness.

Mufti Ali-ud-Din equally hits at the social drawback of the Hindus. According to him, the caste system had divided them into watertight compartments which had affected the ranks of the Brahmanas themselves. The subdivisions even amongst the Brahmanas religated a section of their community upto that of Shudras. However, such subdivisions amongst the Brahmanas were not hereditary in character. The Brahmanas were not free from ordinary social vices of sex and greed. Fraudulent practices, treachery and falsehood were common on their part. They mostly showed aversion to army service. As distinct from the Brahmanas, the Khatris were mostly businessmen. They were a prosperous community but they showed no sense of morality in business. They were equally averse to military service. Despite economic prosperity, they were not very hospitable. In matters of dress, food, manners and etiquettes they did not observe any formality. Accumulation of capital was their main business. Their children were married at a very tender age of 6 to 10. The other two groups of the Vaishyas and the Shudras mostly continued their normal traditional ways of life. There was considerable flexibility and many rose to higher position in life.

As regards the Sikhs, the author comments, they generally shook off the rituals that the Brahamanas fostered on the other Hindu society. They mostly took to agriculture and invariably joined army. Many Sikhs belonged to the *Zamindari* clans. They were highly sensitive for the protection of the honour of their women folk. They did not observe the practice of preparing a *chauka* before eating meals. Meat was their stable diet but they would never eat meat or any animal slaughtered by a Muslim. They did not observe any formality in the matter of dress and social intercourse. Instead of saying 'Ram Ram' like the other Hindus, they would utter *Waheguru Ji Ki Fateh.* In the morning hours, they would recite only the Guru's Bani, i.e., *Japji* and the *Sukhmani*. The main section of the Sikhs was that of the cultivators. A large number of those who embraced Sikhism called themselves *Singh Guru Ji Ka* and were engaged in the trade. They were, by and large, very fond of wearing arms. Those who could well afford liked riding horses and elephants. The Sikhs made extensive use of Gurumukhi and read and wrote in that script. In social life, they indulged in wine and sex. The sections known as the Akalis and *Nihangs* were extremely fanatics.

The above description is only a gist of the description about the common people of the Punjab as provided by Mufti Ali-ud-din's *Ibrat Nama*. This work, written in Persian, even though published in Pakistan, has not been translated into English or any of the regional languages in India or Pakistan. Similarly, Rae Kali Rai and Lala Tulsi Ram's work, *Kitab-i-Sair-i-Punjab* gives a fairly comprehensive account of the religious beliefs and practices, food habits, dress, amusements and recreation, fairs and festivals and above all, the customs and traditions of the commom people, more especially in the rural areas of the Punjab during the mid-19th century. Despite all its drawbacks for the historical portion, it is a highly significant source of information for the period under review. Its importance can be well realised from the fact that the later English works, i.e., Ibbetson's *A Glossary of Tribes and Castes of Punjab,* Griffin and Massey's *Chiefs and Families of Note* and Richard Temples's *Legends of the Punjab* and various other works are based upon it to a great extent. One can equally glean significant passages on the social life from Ganesh Dass Badhera's *Chahar Bagh-i-Punjab.* The *Vars* and the *Kissas* speak of the habits and social out-look of certain sections of the people in a significant manner.

It is significant to observe that even though Persian was the court language of the Lahore Darbar, the common people of all religious faiths, the Muslims, the Hindus and the Sikhs spoke Punjabi which was written both in Arabic and Gurumukhi scripts. All the same, in 1882 A.D., Urdu was introduced by the British government as an official vernacular language, more or less against the wishes of many a sections of the Punjab society.

(6) At the end, it may be reiterated emphatically that right from the 16th century down to at least the mid-19th century, the Nanak *Panth* was regarded as an integral part of the Hindu society. Even though distinct from the other Hindu faiths, viz., the Brahmanical order, Vaishnavism, Shaivism, other bhakti cults and the socio-religious orders like the Jains, Jogis (*faqirs,* i.e., Kanphattas and Augars, etc.), it remained within the Hindu socio-religious structure. As a matter of fact, right from the 8th century onwards, the Muslim writers used the term Hindus (*Hanud*) in India in contrast to the followers of Islam (*Musalmeen*). In the early medieval age, even though Buddhism was well established in Sindh, Multan and other parts of the west Punjab, despite social tension between the Buddhists and the Brahmanas, the Arab accounts insist on covering both as a part of the Hindu society. From 13th century onwards, the Persian sources maintain this concept of the Hindus and Muslims and consider all religious sects in Hindustan which were outside the Islamic religion and its people (*Musalmeen*) as the Hindu people (*Hanud*), though, of course, both were divided into various clannish social groups (*firqas*). It is clear from the hymns of

Guru Nanak and the writings of Guru Gobind Singh that when they appeal for social cohesion and composite human culture, they only mention the Hindus and the Muslims as the two main religious classes in Hindustan and regard their own socio-religious order as a part of the larger Hindu society with multifarious sects. It is evident from the 18th century documents that gradually the term *Khalsaji* or the *Panth* comprised all the Sikhs (*Singhan*) divided for political purposes unto various ethnic, tribal and clannish groups (*qabial* or *qabalian* or *qabilas*) under the Sardars (*Sardaran-i-Khalsa*) with their respective *dals* and territorial *zamindari* and *taaluqadari* jurisdictions (*makanat*) all over the Punjab, cis-Sutlej territories and other regions of *subah* Delhi. As before, the distinction between the *firqas* of *ahi-i-Islam* and the Hindu *aqwam* (*qaums*) is maintained and the Sikh *aqwam* (qaums) are considered as a part of the latter. At the close of the 18th and the early 19th century, Mitza Qatil, a converted Sikh-Muslim in *Halft Tamasha* while giving an account of the creeds, traditions and sects of the Hindus, and of the Musalmans of India regarded "the Sikh disciples of Peshwa Nanak Shah Punjabi as part of the Hindus of the Punjab." This concept is maintained both by the Hindu and Muslim writers in the reigns of Maharaja Ranjit Singh and his successors. It is only after the annexation of the Punjab that the British administrators, while writing their memoranda and reports in the English languages, that they gave connotations to the existing technical aspects of the socio-religious orders so as to make Sikhism as distinct from Hinduism.

Prior to the annexation of Punjab (1849), both the English Governor-Generals of India, Lord Hardinge and Lord Dalhousie, while considering the viability of the annexation of Punjab in their correspondence and respective Minutes had considered the Lahore Government as a Hindu Government. When after the first Anglo-Sikh war, Lord Hardinge advocated the non-annexation of Punjab, his main argument was that this being the last Hindu state in India could well serve as a buffer between "the sutledge and the Khyber", i.e., between the English and the Muslim states of Afghanistan and Iran etc. Both Hardinge and Dalhousie considered the 'Lahore Court', 'Khalsa State, Hindu Government', the Lahore Government as co-terminous and identical. Even as late as 1881-83, when the Report on the Census (1881) was compiled as the first experiment in the Punjab, the English administrator responsible for carrying out the census conceded the fact that it was based on "the initial experience", "infinite diversity of the material to be dealt with" and their own, i.e., the English, "infinite ignorance of that material" as well as "ignorance of the customs and the beliefs of the people." It was meant not only for the guidance of the British Indian officials but it also aimed to feed "European Science" about "the social and religious phenomena" of the Punjab. All the same, in many a region, of the peoples of various castes and clans professing the same religious faith, some got themselves recorded as Hindus while others as Sikhs. As a matter of fact, it is only in the late 19th and 20th century that in the changed political circumstances, the Sikhs have come to be viewed as a separate religious entity as distinct from the Hindu Society.

As a matter of fact, it was only during the British rule in the Punjab, towards the closing years of the 19th century, that under the impact of the Singh Sabha Movement, some politically motivated sections of the Sikh community in the Punjab asserted that they were not Hindus (*Ham Hindu Nahin Hain*). However, before Independence (1947), the evolution of the Punjab policy under the colonial rule led to the emergence of the Sikhs as a separate religious and political entity but never as a nation.

Like Buddhists and Jains, the Nanak *Panth* (16th century) in the Punjab and North India was essentially a part of Hindu community and culture. Both Guru Nanak Dev and Guru Gobind Singh, as exponents of Hindu culture, were great liberal thinkers and preceptors. Guru Nanak was, par excellence, a humanist and a fervent believer in the composite culture. Guru Gobind Singh's saying, 'Reckon all human beings of one race (*Manas ki Zat Ek*) urges non-discrimination amongst various religious faiths and racial peoples and the one-ness of the entire human race. Right from the 16th century down to at least the mid-19th century, even though distinct from the other Hindu faiths, viz., the Brahmanical order, Vaishnavism, Shaivism, other bhakti cults and faiths of the Buddhists, Jains, Jogis etc., it remained within the Hindu socio-religious structure. It is clear from the hymns of Guru Nanak and the writings of Guru Gobind Singh that when they appeal for social cohesion and composite human culture, they only mention the Hindus and the Muslims as the two main religious classes in Hindustan and regard their own socio-religious order as a part of the larger Hindu society with multifarious sects. The continuation of this concept all through the 18th and first half of the 19th century is well confirmed by the contemporary sources.

(7) The criticism of the colonial exploitation and colonial approach to history is, by and large, justified. Even when one may not agree

with C. A. Bayly's generalisation (in Rulers, Townsmen and Bazars: North Indian Society in the Age of British Expansion 1770-1870, Oxford, 1983) to the effect that regional consideration and conditions constituted normal state of affairs in the Indian society, the role of the regional or the regional cum religious factors, even during the 18th century India, however periphant or significant, cannot be denied. It is not only the economic and agrarian factors that brought about the downfall of the Mughal Empire in the 18th Century but along with them, the rise of the regional powers guided by socio-religious and political factors which affected the unified features of the Indian polity.

C. A. Bayly's remarks on the decline of the Mughal Empire and emergence of the regional principalities as an aftermath of Aurangzeb's religious policy is not unfounded. Bayly aptly remarks, "Aurangzeb had departed from the latitudinarian stances of his predecessors and insisted on a more full-blooded Islamic policy among his high officials. But in Gangetic north India, where less than 15 percent of the population were Muslims and were concentrated in the cities, this was a hazardous move. Local conflicts over Hindu and Muslim practice became confounded with the tension and periphery over the destination of revenue and resources."

Similarly, the criticism of Burton Stein for not having accepted the view of the mere agrarian cause responsible for the disintegration of the Mughal Empire is partial. In fact, in this regard, these writers have tried to substantiate what was already written long back by the learned historians J. N. Sarkar, Siri Ram Sharma, W. S. Sardesai and others. One may not agree with the views of Bayly, Burton Stein and the authors of New Cambridge History in many a respect, but to say that they have stressed the religious or ethnic factors leading to the emergence of the independent principalities in the 18th century with a view to inculcate such an apprehension for 21st century India, however despicable, is rather too far fetched an opinion. All the same, it is difficult to agree with any of their views which undermines the role of the Indian Muslim League and Muslim communalism vis. a vis., the Hindu organisations responsible for the partition of India.

II

When anyone rejects certain beliefs, customs or usages and asserts correctness of certain alternatives, it is a revolt in the making, Nanak did that. Now revolts can be peaceful or armed depending on various factors. Nanak's revolt was peaceful. And it could not be anything else but peaceful. At certain stages, certain questions do not arise. So the question of armed revolt of a Hindu reformer, which Nanak was, did not arise.

Now against whom this peaceful revolt of Nanak was directed ? Logically, it was directed against those beliefs, customs or usages he rejected. It was against that condition of minds of the people which perpetuated those beliefs, customs or usages. And against that class of people, the Hindu Pundits, who, day and night must have been exerting their energies for the perpetuation of those practices.

Nanak rejected idolatry, caste distinctions, religious asceticism or renunciation to face the onslaught of Muslim rule. Instead, the people must upgrade themselves in beliefs and practices, to a certain extent, of the rulers themselves. It sounds like Sayyid Ahmad Khan of Muslim India of latter days who wanted to upgrade Muslims in view of their backwardness with reference to the better culture offered by the English.

We can safely say that in the making of Nanak there was a background of almost 500 years annexation of the Punjab by Mahmud of Ghazni (1020, to birth of Nanak 1469), of Muslim influence on the people he was born in. Apart from straight away submission or hostility, it seems that, it was, in the person of Nanak, the main ideological response to Muslim domination by the Hindus of the Punjab. Therefore, to an extent, the aspirations of our forefathers' must have contributed in the making of Nanak.

Sikhism was founded by Guru Nanak, about the end of the 15th century, apparently to blend, in peaceful union, the discordant elements of bitterness and animosity existing between Hinduism and Islam, the religious of the ruled and the ruler. He endeavoured to effect this purpose by means of mild persuasion. The cardinal principle of this teaching was the unity of God and the equality of all men before him. He preached against idolatry and caste distinctions in order to bring Hinduism on to a level with Islam. Keeping the goals of both religions in view, he asserted that salvation could be attained only through upright character and good deeds. He also urged that the object of human life was purity of mind, and declared that asceticism or renunciation of the world was unnecessary. He lost no opportunity to strike a blow at the superciliousness of Hinduism and Islam but his remarks carried with them so much of straight forwardness, sincerity and ready wit that even the bigoted Pandit and Mullah did not feel annoyed with him. He laid stress on a spiritual discipline (*Sadhana*) which required devotion and service. He exercised great influence over large numbers who looked on him as their Guru (or spiritual guide, and with their offerings he established '*Langars*' or free dining halls where crowds of the poor and the helpless were fed.

It is not possible to grow a plant without a favourable environment. What Nanak preached attracted people who felt spiritually elevated and consequently, better equipped for practial tasks of life in the given circumstances. But mere preaching religion and satisfying peoples spiritual requirements have not singled out Nanak for greatness. Without listing others, it is so simple to understand that at any given time there are always many preachers of any religion.

In both cases, insignificance would have been his fate. But the situation is otherwise. We find in Nanak's followers, men of high intellectual calibre. The succeeding Gurus took one or the other steps of original nature and which could not have been possible either without the support of the people or without the commitment of the leaders of the movement. The movement was peaceful as it could not have been otherwise. The second Guru Angad invented 'Guru Mukhi' or Gurumukhi script and the first prose of Sikh religion, i.e., 'Janum Sakhi' of Guru Nanak was written. Amar Das, the third Guru, encouraged inter dining and forbade the practice of sati. Ram Das, the fourth Guru, added to the solidarity of the growing faith by providing it with a sacred tank to which he gave the name Amristar (the tank of nectar). He made it obligatory that his followers contribute one tenth of their incomes towards the common funds of the Guru. Guru Arjun, the martyr, compiled the *Adi Granth* and built a temple in the centre of the tank and named it Harmandir (God's temple). He encouraged his followers to take to the lucrative trades. So there is the innovative leadership who have their following steadily increasing in numbers. The movement seems to fulfill certain needs of a section of the people.

Himself, he was an intellectual of great order who was able to dictate holy book of the religion the *'Adi Granth'*. And he was in a position, at least mentally, to disregard the Mughal Emperor, a no small thing to contemplate. The Guru remained dignified and unrepentant in front of Emperor Jahangir. He had given rupees 5,000, said to be moved by compassion, to Prince Khusru, the rebellious son of the Emperor. The Guru was tortured. He died a martyr. These events at the time of their happening must have looked small but historically, they proved to be of great significance.

The martyrdom of Arjun proved an impetus for further developments... If birth or emergence of Nanak may be termed the origin, then right from the second half of the 15th century (Nanak born 1469) to 1800 i.e., the rise of Ranjeet, this variation of Hindus continued to produce leaders of high calibre. This cannot be an accident or chance in the history of our land. Nothing but the tyrannies of the age on the people of the land was fueling the process of history which produced these men.

In conclusion, we may say that this revolt of Hindus of the Punjab was of local character, therefore it could not have been a counter point to the Mughal imperialism in India. Its character and outward form changed as it progressed and ended up in the formation of Sikh power in the Punjab. It was a peoples' movement and it threw up men of character from amongst the common folk. It tells us as to how far humans can go for a place under the sun. The Hindus of the Punjab dared to think, did not accept Muslim supremacy, upgraded themselves, even taking ideas from their oppressors and continued the struggle. The time came when imperialism weakened and the revolt triumphed.

Chapter 3

Approach to the Study of Culture of the People with Special Reference to Punjab*

Mr. Vice-Chancellor, Dr. Ganda Singh, Fellow Delegates, Ladies and Gentlemen:

I am extremely indebted to the organisers and members of the Punjab History Conference for having chosen me as the General President for its 19th Session to give me, thus, the opportunity to share with you my ideas and thoughts on the History of the Punjab. I am fully conscious of my limitations for addressing from this August forum which has had the most eminent historians as its Presidents in the past. Perhaps my only claim is my association with this organisation right from its very inception as well as my fervent desire and constant endeavour to build it up on sound academic and scientific lines so as to become one of the leading organisations in the country. A few years back, I presided over the Medieval Section of this Conference and now I regard it as a privilege for the great honour done to me.

The most significant aspect in history is the approach to the study of the culture of the people. In the recent years, the canvas and scope of history has been so much widened as to encompass more or less all the facets of culture of mankind. An historian has to underline the currents and cross-currents of political, social, economic, religious, regional and geographical factors which adequately explain the variety in the way of life of the people within and outside the country. He equally aims at covering comparative study of social formations and institutions, more especially with the neighbouring countries and outside world. An Indian historian may as well emphasise the study of such problems which emphasise Indian contact through the ages

---

* Presidential Address at the Punjab History Conference, 19th Session, March, 1985, Punjabi University, Patiala.

under-lining mutual impact and influences on the life of the people and totality of culture. The entire approach has to be scientific and objective so far as possible. The historical processes which have determined the history of mankind are immensely complex and an explanation of any historical situation in the history of a people without reference and analysing the accumulative social, economic and ideological urges of the society at large becomes rather an over-simplification of the historical situation in a period of change.

As a matter of fact, ever since the end of the colonial phase after the Second World War, there has been considerable intellectual temper and human thinking is in deepening crisis. The social scientists and the humanists are fully conscious and well equipped with multifarious tools in the operation of writing about the life and culture of the people settled in different regions of the world. This has thrown a great challenge to the erstwhile complexes of so-called superior civilization of the people of one part of the world in comparison to those of others. A partial or partisan analysis of culture and falsification through the suppression of truth may be well exposed. The use of shibboleths based on complex of superiority of race and culture or preconceived notions based on an individual or a group basis in the historical writings have done more harm than good to the correct appreciation of the life of the people. Of course, historiographic trends have undergone changes from time to time. The writing and reinterpretation of history has been going on from one age to another. It is written afresh not only because new facts and data have been discovered but because the life and culture of the people has to be looked upon from new aspects than done in the past. Today, historiography is passing through a crucial stage. It is well accepted that historical facts of the past cannot be changed. All the same, there is a danger that a historian inspired by political, regional, communal or ideological considerations may attempt to alter the past picture through distortions. There is every danger of making history as an instrument of propaganda for vested ideologies and groups in a community in the name of a nation. "Five Thousand Years of Pakistan" is a ridiculous example in this regard.

The understanding of the concept of culture for a proper scientific study of mankind is essential as culture exists within the society and not outside it. The present day developed means of communications and smallness of the world have left a great impact on the human thought. Even science and technology would not have much relevance without humanistic studies and historical insight. The changing values of mankind and reciprocal appreciation of cultural heritage of different peoples of the world are bound to affect the character of human thinking and the concept of history.

Regional history is a very fruitful exercise as it affords full opportunities for the exploitation of regional source material of multifarious nature. All the same, an objective approach and disciplined methodology of historical research may caution against parochialism and chauvinism. The historical canvas may be much wider wherein regional diversities and identical features with the neighbourhood and on an all India level have to be clearly underlined. The regional concept is essentially a part of a landscape and of a large whole. Notwithstanding regional bias, elements of continuity and change in the socio-economic formation from one phase to another may be equally discerned. With all the desirability for giving a comprehensive account, any historian with imagination has to prescribe limits for himself for investigation of particular aspects and problems of history in this regard.

As the source material on varying aspects of human life available from one period to another is of numerous types and in manifold languages, any reliance on partial or fragmentary material is too risky to give a fully reliable and comprehensive picture of the subject in hand. For any social structural analysis, the examination of the sources on comparative basis and resort to cross-examination is rather essential. A disciplined technique of the study of the sources may as well help in bringing the gap in our knowledge to the largest possible extent. For the study of any subject in hand, it is the principle of priority and the importance of the selection of the source material which has to be essentially kept in mind.

For the medieval ages, we cannot appreciate the culture of the people without going into details of the various aspects of socio-economic pattern in an integrated manner. Though important works based on regional source material covering archaeology, epigraphy, chronicles and archival literature have been produced, an Indian scholar could not possibly work on these regions without proper knowledge of the regional languages. Distinct progress has been made in this direction. The methodology of research needs more of coordination on the part of historians and scholars of other disciplines in the social sciences for analysing the cultural and institutional aspect of the people.

The identity, concept, personality and territorial jurisdiction of the Punjab through the ages is of vital importance. While the Arab accounts (8th to 14th centuries) provide detailed description about the territories of Sind and Multan, there is no reference to the Punjab. Of course, the term Punjab denoting 'the land of five rivers' emerges during the medieval age and finds frequent reference in the Persian literature of the 14th century. As for the purposes of administration and revenue collection, the territories of North India were divided into *shiqs* (also *khittas*). Multan and Lahore are mentioned as separate *shiqs*. At times, the administration of a couple of *shiqs* could be put under the charge of one governorship. Ain-ul-mulk Abdullah Mahru, *Naib-i-Multan*, in his letters (*Insha-i-Mahru*) mentions that earlier under Mohammad bin Tughluq, he had double charge, i.e., the affairs of Multan and *shiqdari* of Lahore (around 740-41 A.H./1340-41 A.D.).[1] However, Mahru does refer to the Punjab in the context of the Mongol inroads.[2] He advises the Sultan (Firuz Tughluq) for the punishment and suppression of Banbhaniyah Umar who, having sold his conscience and religion, was source of disorder in Multan and Gujarat and was also responsible for having brought the Mongols in the large *wilayat* of the Punjab (*wilayat-i-vasih-i-Punjab*). Mahru states that when the army of Multan reached there, the former (Banbhaniyah Umar) took to flight and moved towards the *wilayat* of Gujarat. It seems in the context that the regions of the *shiq* of Multan comprising the *doabs* were a part of the Punjab or at least intimately connected with it. However, later on, the Mughal sources (16th to 18th centuries) identify Punjab with the territorial boundaries of *Darul Saltanat* Lahore or *subah* Lahore or *subah* Punjab or *wilayat-i-Punjab*. The territorial boundaries extend from the river Sutlej in the east to river Indus (*Sind*) in the north west and comprised five *doabs* or *sarkars,* viz., Bet Jalandhar, Bari, Rechna, Chenhat and Sind Sagar. Apart from this, some hilly regions to the north or Bet Jalandhar, not covered in the *doabs* entitled as *Berun-i-Panjnand,* also formed part of the *subah*. The earmarked mountaineous regions (*parganas*) to the north of the *doabs* formed the respective *doabs* or *sarkars*. The Bari Doab, with headquarters at Lahore, formed the core of the Punjab. By the end of the 17th century, five *parganas* of *subah* Multan were also transferred to *subah* Punjab. However, the *doabs,* viz., Bari, Rechna, and Sind Sagar along with *mahals* beyond the five rivers of the Multan territories continued to form part of *subah* Multan.

The territories between the river Jamuna and Sutlej and the trans-Sutlej territories formed parts of the *sarkars* of Delhi, Hissar Firozah and Sirhind of *subah* Delhi. Notwithstanding the fact that during the course of the 18th century, many a Sikh *zamindari*, *misl* and chieftainship were established in the above mentioned territories, they continued to be well within the jurisdiction of *Subah* Delhi.

At the close of the 18th century and nearly four decades of the 19th century, the kingdom of Lahore established by Maharaja Ranjit Singh (1799-1839 A.D.), covered all the territories of the erstwhile Mughal *subahs* of Punjab, Kashmir, Multan, some of the trans-Indus *ilaqas* of *subah* Kabul, viz., Peshawar, Kohat, Bannu and a few tribal regions. Except for the two *subahs* of Kashmir and Multan, all other territories were divided into more or less distinct primary administrative divisions. On the eastern side, the Cis-Sutlej chieftainship viz., the chiefs of Malwa and Sirhind being under the British protection remained outside the territorial boundaries of the kingdom of Lahore. The Lahore *darbar* covered the traditional territories of the Punjab, the *subahs* of Multan and Kashmir as well a few *ilaqas* of Afghanistan. All the same, the concept of the Punjab remained the same as before.

As a matter of fact, the real change in the territorial concept and the traditional boundaries of the Punjab came only after its incorporation in the British Empire. After the first Anglo-Sikh war, the British occupied Lahore in February 1846. In accordance with the treaty signed in March 1846, the Lahore *darbar* ceded to the English East India Company all the territories in the *doab* between the Beas and the Sutlej as well as the hill territories between the Beas and the Indus including Kashmir and Hazara. Kashmir and Hazara were made over to Maharaja Gulab Singh for a payment of rupees seventy-five lakh but later on Hazara was exchanged for the territory near Jammu. After the second Anglo-Sikh War, all other territories of the Lahore Kingdom were annexed to the British Empire (30-31 March, 1849) and were incorporated in the newly formed province of the Punjab. At the same time, the administration of the Cis-Sutlej states as well as districts comprising Thanesar, Ambala, Ludhiana and Ferozpur were merged with the Punjab in 1849. In 1858, the Delhi division of the North Western Provinces comprising the six districts of Delhi, Gurgaon, Panipat, Rohtak, Hissar and Sirsa were also merged with the Punjab. Later on in 1901, the districts of Peshawar, Hazara, Bannu and its Marwat tehsils as well as the trans-Indus part of Dehra Ismail Khan excepting the *ilaqa* of Vehoa were separated from the Punjab so as to form a new North Western Frontier Province. With the transfer of the British Indian capital from Calcutta to Delhi, the Delhi tehsil, along with the Mahrauli *thana* of Ballabgarh, was separated from the Punjab and formed into the Delhi Province. Thus, it is very clear that the Punjab, as it stood on the eve of the partition of India in 1947, has been formed by the British Indian Government purely due to administrative expediency for the stability of its colonial rule in India.

The importance of the relationship between geography and history is well known. Apart from the other features, the trade-routes have had considerable impact not only on the economy but also on the cultural and political aspects of the inter-connected regions. Throughout the ancient and the medieval periods, India enjoyed a very strategic position for international trade routes-both land and sea which connected the mediterranean, Africa, West Asia with South-East Asia and China. These routes served as links between the areas of raw material, production and exchange between the manufacturing centres and the markets. This equally exposed India to the humanising factor of cultural interaction with the peoples or the trading countries.

All through the ages, by land the Punjab was connected with the Central Asian countries through the 'trans-Himalya' network of trade routes which ultimately joined with the so-called "Silk routes" or "Silk roads" (a term coined in the nineteenth century by Baron Ferdinand Von Richtehofen connecting China with the Mediterranean after passing through many a region of Central and West Asian countries. The routes from the Punjab and North-Western India traversed through the Hindu Kush, the Pamirs and the Karakoram.[3] The mountain passes at the North-West of the Indian sub-continent connected the Western Himalayan ranges with the Pamirs (Roof of the World) through Hindu Kush and Alai. The Taxila-Khyber Pass (3,370 feet)-Kabul-Balkh was the major route. It passed through Eastern Afghanistan and the western mountains of Hindu Kush, the easy Shibar Pass (10,778 feet) and the mountain valley of Bamian and Samangan. Though there were other routes from Kabul to Balkh, even shorter, the most convenient one was through Bamian as described above. Balkh was connected in the north with Samarkand and these two cosmopolitan oasis towns cum trade centres of Cental Asia on the silk routes were well connected with Eastern Central Asia and China in the east as well as West Central Asia and the West Asian countries.

Notwithstanding overlapping, the trading emporia of the western and eastern parts of Central Asia were more or less marked. The western portion of Central Asia comprised areas north of Hindu Kush, viz.. Bactria, Transoxiana, Samarkand (Sogdiana) and Ferghana-now-a-days called Western Turkistan covered by the present day Soviet Central Asia as well as North Afghanistan. The eastern portion of Central Asia comprised the regions of Xinjiang along with Tarim Basin known as Eastern Turkistan as well as Chinese Central Asia. On the silk road, the Alai mountains separated the Eastern Central Asia, i.e., the Chinese Central Asia from the Western Central Asia, i.e., the present day Central Asia. The Alai or Kizilsu valley leading to Oxus river and Bactria constituting part of western portion formed a convenient traffic channel from the East to the West.

Another route from north-western India started around Peshawar and passing through Chitral and the Pamirs was connected with Yarkand in the north and Balkh in the west. Still another less important route from north-western Punjab moved towards the difficult Khawak Pass (11,650 feet) of the Hindu Kush Range and passing through it joined the silk route connecting the south-western part of the Tarim Basin with Balkh via Badakshan over the Pamirs, Kashgar and Alai.

Apart from these, the Punjab was also connected with Central Asia through Kashmir. Two distinct, well-trodden routes connected West Punjab with Srinagar (Kashmir)[4], viz., from the Jehlum valley (Hasan Abdal) through the Barahmula gorge and cutting through the Pir Panjal range to Srinagar and secondly, from Gujrat-Bhimbar-Rajouri to Pir Panjal Pass (11,462 feet) and onwards to Srinagar. The latter was the main route usually followed by the Mughal emperors. There were also tracks which connected the Swat valley with Kashmir through the Ghorband valley to Indus and then from the low mountains of Hazara to Jhelum river and joined the aforementioned Barahmula gorge route towards Srinagar. From Srinagar, two main routes followed—one towards north-east to Leh (Ladakh) via Zoji-La Pass and while passing through Taghnak-Karakoram Pass (18,694 feet), it bifurcated, one route going to north-east towards Khotan and yet another to north-west towards Yarkand—both situated on one of the main silk routes of Central Asia. There was also a route from Shigar (Lower Tibat) which probably joined the above route at Taghnak. Srinagar was equally connected with Chitral via the Astor valley, Gilgit valley and the easy Shandur Pass (12,250 feet) and with the Pamirs directly through the Astor valley. From Pamirs, a route led to Tarim Basin in Central Asia.

There were two other major routes which connceted the Punjab with Leh,[5] one from Lahore via Sialkot, Jammu (Jammu region) and after crossing the Banihal Pass and Pir Panjal range towards Srinagar and another from around Nurpur to Kangra, Kulu, Lahul Spiti to Toling in West Tibet and Leh where both these routes joined the main Srinagar-Leh route going towards Khotan and Yarkand on the main Central Asian silk route. This was an easier route for the Chinese Turkistan.

Apart from the Lahore-Kabul-Qandhar-Khurasan route, the Punjab was equally well connected with the West Asian countries through other distinct routes.[6] The important land routes connecting with West Asia were, firstly, from Lahore to Multan-Qandhar (via Duki and Fusharj as well as via Dera Ismail Khan) and then to Khurasan and secondly from Ultan to Iran via Balochistan and Makran. The Multan-Qandhar route was more cumbersome because of the deserts all the way[7] and as such, for Khurasan, the Lahore-Kabul-Qandhar route was preferred.

The real importance of the routes connecting Punjab with West Asia, Himalayan and trans-Himalayan Central Asian territories lies not only in the politico-economic aspect but in the cultural dimension which has been far less emphasised hitherto. All through the ages, Punjab had not only been the gateway of India in its north western portions but ever since the ancient period had developed close cultural ties with the aforementioned territories, more especially with Afghanistan, Iran, Turan, forming part of Central Asia but politically under the Iranian jurisdiction and other West Central Asian territories.[8] The economic nodes along the trade routes with specialised commodities and inhabited by local population ruled by tribal chiefs from time to time with different ethnic lineage and culture influenced not only the life of the local inhabitants but also of the peoples of other territories connected through trade. The economic and cultural interactions affected the process of cultural transformation, at times, in a complex manner. Trade essentially financed the political centres along the inter-territorial trade, routes which evolved cultural synthesis resulting from the historical, religious and material cultures, philosophical and ecological features of different regions. It equally affected the regional artistic and intellectual contribution of ideas. In the ancient period, Buddhism had gone from India to China via Central Asia and by the early medieval age, the Central Asian Buddhist forms and ideas in return affected the Buddhism in Northern India. Notwithstanding the fact that from the 7th to the 10th centuries, along the trade routes from the Punjab to Central Asia and the main silk routes, lived populations adhering to different religions, viz., Hindus, Buddhists, Zoroastrians, Manicheans, Nestorian Christians and Muslims from the 8th century onwards—the archaeological artistic evidence reflects the cultural diversity of the population and the influences of the Indian, Iranian, Chinese and even the Mediterranean arts. There is, in fact, a special relationship between the Buddhist art of North-Western India and Central Asia.

Within Central Asia, the ecology and the socio-economic systems of Eastern and Western Asians were different from each other whereas the former, because of the scarcity of water resources and the prevalence of steppe-desert regions, was more characterised by the pastoral economy; the latter's economy was traditionally based more on agriculture than on pastoralism. Apart from Iranian and Mediterranean influences, it had been equally amenable to Hindu-Buddhist impact from the Punjab and North-Western India. Reciprocally, the socio-economic pattern of Western Central Asia continued to affect the socio-economic orders in the Punjab from the ancient times down to the medieval ages in many a respect. There were even migrations of the peoples-tribes and clans as well as individual families all through the medieval age-which helped in the development of the agricultural economy, process of urbanisation and evolution of the composite and synthetic culture of the Punjab.

Practically all the routes traversed by the merchants and the travellers accompained by the pack animals had to cross difficult streams over the ferries and rope bridges made of twisted twigs but the convenience of the availability of local pack animals, food, porters and above all, the security were the main considerations for following a particular route. The trade caravans often preferred to take longer and easier routes for the safety of the heavily loaded pack animals. From North-Western India to Central Asia, the Hindu Kush-Pamirs with better travel conditions constituted the main cross roads and were preferable to those routes which followed the Hindu Kush passes to the south west and the Karakoram passes to the south-east. However, at times, political developments led to the diversion or intensification of the alternative routes. During the 8th century, the Sino-Tibetan tussle and the Sino-Arab conflict and the ultimate victory of the Arabs ended the Chinese expansionist plan in Gilgit (Little Bolor), Baltistan (Great Bolor) and pushed them from the Pamirs towards Tarim Basin.

The Arab campaigns against Balkh, Samarkand (Sogdiana) and assertion of ascendancy over the Pamirs not only gave set back to Buddhism in these regions but also led to considerable diversion of trade route from the Punjab and North-Western India to the silk routes in Central Asia from the Pamirs to Karakoram The aforementioned routes from the Punjab-Kashmir-Tibet or Punjab-Tibet via Karakoram to Eastern Central Asia came to be heavily traversed and despite difficult climatic conditions, the caravan-traffic continued to be operated till recent times. Apart from various other items, it was from this route that the import of goat fleece from Yarkand and Tibetan highlands led to the development of shawl-industry in Kashmir during the medieval age and in the first half of the 19th century even in Nurpur and Amritsar in the Punjab as well.[9] However, the establishment of strong Indian Mughal Empire during the 16th and 17th centuries, which in the north-west comprised the territories of Afghanistan, Badakhshan and Balkh (occupied by the Mughals in 1646-47 AD) rendered the north-western trade routes across Hindu Kush and the Pamirs to Western Central Asia equally popular.[10] But during the 17th century, the loss of Qandhar to the Safavid Empire of Iran did adversely affect the trade route from Lahore-Multan-Qandhar to West Asian countries. Similarly, during the 18th century, on the decline of the Mughal Empire, the invasion of Nadir Shah (1739 AD) and the recurring Durrani campaigns and the unsettled political conditions in the Punjab[11] not only affected its economy but led to considerable volume of the trade-traffic from the north-west routes to those connecting Punjab with Himachal territories and finally with Srinagar or directly with Leh for onward movement to Central Asia.[12] To this was added the equally disturbed conditions in Georgia, Armenia, Persia and Afghanistan, the money-exchange problem as well as tendency on the part of the local chiefs to charge higher tariff rates.[13]

The most preferred intensified route in this regard was via Nurpur, Kotla, Haripur, Guler, Kangra, Jawalamukhi, Nadaun, Sujanpur-Tira, Mandi, Suket, Sultanpur (Kulu), Lahul and Leh.[14] This route also touched the headquarters of the local chiefs of Western Himachal which was considered to be a part and parcel of the *Kohistan-i-Punjab*.[15] Kangra was as well connected with the other *qasbas* in Himachal territories through internal routes. Kangra was also connected with Srinagar directly which joined the Leh route. From the East Punjab side, another important route was Jalandhar-Hoshiarpur-Kangra which further followed the aforementioned route, Kangra-Kulu-Leh.

Notwithstanding all this, the inter-territorial trade, even though scuttled, continued to operate on the traditional northwestern caravan routes as well for the need of the goods either way, the lure of profit and the income from the tariffs, were the main incentives. As a matter of fact, the *banjara* community operated both on short and long distance routes for transportation of goods on fixed charges.[16] Some of the *banjara* tribes specialised in the carriage of particular articles. By the 17th-19th centuries, the contemporary sources point towards the practice of insurance (*bima*) of the goods being transported on the main routes. The *banjaras* also carried armed guards with them. The zamindars of the regions were required to ensure their free passage in their respective *zamindari* jurisdictions. As the *banjara* class kept up the supply pipeline from one place to another, and hazarded great risk on the insecure routes, it was well respected in society. Whenever a caravan reached a *qasba*, it was received with great warmth. The zamindars often offered robes of honour to the *banjara* chiefs on the safe arrival in their territories. Notwithstanding the disturbed political conditions during the 18th century, the Sikh chiefs in the Punjab fully protected the interest of the merchants both in the plains and the hilly regions.[17] The 18th century *akhbarat* (news-letters) relating to the Punjab show that the Sikh chiefs and the *misaldars* fighting against the Durranis often got information through the business magnates (*sahus* and *sarafs*) regarding the political occurrences and military movements on the part of the Durranis and the local chieftains enroute Kabul-Peshawar-Lahore-Amritsar-Delhi.[18] As the business community was vitally affected by the political cum military situation, the Peshawar *sahus* used to send some of the businessmen as special messengers along with detailed information for their counterparts, i.e., *sahus* and *sarafs* in Lahore, Amritsar, Patiala and those in the main business centres in Rajasthan.[19]

The medieval chronicles and the archival source-material bear testimony to the settlement of the mercantile communities from the Punjab and Multan in the cities of Central and West Asian countries, viz., Kabul, Ghazni, Qandhar, Herat, Mashhad, Yezd, Kachan, Cashin, parts of the Caspian shore and the Persian Gulf.[20] There, they were provided full protection for their properties and enjoyed complete religious freedom. They equally influenced the social concept of those territories. As late as 19th century, the Governor of Bandar Abbas prohibited the cow slaughter in reverence to the sentiments of the Indians settled over there.[21] For the medieval and early modern periods, it is on record that from the 14th century to the late 19th century, the Multani merchants and the Punjabi Khatris not only carried on overland business but many a family had trading settlements on the trade routes from the Punjab right upto Central Asia to Astrakhan and Lake Balkhash.[22]

It is significant to observe the trade routes connecting the Punjab served as the beaten tracks not only for the migration of the peoples from the foreign lands but also for the politico-military campaigns during the ancient and the medieval periods. The Greeks, the Parthians, the Scythians, the Shakas, the Kushans, the Huns, the Arabs, the Turks, the Mughals and the Afghans invaded the lands of Punjab and many of their tribes and clans even settled over there. The archaeological, epigraphic and literary sources completely bear out their socio-economic import and assimilation with cultural life of the people of the Punjab. The new socio- religious and political ideals affected the polity and socio-cultural life of the people. The impact on trade, economy, the growth of the towns, the process of urbanisation, agriculture and agrarian relations amongst the various agricultural and pastoral tribes and clans, horticulture, medicine, arts and crafts was fundamental in character which led to social transformation from one phase to another.

Punjab was connected with the Indian Ocean only through Multan and Sind. For the early medieval period, the Arab accounts fully bear out the fact that the Sind port of Deval (Debal) and the Indus commercial towns of Nerun and Mansurah were well connected with Gujrat, Deccan and the western coast of India. At the same time, they had considerable commercial intercourse with the West Asian countries, African countries and Europe through the Arabian Sea of the Indian Ocean. By the 14th century, with the gradual decline and ultimate disappearance of Debal, its place had already been taken by Lahri Bandar, which was as much a port of Sind as of the Punjab.[23]

The Arab intrusion of the western Indian coast, Sind and north-western frontiers of Hindustan started right from the first half of the 7th century AD but except for occasional realisation of partial tribute, the attempt at occupation proved futile due to the resistance on the part of the local tribes and chiefs. It was in the early 8th century (712 AD) that Mohammad bin Kasim approached Sind after having defeated Raja Dahir of Debal and other local chiefs. Thereafter, the Arabs were successful in the occupation of the territories of Multan but they could not penetrate into the heart of the Punjab territories due to stiff resistance on the part of the chiefs and clans settled therein. However, in due course of time, the Arab territories of Sind came to be divided into two distinct states, Mansurah in the south and Multan in the north, under the rule of the local Muslim tribes with political allegiance to the Caliphs of Baghdad. From around the second half of the 9th century, Multan was ruled by the Sama dynasty. In the last quarter of the 10th century, it came to be governed by the Ismaili Qureshi-a Shia Muslim family, a branch of the same dynasty but with political allegiance to the Fatamite Caliphs of Egypt. This was followed by the Sumra dynasty which ruled over Multan from around the second quarter of the 11th century to the 14th century when it was finally annexed by the Delhi Sultanate in the reign of Muhammad bin Tughluq.

For want of adequate contemporary sources, it is not possible to trace complete history of other territories of the Punjab proper for the early medieval age. However, Arab sources, local archaeological finds and later Persian sources do help us in constructing the main events and features of these centuries. It seems that from the 8th to the early 11th century, the territories of the Punjab were dominated by various local tribal chieftains and various states claimed suzerainty over one part or another in an intermittent manner. The main contestants in the struggle for supremacy over the 'Land of Five Rivers' were the Turki-Hindu-Shahis of Kabul and Udabhandapura, the rajas of Kashmir, the Gurjara-Pratiharas of Kanauj, the locally settled Gurjara families, the *amirs* of Multan and finally the Turkish rulers of Ghazni.[24] The Arab and the Persian sources consider considerable portion of Afghanistan i.e., the Kabul territories (Kabulistan) south of Hindu Kush, Lamghan in the north-east and Safed Koh in the south-east as well as Gandhara region forming part of the Turki-Shahi kingdom with headquarters both at Kapisa and Udabhandapura, as part of Hindustan.[25] After intermittent campaigns, by 870-71 AD, the Arabs were able to capture not only Sijistan and Herat but also Kabul. This gave a death blow to the Turki-Shahi family and the establishment of the Hindu-Shahi rule with capital at Udabhanda Pura, also named as Wahind by the Arab and the Persian chroniclers.[26] The Hindu-Shahi rule covered the territories of Afghanistan with Lamghan in the north-west and the regions upto Safed Koh in the south east. Besides this, it equally covered the Gandhara region on either side of river Indus, the regions of Potwar, Kohat, Bannu as well as the plains of Punjab to the west of river Chenab.

It has also been claimed that by the 10th century, the Gurjara-Pratiharas of Kanauj asserted their suzerainty over the chieftains of the Punjab as well as the Hindu-Shahis of Wahind.[27] As a result of mutual warfare, at times, the *amirs* of Multan equally asserted their suzerainty over them.[28] However, it is clear that by the close of the 10th century, Jayapala of the Hindu Shahis was able to crush recalcitrance on the part of local chiefs in the plains of Punjab[29] and extended his territories from Lamghan (Afghanistan) in the north-west to Sirhind in the south-east, also touching the boundaries of Kashmir in the north and Multan in the south—the largest extent of territories in the Punjab ever claimed by the Hindu-Shahis. However, towards the closing years of the 10th century, with the phenomenal rise of power of the Turks at Ghazni (Afghanistan), its Sultan Subuktgin having defeated Jayapala, the Hindu-Shahi ruler, extended his territories upto Indus (Sind) river. Later on, in the first quarter of the 11th century, the incessant campaigns of Mahmud of Ghazni gave a death blow to the Hindu-Shahi rule at Wahind and the Punjab which was annexed to the Ghaznavid Empire. Multan was also captured by Mahmud of Ghazni but later on the Sumras established their independent rule which continued till the 14th century. It is rather significant to remark that when in 1109 A.D., Anangpal, son of Jayapal, the Hindu-Shahi ruler of the Punjab invited the other chiefs of Northern India to give a united confrontation to Mahmud of Ghazni, the *Amir* of Multan-a Muslim chief also joined the other Indian rulers in a bid for liberation of the Punjab and its Hindu-Shahi dynasty. Of course, the battle was lost.

The socio-cultural life of the people from the 8th to 10th centuries serves as a precursor to the establishment of the Turkish rule in North India. As such, the study of the people in the Hindu states should cover not merely conceptual aspect, but it should essentially encompass the structural development in the socio-economic and cultural fields. There are a number of issues which have still to be gone into based on functional analysis rather than merely on theoretical basis. As to what extent the Indian polity was feudal in character or whether the chieftainships within a big state were autonomous in character or the territories of chieftains in a larger state by themselves were segmented states can be essentially analysed against the nature of the political power as well as demographic and tribal background of the peoples settled in different parts of India.

On cultural plane, from 6th to the early 11th centuries, many a region of the Western Punjab were vitally governed by the political, socio-economic and cultural trends and transformation taking place from one phase to another in the territories of eastern Afghanistan, north-western portions of India, Kashmir and the Jammu region. Other regions on the eastern side were more amenable to influence from the social concepts and values of the Gurjara-Pratiharas of Kanauj. This is clearly borne by the numismatic evidence, the archaeological art finds of sculpture as well as the literary sources.[30] Under the Turki-Shahi rulers, both Buddhism and Hinduism were practised. Even though during this phase Buddhism was the state religion, the ruling classes patronised both Hindu and Buddhist cults. It seems that from the 7th century onwards, the Hindu *Siva* cult (*Umma-Mahesvra* and other forms) and Sun Worship (worship of images of *Surya*) gradually gained ascendancy amongst the masses especially with the help of the Hindu military class under the Turki-Shahis. Later on, with the Hindu take over in the 9th century by the Hindu-Shahis, Hinduism became the main religion. Hinduism and Buddhism were socially compatible. Notwithstanding their basic co-existence over a number of centuries, there was gradual demise of Buddhism, especially due to the economic changes brought about first by the Hindu-Shahis and later on by the Islamic Turkish rulers. During the 11th and 12th centuries, the surviving Buddhist followers found refuge in the territories of Tibet and Nepal.

It would not be correct to surmise that on cultural level, Islam came to be known to Punjab only after the establishment of the Ghaznavid rule in the 11th century. The Arab campaigns into the Punjab territories from the 8th century onwards, especially intermittent tussle amongst the *amirs* of Multan, the Hindu-Shahis and the Gurjara-Pratiharas of Kanauj, the consequent reshuffling in the territorial boundaries as well as the socio-economic intercourse during the peaceful periods were bound to have mutual cultural impact.[31] Even though Multan under the Muslim Samma and Sumra rule had majority of the Shia Muslim population, there was significant Hindu population in the urban centres and Buddhists in the rural territories.[32] It is on record that all through these centuries, Hindu pilgrims from the Punjab and other parts of India visited the sacred temples of Multan.[33] It is also on record that there were Muslim settlements in the territories of the Hindu-Shahis as well as the Gurjara-Pratiharas of Kanauj.[34] The Muslim pockets possessed mosques and enjoyed freedom of worship.[35] They were also governed by their own *Shariat* laws and administered by Muslim *ulema* and *hukam*.[36]

India's classical language, Sanskrit which was generally speaking the language of the royal courts, now ceased to be so but it continued to remain the language of the Brahmanical priests and the *pandits*, of the scholars and intellectuals, but in increasingly smaller circles. Already by about the 9th, 10th and 11th centuries because of general regionalization of Indian social polity, the various regions of India were slowly but surely evolving regional languages of their own, which could be distinguished, more or less, from one another. Indeed, the early medieval period is the period of germination of almost all the regional languages of India except Tamil which is much older, the oldest, in fact, of the Indian regional languages. This is also the period which witnessed the evolution of the regional scripts, generally speaking. The numerical notation was, however, shown not in alphabetical letters but in *anka* which differed in different regions of the country.

But the most significant cultural event of the early medieval age, Sultanate and early Mughal period of Indian history is the growth of the nascent regional languages and their taking recognizable shape and form in terms of grammar and syntax and in that of power of articulation of ideas, facts and feelings. This is clear even from the meagre instances of literary compositions belonging to this period, that have come down to us as well as from the testimony of the Arab writers and of Amir Khusrau. This testimony is very clear on one point, namely, that different regional dialects were spoken in different regions of India for common purposes of life. The regional language which the Arab writers and Amir Khusrau came to confront was the one which was current in what came to be known as Hind, namely, Hindavi; they testify that in their times, the language was already evolved.[37]

The growth of the regional languages and literatures during the medieval period was due to several causes simultaneously in operation. Sanskrit was slowly but surely losing its grips for reasons already referred to. Besides, inside of Brahmanism and Buddhism even, because of expansion of its physical boundaries, more and more of relatively lower orders of society and of protestant sects and cults were entering the folds of the dominant socio-religious communities. Followers of these lower order and protestant and esoteric cults were mostly ignorant of Sanskrit and spoke dialects and languages which had only local and regional vogue. This is very clear in what has come down to us of the language and literature of the Nathapanthi and Vajrayani-Sahajayani *siddhas* and others spread over practically the whole of northern India. Countless number of people belonging to these orders, sects and cults communicated among themselves in their regional, at times, even in an esoteric language of their own alone.

The emergence of the mystic sufi order of Muslim saints whose appeal was primarily to the unorthodox, simple and common but religiously inclined common fold, was a great impetus to the growth of the regional language and dialects of what was known to the sufi saints and Islamic political authorities as *Hindosthani*.

The emergence of the religious leaders of the *Nirguna Sampradaya* in the 14th and 15th centuries, and of what is generally called the *Bhakti* cult, in the 15th and 16th centuries, was perhaps the greatest and most potent cultural factor responsible for the growth of India's regional languages and literatures in medieval India. The leaders of these movement as much as those of the medieval Vaishnava and Saiva movements of the Dravidian South, which were all critical and protestant from a socio-religious point of view and were directed towards the common people, considered that their language of communication could be, for effective purposes, the respective languages of the common people alone. They went on articulating, mainly in lyrics, songs and sayings, their ideas and ideals, hopes and aspirations, woes and yearnings etc., which is one reason why the regional literatures of the period are in the main, religious and devotional or didactic in their content, aim and purpose. More or less similar sentiment is articulated in a couplet of Kabir:

Kabira Samskrit sansar me pandit kare bakhan
bhasha bhakti drdhavahi niyara pada nirvan

Sanskrit can be followed by the *pandits* alone; *bhakti* can never be deep-rooted without *bhasha* nor without *bhasha* can one reach *nirvana*.

According to Arab accounts of the early medieval age, the population of Sind and Multan was predominantly Hindu. The people of Sind spoke Arabic and their own language Sindi (Sindian) which was rather different from the rest of India.[38] The people of Multan spoke Sindi and Arabic. Persian was also well understood.[39] By early 11th century, Al Beruni noted the existence of regional languages all over India though the comments that the common people used the 'neglected' vernacular one while the upper and educated classes used a classical one (i.e. Sanskrit) which was much cultivated.[40] During the 13th century, Amir Khusrau commented that the languages of Hindi had been applied in every way to the common purposes of life and that in every province there was language peculiar to itself, and not borrowed from the other. From Delhi to the west, he mentions the languages of Delhi, Dugar, Kashmiri, Lahori and Sindhi.[41] However, modern scholarship is inclined to believe that since 10th-11th centuries, the Multan region developed rich and diversified literary life. Addahman Multani's poem *Sandeshrasak* was written in local Avahattha (around 1039 AD). At the same time, in the Punjab territories as well as in some other portions of North India, during the early medieval age (8th to 13th centuries), the Nath Jogis and the *siddhas* wrote poetry in the local Hindavi dialects, more especially the *siddhas* during the 10th and 11th centuries modified Apabharamsa into early shape of Hindavi. Delhi and Lahore had distinct dialects forming a part of the Hindavi language. From 11th century onwards, the first impact of the Persian and Arabic languages embodied in the sufi literature was made on the Lahori Hindavi dialect (Punjabi). Apart from the sufi factor, the merchants and the caravans from Punjab to Delhi and back used vocabulary which also affected the language of this region. The use of the Arabic script in the Hindavi language of the Punjab also forms the basis for the growth of the Urdu language at a later stage.

In the Punjab, the sufi saint Shaikh Fariduddin Masud Ganj-i-Shakar (1173-1264) communicated his teachings to the simple folk in Hindavi. His verses, later on incorporated in the *Adi Granth,* are in the Punjabi dialects of Multani and Lehndi though Hindi and Persian words intelligible to the people also find place.[42] This is the first recorded poetry in the Punjabi language. Philosophical in content, similies were taken from the every-day life and social customs of the people. The style is simple, natural and forceful.

Apart from Nanak's own composed sayings, the *Adi Granth* compiled in the early 17th century comprises verses from the teachings of many a *bhagat*. In the preceding centuries, the evolved Hindustani language (*Khari boli*) of the Nath Panth jogis had equally influenced the Punjabi language. Nanak's own language is basically Punjabi (Hindavi spoken in the Punjab) but he freely uses nouns and words from *brajbhasha, khari boli,* Persian and Arabic.

In fact the *slokas* of Baba Farid and the hymns of the first six Gurus covering nearly four centuries form a distinct phase in the poetic diction of the Punjabi language. The later half of the 17th century *bani* of Guru Tegh Bahadur (59 *shabads* and 57 *slokas*), as incorporated in the *Guru Granth Sahib*, the *Dassam Granth* of Guru Gobind Singh and Sainapat's *Sri Gur Sobha* bear the impact of the neo-classical style with an emphasis on *Braji* 'Hindi' and *Khari-boli* in the Punjabi language.This was but natural as these writings reflected the language of the people of the regions where the Gurus lived. Apart from it, the Punjabi prose (in Gurmukhi) both in the *kitabi (nastalik)* and *shikasta (trimukhi, chaprela* or *chalant*-running style) was evolved in the course of the 17th century. This is well confirmed by the *nishans* (letters bearing the signatures of the Gurus) and *hukamnamas* issued by the Gurus from time to time. The *chalant nastalik* style was effectively developed by Guru Tegh Bahadur. Guru Gobind Singh adopted it on an extensive scale so as to make it popular one. In the course of the 18th century, the Punjabi poetry, both in Gurumukhi and Arabic scripts, became extremely popular especially amongst the mystic writers. *Kafian Shah Husain* (Gurmukhi), *Mujmua Abyat Sultan Bahu* (Urdu), Bullhe Shah's *Qanun-i-Ishq*, *Mukammal Majmua Abyat Ali Haider*, Fard Faqir's *Darya-e-Marfat* and *Roshan Dil*, Hashim Shah's *Shirin Farhad* and *Qissa Sassi-Punnu* mark the epoch of the Punjabi poetry.

The concept of sufism as a social order was equally common to India and the West Asian and the Central Asian cultures. It emphasized the concept of *tauhid* and *vadha-vujud* (He is everywhere and yet hidden) and the associated concept of the exile of the soul and its longing for return.

Of the sufi *silsilahs*, two of them, namely the Suhrawardi and the Chistia had entered India by the llth-l2th centuries. It was in the Punjab that the first treatise on sufism, the *Kashf-ul-Mahjoob* was written in Persian by Shaikh Abdul Hasan Al-Hujwari, popularly known as Data Ganj Bakhsh of Lahore. Shaikh Bahauddin Zakaria Multani, the follower of Suhrawardi order, also established *khanqahs* at Multan and Sind. Khwaja Muinuddin established the Chistia order at Ajmer (Rajasthan). Baba Farid Ganj-i-Shakar, the representative of Khwaja Qutubuddin Bakhtiyar Kaki of Delhi, established the Chistia seat at Ajodhan (Pak Pattan) in the Punjab. During the 12th century, the Chistia *Silsilah* in India had two great saints in Khwaja Muinuddin Chisti of Ajmer and Baba Farid Ganj-i-Shakar of Ajodhan who laid the foundations of the order on love and service for man and direct spiritual communion with God.[43]

The fact that majority of the Muslims were converts to Islam did not detract them from following many of the Hindu practices in the rural society. The Hindus also came to have reverence for the Muslim saints. The sufis enjoyed special popularity amongst both Muslims and Hindus. They studied the religious and philosophical systems of the Hindus, the epics and the folklore of the country and spoke local dialects like Multani, Sindhi, Punjabi, Hindi and others. Hinduism and *Vedanta* had a great impact on sufism. The influence of Hinduism is specially noticeable on the sufi order of Chistias. They came in contact with the yogis and sadhus and borrowed from them the practice of music and singing during prayers. This can be further confirmed by the institutional study of the socio-economic structure of the early medieval age.

For the nature and the impact of the Ghaznavid rule in the Punjab (llth-l2th centuries), very little work has been done so far. The Persian chronicles give details about the campaigns of Mahmud of Ghazni and for the period thereafter one could outline the political trends till the establishment of the Turkish rule at the close of the 12th century. Of course, during the early 11th century, Al-Beruni in his account on India in *Kitabul Hind* (written, in Arabic) makes his observations on the social structure, philosophy, mode and ways of life of the Hindus, their manners and customs, languages, prejudices against the foreigners, especially the Muslims, haughtiness and superiority complex in respect of the achievements in the sciences.[44] Al-Beruni states that Mahmud of Ghazni through this military campaigns and exploits "utterly ruined the prosperity of this country (India)" and "the Hindus became, like atoms of dust scattered in all directions." Al-Beruni comments this very fact and accounted for the most inverterate aversion of the Hindus towards the Muslims.[45] He further comments that this also explained the reason that the Hindu scientists had retired far away from the parts of the country conquered by Mahmud to places beyond his reach, to Kashmir, Benaras and other places.[46]

According to the earlier Arab accounts and AI-Beruni, the prevalence of the caste system amongst the Hindus brought about considerable compartmentalisation in the social order. Ibn Khurdabah (later half of 9th century) had noted the prevalance of 7 castes in the Hindu society, i.e., the Shakshris (Kshatriays), Barahimah (Brahmins), Kastris (Khatris), Shudras, Besh (Vaishyas), Shandals (Chandals) and the Zambs (Doms).[47] However, AI-Beruni (early 11th century) mentions only four traditional castes, i.e., Brahmin, Kshatriay, Vaishya and Sudra. Al-Beruni does not reckon Antyaja, i.e., the people belonging to craft or profession as members of any caste. At the same time, Hadi, Dome

(Domba), Candala and Badhtau are not reckoned amongst any caste or guild.[48] Al-Beruni's itinerary remained confined to the territories of the West Punjab and for his treatise, he mostly utilised the earlier Hindu texts available to him at Multan. As such, his reflections on the society cannot be taken as an exact portrayal of early 11th century India and his observations about Indian society are not free from complexes.

One would be naive to believe that the Ghaznavid rule in the Punjab, except for administrative governance and realisation of the revenues, was sterile in character. In fact, there was considerable social transformation. *Divan-i-Masud Saad Salman* sheds significant light on the cultural traits of some classes of the society.[49] Born in Lahore, Saad Salman lived and wrote under six Ghaznavid rulers in the Punjab (C. 1038-1127 AD). He was the most eminent poet of the times and preceded Amir Khusrau of Delhi by nearly two centuries. It is believed that Saad Salman compiled his works in three languages, viz., *Parsi* (Persian), *Tazi* (Arabic) and *Hindavi* (Hindustani). It is rather unfortunate that his *Hindavi Divan* is not traceable. However, his *Davazdah-Maha* in Persian has been considered as the earliest reference to *Barah-Masa*, the popular folk form of poetry and music in North India.

Masud Saad Salman's *Qasaid* and *Habsiyat* (prison poems) are well known.[50] Some of the poems give an interesting account of the sufi and secular music, the *majalis* (musical gatherings), the musical instruments and their enchanting tunes and the well known male and female musicians of his time. Saad Salman mentions his own visit and that of Pari-Bani, the female artist to Alander (Jalandhar) which was next in importance to Lahore. This equally shows that Jalandhar was a part of the Ghaznavid state in the Punjab. While giving description about the royal musical concert (*shahi majlis*), the author also mentions musical instruments, viz., Chang, Barbat, Chighanah, Unqa, Surnay, Nay, Jabah (musical box, i.e., the barrel-organ) and the choicest musical songs and tunes viz., Qawwali, Qanl and Bangs (Tar). In the *majlis*, Wine (*mai*), *Meena* and *Saqi* went together with *Saror-u-Raqs* (*mujra*-song and dance). The author also refers to the amassing of wealth by the ruling elite and indulgence in extravagance, the pimps, the dealers in female flesh, the gambling dens, the corruption amongst the officials from *mufti* down to the ordinary policeman.

In fact, music occupied an important part of the cultural life in medieval India. For the Delhi Sultanate period, Amir Khusrau speaks of the Indian melodies and musical instruments which placed the Indian music in an enviable position. The Jabah, Alawan, Tala, Hindi, Mandal, Ajab-Rud, Chang, Rabab, Nay and Duff were played in the musical concerts (*majalis*).[51] In *Qiran-us-Sadain*, Amir Khusrau provides detailed description about each one of these instruments. The Sultans and the Indian chiefs (chief zamindars) patronised groups of artists (mandalis) and held regular musical concerts (*majalis*) where vocalists and instrumentalists displayed their skill. The musical halls were specially designed for the artists and the audience where full decorum was observed. Many a foreign artists settled in India added to the richness of the music. The sufis permitted mystical music which helped in the creation of sama, an ecstatic state. The reciters of Quran (*muqriyan*), *qawwals* and the instrumentalists were an integral part of the sufi *khanaqahs* of the Chistia Order. During the bhakti phase, music played an important role in the *kirtans* arranged by the *bhagats*.

This is equally true of the Sikh religion. In his religious discourses, Guru Nanak is always shown accompanied by the two rebeck players. The hymns of the *Adi Granth*, those incorporated in the *Janam-Sakhis* and other Sikh literature are replete with *Ragas* of various types. In fact, it is high time that with an inter-disciplinary approach, the theologians, the musicologists and historians were to work out in detail the relationship and the nature of music associated with the Sikh religious literature.

In the later half of the 17th century, Nawab Saif Khan Faqirullah in *Raga Darpana* (also referred as *Mankutuhal*) detailed musical treatise[52] on India underlines the distinct contribution made by Sheikh Bahauddin Zakariya Multani in the composition of the melodies. *Raga Multani* was his creation. Following him, Nayak Bakshoo mixed *Malsiri* in *Dhanasiri* to bring about *Multani Dhanasiri*. *Kafi* was sung in Sind to express sentiments of love and affection. In Lahore and the adjoining territories, *Chhand*—constituted of a few lines—was sung. Hazrat Sheikh Bahauddin Zakariya Multani gave it the Persian name of *Chhand* and adopted this poetic form for musical rendering. Its theme comprises praise for the All-Merciful as well as love and humility of man before the Creator. In the Punjab countryside, *tappa* (also *dappa*) was sung in the local language. It was made up of two to four single lines or even more, but each set of two rhymes separately. The theme was usually didactic. Of the instruments, *Sarangi, Rabab* and *Tambura* were popular in the Punjab. Though the Kashmir music was mostly influenced by Persia, *Shahnaz* was analogous to *Sri Raga* which the people of the Punjab sang.

Music was popular and patronised by the chieftains in the Punjab throughout the 18th and first half of the 19th century. Ram Sukh Rao in *Sri Fateh Singh Partap Prabhakar* has given comprehensive account of music along with a theoretical and philosophical basis of the Indian classical music.[53] He has also defined the *ragas* of different types. He equally refers to rewards given to the *rababis* of the *gurdwaras*, musical concerts at the court and the popular song of *puch kara* at the marriage procession. He also compiled a separate treatise on music *Sri Radha-Govind-Sangit-Sar*.

From the 13th century onwards, the Turkish occupation of North India gave a fresh impetus to crafts and industries. This had great impact on the socio-economic life of the people. Apart from the ancient use of whorls and spindles rotated by hand and the cotton-gin, the spinning wheel (*charkha*) was quite in common use with the women by the middle of the 14th century. The professional class of cotton-cleaners (*naddaf*) cleaned and made the cotton fine with bowstring device (midaft a wooden implement with which the cotton cleaner strikes the bowstring to make the cotton fine). This inevitably led to greater commodity production of cotton crop and textile industry in coarse cloth both for domestic and commercial purpose.

Cotton and silk textile industries, craftsmanship of war weapons, leather works, gold work, embroidery, tailoring and house-hold utensils representing cohesion of the West Asian, Central Asian and Indian cultures flourished at a tremendous pace from the 13th-14th centuries onwards.

The irrigation of land through wells has been known to India since ancient times. The wells named *araghatta* and *udhataghati* did operate through pots of wheel but it is difficult to say if the Persian wheel (*saqiva*) was in vogue. It seems that from the 13-14th centuries onwards, 'Persian wheel' became quite popular in North-Western India, especially in Sindh and in the Punjab. It equally helped the process of transformation of some of the pastoral and animal breeding tribes to agricultural communities.

As regards writing material, paper industry developed from the 13th century onwards. Though the use of paper was well known to the Arab culture since 8th century, the Indians mostly used date and palm leaves as well as bark of the *tuz* tree, as writing material during the early medieval ages.[54] From the 13th century onwards, the use of writing paper became quite common though its scarcity is confirmed by the fact that written papers were washed off for re-writing.[55] From the 16th century onwards, paper industry developed tremendously so as to export it even to West Asia. Sialkot, in the Punjab, developed as an important manufacturing centre of paper industry.

For the early medieval ages, the Arab writers have given a favourable account of the development of science in India. After the 13th century, the fusion between the Hindu scientific heritage and the scientific knowledge of the Islamic world led to further development in the field of science and technology.[56] In Civil Engineering, the removal of Asoka's Pillar from Topra and its transportation and installation at Ferozabad (Delhi) by Firuz Shah Tughluq is a unique engineering feat.[57] In building industry, the use of time-mortar and domed roofing grew from the 14th century onwards. Water cooling process was known to all through the ages. During the medieval age, the cooling process was developod through the medium of saltpetre.

In military technology, the Arabs had developed the use of catapults (*manjanik*) for discharging stones, naphtha weapons and appliances for shooting fire arrows used against the Indian army in Sindh in early 8th century.[58] The Hindu chiefs in the Punjab also learnt them in the following centuries. The use of light cavalry with coats of mail for the horses, stirrup and horse shoe—an essential equipment of the Turkish army in the early 13th century, gained ground amongst the armed forces of the Indian chiefs throughout India.[59] In the 16th century, Babur introduced artillery in the Indian art of warfare. Though the Arabian horses continued to be imported all through the centuries, horse breeding was considerably developed in some of the regions in the *doabs* of Bet Jalandhar, Chenhat and Sind Sagar. Cross breeding with Persian and Arabian horses was practised for the further improvement of the breed. The *subah* of Lahore was known for horse studs and supplied the best cavalry to the Mughal state.[60]

It is rather significant to underline the elements of continuity and change in the agrarian relations and structure in the Punjab from the pre-Ghaznavid to the Ghaznavid, Turkish, Afghan and Mughal phases during the medieval age. There is no denying the fact that the Ghaznavid and Delhi Sultanate laid considerable emphasis on the organisation of the military cum revenue machinery for the collection of the land revenue in the Punjab. But it seems rather doubtful that the Muslim fiscal ideas based on Islamic theory of taxation relating to state demand and methods of assessment were really enforced in actual practice.[61] Of course, Persian names came to be applied to various revenue practices and institutions. The rural areas were inhabited by different tribes and clans in different regions and the village communities were governed by the regional and tribal practices undergoing changes from time to time. In the ancient and early medieval ages (pre-Ghaznavid), the tribal conquests by the Huns, the Gujars and the Rajputs led to the reshuffling in the clannish landed interests imposed on the settled villages, new relationship between the dominant clans with the intermediary landed rights and the other cultivating families in the villages, the colonisation of the new villages settled purely by the families of the dominant clans or with the help of the cultivating families of the other castes, the settlement of villages by the religious assignees and concentration of the professional non-agricultural castes adept in certain crafts in the particular villages and on regional inland trade routes. During the Ghaznavid and the Sultanate periods, where the Hindu chiefs were completely suppressed, they assumed the role of landed intermediaries as dominant clans of the rural society. In the course of centuries, the descendants and septs of the erstwhile ruling families were reduced to the position of the petty zamindars. Many dominant clans accepted Islam and continued to possess *zamindari* rights. On the Turkish conquest, some of the Rajput families fled from the plains and set up new chieftainship in the sub-Himalayan ranges and other portions of north India. Even though the term zamindar or *Zamindari* came into vogue during the Turkish rule, it can be well maintained that the institution of *zamindari* with its indigenous socio-economic features can be well traced to the pre-Ghaznavid period in the Punjab. However, the institution of *zamindari* with its manifold aspects found acceptance during the Sultanate period and the Mughal age.[62]

The letters of 'Ain-ud-din' Abdullah Mahru (*Insha-i.Mahru*) clearly bring out the pragmatic taxation policy of the Delhi Sultanate under the Khaljis and the Tughluqs.[63] They emphasise the fact that where the taxation policy cannot be run in consonance with *shariat*, it may well be supported based on expediency and practice as warranted by the *fiqh*. In a letter on matters of *fiqh* addressed to Maulana Shams-ud-din-Mutawakkil, Mahru tries to prove the inadequacy of *kharaj* (taxes) as permitted by the *shariat* to meet the state expenditure. He justifies the heavier incidence of *kharaj* (taxation) than permitted by *shariat* due to financial exigencies. He vehemently argues that the existing *kharaj* imposed on the *riaya* since long standing period (*qadimulayam*) could not be waived. For the legality of extra *sharai kharaj* (taxation), he takes a stand on *Kafi-al Kafi fi'l fiqh* by Mohammad bin Mohammad-al-Maraazi—a well-known work on *fiqh*. Mahru also argues the legality of price control as an emergency measure. He fully justifies the state purchase and selling of certain articles which would benefit the *bait-ul-mal*. In another letter addressed to Maulana Shihabuddin while citing the case of the administration in the territory of Multan, Mahru argues that previously Imad-ul-Mulk's mal administration as well as abolition of certain taxes by Mohammad bin Tughluq and the continuation of those remissions by Firuz Tughluq had led to the decline of the revenues and as such full demand of the *ulema*, sufis relating to the *madad-i-maash* grants could not be met. For such grants, he underlines the state policy wherein only half of the revenue paying and half fallow cultivable land (*kahl*) could be assigned. Here, too, Mahru stresses the fact that the incidence of *mahsul* cannot be determined purely from the *shariat* angle and that it has to take into cognisance the continuing customary practice of the territory. He also outlines the guidelines on which revenues could be realised by the principal *riaya* (*dumbal, dahakin, wa zamidaran*). In the territories assignable to the soldiers (*wajah-i-lashkar*), half of the revenues may be realised in cash and half in kind.

Another important letter of Mahru underlines the state policy towards the development of irrigation. He clarifies that digging of the main canals from the rivers may be the responsibility of the *bait-ul-mal* but in case *bait-ul-mal* is not in a position to bear the expenses for the digging and repair of certain types of canals, expenses may be charged from the people (*khalq*). He spells out the nature of such irrigation canals and reiterates that any deviation from this practice will adversely affect cultivation and the people at large. Even the religious assignees (*ulma wa mashaikh*) availing of the canal water for the irrigation of their villages could not be exempted from sharing expenses for such purpose as this was not the sole responsibility of *bait-ul-mal*. For the adoption of this policy, he quotes Caliph Umar in support of his statement for implementation. Further, in another letter, Mahru, as against the arguments of the *qazis*, underlines the policy for the realisation of the revenues in *iqtas* and *madad-i-maash*. He makes a clear distinction between the *jizya* and agricultural sources of revenue for the purpose of assignment. Accordingly, the income from *jizya* could not belong to the religious assignees or owners of the villages (*malik deh*) and had to be deposited in the state treasury. Other letters as well fully bring out the rights and privileges of the *muqtas* and *madad-i-maash* assignees during the Sultanate period. However, theoretical controversy with regard to the land rights continued to persist throughout the medieval period. Even during the early Mughal phase, Jalal-ud-din Thanesari in *Risala-dar-bai-Arazi* reopened the question of land ownership and the rights of the *madad-i-maash* assignees from the purely theoretical *shariat* angle.[64] While advancing the arguments from the *Hanafite* and the *Shafite* schools and numerous *fatawas* of the Indian Muslim jurists, past as well as contemporary, Jalal-ud-din Thanesari argued that there was no evidence to show that at the initial state of the conquest of India by Islam, the land was either distributed amongst the victors or restored to its original owners. As against such revivalist contention, the Turkish rule on its conquest of North India had accepted the land rights of the various classes based on expediency rather than being influenced by the theoretical canons of the *shariat*.

For the Sultanate period, information is available for the agrarian administration, the methods of land revenue assessment, the magnitude of the state demand and the nature. of land grants.[65] Four methods of assessment, viz., *batai* (*hukam-i-hasil*), appraisement (*hukam-i-mushada*), measurement (*hukum-i-misahat*) and lump sum payment (*muqtai*) were in vogue during this period. The assessment of land revenue based on the measurement of land was specially encouraged by Alauddin Khalji and Sher Shah Suri. The role of the cash nexus also grew in the latter's period but the real breakthrough in the agrarian economy comes during the Mughal age. Even though in the recent years, some original work has been produced on the Mughal agrarian system for whole of North India, no worthwhile attempt has been made on regional basis for the Punjab, either for the Sultanate or Mughal period. As a matter of fact, the multiplication of the sources of various types from the mid 16th to the mid 19th century provides not only lot of information on the subject but also offers a real challenge to a professional historians so as to work out the agrarian economy of the Punjab for these centuries in a coordinated and scientific manner. Some work on the elements of continuity and change in land ownership and rights from the Mughal age to the early British administration in India has already been done[66] but there are various other aspects of the Punjab agrarian society which have still to be worked out in detail.

The agrarian economy in the Punjab has always been governed by its geographical features and the monsoons. The annual rainfall increases from west to east, around 10 to 16 inches in Multan, gradually increasing to 20 inches in the other regions but with only 5 to 10 inches in the South-East tracts while the precipitation increases Sutlej eastwards. As such, the government's share of the gross produce in respect of *mal-o-jihat* and *sair-i-jihat* was fixed at varied rates determined in accordance with a detailed classification of land taking into consideration the nature of the productivity of the soil, the means of irrigation, if any, the outlay of personal and plough-oxen or labour necessary for the cultivation of the land, the nature of the crops, other facilities for cultivation conditioned by the local geographical features in different parts and, above all, on the personal condition of the *riaya* and his holding.[67] The irrigated and *barani* crops were assessed at separate rates. Though the traditional methods of land revenue assessment continued, the introduction of the *zabti* system based on the measurement of land and assessment per unit of bigha, especially for the cash crops (*jins-i-kamil*) is a distinct contribution of the Mughal age. Another distinguishing feature of the period is the extension of the irrigation facilities to the cultivators for the development of the agricultural economy in the Punjab. The sources of information for the development of irrigation facilities are adequately more detailed for the Punjab than any region of North India. The traditional well irrigation (*chahi*) was known to the major territories in the Punjab. Both lined and unlined (*basta* and *kham*) wells are known to have existed. Though the well digging was an individual responsibility of the *riaya*, the Mughal government always financed the project with the advance of the *taqavi* (agricultural loan). The well digging operations were conducted by a class of diggers as well as on joint community basis. By and large, the *riaya,* i.e., the *zamindari* families and other peasant proprietor *riaya* possessed their own wells. The *muzarian* (the occupancy tenants also constituting *riaya*) may or may not possess their own wells. In the latter situtation, they had to pay fixed annual rent for the utilisation of the wells situated on their lands.

There were regions in the Punjab where the wells by themselves could not mature large areas without supplementing from the river floods (*sailab*) in autumn or irrigation from inundation canals or embankments. In the plains, where conveniently available, the water was stored in the reservoirs, ponds and lakes for irrigation and spread out to the fields through water ditches. Even though the regularly constructed main canals were fewer in number and confined to some regions of the Punjab, the irrigation from the inundation water canals and channels from the main rivers or rivulets was the most prominent feature of the agrarian life. Indigenous engineering methods helped the construction of inundation channels and more or less perennial canals utilising the river water whenever its level was high enough to permit its regular flow in the channels. In case of inundation channels, there were usually no *bundhs* (weirs). The archaeological and physical remains of the *nalas* and the channels in the 19th century point towards such practices.

The concept of the *nahr* in the pre-colonial era is different than the later times or even today. In the Punjab, by and large, regions with small and uncertain rainfall confronting the peasants with drought and famine, were covered by the network of perennial canals or canals which would flow for the major portion of the year. Though the chronicles attach importance to the construction of a few canals, viz., the West Jamuna and the Lahore, i.e., Upper Bari, scattered regional contemporary sources point towards the existence of many a perennial small canals in either parched areas or at places where constant water was available from the streams and the *nalas*. Old canals were cleared, remodelled and extended; even canals were constructed by the Mughal state and the Mughal *jagirdars* for stepping up the agricultural and horticultural production.

Apart from the main West Jamuna and the Lahore, i. e., the Upper Bari Doab Canal, there are a number of small canals traceable from the contemporary sources, viz., from Shahpur to Shalimar in Lahore (Ravi Canal); Shahpur to *pargana* Pathankot (Ravi Canal); Shahpur to *pargana* Batala (Ravi Canal); Shahpur to *pargana* Patti Haibatpur (Ravi Canal); from Tawi to Ibrahimabad near Sodhara; Sialkot Canal—a branch of river Aik; and *Nahri-i-Chautung* covering the *parganas* of *chaklas* of Hissar and Sirhind (*subah* Delhi) which led to the growth of the agricultural production in the irrigated regions. With the developed technique of archaeological explorations, it is possible to trace such small canals in the other *doabs* of West Punjab and Multan (Pakistan) for which stray references are available in the sources till the mid-19th century.

Both under the Mughals and the Lahore Darbar under Ranjit Singh, the administration of the canal irrigation formed an integral part of the revenue administration of the local government. The *darogha-i-ab-nahar* (canal *darogha*), the *mir-i-ab* (expert irrigation engineer), the *mehmaran* (masons) in cooperation with the local *jagirdars* and zamindars managed the administration of irrigation as well as for equitable water distribution to the cultivators.

In fact, the real basis of irrigation administration was cooperation between the government and the *riaya*. The headquarters of the canal, the main lines and branches, and the distributaries were all constructed and maintained by the state administration but the water courses and the field channels were constructed and invariably maintained by the *riaya* (primary zamindars, peasant proprietor, *riaya* and the *muzarian*). In regions close to the main rivers and streams, the construction of the canals, the water courses and the *bunds* was the joint responsibility of the state and *riaya*.

During the 16th-17th centuries, the enhanced agricultural production and industrial goods in the Punjab eroded the concept of the village self-sufficiency and subsistence economy in the developed regions. The interdependence of groups of adjacent villages on the local *mandis,* both for commercial crops and non-agricultural products, led to an integrated pattern of rural cum urban, inter-provincial and foreign trade with favourable balance.[68] This exercised great impact on the agricultural development, rural growth and process of urbanisation. In the *subahs* of Lahore and Multan covering the territories of the Punjab, the production of wheat, sugarcane, opium and indigo affected the growth of economy. Similary, the production of industrial goods like embroidered muslin, swords and daggers in the *Chenhat Doab*; shawls, fine calico, stripped silk, satin embroidery, carpets, coarse wooden stuffs, felts, leather, paper, swords, bows and arrows in the *Rechna Doab*; chintz, calico muslin and gold brocades in the Jalandar *Doab* in *subah* Lahore; and calico, chintz, woollen and cotton carpets and bows in the *Bari Doab* of *subah* Multan moulded the character of both the inland and foreign trade. The trading communities had a network of establishments in the rural and urban commercial centres. The *bharawala* firms contracted for carriage of goods for inland, provincial and inter-provincial trade both by road through caravans and through river system. The goods could be insured and payment by means of *hundi* was widely operative in the business circles.

The Indus river system connected the rural areas, the main cities of the *subahs* of Lahore, Multan, Sind and Kashmir. From Lahore to Thatta with its harbour, Lahari Bandar at the mouth of the Indus—one of the largest trading centres in India, goods moved in two ways, one by the river Ravi upto Multan and the river Sind upto Thatta, the other by land. As the journey was down stream, it took less number of days and involved less expenditure. The return journey of upward stream would take over three months, more than double the time needed for going down. From Lahore and Multan, cloth goods, opium, sugar, sulphur and nutgall came down the Indus by boats. Caravans of camels brought merchandise from Agra to Lahore and then to Bhakkar on the river, which was about 15 days distance from the port of Lahari Bandar. The Indus system and the Ravi carried a large trade in shallow draught vessels of about 60 tons and more. After the rainy season was over, many boats plied between Lahore and the commercial centres of Thatta. The voyage took about 40 days via Multan, Bhakkar and Rohri. The *Ain-i-Akbari* places the number of boats that plied the Indus about 40,000. Kashmir trade was also served by the rivers Jhelum and Ravi and linked it with Lahore and Multan so as to secure access to foreign markets through the port of Lahri Bandar. As such, there was considerable commercial traffic through river navigation as the cost of the maintenance of cargo boats was lesser than the oxen-driven carts and the freight charges were much cheaper in comparison to road transportation. It was also a quicker means of transport. The boat building industry was available around all the main rivers, though Wazirabad on the bank of the Chenab (*Rechna Doab*) was a big centre for this purpose.

The Punjab salt was supplied over long distances. The *zamindari* of the salt mountains at Kheora and Sind Sagar belonged to the *janjua* tribe. The salt extraction was undertaken by the professional caste—the *alasha-khash* people. As the state imposed heavy duty on it, an *amin-i-namak* vested with the *faujdari* powers was appointed for the administration of the *parganas* comprising the salt range. In the rural areas, there were pastoral tribes specialised in animal and bird rearing. The breeding of excellent qualities of buffaloes and horses was done specially in the *doabs* of Jallandar, Chenhat and Sind Sagar.

During the early medieval ages, Hindu mysticism found expression in the cult of Naths which emphasised the practice of certain physical, mental and psychical exercises in order to attain liberation from the wheel of rebirth. Nathism itself appears to be older than Matsyendranath and Gorakhnath (10th century A.D.) and the terminology adopted by this cult, i.e., *sahaj, sunn, surti, sabda,* etc. may as well be traced to yoga schools of ancient times. Matsyendra and Gorakh, the great exponents of a school of mystic yogis, were not the founders of a new religion nor were they social reformers. Gorokhnath and the Nath cult grew quite popular from the 10th century onwards. The followers of this sect were the jogis of whom those who went through the last stage of initiation were named *Kanphatas* (with pierced ear lobes and large earings) while others were known as *aughars*. The medieval Indian gnosticism owes much to *Avadhuta* Gorakh.

In North India, from the 13th century onwards, there is revival of religious devotion in the form of *bhakti* which is coeval with social change. The distinguishing feature of the *bhakti* movement is a practical and devotional mysticism intimately interwoven with the daily life and spiritual needs of all classes of men and women. The devotional worship (*bhakti*) was open to all castes. Moreover, equally significant was the fact that the medium of expression of religious thought and devotional worship was the regional vernacular language of the people.

Kabir (15th-16th centuries) finds a prominent position in the *Adi-Granth*. He represented more of the Sant tradition evolved as the synthesis of the vaisnava concept of love in *bhakti*, the tantric *hatha-yoga* technique and the sufi concept in North India during the medieval ages. He refuted the conventional social pattern, the ceremonial aspect and external authority of the religion whether Hinduism or Islam. Kabir rejected all exterior forms, ceremonies, caste distinctions, sacred languages and scriptures. True *bhakti* was not ritual but something nobler. Love was offered direct to Supreme God Himself through strictly inward meditation and devotion. For Kabir, the Guru is the *Satguru*.

In the Punjab, Guru Nanak (15th-16th centuries) also took inspiration from the Sant path. However, Nanak's approach to monotheistic religion based on experience was clearer, more consistent and comprehensive. Nanak's thought revolves as much around God as man and the social order. Kabir and Nanak are strict monotheists and their monotheism is strictly related to man and his society. According to them everything that exists emnates from God and nothing outside His domain. Everything that happens is in accordance with His Law (*hukam*). Both good and evil are His own creation and both operate under His Law (*hukam*). The whole creation is in Him. He resides in the heart of every man. Thus, from the fatherhood of God, Kabir and Nanak directly derive the brotherhood of man to be created on earth. Both Kabir and Nanak believe that God made man to be happy and to be in tune with his Creator but in actual fact he is alienated from Him and is therefore unhappy, suffering and miserable. The whole world is smouldering. They have diagnosed the cause of man's alienation from God resulting in his suffering. He is suffering because he is in the bondage of *maya* and victim of egoism. *Maya* and egoism, both reflection of each other, are the root cause of all evil in life. The reflection of *maya* in the mind of man is egoism which perverts his mind and makes him inhuman. It not only alienates him from God, it alienates man from other man. It dries up from his heart the love of fellowmen and instead feeds it with egoistic motives, greed, pride, anger, lust and love of wealth and callous selfishness. Kabir and Nanak declared these egoistic motives as deadly sins. They bring no happiness to man nor do they help him in his self fulfilment.

According to Nanak, the solution of man's problems on earth lies in the annulment of his alienation from God and return to the path shown by Him. For this purpose, *Sat Guru*, the true Guru's lead is essential. He alone knows the true path and He alone can guide man on to it. He alone is custodian of *Nam* and He alone expresses that in *sabad*. God reveals the truth through *Sat Guru* and his word. With the help of *Sat Guru* and *sabad*, man becomes the embodiment of Nam. Sat Guru's *sabad* burns egoism from the heart of man and a complete human moral transformation takes place in him. In place of alienation from everyone else, love for all pervades in his heart. To be in line with his Creator means to be intune with His creation and to be one with mankind. In Nanak's eyes, in the contemporary society, the *pandits, jogis, bairagis, shaikhs, quazis* and *mullas* laying emphasis on scriptures and ritual prayers were not 'true' Hindus or Muslims. Only a person who followed the interior discipline with the help of the true Guru and adopted God's Name and His Law (*hukam*) could be a 'true' Hindu or 'true' Muslim. In Nanak's *bhakti*, devotion is that of God Himself and not of any *avatar*. Different castes may be sincere in their vocations but the highest duty of all is to repeat the name of the Lord. God has no 'caste' and in His eyes, 'caste' and 'birth' are totally irrelevant to one's salvation.

Motivated as man is under egoism, he degrades woman to the position of a chattel and uses her for satisfaction of his lust, thus degrading from the position of fellow human being. Nanak restores woman to her original status as a fellow human being and proper womanhood. He also disapproves the custom of *sati*.

Guru Nanak was par excellence a humanist, a liberal thinker and a fervent believer in the composite culture. The concept of selfless service (*sewa*), dignity of labour for one's own living and sharing with the needy, the institutions of *dharamsala* as precursor to the *gurdwara*, *sangat* (organised fellowship), *pangat* (sitting in rows), *langar* (common kichen) and *Nam simran* as embodied in the *Adi Granth* became essential features of the *Nanak Panth,* i.e., Sikhism as further evolved in the course of centuries. Nanak's liberal thought finds echo in Akbar's liberal thinking as outlined by Abul Fazl in the *Sulha-i-Kul* policy, thoughts recorded for an inscription for a temple in Kashmir and in Dara Shikoh's *Majma ul Bahrain*.[69] This is equally true of the writings of Guru Gobind Singh and the 17th-18th centuries Muslim sufi thinkers in the Punjab as cited below:

Many have become shaven-headed *sanyasis* (recluses), many have become *jogis* (ascetics).

Many have taken to *brahmcharia* (celibacy), many have become *jatis* (with long twisted hair).

Many are Hindus, Turks, others Rafiji, Imam and Shafi.

But reckon all human beings of one race.

He (God named as) *Karta* (Doer), *Karim* (Kind-bestower), as well as *Raziq* (Sustainer) and *Rahim* (Merciful) is the same. They are all basically one and that is Brahma incarnate. (Do not make any basic difference amongst them).

We should serve only One (Supreme God) and all human beings have the same *Guru Dev* (Preceptor).

They (different names of God) have all the same form and we should acknowledge one Light (*Joti*-God).[70]

They are neither Hindav (Hindus) nor Turka (Muslims).

Different people have started different *mat* (faiths).

But every individual cannot succeed in propagating his own (separate) *panth* (religious order).

As each one's concept becomes contradictory.[71]

NUN: Neither are they (the true sufis) Hindus, nor are they *Mumin* (Muslims), nor do they offer *sajda* (bow in obeisance) according to Islamic establishment (mosque), O He.

Those who have not wasted their lives can behold *Maula* (God) in every breath (of their lives), O He.

Those who are wise appear mad (in the eyes of conventionally religious). Those ones who merge their identity with *Sain* (God) are really wise, O He.

Oh, Bahu, I hail those who have opted for the game of love (of God).[72]

You grazed the cattle in Brindaban (in the form of Lord Krishna).

You celebrated the victory on the conquest of Lanka (in the form of Lord Rama).

You came as pilgrim to Mecca (in the form of Prophet).

What wonderful forms you assumed!

From whom are you trying to hide yourself ?[73]

I am neither a Hindu nor a Musalman. Let us sit to spin and abandon pride.

Neither I am a Sunni nor a Shia. I have adopted the *marg* (path) of Sulha-Kul (peace with all).

(Spiritually) Neither I am hungry (poor), nor I am satisfied one (rich). Neither I am naked (raw) nor I am clothed (delivered).

Neither I am crying nor am I laughing. Neither I am desolate nor I am settled.

(In the conventional sense) Neither I am a sinner nor I am pious. Neither I acknowledge the established concepts of sin nor that of piety.

Bullah Shah is devoted only to God (Hari) abandoning both the Hindus and the Turks (Muslims).[74]

The 18th century is a crucial period in the history of the Punjab. As most of the Mughal and the Durrani Persian chronicles as well as the official documents compiled by the *Insha* experts (munishies) looked up the problems from the imperial angle emphasising the disruptive forces with fissiparous tendencies, the distinguishing features of the local and regional, socio-religious cum political groups remained in the background with only peripheral description. Even though the historians have by and large utilised these sources along with the 19th century source material in Persian and Gurmukhi, the emphasis has been mostly on the political history with religious tenor. A detailed study of the social groups in manifold aspects, socio-economic institutions and polity still awaits further probing equally taking into consideration the *akhbarat* (letters and news letters and kindred documents) despatched by the vakils and newswriters to the English East India Company, Mughal Court, (in Persian), Maratha Peshwas (in Persian and Marathi), Rajasthan chiefs, especially the Jaipur Darbar (*arzdashts, vakil* reports and miscellaneous correspondence in Rajasthani and Hindi). The Baba Jassa Singh Ahluwalia Bi-Centenary Committee has laid the historians under gratitude by mobilising the 18th century source material from Rajasthan, Gujarat and Maharashtra. Its utilisation along with the known sources from the 17th to the 19th centuries is bound to give a new dimension and perspective to the historical analysis of the 18th century Punjab.

The gradual transformation of the socio-religious character of the Nanak-Panth into a socio-religious cum political aspect of the Sikh community comprising followers from various clans (*aqwam*) and castes (*jatis*) during the course of the 17th and 18th centuries is a significant feature of the social change. Initially, the *Nanak-Panth* mostly comprised the Khatris, petty traders, artisans and craftsmen, low caste Hindus and a section of the poor peasantry, more especially from the Majah territories. The *hukamnamas* of the Gurus reveal that the *sangat* of the Gurus (Sikhs) were equally drawn from the prosperous commercial classes and other sections of the peasantry as well. They were drawn not only from the regions of the Punjab but from the cis-Sutlej territories, the regions around Delhi and other places in India. The socio-economic phenomenon involving the emergence of the new dominant clans in the landed structure in the Punjab and territories of Delhi, the conversion of these clans, more especially the peasantry to Sikhism in the course of the 17th and 18th centuries, added a new dimension to the character the Sikh community. The initiation of the *Khalsa* by Guru Gobind Singh, the armed struggle by Banda Bahadur in the territories of *subah* Delhi, hilly and plain regions of the Punjab against the Mughal state in the early 18th century, the later division of the *Khalsa* unto *Bandais* (after Banda's death) and the *Tat Khalsa*, the ultimate supremacy of the latter further moulded the militant character of the *Singhan* for safeguarding the interests of the *Panth*. Apart from this, a number of influential Hindus belonging to commercial class and officialdom became the Sikhs of the Guru.

As a matter of fact, the emergence of the Sikhs as a political force has to be viewed in the larger context of the dissolution of the old political order and the rise of the Marathas, Bundelas, Rajputs, the Jats and Afghans in other parts of India. By and large, during the 16th and 17th centuries, the Mughal polity had depended upon the Mughal-Rajput alliance and its own elitist nobility for the governance and stability of the Empire. But during the 18th century, other socio-political people fought against such an order and shook the foundations of the Empire to the point of dismemberment. This had great impact on the political, economic and social developments of the period with mutual inter-action. Notwithstanding all this, there is considerable element of continuity in the traditional form of regional polity, administration and economic system. The emergence of the Sikh *misls* based on the traditional territorial *zamindari* pattern with landed hierarchy, the suppression of the other landed castes unto *khud kasht* riaya and *muzarian* for the realisation of the revenues and extraction of the surplus produce, the inter-*misl* rivalry and mutual warfare, the attempt on the part of a powerful *misl* for the establishment of its suzerainty in the name of the *Panth*, the realisation of *malia* (*mamla*), *nazrana* etc. from the suppressed *misls* and chiefs is a continuous feature till the emergency the Lahore kingdom under Ranjit Singh by the end of the 18th and early 19th century.

The 18th century Punjab politics assumed triangular character with three main contestants viz., the Mughals, the Sikh *misls* and the Durranis of Kabul. During the first half of the century, it is mostly the Sikh-Mughal tussle. But during the second half of the century, the Mughal sovereign's rights over the Punjab territories had practically vanished and the Durrani rule of Kabul had stepped in. Apart from the occupation of Kashmir and Multan, the Durannis claimed political sovereignty over the Punjab territories and realised *peshkash* more or less on the Mughal pattern. However, the Durrani rule was rather intermittent and the Sikh *misls* always tried to assert as *de facto* power. During the last three decades of the 18th century, even though the Durranis continued to claim political sovereignty, their effective administrative control was minimal.[75] The Durranis continued to claim only *de jure* political rights. In fact, the Lahore Darbar of Ranjit Singh claimed both *de jure* and *de facto* rights as successor to the Durrani rule.

During the 18th century, the role of the Sikh *misls,* especially that of Baba Jassa Singh Ahluwalia who was selected as *mukhi sardar* and was bestowed the title of *Nawab* and *Panth ke malik* by the *Panth* itself and who got the Hari Mandir of Amritsar reconstructed after demolition by Ahmad Shah Durrani, stands unparalleled for the liberation of the Punjab from the Duranni rule.[76] He is the real precursor to Ranjit Singh in this regard. At the same time, the 18th century Sikh polity was by no means confined to the territories of the Punjab. The Sikh Sardars and Baba Jassa Singh in particular were as much interested in the territorial superior *zamindari* claims and suzerainty over the cis-Sutlej territories, Sutlej-Jamuna regions (*subah* Delhi), territories to the North and around Delhi itself and even Rajasthan as other powers of the times viz., the Marathas, the Rohilas and the Jats. According to *Jassa Singh Binod*, Baba Jassa Singh's military expeditions covered the territories of Bharatpur, Bikaner and Jaipur chieftains for the realisation of the revenues viz., *malia* and *nazrana* etc. This gives absolutely a new perspective of the Sikh polity.

The commercial set up in the Punjab during the 18th century practically ran on the same lines as during the 17th century.[77] The view that the campaigns of Nadir Shah and Ahmad Shah Abdali and the internal political disturbances ruined the cottage industries and commercial life is not fully borne out by the contemporary sources. There is no denying the fact that during the periods of foreign incursions, the commercial life in the urban centres was disrupted and the food grain prices, the freight charges by the caravans and insurance rates went up but such sharp commercial panic or set back was temporary in nature. The economic effects of these campaigns were not profound or lasting as the rulers themselves were always interested in the restoration of commercial and agrarian normalcy. If the ruination of the Mughal nobility resulted in the lack of patronage to industrial goods, the deficiency was gradually made up by the newly established chieftain and *zamindari* families who equally patronised the craftmanship. However, under Ranjit Singh the Punjab economy regarding agrarian as well as trade and commerce, both internal and external, fully recovered and was further developed.

The Punjab under Maharaja Ranjit Singh and his successors (1799-1849 AD) has attracted the largest attention on the part of the British and the Indian historians. This is essentially due to the fact that the British took over the territories of the *Dar-ul-Sultanat* of Lahore from the Sikh rule and were tempted to write the past history of the Sikh community. A number of Indian writers produced works both in Persian and the vernecular languages. In fact, during the Sikh regime itself, a number of historical accounts in the Persian language were prepared both by the Hindu and Muslim historians. The students of the Punjab history are fortunate to have inherited all these sources to which can be added the original archival source-material comprising the *Khalsa Darbar Records*, the correspondence of various categories (in Persian) under the Bhandari Collection available at State Archives, Patiala as well as the English reports of multifarious nature. A few good works on Ranjit Singh, his successors and the circumstances leading for the annexation of the Punjab by the East India Company have been attempted. All the same, with rare exception,[78] not much analytical work has been done so as to cover various socio-economic and cultural aspects of the people of the Punjab under the Sikh rule. It may be essentially borne in mind that the later Settlement Report by the British writers covering this historical portion do not constitute authentic history unless supported by the contemporary evidence. The contemporary sources provide detailed description about the economic development, nature of social transformation in respect of the land rights of the landed classes of various tribes and clans, revenue practices, new ventures for the extension of irrigation, especially in the trans Indus *ilaqas* of Peshawar, the territories of Multan and Bari *Doab*, mines and industries all over the kingdom as well as internal and foreign trade. A professional historian has to be fully conversant with the technical terminology and the change in connotation, if any, during this period. An internal landed structure of chieftains of the hills (*zamindaran-i-kohistan-Punjab*) and the plains as well as the administrative cum financial relationship with the latter needs to be worked on micro level with variations in different regions in the Punjab.[79] Above all, the contribution in the fine arts and architecture, the nature of the state, the extent to which cultural synthesis and composite culture was achieved in a unique manner requires special attention on the part of the historians.

It may be reiterated emphatically that right from the 16th century down to at least the mid-19th century, the *Nanak Panth* was regarded as an integral part of the Hindu society. Even though distinct from the other Hindu faiths viz., the Brahmanical order, Vaishnavism, Shivaism, other bhagti cults and the socio-religious orders like the Jains, Jogis (faqirs, i.e. Kanphattas and Angars, etc.) it remained within the Hindu socio-religious structure. As a matter of fact, right from the 8th century onwards, the Muslim writers used the term Hindus (*Hanud*) in India in contrast to the followers of Islam (*Musalmin*). In the early medieval age, even though Buddhism was well established in Sind, Multan and other parts of the west Punjab, despite social tension between the Buddhists and the Brahmans, the Arab accounts insist on covering both as a part of the Hindu society. From 13th century onwards, the Persian sources maintain this concept of the Hindus and Muslims and consider all religious sects in Hindustan which were outside the Islamic religion and its people (*Musalmin*) as the Hindu people (*Hanud*), though, of course, both were divided into various clannish social groups (*firqas*). It is clear from the hymns of Guru Nanak and the writings of Guru Gobind Singh that when they appeal for social cohesion and composite human culture, they only mention the Hindus and the Muslims as the two main religious classes in Hindustan and regard their own socio-religious order as a part of the larger Hindu society with multifarious sects.[80] It is evident from the 18th century documents that gradually the term *Khalsaji* or the *Panth* comprised all the Sikhs

(*Singhan*) divided for political purposes unto various ethnic, tribal and clannish groups (*qabial* or *qabalian* or *qabilas*) under the *Sardars* (*Sardaran-i-Khalsa*) with their respective *dals* and territorial *zamindari* and *taaulqadari* jurisdictions (*makanat*) all over the Punjab, cis-Sutlej territories and other regions of *subab* Delhi.[81] As before, the distinction between the *firqas* of *ahl-i-Islam* and the Hindu *aqwam* (*qaums*) is maintained with the Sikh *aqwam* (*qaums*) as a part of the latter. At the close of the 18th and the early 19th century, Mirza Qatil, a converted Muslim in *Haft Tamasha,* while giving an account of the creeds, traditions and sects of the Hindus,[82] and of the Musalmans of India, regarded "the Sikh disciples of Peshwa Nanak Shah Punjabi" as part of the Hindus of the Punjab. This concept is maintained both by the Hindu and Muslim writers in the reigns of Maharaja Ranjit Singh and his successors. It is only after the annexation of the Punjab that the British administrators while writing their memoranda and reports in the English language that they gave connotations to the existing technical aspects of the socio-religious orders so as to make Sikhism as distinct from Hinduism. Even as late as 1881-83, when the Report on the Census (1881) was compiled as the first experiment in the Punjab, the English administrator responsible for carrying out the Census conceded the fact that it was based on "the initial experience", "infinite diversity of the material to be dealt with" and their own, i.e., the English, "infinite ignorance of that material" as well as "ignorance of the customs and the beliefs of the people." It was meant not only for the guidance of the British Indian officials but it also aimed to feed "European Science" about "the social and religious phenomena" of the Punjab.[83] All the same, in many a region, of the people of various castes and clans professing the same religious faith, some got themselves recorded as Hindus while others as Sikhs.[84]

For the post-colonial period down to the partition of the Punjab in 1947, it may be briefly stated that the nature of the colonial rule as a part of the British Raj in India, the social and economic transformation of the people of the Punjab along with the variant factors from the other part of the British Indian Empire, the relations amongst the various religious communities, both in the rural areas and the urban centres, need an unbiased further probing in detail. Viewing the problem in the historical context, as already outlined, is it not worth saying that the unfortunate so-called 'two nation theory' responsible for the partition of the people of the Punjab was ill-conceived ?

I am extremely obliged to the senior historians in the Punjab for having guided me on various problems relating to the history of the Punjab. I thank you all, ladies and gentlemen, for the courtesy and kindness extended to me and above all for tbe patient hearing given to me.

References

1. Sheikh Abdur Rashid (ed.), *Insha-i-Mahru* (Persian text), Lahore, 1965, letter No. 48, pp. 105-106.
2. *Ibid.*, Letter No. 46, pp. 100-103, *Tarikh-i-Masumi* (Persian text), Bombay, 1938, p. 59; For the territorial boundaries of pre-British Punjab, also see Khushwaqat Rai, *Tarikh-i- Sikhan*, Ms. No. SHR 1274, Khalsa College, Amritsar, pp. 83-85; Bute Shah, *Twarikh-i-Punjab*, Ms. No. 1288, Amritsar, I p. 4.
3. Deborah. E. Klimburg-Salter (ed.), *The Silk Route and the Diamond Path, Esoteric Buddhist Art on the Trans-Himalayan Trade Routes*, UCLA Art Council, U.S.A., 1982, pp. 19-51, 83-90, 112-119, 153-156, 205-208; Irfan Habib, *The Atlas of the Mughal Empire*, Delhi, 1982; Notes-Political, Economic on Afghanistan, Kashmir, Punjab and Sind, pp. 1-16.
4. For these two routes, see Abul Fazl, *Akbar Nama*, Bib. Ind., Calcutta, 1873-87, Vol. II, pp. 538-542; *Tuzk-i-Jahangiri*, tr. A. Rodgers, ed., H. Beveridge, Delhi, II, p. 139; Abdul Hamid Lahori, *Padshahnama*, Bib. Ind., Calcutta, 1866-72, I, ii, pp. 15-21; De Lact, *The Empire of the Great Mogol*, tr. J.S. Hoyland, 1928, p. 57; Muhammad Kazim, *Alamgir Nama*, Bib. Ind., Calcutta, 1865-73, pp. 820-827.
5. William Moorcraft and George Trebeck, *Travels in Himalayan Provinces of Hindoostan and the Punjab, in Ladakh and Kashmir, in Peshawur, Kabul, Kundus and Bokhara (1819- 1825)*, London, 1841 (henceforth Moorcraft), p. 141; Foreign Frontier, National Archives of India, New Delhi (NAI), 35. July 30, 1842. Foreign Secret, NAI, 832-33, December 26, 1846; Foreign Political, NAI A, 50-53, September, 1866; 125-127, January, 1867; Foreign General, NAI, 246, November 12, 1867; 246, January 12, 1868; B-62, January 24, 1868; B, 128-131, October, 1898.
6. *Babur Nama*, tr. A.S. Beveridge, Delhi (Reprint), 1967, p. 202; Francisco Pelsaert, *The Remonstrantie-Jahangir's India*, tr. W.H. Moreland and P. Geyl, Delhi (Reprint), 1972, p. 6; J. B. Travenier, *Travels in India*, tr. V. Ball, London, 1889, Vol. I, p. 90. (henceforth Travenier).
7. Travenier, I. p. 90.
8. *Op. cit.*, No. 5.
9. Moorcraft, I, p. 111; pp. 112-113; Foreign Frontier, NAI, *op. cit.*, No. 5.
10. *Op. cit.*, Nos. 4 and 6.
11. *Safar Nama-i-Anand Ram Mukhlis*, A.H 1164/1751 AD, (ed.), Sayyid Athar

Ali, Rampur, 1946, pp. 69 & 82; Kanwar Prem Kishor Firaqi, *Waqai Alam Shahi* (ed.), Imtiaz Ali Khan Arshi, 1949, pp. 33, 48, 50, 64-65, 72-73, 90-101, 117, 124, 126-127, 135 & 142; *Calender of Persian Correspondence*, NAI, VIII, para 234, p. 97; Capt. F.V. Raper, *Asiatic Researches*, Calcutta, 1810, II, p. 453, XI, p. 953; For details, also see B. R. Grover, "An Integrated Pattern of Commercial Life in the Rural Society of North India during the 17th and 18th Centuries," *IHRC, Proceedings*, Thirty Seventh Session, Vol. XXXVII, Delhi, 1966, pp. 121-153. (Henceforth Grover, An integrated Pattern of Commercial Life); C.A. Bayly, *Rulers, Towns' Men and Bazars, North Indian Society in the Age of British Expansion*, Cambridge, 1983, pp. 29, 68-73, 157-160.

12. Moorcraft, I, pp. 141-142; also other references, *op. cit.*, No.5.
13. Bartholomew Plaisted, *A Journal from Calcutta in Bengal, by Sea to Busserah*, etc., London, 1758 (2nd ed.), pp. 11, 97-98; George Forster, *A Journey from Bengal to England*, etc., 1782, (henceforth Forster), II, p. 178; Dow, *The History of Hindustan*, I, pp. CXIV-CXVI; William Bolts, *Considerations on Indian Affairs*, etc., London, 1772, pp. 195-197.
14. *Op. cit.*, No. 12.
15. B. R. Grover, "Relationship between the Sovereign State (the Mughals and the Afghans) and the Punjab Hill Chiefs during the 17th and 18th Centuries: A Case Study of Chamba Chieftainship based on Bhuri Singh Museum, Chamba Documents", *Proceedings Punjab History Conference*, XVII Session, March 12-14, 1982, pp. 94-102; "Relationship between the Lahore Darbar and the Punjab Hill Chiefs during the first half of the 19th century till 1848", *Proceedings Punjab History Conference*, XVII Session, October 8-10, 1982, pp. 230-240.
16. For details of transportation of commodities by the banjara community, *bima* system and the role of the local zamindars, see Grover, "An Integrated Pattern of Commercial Life", *op. cit.*, No. 11, pp. 132-136.
17. Polier, 1785 AD, in Ganda Singh (ed), *Early European Accounts*, pp. 87-88.
18. Persian *Akhbarat*, NAI; *Akhbar* (Amritsar) No. OR 538, dated 10th *Jamada* II, A.H. 1211/11 December, 1796 AD; *Akhbar* (Shah Jahan Abad), No. OR 375, 29th *Zilhija*, A.H. 1211/11th July, 1797 AD.
19. *Ibid. Akhbar* (Amritsar) No. OR, 22 dated 18th *Jamada* II, A.H. 1211/17 December, 1796 AD; *Akhbar* No. OR 102, 3rd February, 1797 AD.
20. Forster, II, pp. 79, 98, 103, 135, 166, 259-267; Pennant, A *View of Hindoostan*, Eastern Hindustan, London, 1798, I, p. 38.
21. Bartholomew Plaisted, *op. cit.*, No. 13, p. 9.
22. Ziaal-Din Barni, *Tarikh-i-Feroz Shahi* (Parsian text) (ed.), Saiyid Ahmad Khan; A.S, B., Calcutta, 1862 (henceforth Barni), pp. 309-11; Forster, I, p. 220.

23. The author of *Tarikh-i-Tahiri* (British Museum, OR 1685, fol. 12a) says that the river Sind below the region of Bhakhar was named as Punjab. Also, Elliot and Dowson, *History of India as told by its Historians*, I, p. 256; *Ain-i-Akbari*, (tr. H.S. Jarrett, R.A.B., Calcutta, II, p. 339) puts the number of boats which plied on the Ravi-Indus System at 40,000; Also De Laet, *op. cit.*, No. 2, p. 51; Richard Steele and John Crowther, Samuel Purchas: *Purchas* his Pilgrims, while travelling from Ajmer to Ispahan in 1614 AD consider Lahore associated with the Portuguese trade "as being the centre of all Indian traffique. And here they embarqued the same downe the river for Thata whence they were transported for Ormus and Persia. The merchants also passing that way be wixt Persia and India payed them freight..."; M.R. Haig (*The Indus Delta Country—A Memoir Chiefly on the Ancient Geography and History*, London, 1894, pp. 77-79) comments that Al Beruni in the early 11th century puts Lahari Bandar as "Laharani, which is equivalent to later Lahori; for Lohawar was the ancient capital of the Punjab and the only one known to Al Beruni. Lohawarani, or Loharani...was thus a name indicating the connection between the port and the capital; as in course of time Lohawar became Lahor, so the name of the port was transformed from Loharani to Lahori". Haig agrees that this is not a plausible explanation as the indigenous name was Lahari, derived from the tribe of Lahar settled in the part of the Delta. All the same he argues that the association of the port with Lahori outside of Sind in northern India speaks for the popular image of the port for the commercial traffic of the Punjab.
24. *Hudud al Alam* (Persian text), Leningrad, 1930, fols. 14a-16a, tr. and commentary, V. Minorsky, 'The Regions of the world', *A Persain Geograghy*, London, 1937, (henceforth *Hudud al Alam*), pp. 86-92, 235-54; Al Beruni, *Kitab-ul-Hind*, tr. E.C. Sachau, *Al Biruni's India,* 2 vols., London, 190, I, pp. 206-59, II, p. 206 (henceforth Al Beruni); Kalhana, *Rajatarangini*, tr. M A. Stein, 1961, V. pp. 141-55, VII, pp. 47-63; Al Masudi, 'Murujadh-Dhahab wa Maadin-al-Jawhar' (Arabic text) vide Maulana Masud Ali Nadvi, *Hindustan Arabun Ki Nazar Me*, Azamgarh, Vol. I. 1960. Vol II, 1962 (henceforth Nadvi). I, pp. 279-280; Al Sharifal Idrisi, *Kitab Nuzhatal Mushataq Fikhtiraq al-Afaq*, Leiden 1960, tr. S. Maqbul Ahmad, *India and Neighbouring Countries etc.* (relevant passages), pp. 64-66. Also see *The Age of imperial Konauj*, Bhartiya Vidya Bhawan Series, Bombay, 1955, pp. 112-115; Yogendra Mishra, *The Hindu Sahis of Afghanistan and the Punjab* 865-1026 AD, Patna, 1972, pp. 25-29, 97; D.B. Pandey, The *Shahis of Afghanistan and the Punjab*, Delhi, 1973, pp. 1-39, 57-71, 101-122.
25. *Ibid*.
26. *Ibid*.; also Bishari Magdisi (Arabic text) vide Nadvi, I, p. 383.
27. *Hudud al Alam*, fols. 14a-16a.
28. *Ibid*. The author claims that the Amir of Multan claimed suzerainty over

Lahore. But the geographical description associated with it having great number of pine trees, almond trees and walnut trees does not justify its identity with the present day Lahore, the capital of West Punjab (Pakistan). It seems in the context that a city named Lauhawar was also located in the Gandhara region. This is well confirmed by Al Biladauri, *Kitab Futuh-al-Buldan* which according to him lay between Multan and Kabul. Also see Lieut. Col. K.A. Rashid, 'Proceedings of Pakistan History Conference', Vth Session, Khairpur, 1955, p. 131; *Lahore Fort Excavations*, *Pakistan Archaeology*, No. 5, 1965, pp. 156-60. It has also been considered that a village/*qasba* may have existed on the present day site of Lahore since ancient times but it developed as a city or was named as Lahore only in the course of 10th century AD. Also see *Mansur Adab-ul-Mulk wa Kifayatul-Mamluk*, partly published and tr., M. Nazim, J.R.A.S.,

29. Great Britain and Ireland, July, 1927, pp. 486-93.

30. *Ibid.*

31. *Epigraphica Indica*, I, pp. 184-90, 244-250. Buzarg bin Shaharyar, *Ajaibal Hind*, (Arabic text) vide Nadvi, I, p. 193; also *op. cit.*, Nos. 24-28.

32. *Istakhri* (Arabic text) vide Nadvi, I, pp. 368-70; 373-74; Abdul Karim Shahstani Nadvi, II, pp. 15-18, 71-72; *Al Idrisi*, Nadvi, II, pp. 187-191, 194-196, 201.

33. *Ibid.*

34. *Hudud al Alam*, fols. 14a-16a; Bishari Al Magdisi; *Kitab Ahsan al Taqasimti Maritat al Aqlim* (Arabic text) Leiden, 1906, pp. 480-85; also Nadvi, I, pp. 387-88.

35. *Ibid.*

36. *Ibid.*

37. *Al Beruni* I, pp. 17-18, 172-73; Amir Khusrau, *Mathnavi-i Nuh-Sipehr*, Ms. No. 866, Azad Library, A.M.U., Aligarh, *Sipehr* No. III; *Ashika*,, tr. Elliot and Dowson, III, p. 556.

38. *Al Beruni*, I, p. 82; Al Masudi, Leiden, I, p. 377; Nadvi, I, pp. 288-89; Bishari, Leiden, p. 481.

39. Ibn Haukal, Leiden, p. 226; Bishari vide Nadvi, I, pp. 389-90.

40. *Al Beruni*, No. 37.

41. *Ibid.*

42. G.S. Talib (ed.) (a) *Baba Sheikh Farid, Life and Teachings,* New Delhi, 1973 (Urdu version of *Sloks,* pp. 62-83); (b) *Perspectives on Sheikh Farid,* Patiala, 1975, pp. 129-38, 221-52.

43. For details, also see B.R. Grover, 'Baba Farid—a Man of the Masses', *Ibid.,* (a) pp. 79-82; B.R. Grover, 'Farid Speaks the Human Truth', *Ibid.,* (b), pp. 149-56.

44. *Al Beruni,* I, pp. 17-23, 101, 173, 179-85.

45. *Ibid.*, p. 22.
46. *Ibid.*
47. Ibn Khurdadbah, *Kitabu-L Masalik wa-L Mamalik,* Leiden, 1869, p. 17; Nadvi, I, pp. 25-26.
48. *Al Beruni,* I, p. 101.
49. I am extremely grateful to Shri Shahab Sarmadi (Aligarh) for having drawn my attention to the works of Masud Saad Salman, important works on music during the medieval Indian times and giving me the required information.
50. Masud Saad Salman, Persian *Divan,* complied by Dr. Rashid Yasmi, Tehran, 1879.
51. Amir Khusrau, *Qiran-u-Sadain,* ms. No. 125 (2), Azad Library, A.M.U., Aligarh, fols. 87a-95a-b; *Aijaz-i-Khusrawi,* Lucknow, pp. 241, 275-91.
52. Nawab Saif Khan, Faqirullah, *Raga Darpana* alias *Mankutuhal,* Azad Library, Lytton, ms. No. 41; Subhan mss. Nos. 780-4/113, 780-4/10, pp. 23-24, 26-29, 55-56, 59-61, 87-100, 111.
53. Ram Sukh Rao, *Sri Fateh Singh Partap Prabhakar,* (ed.), J. Kaur, Patiala, 1980, pp. 284-99.
54. *Al Beruni,* I, p. 70.
55. Amir Khusrau, *Qiran-u-Sadain,* pp. 228; Barni, pp. 64, 70.
56. *Al Beruni,* I, p. 188; *Sirat-i-Firoz Shahi,* ms. Khuda Baksh Library, Patna, fols. 156a onwards; *Ain-i Akbari,* tr. Blochmann 1866-67, Calcutta, I, pp. 119-21.
57. Afif, *Tarikh-i Feroz Shahi,* Bib. Ind. Calcutta (henceforth Afif), pp. 308-13.
58. *Chach Namah,* tr. Mirza Kalich Beg, Karachi, 1900, pp. 76, 81-83, 138, 143.
59. Adabu-i-Harbu-Sh Sujaat, Tehran, 1346 A.H., pp. 191, 421-27.
60. *Ain-i-Akbari, op. cit.,* No. 56, pp. 140, 538; Sujan Rai Bhandari, *Khulasat-ut-Tawarikh,* ed. Zafar Hasan, Delhi, 1918, pp. 66, 75.
61. Also see for details, B.R. Grover, 'Elements of Continuity and Change in Land Ownership and Rights from the Mughal Age to the Early British Administration in India', *Proceedings of the Indian History Congress,* Presidential Address, Medieval India Section, 37th Session, Calicut, 1976 (henceforth 'Elements of Continuity and Change in Land Ownership and Rights' etc), pp. 143-178.
62. *Ibid.,* also see B.R. Grover, 'Nature of Land Rights in Mughal India', I.E. SHR, II, No 3, 1963, pp. 1-23.
63. *Insha-i-Mahru, op. cit.,* No. 1, for details, see Letters Nos. 28, 31 and 144, pp. 61-63, 73-80 and 204-05 respectively.
64. *Rasala-dar-bai Arazi,* ms. Azad Library, A.M.U. Aligarh, Shaifta Collection, *Fiqh,* Arabia, NO. 24/26, also B.R. Grover, *op. cit.,* No. 61.

65. For details, Barni, pp. 287-91, 429-30, 472-80, 497-99, *Sirat-i-Feroz Shahi, op. cit.,* No. 56, fols. 37a-b, 71b-72a, 86a-87a, 147a, 105b-106a; Afif, pp. 94-96, 98-100, 129-31.
66. For details, see, B.R. Grover, 'An Integrated Pattern of Commercial Life' *op. cit.,* No. 11.
67. B.R. Grover, 'Classification of Agrarian Land Under Akbar', *Proceedings of Indian History Congress,* Aligarh, 1961.
68. For details, see B.R. Grover, 'An Integrated Pattern of commercial Life', *op. cit.,* No. 11.
69. Dara Shikoh, *Majma-ul-Bahrain* (ed. Mahfuz-ul-Haq) or the *Making of the Two Oceans,* edited in the original Persian with English translation, Notes and Variants, Calcutta, 1929.
70. *Dassam Granth,* 15/85 vide Maheem Singh, *Guru Gobind Singh aur un ki Hindi Kavita,* p. 100, tr. Grover.
71. *Ibid.,* 2 Sankhaya-7, Nihkalanki Avtar, 24 Avtar, p. 107, tr. Grover.
72. Bullhe Shah, *Kanun-i-Ishq* (Urdu), Vol. II, Kafi 73, tr. Grover.
73. *Ibid.,* kafi 90.
74. *Majmua Abyat Sultan Bahu,* (Urdu), p. 22, tr. Grover.
75. For details, see B.R. Grover, *op. cit.,* No. 15.
76. For details, see Ram Sukh Rao. ms. No. M/772, Punjab State Archives, Patiala; *Sri Fateh Singh Partap Prabhakar, op. cit.,* pp. 284-99.
77. B.R. Grover, *op. cit.,* No. 11.
78. Indu Banga, *Agrarian System of the Sikhs,* New Delhi, 1978, p. 115.
79. B.R. Grover, *op. cit.,* No. 15.
80. *Ibid.,* Nos. 70-71.
81. For details, see Persian *Akhbarat,* N.A.I.; Persian documents Pt. I, Text (ed. P. Saran), Asia Publishing House, Bombay, 1966; *Persain Records of Maratha History,* I, Delhi Affairs, News Letters, tr. J. N. Sarkar, Bombay, 1953; *Calender of Persian Correspondence,* N.A.I. vol. II, 1767-69, Calcutta, 1914, vol. III, 1770-72; also *op. cit.,* Nos. 18-19.
82. Mirza Muhammad Hasan with the poetical name *(takhlus)* of Qatil, Mirza, *Haft Tamasha,* British Museum, Rieu, ms. No. 476. Originally, a Hindu from a khatri family, named Davali Singh, was converted to Islam at the age of eighteen. Apart from other books and a *Divan,* he wrote *Haft Tamasha* (Seven Chapters) and dealt at length with the creeds, traditions and sects of the Hindus and of the Musalmans of India as well as curious facts relating to Indian *Faqirs.* He died in 1233 A.H./1817-18 AD.
83. Denzil Ibbetson, Preface to the Report on the Census of 1881, dated 15th August, 1883 reproduced in *Punjab Castes,* Lahore, 1916, pp. iii-viii.
84. *Ibid.,* pp. 1-37, 102-31, 214-38.

Chapter 4

Historiography – Medieval Punjab*

When I first received Sardar Ganda Singh's letter asking me to preside over the medieval section of the Punjab History Conference, I felt somewhat surprised because I had not written anything on the history of medieval or modern Punjab. But then I thought that, perhaps, I had been invited on account of my long teaching experience and the little work that I had done on the history and culture of the neighbouring State of Kashmir. Anyhow, whatever the reason, I am conscious of the honour which the organizers of the Conference have done to me, and I am most greateful to them for it.

I should like to congratulate the Department of Punjab Historical Studies, Punjabi University, for organizing a Punjab History Conference of which this is the second session, because this would give great encouragement to the study of the history and culture of the Punjab. There are some Indian historians who are rather suspicious of provincial or regional histories on the ground that they encourage local loyalties and detract from their loyalty to the country. But this is a wrong view, for loyalty to one's family, group, town or region is only natural, and instead of weakening national sentiments, it nourishes and strengthens it. In fact, it will not be wrong to say that those who have no attachment to their family, group, town or province, cannot have any deep feeling for their country. Moreover, it must be remembered that for reconstructing the history of India, a study of the history of different areas is necessary because the general histories – and I am referring here only to those of medieval India being mainly concerned with the activities of the central government – do not deal completely with the different parts of the empire or the contemporary provincial dynasties. An intensive study of the local

* Presidential Address (Medieval Section) Panjab University History Conference, 10th Session, Feb. 1976, Punjabi University, Patiala.

histories would not only throw light on many an hitherto unknown or little known facts about the Sultanate of Delhi or the Mughal Empire, but it will enable us to reconstruct the history of medieval India as a whole. It is a matter of great satisfaction that already in some of the States like Bihar, Bengal, Mysore and Gujarat, works on their history and culture have been published, while in others, like Punjab and Kashmir, such studies have been undertaken.

The writing of a history of the Punjab is comparatively much more difficult than the writing of a history of other parts of India like Sindh, Gujarat, Kashmir, Malwa (now a part of Madhya Pradesh), Bengal, the Deccan and South India. This is because the Punjab as a whole, unlike these areas, hardly ever enjoyed independence during the medieval times and, consequently, it did not have, its own chroniclers until the rise of the Sikh movement. It was a part of the kingdom of Delhi, and the medieval historians did not, therefore, treat it separately except in relation to the central government.

Despite this deficiency, sufficient material is available, particularly from about the early part of the sixteenth century, for the writing of a history of medieval Punjab. First, there are the usual histories of the Sultanate of Delhi and the Mughal Empire which, if carefully studied, would yield useful material despite the fact that they do not treat the Punjab separately. Secondly, there are a large number of Sufi works which throw light on the social and religious history of the period. For a history of the Chishti and Suhrawardy Orders in the Punjab during the early period, Amir Hasan's *Fawaid-ul-Fuad*; Nasir-ud-Din Chiragh Dehlavi's *Khair-ul Majalis* and Amir Khurd's *Siyar-ul-Auliya* are important. For the Naqshbandi Order and for the movement of Shaikh Ahmad Sirhindi, Muhammad Hashim's *Zubdat-ul-Maqamat, Maktubat-i-Baqi Billah, Maktubat-i-Imam Rabbani* and Badru-ud-Din's *Hazrat-ul-Quddus* are the basic sources. For the eighteenth century Chishti saints, Haji Najm-ud-Din's *Manaqib-ul-Mahbubin* should be consulted. Thirdly, there are a large number of non-Persian sources mentioned in Dr. Saran's recent publication entitled *Descriptive Catalogue of non-Persian sources on Medieval Indian History.* However, it is impossible to assess their importance merely by their titles because the editor has not cared to evaluate them. Sardar Ganda Singh has also referred to a number of non-Persian works beginning from about the end of the fifteenth century, particularly in the Punjabi Language, in a paper shortly to be published which he wrote for the Seminar on *Historians of Medieval India* held during the first week of this year at the Jamia Millia Islamia, New Delhi. These works, both published and unpublished, appear to be very important for the life and teachings of the Sikh Gurus, Mughal-Sikh relations, and the social and economic history of the period.

Lastly, there are a large number of Mughal *farmans* which throw light on the religious policy of the Mughal emperors and on the economic life of the people. Some of these *farmans* have been acquired by the Punjab University, Chandigarh, while others are still, I believe, in Pathankot. They reveal that the *madat-i-maash* grants were not only given to Muslims but also to non-Muslims. The *madat-i-maash* grants, which are in the India Office, are useful for an understanding of the commercial life of the period. The Rajasthan Archives are rich in material dealing with the various aspects of the revenue administration of the Punjab, particularly of its eastern part. They have been utilized by the speaker Professor B. R. Grover of the History Department, Jamia Millia, in some of his published papers.

In the period under review, the Punjab did not form a separate province, but was a region comprising smaller divisions which were directly ruled from Delhi or Agra. Under Muiz-ud-Din, the administrative units were Bhera, Sialkot, Lahore, Multan, the *vilayat* of Kohram and Samana and Hansi. During the first half of the thirteenth century, the *iqtas* and *vilayats* were: the *vilayat* of Lahore, including Bhera and Sialkot; Multan, including Uch in upper Sindh; the *vilayat* of Kohram and Samana; and the vilayat of Hansi. Balban made some changes, and in 1360, the *Shiq* of Sirhind was created from the large *shiq* of Samana and Suman by Firuz Shah. The Sayyids, Lodis and Surs also made changes. Under the Mughals, the districts of East Punjab upto the Sutlej were parts of the subah of Delhi, while the rest of the Punjab consisted of the subah of Lahore and the subah of Multan (this included upper Sindh also). But in spite of these administrative divisions, the Land of the Five Rivers had always its separate geographical, linguistic and cultural identity, and the word Punjab has been constantly referred to in this sense by the chroniclers.

Few parts of this sub-continent have been, until the modern age, so intensely subjected to foreign impact as the Punjab. We know a great deal about the common characteristics of the Indus Valley civilizations of Persia, Babylon, Egypt and Crete, but we are ignorant of the nature and extent of the cultural exchanges that took place between them. However, when we come to historical times, the picture becomes clear. The Punjab was ruled for nearly two centuries by the

Achaemenan dynasty and, in consequence, it came under the cultural influence of Persia. Later, it fell under Greek influence (190-40 B.C.). Then in the eighth century came Islam whose impact was more profound and abiding than that of the previous cultures. It infused new blood in the country and brought about changes in religious beliefs and social life as well as in dress and in diet. It brought into existence a new language, which was later on called Urdu, and it enriched the language of the people, namely, Punjabi. It gave a great impetus to the Bhakti Movement, and it was, among others, an important factor which led to the birth of the Sikh religion. The social, religious and cultural ideas of Islam seeped through the Punjab to other parts of India as well.

However, we must remember that this traffic was not one-sided. Every one who entered the Punjab was influenced by Indian culture and religion. Similarly, the Muslims who came to the Punjab, adopted many of the local customs and religious beliefs; and the Perso-Islamic culture, which they had brought with them, became considerably transformed in its Indian setting. Some work has been done on the influence of Islam and Hinduism on each other, but this is of a general nature and does not relate to the Punjab specifically. Being a frontier province, its problems were somewhat different from those of the rest of India, and therefore, require a separate study.

A great deal of work has been done on Sikhism by European scholars as well as Sikh scholars but there is no study of the Muslim religious movements in the Punjab. The Ismailiya, a Shiite sect of Islam, played an important role in the social and political history of medieval Islam from the tenth to the middle of the thirteenth century. A great deal of work has been done by the Orientalists on the Ismailites outside India, but practically nothing has been written on the social and political organization of the Ismailities of Multan, who held the greater part of Upper Sindh for nearly two centuries. They were massacred by Sultan Mahmud of Ghaznin who occupied Multan and imposed a Sunni ruler on the town. But after his death they re-occupied it and ruled until Muiz-ud-Din captured the place in 1175. He, however, failed to crush them, for they continued their activities and remained a thorn in the side of the Sultanate for a long time.

The Chishti Order was introduced into the Punjab in the thirteenth century. Professor Khaliq Ahmad Nizami has written a biography of Baba Farid of Pakpattan and has described the Chishti Order in the thirteenth and fourteenth centuries, but we are ignorant of the nature and extent of its influence and of its subsequent history in the Punjab.

The Suhrawardy Order was first introduced into the Punjab by Shaikh Shihab-ud-Din Zakariyya (1182-83-1262) who firmly established it in the Punjab and in Sindh. It is worthwhile investigating why its influence remained confined to this area, and never had much influence in the Indo-Gangetic plain. Another order, which had considerable impact on the Punjab, was the Naqshbandi. Besides, Shaikh Ahmed Sirhindi, a follower of this order, started his revivalist movement in the Punjab, and from here it spread to other parts of India. Dr. Athar Abaas Rizvi has described the ideas and activities of Sirhindi and other Naqshbandis in a recent publication entitled *Muslim Revivalist Movements in Northern India in the Sixteenth and Seventeenth Centuries,* but a more detailed and deeper analysis of the Muslim religious movements of this period is called for. It would also be interesting to investigate how much Sayyid Ahmad Brelvi owed to be Naqshbandis and, in particular, to Sirhindi for his ideas.

Another aspect that requires to be studied is the culture of medieval Punjab. Before the establishment of Mughal rule, the Punjab did not seem to possess any buildings of architectural significance, except in Multan, where a number of tombs were constructed in the twelfth and thirteenth centuries. That the rest of the Punjab is devoid of monuments of the period of the Sultanate is probably due to the absence of a local dynasty, constant foreign invasions and internal turmoil. It was only with the coming of the Mughals that the Punjab enjoyed a long period of peace, and Lahore became virtually a second capital because it lay on the route to Kashmir and Kabul, the two valuable Mughal possessions. In consequence, a large number of buildings were erected in Lahore during this period. Lahore cultivated an independent architectural tradition and showed considerable individuality. Percy Brown has made a short study of the Mughal buildings of Lahore but they require a detailed analysis.

Persian came to the Punjab with the Ghaznavids, and the later Ghaznavids were patrons of learning. The greatest Persian poet of this period was Masud Saad Salman (1046-1121). He was born in Lahore and wrote verses both in Hindi and Sanskrit which are no longer extant but his poetical work in Persian has been published in Tehran. Another great poet was Abul Farj Rumi (d. 1091). Baba Farid of Pakpattan, a great Sufi saint of the Chishti Order, was not only an erudite scholar but also a poet who wrote verses in Persian, Arabic and in the local dialect. Of the Mughal period, two persons deserve to be mentioned. Abul Barkat Munir Lahori (1609-45) whose letters are famous, is said to have written one hundred thousand verses which included *ghazals, masnavis* and *qasidas*. Another prominent poet and prose writer of this period was Chandra Bhan Brahman (d. 1662). He was born in Lahore and served first Shahjahan and then Dara Shikoh.

Since the language of court and culture was Persian, the development of Punjabi was greatly hampered. Besides, there were no local dynasties to patronise it as happened in the case of Gujrati, Bengali, Kannada, Marathi and Telugu. In spite of this, the Punjabi language continued to be enriched because the Sufi saints and the Sikh Gurus used it as a vehicle for communicating their thoughts and feelings to the common people, and to make it more effective, they wrote in verse form. But owing to the domination of Persian, not much prose literature could be produced in Punjabi during this period.

The Punjab was strategically an extremely important part of the empire of Delhi. Being the western most area, it had to bear the chief brunt of invasions from beyond the north-west. Under the great Mughals, however, the political frontiers having been pushed back, it was Kabul, Qandhar and Ghazanin which formed the main line of defence. But when this line crumbled, first by the loss of Qandhar in 1649 and then of Kabul and Ghaznin in 1738, the Punjab again became directly exposed to the invasions from beyond the Sulaiman Range.

The commercial importance of the Punjab is evident from the fact that before the annexation of Gujrat by Ala-ud-Din Khilji, it was the main centre of foreign trade of the Sultanate of Delhi. The Punjabi merchants traded with Khotan, Yarqand and Kashgar through Kashmir, and with Persia, Samarqand and Bokhara through the easily accessible Gomal Pass. It seems that despite the constant Mongol invasions in the thirteenth century, foreign and internal trade did not stop. Merchants continued to deal in horses, slaves, cloth, carpets, shawls and other commodities. Muslim merchants from Lahore, in the reign of Bahram, the third son of Iltumish, journeyed to do business with the Hindus of Gujrat and made huge profits. Owing to the Portuguese domination of the Indian waters and the Persian Gulf in the sixteenth century, the overland Indo-Persian land route became more frequented. During the early years of the seventeenth century, 14,000 camels loden with goods passed annually from India via Qandhar into Persia. Owing to the increase of foreign trade, the Punjab and its towns became prosperous. In the time of Sher Shah and his son, Islam Shah, "Lahore was a large and flourishing city, the centre of rich trade, and amply furnished with every useful and costly production of the times." Terry speaks of the Punjab as "a large province, and most fruitful. Lahore is the chief city thereof, built very large, and abounds both in people and riches, one of the principal cities of trade in all India." Father Monserrate even declared that Lahore was not second to any city in Europe or Asia, that every kind of merchandize was to be found in its shops, and that the streets were blocked by dense crowds. However, from the early part of the eighteenth century, owing to the Mughal-Sikh conflicts, the Maratha raids and foreign invasions, Lahore greatly suffered, and the once prosperous and flourishing city became impoverished.

In conclusion, I should like to refer to a tendency common among the students of Indian history these days to blame the past, particularly the medieval past, for the misfortunes of the present. It is true that the medieval age in India was at times characterised by serious religious differences and conflicts-though sometimes these conflicts were basically economic and political and took on a religious garb but we should not forget that there were also wide areas of agreement. Hindus, Muslims and Sikhs lived side by side in peace and harmony, participating in each other's social gatherings and festivals and visiting each other's sacred places. Baba Farid and other Muslim saints met Hindu Yogis and had friendly discussions with them. The Sufi saints and the Sikh Gurus had also cordial relations with each other; and it is not without great significance that Mian Mir, a Muslim saint, was invited to lay the foundations of the Golden Temple at Amritsar. That despite these facts it was intolerance and disagreement which got the upper hand and asserted themselves, is no fault of the past, but is due to the failings and the bankruptcy of the present.

Some Indian historians are also inclined to exaggerate the defects of the medieval age and belittle or gloss over its achievements. Here again, we must admit that the medieval age was at times characterised by violence, injustice, cruelty, waste and many other evils. But it had also great achievements to its credit. It opened India's doors to foreign influences, whose impact on her was profound and far-reaching. It challenged some of the basic assumptions of Hindu society and thus gave rise to a mood of inquiry and reform. It made great contribution to administration, art and architecture, music, social refinement, poetry, historiography and mysticism. Now if we ignore all this, we would be doing great harm to ourselves. Scholars in the Punjab are at present feverishly busy writing about their past and evaluating it. It is hoped that, while they are free to judge the past, because without this their accounts would be more dull and dry stuff, they would not lose their sense of proportion and historical perspective, for otherwise they would not be able to give us a true history of the Punjab.

Chapter 5

Farid Speaks the Human Truth*

Sheikh Fariduddin Masud Ganj-i-Shakar, popularly known as Baba Farid, the great Chisti Sufi has left a great impact on the cultural life of the medieval Panjab. Undeniably, Farid occupies an esteemed position in the Chistia *Silsilah* which during the medieval age claimed popularity and institutional organisation in most of the regions in India. Farid ranks with Khwaja Muinuddin Chisti and Sheikh Nizamuddin Auliya, the great luminaries who have moulded the character of the medieval Indian culture. However, on regional basis, the cultural heritage of the Panjab owes much to Farid. Farid speaks of the fundamental truth of human life irrespective of the division of the social structure on religious basis.

Farid was a noble product of Sufism which made an appeal to the Holy Quran and the *Sunnah* in its exploration of the spiritual world and man's place in society. The Quran and the *Sunnah* cover not only the spiritual aspect of man's life but comprise the totality of man in respect of his social behaviour.[1] The Prophet Muhammad had aimed at a cultural revolution of the entire social order in respect of religion, socio-economic relations and political set-up. Submission to God and the ideal of ultimate union of man with Him demanded perfection in the personality of man (*tazkiya*). For its achievement, not only piety and virtue but confirmity to an egalitarian order based on justice and equity were essential prerequisites.

Sufism[2] had no dogma. Even though all sufic searched for truth, in the soul's eternal yearning to have direct experience of the Ultimate Reality, one sufi may differ from another in thought and action. The *tariqah* covered a wide range of thought and feeling and emphasis on its one aspect or another depended upon the comprehension of the

---

* Presented at Seminar on Baba Shaikh Farid, November 16-17, 1973, at New Delhi.

sufi. The importance of the prayer and fast veried in degree with an individual sufi. The canvass of the sufi thought is very large. It dealt as much with metaphysical speculation and the philosophic idea as with the social concept. The ideas of sufism were equally influenced by the contemporary socio-economic order and political set-up.

In its early stages, the sufi mind repelled against the fermalism, hair-splitting Islamic theology, the rigidity of the interpretation of the Muslim jurisprudence. A sufi had a passion for direct experience with the Supreme Being and the religious truth. Above all, this sufi conscience rebelled against the injustices of the social order which accepted the difference between the theory and practice of the Islamic ideas and principles. It is this trait of sufism which is essentially coeval with 'social concern' which needs emphasis. It originated at an early stage of the development of Islam, more especially after the establishment of the Omayyad empire.[3] The political structure of Islam underwent a revolutionary change and led to the separation of religion and politics. A service for the state was distinct from the service for the religion. This undermined the erstwhile welfare concept of the Muslim state. The territorial wars and the expansion of empire led to atrocities and resulted in marked cleavage in the governing classes and the 'ruled'. The socio-political order governed by sheer mundane motives was a clear deviation from the original Islamic principles of the social order. The early sufi emphasis on 'fear from God' and penance was a 'quiet way' of resentment against the 'unIslamic' cleavage in the social order.

The resentment against the social structure based on marked division between the 'privileged' governing classes and the poor people becomes more pronounced and a marked feature of sufism from the 11th -12th centuries onwards. The view expressed hitherto that the political conquest of Islam brought in its wake an egalitarian concept of socio-economic order in the conquered territories cannot be accepted on the basic of the available contemporary evidence. In the seventh century A.D., Persia[4], the cradle of sufism, became a part of the Muslim world and a new theory of state common to the other Muslim territories was evolved. Islam was a unifying force for a new civilization of the Muslim world. Islam offered the mass of people release from conditions of social inferiority. If Islam offered to influence tha social and economic institutions, on its own, the islamic theory was modified by the prevalent pro-Islamic social concept and customs of the conquered territories. The pre-Islamic Persian social order under the Sasanian dynasty attached sanctity to family ties, private property and landed estates. There was a marked distinction between the different classes of society. Each class had its own assigned place in the social order. Islam itself recognised the concept of private property and materially affected the development of landed property and land tenure. In practice, the pre-Islamic landed hierarchy was maintained. The social class division was not only recognised but further accentuated by the taxation and administrative policy of the Seljuks. In the commercial sphere, trade and commercial taxes were continued to be lived on the pre-Islamic Sasanian pattern and excepting the privileged, all paid poll-tax in accordance with an income oriented slab. Same is true of the society in Afghanistan. Even though the administrative concept evolved by the Turkish elite in South Asian Muslim countries left a large measure of autonomy in law and custom to the economically productive sections of the population, the concept of ownership of land subject to the payment of *Kharaj,* the land owing class constituting the *rais,* the *iqta* and the *muqta* system for the collection of revenue created marked cleavage in the social classes in respect of privilege and financial mainstay.[5]

The political conquest of Sindh (8th century) by the Arabs and Panjab (11th century) and the whole of North India (12th-13th centuries) by the Turks did not materially affect the Hindu agrarian structure based on hierarchical pattern of landed intermediaries. Except for the imposition of *Jizya* upon the non-Muslims, it is very doubtful if the Turkish rule brought about any fundamental changes in the existing pre-Muslim agrarian administration. In the initial stages, the Muslim emigrees to India largely belonged to the professional classes and did not involve any economic and social displacement of the agrarian population. The caste distinction was applicable as much to the Hindus as to the converted Muslim society. So the social class division was confirmed by the Turkish government.

The sufi mind resented against the very character and development of the Islamic culture which, to its view, was not in consonance with the original concept of the *Shariat* and the *Sunnah.* It revolted against the prevalent social disparities in the life of man and essentially viewed the poorer sections of the society with sympathy and consideration. In the early 13th century, another factor accentuated the depth of the sufi thought. This was the Mongol deluge which completely devasted the Muslim cultural life in South West Asia and the Western Panjab. The sufi mind took up the challenge and questioned the very basis and purpose of human life and culture.

Farid belonged to the Chistis *Silsilah* of sufism founded in India by Sheikh Hasarat Khwaja Nizamuddin Auliya in Ajmer.[6] Farid was the representative (*Khalifa*) of Khawaja Qutb-uddin Bakhtiyar Kaki, the founder of the *Silsilah* in Delhi. Through the Chistia *Silsilah* was essentially Indian in character, it had significantly identified thoughts with the contemporary sufism in Persia. Farid, being a product of his age, assimilated in himself the highest qualities of Persian and Indian sufism. Many of his ideas are identical with Khwaja Fariduddin Attar and Maulana Jalal-uddin Rumi (ob. 1273), the great sufi posts of the age. With them the Centre of thought remains man as a social being and love of God. The concept of Wahdat-ul-Wajud meant that everything was God and of the same essence. When God was omnipresent, there was God in man himself. Submission to God and love for Him could be realised only through love for man. How was it possible to realise if man were to suffer at the hands of another man ? Attar speaks in the name of humanity:

چیست انسانی تپیدن در غم همسائگاں

خوار دیدن خویش را از خواری ابنارے جنس

(What is humanity ? It is to suffer pain at the distress of our neighbours; and to feel humilated at the humiliation of the human race). Attar also speaks of one God who is not in the hands of any single section of the people. He is within the reach of every person.

خدا را جز خدا یک و دستِ کس نیست

که در خود و خدا هم اوست کس نیست[7]

There is one God and is not confirmed in the hands of a single person (or a single section of people). Only he is capable of being God and none other.

When Nizamuddin Auliya saw the Hindus praying and taking a dip in the Jamna river, he uttered the same truth :

ھر قوم راست راھے دینے و قبلہ گاھی[8]

(Every community has its own path of religion and place of worship).

Attar says that man is not separate from God Himself as God Himself is present in man.

تو از دریا جدائی و بن عجب بین

ز تو یک لحظہ این دریا جدا نیست[9]

You are not seperate from the ocean (of divinity). It is no surprise as you are not seperated from this ocean for a moment.

Farid also expresses the same idea when he says :

Farid, why wanderest thou from forest to forest, breaking down the thorns of the trees ?

The Lord abides in the heart, why seekest thou Kin in the forest ?

Maulana Rumi says that the virtue of real *kaba* and *haj* lies in helping the poor and sympathising with him. For his going to *kaba* is not as great a virtue as pleasing and helping a poor man.

ھزاراں کعبہ بیک دل نرسد

دِل بدستِ آور کہ این حجِ اکبر است[10]

(Thousands of Kabas are not equal to pleasing one soul. You please another man and this is the greatest haj). Maulana Rumi equally speaks of the presence of God in a pure human heart.

خویش را صافی کُن از اوصاف خود

تا بِني ذاتِ پاک صاف خود[11]

(You should purify yourself with your own good acts and character so that you may see your own pure self).

آبینه دل جوں شود صافی و پاک
نفسیا بنی بروں از آب و خاک[12]

(Only when the mirror of the heart becomes clean and pure, you can see the layer even below the water and the land).

Farid's contribution to the Sufi thought and movement in India is remarkable. His love for man and God and egalitarian concept gave a new lease of life to sufism in the medieval Indian society. Unlike Attar and Rumi, Farid has not left behind much of the poetical *Sufi* thought unless we were to accept the view that Farid was the author to the *Slokas* entitled, *'Salok Baba Farid Ke'* incorporated in the *Adhi Granth*. It has also been suggested that probably Sheikh Brahm (Ibrahim), a descendant of Farid and a contemporary of Guru Nanak, was the author of those *Slokas*.[13] The collection of the Slokas composed in local Punjabi dialect (Multani) was presented by Sheikh Ibrahim to Nanak who also held spiritual dialogues with him. There is no denying the fact that Nanak was in close touch with the Farid School of thought. Notwithstanding the controvercy about the composition, what really important is the substance of the *Slokas* as representing Farid's ideas accepted by his followers. Guru Nanak carefully scrutinised and accepted the *Slokas* which fell in line with his own ideas. To Nanak they represented Farid's thought and reflections on human truth. Nanak attached the highest importance to Farid's concept of human life love of God and humanity, the pity on the man's waste of short span of life in frivolous pursuits of worldly riches, sympathy for man's suffering due to injustice, man's forgetfulness of the inevitability of death, consequences of evil deeds of life, forgiveness, charity, honesty and a search for higher values and meaningful way of life.[14] Nanak, the seeker of truth, accepted Farid's *bani* as his own *bani*. This is the highest tribute that Nanak could pay to Farid, the exponent of human truth. Even though Farid was a great scholar and valued knowledge, he did not write any book. However, the sufi literature comprising *Fawaid-ul-Fuad, Siyar-ul-Auliya* and *Khairul Majalis* goes in complete harmony with the above mentioned *Slokas* incorporated in the *Adhi Granth*. Taking all these sources in coordination, one could draw an authentic picture of Farid's ideas and thought.

Farid's view of *tariqat* (true path of life) lies in the inner qualities of man, prayers, patience, charity, love of man and God.[15] But this is not mere spiritualism. In his concept of sufism, Farid shows serious concern with the contemporary society. Though he talks in the Islamic idiom, his social concern is universal which cuts across caste, communal and religious barriers. In his *Jamat Khana,* no discrimination is made between man and man on any ground whatsoever as in his eyes all human beings are equal.[16] The *Jamat Khana* and the *Khanqal* life is free from all social complexes, caste and creed inhibitions. The rich and the poor, the old and young, the officials and the non-officials, the Muslims and the non-Muslims, the faqirs and the jogis, the foreigners and the natives find equal treatment in every respect, viz., food, accommodation and dignity. Every person being a creature of God has his own worth and dignity which must be respected on an equal basis. This way of life in the *Jamat Khana* is a pointer to Farid's concept of the social order he would like to be established. He denounces the society which had contempt for low-born persons even within the Muslim community. He indicts the socio-political order based on sharp disparity and injustice. He deals with the problems of the suffering humanity. Farid is humanist but his humanism is not for supernatural society but for this very earthly world. He wants to relieve the suffering man of the pain, to infuse him with energry so that he may face the hazards of this life and live in peace. Farid is not an eseapist. He clearly identifies himself with the poor and the weaker sections of the society. His sympathy for the poor and the needy persons is not sheer out of his noble nature. It is borne out of consciousness of the suffering of poor and their helplessness at the hands of a perverted social order which is 'unIslamic' in character. Farid points out the disparity between the rich and the poor classes and warns the former about the ultimate fath in religious term.

فرید! آب نہ آٹا اگلبد اک نہ ناہی لون

اگے گئے سنجا بیں چوبا کھاسی کون [17]

(Farid some have a good deal of flour and some have not even salt when they both go into the yond it shall be known who shall suffer the strokes ?)

Farid's concept of God[18] is based on personal experience, meditation and intuition. Self-purification is essential for the realisation of God.

Fast is a means to freedom from such physical needs which may otherwise lead to greed and vice. Through meditation one can realise his identity and pave the way for love for God. His God is both transcendant and immenent. It is equally omnipotent. Prayers mean communication with the Eternal. As God is a living reality, through prayers, Farid feels his presence with Him. A devoted person is one who loves God.

For Farid, the real aim of life is love of man and God. The love of man is possible only if one loves God in true sense. Greed, avarice, the amassing of wealth and riches detract the man from the path of love of God and union with Him. Love of God and greed cannot go together.[19] Farid distinguishes between right path of life with honest and moderate means and the riches acquired through greed. The former is a legitimate way of life while the latter is morally and socially wrong for through greed, one man may gather wealth only at cost of another starving man. Riches collected through greed are like sugar-coated poison. Farid compares such riches to poisoneous vegetable coated with sugar.

فریدا! اے وس گندلاں دھریاں کھنڈلواڑ
ایک راہے دے رہ گئے ایک رادھی گئے اُجاڑ [20]

Farid says that with greed, the love for God remains false.
When there is avarice what love can there be then ?
If there is avarice, then false is the love.[21]

Farids thinks that the greed in mind for acquiring riches is like an impure blood in the body. The blood of greed in the body is the main obstacle to union with God.

فریدا! رتی رت نہ نکلے جے تن چیرے کوے
جوتن رتے رب سیوتِن تن رت نہ ہوئے [22]

(They who are imbued with their spouse, they have not the blood of greed in their body.

When the Lords fear enters into the body, it grows lean and the bleed of avarice departs from within).

اے تن سبو رت ہے رت بن تن نہ ہوے

جو ھہ رتے اپنے ہنت تن لوب رت نہ ہوئے [22a]

(Every body has blood and there is nobody without blood; only these who love God do not have the blood of greed in their body).

Thus, to Farid, honest and moderate living free from avarice gives real contentment in life. Farid's concept of contentnent is not denial of necessary means of living. It is the elimination of great avarice and lust for wealth. A contented man would not east an eye on the ill-gotten wealth of the other avaricious persons who have gone astray from the right path. Farid sums up this concept of contentment by comparing the food of righteous and contented person to the 'bread of wood' and the ill-gotten prosperity to 'buttered bread'

فرید! روٹی میری کھاٹھ کی لاون میری بھوک [23]

جناں کھادی چوپڑی گھنے سہن کے دکھ

روکھی سوکھی کھاکے ٹھنڈا پانی پیو

فرید! دیکھ پرائی چوپڑی نہ ترسائے جیو

Farid my bread is made of wood and hunger is my cooked vegetable.

They who eat buttered bread shall suffer great pain. Eat thou the hard dry bread and drink the cold water Farid seeing another's buttered bread let not thy mind long for it.

If a person follows a right path, he is entitled to wealth after union with God and that is the real wealth.

فرید! رب کجوری پکاں ماکھیا نہیں وہین [24]

جو جو وبجھے ڈسبیڑا سو عُمر ہتھ پون

Farid equally ridicules in the inhibitions in mind because of caste complexes. He advocates a castelese social order.

فرید! من میدان کر ٹولے بیٹے لا[25]

اے مول نہ آوسی دوزخ سندھی پا

As a Chisti sufi, Farid has an implicit faith in the relationship between the *Sheikh* and the *murdhid*. The *Sheikh* has an entitled statue whose command is like a command of the Prophet. Farid says that it is only throgh the guidance of the *Pir* that a *murid* can obtain union with God. Here Rumi and Farid speak the same language.

Rumi says :

گر نباشد سایہ پیرا فضول[26]

بس ترا سرگشتہ دارد بایک غول

(If you do not have the shadow of a Pir, you are likely to be led astray).

Farid says :

There is only one God. By the true Guru's grace. He is obtained.[27]

The persons who are blessed by the Guru, they suffer not even a scratch.[28]

Farid's greatest contribution to the sufi life lies in the fact that with strict self-discipline, he practiced what he preached. There was complete unaminity between his thought and deeds. He stood as a symbol of harmony among the discordant elements in the society. He is essentially a man of the masses and carried the message of sufism to them. He rendered invaluable service to the communication of the institutional set-up of the Chistis order which is essentially in character and development. His thought has left a permanent mark on the cultural history of the Panjab. He spoke the human truth that was well recognised by Nanak and has left an important legacy to the people of the Panjab and India as a whole.

References

1. M. Abdul Haq Ansari, Islam, Faith and Practice, Theology and Ethics, *Islam,* Patiala, 1939, pp. 1-29.
2. K. A. Nizami, Mysticism, *Islam,* Patiala, 1969, pp. 50-74; M. Mujeeb, Sufism in India, *Influence of Islam on Indian Society,* Meerut, 1972, pp. 59-62; M. Mujeeb, Sufis and Sufism vide *The Indian Muslims,* London, 1967, pp. 113-167.
3. K. A. Nizami, *Tarikh-i-Kushaikh-i-Chist* (Urdu), Delhi, 1953, pp. 16-134.
4. For detailed discussion, A. K. S. Lambton, *Landlord and Peasant in Persia,* London, 1953, pp. 1-30.
5. *Ibid.,* pp. 31-104.
6. For detailed account, K. A. Nizami, vide f. n. 3, *The Life and Times of Shaikh Farid-ud-Din Ganj-i-Shakar,* Aligarh, 1955.
7. Shibli Nomani, *Sherul Ajam,* Azamgarh, 1947, Vol. II, p. 14.
8. *Ibid.,* p. 115.
9. *Ibid.,* p. 12.
10. *Masnavi Maulvi Manavi,* Bombay.
11. Shibli Nomani, *Sawaneh Maulana Rum,* Delhi, p. 177.
12. *Ibid.,* p. 124.
13. K. A. Nizami, *The Life and Times of Shaikh Fariduddin Ganj-i-Shakar,* Aligarh, 1955, Appendix C, pp. 121-22.
14. *Shri Guru Granth Sahib* (English and Punjabi Translation) by Man Mohan Singh, Amritsar, 1960, Vol. VIII, Salokas of Shaikh Farid, pp. 4547-4569.
15. Also see Grover, B. R., Baba Farid, A Man of the Masses, *Commemoration Volume, Hazrat Baba Sheikh Farid*, Patiala, 1973.
16. K. A. Nizami, vide f. n. 13, pp. 46-55, 110-115.
17. Salok Baba Farid Ke, Salok No. 44, vide Adhi Granth; also f. n. 14. I am extremely grateful to Prof. Kishan Singh (University of Delhi) for helping me in the translation and analysis of the Punjabi Script of the Saloks.
18. See f. n. 14.
19. See f. n. 21.
20. Salok Baba Farid Ke vide f. n. 17, Salok No. 37.
21. *Shri Guru Granth Sahib* vide f. n. 14, p. 4551.
22. Salok Baba Farid Ke vide f. n. 17, Salok No. 51.

22a. *Ibid.,* Salok No 52; f. n. 14, p. 4557.

23. *Ibid.,* Salokas No. 28-29, f. n. 14, p. 4553.
24. *Ibid.,* Salok No. 89.

25. *Ibid.*, Salok No. 74.
26. See f. n.10, p. 92.
27. Salok Baba Farid Ke, Salok no. 1, *Shri Guru Granth Sahib*, vide f. n. 14, p. 4547.
28. *Shri Guru Granth Sahib,* vide f. n. 14, p. 4563.

Chapter 6

Nanak Panth

*The Emergence of Nanak Panth - A Hindu Sect and Its Evolution unto Khalsa from the Sixteenth to Nineteenth Centuries**

(Based on the Contemporary Persian and Gurumukhi (Punjabi) Source-Material)

In the annals of India History and Culture, Guru Nanak Dev, the founder of the *Nanak Panth,* occupies a unique position in the socio-religious life of the people of India. He was a great Hindu religious thinker and revolutionary, both in thought and action. Though basically devoted to the Bhakti school of thought, he evolved afresh socio-religious philosophy and code of conduct to be pursued both by the elite and the common people.

In the Punjab, Guru Nanak (fifteenth-sixteenth centuries) also took inspiration from the *Sant panth*. However, Nanak's approach to monotheistic religion based on experience was clearer, more consistent and comprehensive.[1] Nanak's thought revolved as much around God as man and the social order. Kabir and Nanak were strict monotheists and their monotheism is strictly related to man and his society. According to them everything is related to man and his society. As such, to them everything that exists emnates from God and nothing outside His domain. Everything that happens is in accordance with His Law (*hukam*). Both good and evil are His own creation and both operate under His Law (*hukam*). The whole creation is in Him. He existed in the heart of every man. Thus from the fatherhood of God, Kabir and Nanak directly derive the brotherhood of man to be created on earth.

---

* Research Article presented at the XXXVIth International Congress of Asian and North-African Studies, Montreal, (Canada), 27th August-2nd September, 2000.

According to Nanak, the solution of man's problems on earth lies in the annulment of his alienation from God and return to the path shown by Him. For this purpose, *Sat Guru*, the true Guru lead is essential. He alone knows the true path and He alone can guide man on to it. He alone is custodian of *Nam* and He alone expresses that in *sabad*. God reveals the truth through *Sat Guru* and his word. With the help of *Sat Guru* and *sabad*, man becomes the embodiment of *Nam*. Sat Guru's *sabad* burns egoism from the heart of man and a complete human transformation takes place in him. In place of alienation from everyone else, love for all pervades in his heart. To be in line with his Creator means to be in tune with His creation and to be one with mankind. In Nanak's eyes, in the contemporary society, the *pandits, jogis, bairagis, shaikhs, qazis* and *mullahs* laying emphasis on scriptures and ritual prayers were not 'true Hindus or Muslims'. Only a person who followed the interior discipline with the help of the true Guru and adopted God's Name and His Law (*hukam*) could be a 'true' Hindu or 'true' Muslim. In Nanak's *bhakti*, devotion is that of God Himself and not of any *avatar*. Different castes may be sincere in their vocations but the highest duty of all is to recite the name of the Lord. God has no 'caste' and in His eyes 'caste' and 'birth' are totally irrelevant to one's salvation.

Guru Nanak was par excellence a humanist, a liberal thinker and a fervent believer in the composite culture. The concept of selfless service (*sewa*), dignity of labour for one's own living and sharing with the needy, the institutions of *dharamasala* as precursor to the *gurdwara*, *sangat* (organised fellowship), *pangat* (sitting in rows), *langar* (common kitchen) and *Nam simran* as embodied in the *Adi Granth* became essential features of the *Nanak Panth,* i.e., Sikhism as further evolved in the course of centuries. Nanak's liberal thought finds echo in Akbar's liberal thinking as outlined by Abul Fazl in the *Sulha-i-Kul* policy, thoughts recorded for an inscription for a temple in Kashmir and in Dara Shikoh's *Majma ul Baharain*.[2] This is equally true of the writings of Guru Gobind Singh as cited below.

> Many have become shaven-headed *sanyasis* (recluses), many have Become *jogis* (ascetics).
>
> Many have taken to *brahmcharia* (celibacy), many have become *jatis* (with long twisted hair).
>
> Many are Hindus, Turks, other Rafiji, Imam and Shafi. But recon all human beings of one race.

He (God named as) *Karta* (Doer), *Karim* (Kind-bestower), as well as *Raziq* (Sustainer) and *Rahim* (Merciful) is the same. They are all basically one and that is Brahma incarnate. (Do not make any basic difference amongst them).

We should serve only one (Supreme God) and all human beings have the same *Guru Dev* (Preceptor).

They (different names of God) have all the same form and we should acknowledge one Light (*Joti*-God).[3]

They are neither Hindav (Hindus) nor Turka (Muslims). Different people have started different *mat* (faiths). But every individual cannot succeed in propagating his (separate) *panth* (religious order).

As each one's concept becomes contradictory.[4]

When anyone rejects certain beliefs, customs or usages and asserts correctness of certain alternatives, it is a revolt in the making. Nanak did that. Now revolts can be peaceful or armed depending on various factors. Nanak's revolt was peaceful. And it could not be anything else but peaceful. At certain stages, certain questions do not arise. So the question of armed revolt of a Hindu reformer, which Nanak was, did not arise.

Nanak rejected caste distinctions, religious asceticism or renunciation. The cardinal principle of this teaching was the unity of God and the equality of all men before Him. He preached against caste distinction prevalant in Hinduism. Keeping the goals of both religions in view, he asserted that salvation could be attained only through upright character and good deeds. He also urged that the object of human life was purity of mind, and declared that asceticism or renunciation of the world was unnecessary. He lost no opportunity to strike a blow at the superstitiousness of Hinduism and Islam. Guru Nanak Dev was highly critical of such Hindus who were wedded to the Brahmanical rituals. In fact, it can be well discerned from the *Adi Granth* that Guru Nanak as spiritual saint was a great revolutionary who made distinct contribution to the Hindu social structure (by no means confined to Brahmanical interpretation of the way of life) and society.

The gradual transformation of the socio-religious character of the *Nanak-Panth* into a socio-religious cum political aspect of the Sikh community comprising followers from various clans and castes (*jatis*) during the course of the seventeenth and eighteenth centuries is a significant feature of the social change. Initially, the *Nanak-Panth* mostly comprised the Khatris, petty traders, artisans and craftsmen, low caste Hindus and a section of the poor peasantry, more especially from the Majah territories. The *hukamnamas* of the Gurus reveal that the *sangat* of the Gurus (Sikhs) were equally drawn from the prosperous commercial classes and other sections of the peasantry as well. They were drawn not only from the regions of the Punjab but from the cis-Sutlej territories, the regions around Delhi and other places in India. The socio-economic phenomenon involving the emergence of the new dominant clans in the landed structure in the Punjab and territories of Delhi, the conversion of these clans, more especially the peasantry to Sikhism in the course of the seventeenth and eighteenth centuries, added a new dimension to the character of the Sikh community. The initiation of the *Khalsa* by Guru Gobind Singh, the armed struggle by Banda Bahadur in the territories of *Subah* Delhi, hilly and plain regions of the Punjab against the Mughal state in the early eighteenth century, the later division of the *Khalsa* unto *Bandais* (after Banda's death) and the *Tat Khalsa*, the ultimate supremacy of the latter further moulded the militant character of the *Singhan* for safeguarding the interests of the *Panth*. Apart from this, a number of influential Hindus belonging to commercial class and officialdom became the Sikhs of the Guru.

Even though Guru Nanak Dev, as recorded in his hymns, embodied in the *Adi Granth*, condemned the atrocities of Babur, the first Mughal monarch as well as the inefficiency and callousness of Ibrahim Lodhi, all through the Mughal age he was considered as a medicant *(darwaish)* with liberal attitude towards all religious faiths inclusive of Islam. As such, he commanded great respect all through the medieval age. It is on this account that the followers of the *Nanak Panth* (Sikhs) were bestowed rent free (*muafi*) land at Amritsar (*Guru Ka Chak*) for the construction of Harimandir Sahib (later named as Golden Temple) and sacred tank etc. by Akbar the Great. Similarly, later on during the reign of Shah Jahan, rent free *(muafi)* grant of land was given to the Sodhis, the followers of Nanak, the *Darwaish* at Kartarpur (near Jullundar, Punjab) for the construction of a Gurudawara as well as preservation of the manuscript (*Ber*) of the *Adi Granth*.

Notwithstanding its pacific nature in the initial stages, impelled by political circumstances, there was gradual transformation of the *Nanak Panth* during the course of the sixteenth and seventeenth centuries of the Mughal rule. In this respect, the two landmarks which ultimately changed the very character of the *Panth* were the execution of the fifth Guru Arjun Dev at the hands of the Mughal monarch Jahangir and the execution of the ninth Guru Tegh Bahadur (1675) during the reign of Aurangzeb. Jahangir mentions in his Memoirs, "...In Goindwal...there was a Hindu named Arjun, in the garment of Sainthood and sanctity, so much so that he had captured many of the simple hearted Hindus, even of the ignorant and foolish followers of Islam. They call him Guru...For three or four generations they had kept this shop warm. Many times it occurred to me to put a stop to this vain affair and to bring him into the assembly of Islam".[5] After the execution of Guru Arjun Dev, the sixth Guru Har Gobind (1606-1644) kept up the tradition of the latter for arrangement of horses and retainers. He also wore two swords of "Miri", i.e., temporal power and "Piri", i.e., spiritual power. Next to the Harimandir Sahib, he also raised a platform called 'Akal Takht', the seat of temporal authority. He had also a few conflicts with the Mughal State.

The ninth Guru Tegh Bahadur (1664-1675) opted to stay at a comparatively safer place, Kiratpur, and laid the foundation of a new town of Anandpur. As he had espoused the cause of the Kashmiri Brahamins against the tyranny of the Mughal rule and fanatical policy of Aurangzeb, he was executed at Delhi. His son and successor, the tenth Guru, Guru Gobind Singh, settled at Anandpur which was a part of Kulher (present Bilaspur in Himachal Pradesh) State, Sarkar Sirhind, *Subah* Delhi. He also maintained private retainers and armed establishment. The Sikhs called him 'Sacha Padshah'. As he used to have religious gatherings, the Mughal Government wanted to oust him from there. He came in conflict both with the Hill Chiefs and the Mughal State. On the Baisakhi day, 30th March, 1699, the Guru abolished the *masand* system and instituted the Khalsa. Guru Gobind Singh considered himself a true successor of Nanak and believed to have been chosen by God to establish the *panth* of Nanak. He wrote in his own autobiography *Bachittar Natik* that he had taken birth for the purpose of spreading the faith, saving the saints, and expatriating all tyrants.

The term Khalsa is not derived from *Khalis,* i.e., pure, as is usually understood. In fact, it is analogous to the Mughal revenue terminology wherein the revenues of the Khalsa territories went directly to the State treasury and were not assigned in any *tankhawah* (salary) jagir. Here Khalsa meant direct relationship with the Guru. As such, Guru Gobind Singh in a symbolic manner selected five willing followers who would lay down their lives for the sake of 'Dharma'. The selection was made regardless of the caste and region, from different places of the country, i.e., a khatri from Lahore, a jat from Delhi, washerman from Dwarka, a cook from Jagannath and a barbar from Bidar. The Guru discarded the earlier method of *Charan Pahul,* i.e., washing of the Guru's feet. *Khandah pahul,* i.e., sweet water stirred with double edged *Khanda* was adopted. The Guru called the five followers as the five beloved ones (*panj-piaras*) and himself took *pahul* from each one of them, thereby merging his person with the disciples. The baptised Sikhs were to wear their "Keshas" as well as arms. As such, the Khalsa became the Guru and Guru became the Khalsa.

The importance of *Dasam Granth* of Guru Gobind Singh from the perspectives of religion, history and literature is undeniable. Many of its compositions relate not only to the life of Guru Gobind Singh with biographical significance, but even to the thought and ideas of the Guru which are of primary importance. As the *Dasam Granth* also comprises some of the major systems of religious beliefs in India, especially the *Shakta*, the *Vaishnava* and the *Shaiva*, these can be well related to the Guru's own beliefs and faith. The recently discovered manuscript of the *Dasam Granth* compiled during the first half of the nineteenth century comprises forty illustrations and paintings of the Kashmiri school.[5a] Apart from the paintings of Guru Nanak and Guru Gobind Singh, they cover Lord Shiva, Hanuman and various other Hindu deities. These equally reflect the conceptual relationship and faith of the Guru in them. It is also well accepted that before launching the institution of the Khalsa and waging a concerted and effective war against the Mughals, Guru Gobind Singh offered prayers at the Naina Devi temple and sought blessings from the Goddess Naina Devi for success in his mission of *Dharam Yud*.

Varying versions about the Khalsa were given even during the course of the eighteenth and nineteenth centuries. Of these, for the sake of illustration, only a few typical examples may be taken up. Ahmad Shah Batalia[5b] attributes the beginning of the Singhs (*Singhan*) to the institution of the Khalsa. He calls the Singhs (*Singhan*) as a group of the Hindus who also claimed to be followers of the earlier faith of Baba Nanak Bedi (*Nanak Panth*). The followers of the Khalsa were named as Singhs (*Singhan*) and professed, more or less, a new faith for the fulfilment of the mission of the Khalsa. Having traced the history of the past Gurus, Ahmad Shah Batalia deals with the life and mission of Guru Gobind Singh and thereafter stresses the militant character of the Khalsa all through the eighteenth century, the establishment of the *misils* and ultimately the rule of Maharaja Ranjit Singh (1799-1839).

Ganesh Das Badhera's description[6] of the Sikhs, the Khalsa and Singhs (*Singhan*) and the role played by them during the course of the eighteenth century and that of Maharaja Ranjit Singh is more apt and objective than many of the writers. He calls the community of the Sikhs (*quam-i-sikhan*) as a part and parcel of the Hindu society. He equally considers the Khalsa community (*quam-i-khalsa*) as synonymous with the Sikhs. He considers Baba Nanak as *Darwesh* (medicant) and his faith (*Nanak Panth*) absolutely tolerant without any fanaticism. He regards that Guru Gobind Singh belonged to the organisation and faith (*Silsala*) of Nanak Shah, the *Darwaish*. He has given a well defined code of conduct of the Khalsa (*Ain-i-Khalsa*) with details of the *pahul*, adoption of the name of the Singh, uncut hair, turban, citation of Akal Purakh, Sukhmani, Japji, etc. He considers this as more or less a new faith of the *Singhan* and the Khalsa. He has well defined the term Khalsa itself, i.e., *Khalsa* with direct linkage between the Singhs and the Guru. He has equally dealt with the institutions of *Dal Khalsa*, *Sarbat Khalsa* and the detailed role played by Banda Bahadur and these institutions during the course of the eighteenth century. According to him, the Hindus were inseparable from the Singhs, Khalsa and its organisational set up which were essentially a part of the Hindu Society (*ahl-i-Hunud*).

Another scholar of the nineteenth century, Pandit Raja Ram Tuti provides detailed description of the establishment of the Khalsa and the Singhs (*Singhan*) with a new faith and militant character to fight against the Mughal oppression. He also makes the Hindus as the basis of the Khalsa and the Singhs (*Singhan*) who played crucial role in the eighteenth century, both against the Mughals and the Abdalis.[7]

The decline of the Mughal Empire during the eighteenth century led to the dissolution of the old political order and emergence of new socio-political forces in various parts of India. In the Punjab as well as in territories of *chakla* Sirhind forming a part of *subah* Delhi, ever since the creation of the *Khalsa* by Guru Gobind Singh (1699), the Singhs (*Singhan*) gradually emerged as a vital force which undermined the traditional Mughal administrative institutions and polity. Guru Gobind Singh, imbued with the spirit of justice and freedom, fought against the Hill chiefs as well as the local Mughal oppression. Due to his untimely death (1708), his mission was carried on by Banda *Biragi* (1708-1716). By the early eigthteenth century, the social base of *Nanak Panth*/Sikhism had undergone a revolutionary change so as to cover not only the urban khatris but the jats, a few Gujar communities and other Hindu professional as well as low-castes from the rural regions. As khatris, even though devoted *Nanak-Panthis*, mostly belonged to the commercial petty trading class and held revenue/administrative posts, they had, by and large, pro-establishment leanings and a period of turmoil much less suited their interests. On the other hand, the rural Jats comprising the petty village zamindars, the peasant proprietors, the varying categories of the cultivators as well as a few Gujar communities, artisans and the other vocational castes being devout Singhs were well prone and fairly equipped to participate in a conflict involving evasion of the payment of the revenues to the Mughal State, plunder and even armed conflict with the State. As such, Banda was able to raise a large army from the rural areas for his military operational purposes. As known from the contemporary sources, he commanded major support from the Jat peasantry, some Gujar peasant communities, as well as the *banjaras*.[8] The Hindu *faqirs, yogis, sanyasis* and *bairagis*,[9] many of whom followed the *Nanak Panth,* equally lent moral and indirect support to him. Many a Hindu Rajput Hill Chieftain of the *subahs* of Punjab and Delhi (in Uttar Pradesh) and numerous people in these territories with varying castes supported Banda in his designs.[10]

Starting his operational activities from Kharkauda, Sonepat and Panipat (Haryana) for suppression and occupation of the Mughal territories in *subah* Delhi both sides of the main canal (*Shah Nahr*) and river Jamuna inclusive of the parganas of *sarkar* Saharanpur as well as *chakla* Sirhind,[11] Banda sacked the town of Sirhind and killed Wazir Khan, the *faujdar* who had been responsible for the execution of the sons of Guru Gobind Singh and struck coin in the name of Guru Nanak and Guru Gobind Singh which was a signal for the overthrow of the Mughal authority and assumption of sovereignty by the *Khalsa*.[12] Apart from the devastation caused by him, for a short span of period, he established his own authority, removed many a landed intermediary of higher strata who continued to owe allegiance to the Mughal State and realised the revenues from the *ra'aya* through the petty and primary village zamindars who supported him.[13] In the Punjab, his refectory itinerary aimed at the occupation of many a *pargana* for the realisation of the revenues covered *Beth*-Jalandhar and *Bari doabs*, though there were insurrections on the part of his supporters in the *Rechna doab* as well.[14] The fact that Banda was able to withstand the mighty Mughal Empire for nearly seven years cannot be explained merely on grounds of tenacity of his character and strategic military warfare. It rather reveals the seriousness and magnitude of the socio-economic grievances felt by some communities, especially the Singhs/Sikhs in the territories of Haryana (*subah* Delhi) and Punjab. After Banda was captured (1715) and brought to Delhi, he was executed (1716) along with 1300 disciples of the Guru of which each one vied with another for earlier execution for the attainment of salvation.[15] Banda's three-year-old son sitting in his lap was killed and the liver of the deceased child was put in Banda's mouth before he himself was torn to pieces.[16] Banda's wife was converted to Islam and became one of the slaves of the royal seraglio.[17]

All this left a scar on the heart of the Singhs/Sikhs, many of whom in due course of time organised themselves into small *jathas* (armed bands) as free-booters. One of such *jathas* was formed by Sardar Kapur Singh, Virkh Jat of village Kalokain to the west of river Ravi (in District Sheikhupura). However, as the lawless activities of the Singhs (*Singhan*) did not stop, a represssive policy was renewed for crushing their activities.[18] Bhai Mani Singh, the chief *granthi* of Harimandir Sahib, was also executed in 1738 A.D.

Nadir Shah's invasion (1739-40) and the capture of Delhi shook the foundations of the Mughal Empire and led to desolation of many a town in the Punjab and a period of uncertainty as well as serious financial crisis. Nadir Shah's invasion broke the neck of the Mughal State and accelerated the aggressive character of the Sikh groups (*grohs*) for plunder and forcible realisation of the revenue from the village zamindars. The Singhs (*Singhan*) exploited the situation in the Punjab while Nadir Shah remained in occupation of Delhi for a few months. However, so long a Zakariya Khan remained the *subadar* of Punjab (1726-45), he kept the situation under control but thereafter it became rather chaotic.[19]

It was around this period that Jassa Singh Ahluwalia started playing an active role for fighting against the Mughal oppression and for safeguarding the cause of the Singh/Sikh community. In his childhood, he, along with his mother, stayed for a few years with Mata Sundri, widow of Guru Gobind Singh and later on took up service with Sardar Kapur Singh Faizullahpuria. Having received hard training in the art of warfare, he distinguished himself as the ablest lieutenant of Sardar Kapur Singh.

The next significant phase fraught with political and economic changes of fundamental character in the eighteenth century history of North India started with the foreign incursions by Ahmad Shah Durrani from 1747-48 A.D. onwards. This period is as well marked by the dominant role by the Sikh Sardars in the agrarian and political set-up in the territories of the Punjab and cis-Sutlej as well as Jamuna Ganga *doab* regions forming a part of *Subah* Delhi. Sardar Jassa Singh Ahluwalia participated in most of the campaigns directed against the Durranis. As after the death of his mentor Sardar Kapur Singh Faizullahpuria in 1753, its *Sardari* descended on the latter's nephew, Sardar Khushal Singh, Sardar Jassa Singh Ahluwalia formed his own *Dal* comprising his *khas-fauj* as well as the *misldars* and Sikh horsemen affiliated to his *Sardari*. On numerous occasions, he joined the *Dal Khalsa* and operated against the *faujdars* of Jalandar *doab*, *chakla* Sirhind as well as against the *subadar* of Lahore and Ahmad Shah Abdali.[20] The Singh/Sikh Sardars had the best of cavalry force which was swift in action but they could not afford to fight a pitched battle against Ahmad Shah Durrani because of the latter's superiority of artillery fire and large number of regular forces at command. So the Singh Sardars (*Singhan*) usually adopted guerilla warfare and struck at the isolated or the rear wings of Abdali's forces and decamped with the booty. However, there are instances when they successfully fought even pitched battles against the forces of Abdali's generals, Lahore Governors and the *faujdars*.[21]

The *Dal Khalsa,* under the leadership of Sardar Jassa Singh Ahluwalia, attacked and captured Sirhind (14th January, 1764) and killed Zain Khan, the *faujdar* of *chakla* Sirhind.[22] Later, on his return journey from the campaign (December, 1764-March 1765), Ahmad Shah Abdali met with severe opposition in the Jalandhar *doab* with Sardar Jassa Singh Ahluwalia in the centre.[23] After Abdali's return to Kabul and during the same year (1765), the Singh/Sikh Sardars, i.e., Gujar Singh, Lehna Singh, Sobha Singh and Jai Singh Kanhiya expelled Abdali's representative and occupied the city of Lahore which they partitioned amongst themselves. Coin was also struck in the name of the Gurus, Nanak and Gobind Singh, with the same wording as earlier inscribed by Banda at Sirhind during his insurrection against the Mughal State.[24]

As a matter of fact, the most significant feature of the political and economic order of the eighteenth century is the establishment of the institution of *misldari* and *sardari* which fundamentally altered the character of armed struggle of the Singhs/Sikhs against the Mughals and the Durranis as well as the revenue administration of the agrarian society. By and large, this was a new rural class and quite distinct from the traditional landed intermediaries and zamindars. Even though the Singh/Sikh *grohs* (mobile armed bands) had operated all through the first half of the eighteenth century, it is their linkage with the land and distribution of the surplus produce of the same amongst the Singh/ Sikh fighting forces, the *misldars* and the Sardars which distinguished the latter from the earlier evolutionary phase of the mere pillage and plunder of the booty.

The so far known contemporary eighteenth century Persian, Marathi and English sources[25] do not use the term *misl*. The Persian *Akhbar* usually refers to the Sikh Sardars (*Sardaran-i-Sikhan*) or the Sikh Sardars in groups (*Jamai-i-Sardaran/Sardaran-i-Jamai Sikhan*) or even with his *Dal*. As an individual Sardar who in the later sources is put as chief of a *misl* is simply described as a Sardar of the Sikhs (*Sardar-i-Sikhan*). The Marathi sources simply refer to the Sikhs or their Sardars. The English sources mention only the Sikhs or some of their distinguished leaders as Sardars. These sources bring out the role played by the particular Sardars in different military campaigns as well as for territorial acquisition on their part at different phases in the course of the later half of the eighteenth century. Based on ties of kinship and the local territorial proximity, the *misl* denoted a group of Sikhs (*groh-i-Sikhan*) under the leadership of a prominent Sardar for military operations, both for defence and offence, territorial acquisition for the enjoyment of the revenues (surplus produce) and the division of the same amongst its male family members as well as the other constituent male members of the group (*groh*).[26]

For military operational purposes, a few *misl* Sardars would combine under the leadership of a chief Sardar who was as well a Sardar of one of the *misls*. As such, the amalgamation of the constituent *misldars*, units under the command of a chief Sardar would be considered as the latter's *Dal*. The combination of the *misl* Sardars under the command of a chief Sardar was purely on an *ad-hoc* basis for a specific campaign.[27] At times, for the purpose of defence or offence, more particularly at critical junctures for operation against the Durranis or the Mughals, the chief Sardars (*Sardaran-i-umda*), after mutual consultation (*Gurumata*) at a joint meetings and in accordance with the decision taken, joined together for a United action under the leadership of one of the chief Sardars.[28] Such a combination on the part of most of the chief Sardars and their constituent *misls* was named *Dal Khalsa*.

The eighteenth century Persian *Akhbar* ordinarily describe the chief Sikh Sardars as *Sardaran-i-Sikhan* or *Sardaran-i-umda* and their *Dal* as *Dal-i-Sikhan* but after the *Gurumata* was taken, they are described as *Sardaran-i-Khalsa* or *Khalsa Ji* and their *Dal* is put as *Dal Khalsa*.[29] The *Gurumata* had as well the sanction of the faith (*Guru Panth*) and was binding on as the participants. In fact, *Gurumata* meant mutual consultation (*mashwara/mashwart salah*) at a gathering of the Sardars for taking decision and adopting course of action regarding a particular matter. The gathered Sardars as the *Khalsa* embodied the form of the Guru. As such, after due deliberation (*masalhat*) and mutual consultation (*mashwarat/Gurumata*), decision was taken which was mandatory (*hukam*) in character to be implemented by all the participating Sardars.

As the Durrani government claimed its own rights over Punjab and cis-Sutlej territories, it equally asserted its claim for the realisation of *muamala* (revenues) from the territories held by the chief Sardars and the *misl* Sardars unless they were reckoned by the Durrani state as revenue-free lands. This led to a continual struggle between the *Singhan*/Sikh Sardars and the local Durrani administration all through the later half of the eighteenth century.

Of the Punjabi sources written in *Gurumukhi* script which cover the eighteenth century period relating to Sardar Jassa Singh Ahluwalia and the other Sikh Sardars, Ram Sukh Rao's *Sri Jassa Singh Binod*, *Sri Bhag Singh Chandgruday*, *Sri Fateh Singh Partap Prabhakar* as well as Ratan Singh Bhangu's *Panth Prakash* copiously utilised by the scholars need special consideration. By the time, Ram Sukh Rao wrote about Sardar Jassa Singh Ahluwalia and Raja Bhag Singh, the *Khalsa Sarkar* was already triumphant and Maharaja Ranjit Singh had not only expelled the Afghans from the Punjab root and branch but had also annexed Multan, Kashmir and even territories beyond Indus inclusive of Peshawar.

Ordinarily, the medieval chronicles that deal mostly with the political history and aspects of the social life of the people have to be gleaned from their accounts. However, Mufti Ali-ud-din, a resident of Lahore, in his *Ibrat Nama* (1854) has dealt with the social life of the common people during the reign for Maharaja Ranjit Singh and thereafter in a comprehensive manner.[30]

As regards the Sikhs, the author comments, they generally shook off the rituals that the Brahmanas fostered on the other Hindu society.

They mostly took to agriculture and invariably joined army. Many Sikhs belonged to the zamindari clans. They were highly sensitive for the protection of the honour of their womenfolk. They did not observe the practice of preparing a *chauka* before eating meals. Meat was their staple diet but they would never eat meat of any animal slaughtered by a Muslim. They did not observe any formality in the matter of dress and social intercourse. Instead of saying 'Ram Ram' like the other Hindus, they would utter *Waheguruji ki Fateh*. In the morning hours, they would recite only the Guru's Bani, i.e. *Japji* and the *Sukhmani*. The main section of the Sikhs was that of the cultivators. A large number of those who embraced Sikhism called themselves *Singh Guruji Ka* and were engaged in the trade. They were, by and large, very fond of wearing arms. Those who could well afford liked riding horses and elephants. The Sikhs made extensive use of Gurumukhi and read and wrote in that script. In social life, they indulged in wine and sex. The sections known as the Akalis and Nihangs were extremely fanatics.

The above description is only a gist of the description about the common people of the Punjab as provided by Mufti Ali-ud-din's *Ibrat Nama*. This work written in Persian, even though published in Pakistan, has not been translated into English or any of the regional languages in India or Pakistan.

It is significant to observe that even though Persian was the court language of the Lahore Darbar, the common people of all religious faiths, the Muslims, the Hindus and the Sikhs spoke Punjabi which was written both in Arabic and Gurumukhi scripts. All the same, in 1882 A.D., Urdu was introduced by the British Government as an official vernacular language, more or less, against the wishes of many a section of the Punjab society.

At the end, it may be reiterated emphatically that right from the sixteenth century down to at least the mid-nineteenth century, the Nanak *Panth* was regarded as an integral part of the Hindu society. Even though distinct from the other Hindu faiths viz., the Brahmnical order, Vaishnavism, other Shaivism, other bhakti cults and the socio-religious orders like the Jains, Jogis (*faqirs*, i.e. *Kanphattas* and *Augars*, etc.), it remained within the Hindu socio-religious structure. As a matter of fact, right from the eighth century onwards, the Muslim writers used the term Hindus (*Hunud*) in India in contrast to the followers of Islam (*Musalmin*). In the early medieval age, even though Buddhism was well established in Sindh, Multan and other parts of the west Punjab, despite special tension between the Buddhists and the Brahmans, the Arab accounts insist on covering both as a part of the Hindu Society. From thirteenth century onwards, the Persian sources maintain this concept of the Hindus and Muslims and consider all religious sects in Hindustan which were outside the Islamic religion and its people (*Musalmin*) as the Hindu people (*Hunud*), though, of course, both were divided into various clannish social groups (*firqas*). It is clear from the hymns of Guru Nanak and the writings of Guru Gobind Singh that when they appeal for social cohesion and composite human culture, they only mention the Hindus and the Muslims as the two main religious classes in Hindustan and regard their own socio-religious order as a part of the larger Hindu society with multifarious sects.[31]

It is evident from the eighteenth century documents that gradually the term *Khalsaji* or the *Panth* comprised all the Sikhs (*Singhan*) divided for political purposes unto various ethnic, tribal and clannish groups (*qabial* or *qabalian* or *qabilas*) under the Sardars (*Sardaran-i-Khalsa*) with their respective *dals* and territorial *zamindari* and *taaulqadari* jurisdictions (*makanat*) all over the Punjab, cis-Sutlej territories and other regions of *subah* Delhi.[32] As before, the distinction between the *firqas* of *ahl-I-Islam* and the Hindu *aqwam* (*qaums*) is maintained and the Sikh *aqwam* (*qaums*) are considered as a part of the latter. At the close of the eighteenth and the early nineteenth century, Mirza Qatil, a converted Sikh-Muslim in *Halft Tamasha,* while giving an account of the creeds, traditions and sects of the Hindus,[33] and of the Musalmans of India, regarded "the Sikh disciples of Peshwa Nanak Shah Punjabi as part of the Hindus of the Punjab". This concept is maintained both by the Hindu and Muslim writers in the reigns of Maharaja Ranjit Singh and his successors. It is only after the annexation of the Punjab that the British administrators while writing their memoranda and reports in the English language that they gave connotations to the existing technical aspects of the socio-religious orders so as to make Sikhism as distinct from Hinduism.

Prior to the annexation of Punjab (1849), both English Governor-Generals of India, Lord Hardinge and Lord Dalhousie, while considering the viability of the annexation of Punjab in their correspondence and respective Minutes, considered the Lahore Government as a Hindu Government. When after the first Anglo-Sikh war, Lord Hardinge advocated the non-annexation of Punjab, his main argument was that this being the "last Hindu state in India" could well serve as a buffer between "the Sutledge and the Khyber", i.e., between the English and the Muslim states of Afghanistan and Iran etc. Both Hardinge and Dalhousie considered the 'Lahore Court', 'Khalsa State', 'Hindu Government' and the 'Lahore Government' as co-terminous and identical. Even as late as 1881-83, when the Report on the Census (1881) was compiled as the first experiment in the Punjab, the English administrator responsible for carrying out the census conceded the fact that it was based on "the initial experience", "infinite diversity of the material to be dealt with" and their own, i.e., the English, "infinite ignorance of that material" as well as "ignorance of the customs and the beliefs of the people". It was meant not only for the guidance of the British Indian officials but it also aimed to feed "European Science" about "the social and religious phenomenon" of the Punjab.[34] All the same, in many a region, of the people of various castes and clans professing the same religious faith, some got themselves recorded as Hindus while others as Sikhs.[35] As a matter of fact, it is only in the late nineteenth and twentieth century that in the changed political circumstances the Sikhs have come to be viewed as a separate religious entity as distinct from the Hindu Society.

It is recorded in *Jassa Singh Binod* that when Sardar Jassa Singh Ahluwalia died in 1783 A.D., on the basis of his last wish, both the Brahmans/Pundits and the Granthis performed his last rites. Many of the Sikh princely states like the Kapurthala and Patiala, which emerged during the course of the eighteenth century, continued to observe all Hindu festivals like the Holi, Dussehra and Diwali. Although the rulers of Patiala claimed themselves to be Sikhs, they had been conducting certain traditional Hindu Pujas during Dussehra.[36] This is further endorsed by the numismatic evidence as at the time of such festivals, coins were struck by the Maharajas and offered to the Hindu deities. It is clear from the State records that the Patiala rulers had been using both gold and silver coins specially minted for these occasions. Many of these coins pertain to this period 1958, 1993-94 *Samvat*/1901, 1936-37 A.D.[37] At the same time, the numismatic evidence clearly bears out that apart from the use of the words Khalsa, Nanak and Gobind Singh, the Pipal tree leaves are also inscribed on the coins which clearly show the traditional Hindu/Brahamanical impact on the currency. This is specially true of the Kashmir coins 1876-1879 Samvat/1820-22 A.D., coins issued at Peshawar (1892-93 Samvat/1837-38 A.D.) during the governorship of Hari Singh Nalwa during Maharaja

Ranjit Singh's reign as well as post-Ranjit Singh period (1839-1849 A.D.). For the period 1840-49, Hindu symbols like Trisul, Om, Chattar, Sat, Shiv and Ramji were inscribed on the Sikh coins which were struck in the name of the Sikh Gurus.

References

1. The entire analysis of Guru Nanak Dev *Bani* is based on the *Adi Granth* compiled by Guru Arjun Dev in 1604 A.D.
2. Dara Shikoh, *Majma-ul-Bahrain* (ed. Mahfuz-ul-Haq) or the Making of the Two Oceans, edited in the original Persian with English translation, Notes and Variants, Calcutta, 1929.
3. *Dassam Granth*, 15/85 vide Maheem Singh, *Guru Gobind Singh aur un ki Hindi Kavita*, p. 100, tr. Grover.
4. *Ibid.*, 2 Sankhaya-7, Nihakalanki Avtar, 24 Avtar, p. 107. Tr. Grover.
5. *Tauzak-i-Jahangiri* (Tr. Alexander Rogers), 1978, New Delhi, p.72.

5a. *Dasam Granth* (manuscript in Hindi and one letter entitled *Zafar Nama* of Guru Gobind Singh in Persian with Punjabi script; Total folios 736), National Museum, New Delhi, No.94.13.

5b. Ahmad Shah Batalia's account entitled *Zikar-i-Guruan wa Ibtdai-Singhan wa Mahzab-i-Aaishan* put as an Appendix (*tatima*) of Vol. I, pp. 1-44 of Sohan Lal Suri's *Umadat-ut-Twarikh*, (Persian text), Lahore, 1885-1889.

6. Ganesh Das Badhera, *Char Bagh-i-Punjab* (Persian text), ed. Kirpal Singh, Amritsar, 1965, pp. 105-137.
7. Pandit Raja Ram Tuti *Ahwal-I-Singhan* i.e. *Halat-i-Mazhab Wa Hakumat Singhan*, Ms. National Museum, New Delhi, No.81. 689.
8. Rajasthan Archives, Bikaner, (previously) located at Jaipur where the present writer consulted them. *Akhbar Darbar-i-Maula* (henceforth *Akhbar*), dated 7 *Jamada* II, A.H. 1122, 4th R.Y Bahadur Shah (henceforth B.S.) 23 July, 1710 A.D. refers to the peasant followers of the Guru (Banda) in chakla Sirhind and *sarkar* Saharanpur; *Akhbar,* dated 24 *Jamada* I, A. H. 1127, 4th R.Y. Farrukhsiyar (henceforth F.S.), 17 May, 1715 A.D. refers to the rebels of Brar sub-caste (Jats). As regards Gujars, *Akhbar,* dated 16 *Jamada* I, A.H. 1122, 4th R.Y B.S./2 July, 1710 refers to the establishment of *thanas* by the rebel *Guru* (Banda) at Rampura, Saharanpur, Buria, etc. (sarkar Saharanpur) with the help of the *qanungos* and the rebellious Gujars. Earlier *Akhbar,* dated *Jamada* I, A.H. 1122, 4th R.Y B.S., while referring to the establishment of the *thanas* by Banda at Rampur, Nanota, Jhujhana, Bakur Barsadua, Sadhaura, Karana, Budhana Kandhala and Buria (all in *sarkar* Saharanpur) states that the wayfarers and the *qanungos* of Saharanpur had collaborated with Banda. Here, the caste of the *qanungos* in this region are mentioned as Kaiyasths. At a few places, the Gujar zamindars supported

the Mughal Government. *Akhbar,* dated 3 *Zulhijja* A.H. 1123, 6th R.Y. B.S./1 January, 1712 A.D. states that after Banda's clash with Muhammad Amin Khan Bahadur and the flight of Banda's forces, those of the Sikhs who crossed the river were killed by the Gujar zamindars. However, the *banjara* community seems to have given consistent support to Banda. *Akhbar,* dated 19 *Shawwal*, A.H. 1122, 4th R.Y B.S./30 November, 1710 A.D. while narrating the Mughal operation against Banda at Dabar and Taragarh etc., states that the villages were plundered by the *banjaras*. *Akhbar,* dated 10 *Ramazan*, A.H. 1123, 5th R.Y B.S./11 October 1711 A.D. states that forty *Nanak Prasat* (Sikhs) *banjaras* were captured from the areas surrounding Multan and were brought to the *kotwali* (at Delhi). As the *banjaras* declined the offer to accept Islam, they were killed. *Akhbar,* dated 10 *Shaban*, A.H. 1126, 3rd R.Y F.S./10 August, 1714 A.D. states that the rebel Guru (*Banda*) with the help of the forces of the zamindars of Srinagar (Garhwal) and collaboration of the *banjaras* had passed through the hills and gone in the direction of Bareilli and Muradabad. *Akhbar,* dated 12 *Rajab*, A.H. 1127, 4th R.Y F.S./3 July, 1715 A.D. states that most of the *banjaras* staying in the *taalluqas* of Heer Chand, Daya Damna and the *zamindaries* of the *khalisa mahals* in *chakla* Kangra were Nanak-worshippers and acting as the spies provided the rebels (followers of Banda) with food-grains, arrows and rifles.

9. *Akhbar,* dated 27 *Ramazan*, A.H. 1123, 5th R.Y.B.S./ 28, October 1711 A.D. states that the Hindu *faqirs*, *yogis*, *sanyasis* and *bairagis* conveyed the imperial news to the rebel Guru (Banda).

10. Rajasthan Archives, Bikaner, (earlier at Jaipur States, Old Historical Records Office), *Arzdashts* (in Rajasthani) from Diwan Bhikhani Das to the Maharaja (Mirza Raja Sawai Jai Singh) describe Shyam Singh Khatri, the *diwan* of the Raja of Nahan as a Sikh of the Guru. Both the *diwan* and the Raja were arrested by the Mughal State on suspicion of alleged help to Banda and for not having revealed the whereabouts of the latter in the Sirmur hills. The contemporary *Akhbar* clearly bear out the collaboration or association on the part of many a zamindar (chiefs) and the people of their territories comprising the Nanak-worshippers as well. The *Akhbar* especially mention Kehlur (Bilaspur) vide, dated 25 *Zulhijja*, A.H. 1123, 6th R.Y.B.S./23 January, 1712 A.D. 14 *Muharram*, A.H. 1124, 6th R.Y.B.S./11 February, 1712 A.D. On dchah, *Ibid*; Kulu vide 18 *Ramazan*, A.H. 1123, 5th R.Y.B.S./19 October, 1711 A.D; Garhwal (Srinagar) vide 23 *Rabi* I, A.H. 1128, 5th R.Y.F.S./13 March, 1716 A.D. Apart from these, a few other *Akhbar* refer to the prevelance of Nanak-worshippers or sympathisers of Banda in the Jammu Hill territories and Rajauri.

11. Of the numerous *Akhbar*, see dated 1 *Zulhijja*, A.H. 1120-21, 3rd R.Y.B.S./ 31 January, 1709 A.D; also Mir Mubarak Ullah entitled Iradat Khan's *Tarikh-i-Iradat Khan*, (originally named *Bahadur Shah Nama* known as Tazikara-i-Iradat Khan as well. It was written in 1714 A.D. and as such the

author was contemporary of Banda who had not been even captured till then). Edited by Ghulam Rasul Menr, Lahore (Pakistan), 1971, pp. 95-96, 100-105, also *op.cit.* No.1.

12. *Akhbar*, dated 30 *Zulada*, A.H. 1122, 4th R.Y.B.S./4th January, 1711 A.D. It uses the term *Khalsa* Sikhs and also gives wording of the inscription on the mohar. Also *Tarikh-i-Iradat Khan, Ibid.*

13. *Ibid.*

14. Of the numerous *Akhbar*, see, dated 2 *Safar*, A.H. 1123, 5th R.Y.B.S./11 March, 1711 A.D; 29 *Safar*, A.H. 1123, 5th R.Y.B.S./7 April, 1711 A.D; 28 *Safar* I, A.H. 1123, 5th R.Y.B.S./4 June, 1711 A.D; 24 *Jamada* I, A.H. 1123, 5th R.Y.B.S./29 June, 1711 A.D. Also *Tarikh-i- Iradat Khan, Ibid.*

15. *Akhbar*, dated 26 *Zulhijja* A.H. 1127, 4th R.Y.F.S./12 December 1715 A.D. (Banda captured); 1 *Rajab*, A.H. 1128, 5th R.Y.F.S./10 June, 1716 A.D. (Banda executed). For details of execution, Shiv Das Lakhnawi, *Shah Nama Munewar Kalam*, tr. S.H. Askri, Patna, 1980, *Waqi*, pp. 15-18.

16. *Ibid.*

17. *Ibid.*

18. *Ibid*, pp. 222-23.

19. Mukhlis, *op. cit.*, No.12, pp. 105-107; 114-16.

20. *Jassa Singh Binod*, fols. 68a-70b, 77a-b 80b, 81b, 86a-89b, 90a-91b, 93a-94b, 116b,. *Akhbar,* dated 2 *Shawwal* A.H. 1177/4 April, 1764 A.D., dated 20 *Zulqada* A.H. 1182/20 March, 1769 A.D.; for direct reference to Jassa Singh's *Dal*, *Akhbar,* dated 5 *Ramazan*, A.H. 1183/21 January, 1770 A.D.

21. At times, the Sikh Sardars had much larger forces than those of Ahmad Shah Abdali vide *Akhbar* 29 *Sha'ban* A.H. 1177/3 March, 1764 A.D. Still the Sikh Sardars avoided direct pitched battle against Abdali and the reporter (*waqainawis*) considers inability on their part for such pitched battle vide *Akhbar,* 17 *Ramazan* A.H. 1178/10 March, 1765 A.D. Also *Persian Records of Maratha History*, I: *Delhi Affairs*: (1761-1788) *News Letters*. From Persian Collection, tr. J.N. Sarkar, Bombay, 1953 (henceforth *Persian Records of Maratha History*), A 4a Delhi *Akhbarat* to Peshwa, 4th *Ramazan*, 3rd February, 1767, pp. 10-11. However, for other such battles against the local *subadars* and *faujdars* etc. in which Sardar Jassa Singh participated, of the numerious *Akhbar*, see 29 *Shaban*, A.H. 1177/3 March, 1764 A.D.; 28 *Zulhijja* A.H. 1177/28 June, 1764 A.D.; 13 *Jamada* I, A.H. 1178/8 November, 1764 A.D.

22. Rajwade, *Marathyanchya Itihasachi Sadhana*, (henceforth MIS), VI, Letter No.384; *Akhbar,* dated 29 *Shaban*, A.H. 1177/3 March, 1764 A.D.

23. *Ibid.*

24. Qazi Nur Muhammad, *Jang Namah*, ed. Ganda Singh, Amritsar, 1939, pp. 128-164.

25. News Letter sent to Peshwa Daftar, Pune; 29 No.55, dated April 1764 states that the Sikhs had set up their rule at Lahore and had settled rightly; *Chahar Bagh-i-Punjab*, p. 130.

26. Only a few instances may be cited. For the Sikh sardars in groups, i.e., *Sardaran-i-Sardan* or *Sardaren-i-Jamai Sikhan*, *Akhbar,* dated 20 *Muharram*, A.H. 1176/13 August, 1762 A.D. *Rabi* Ii, A.H. 1177/11 October, 1763/20 *Muharram*, A.H. 1177/31 July, 1763 A.D., 2 *Shawwal* A.H. 1177/4 April, 1764 A.D. respectively. For the group (here in the sense of *Dal*) of Sikhs affiliated to Sardar Jassa Singh, i.e., *Jamai-Jassa Singh* etc; Jassa Singh etc. *Jamai/Jamburi-Sikhan*; *Akhbar,* dated 29 *Shaban* A.H. 1177/3 March, 1764 A.D. 20 *Shawwal*, A.H. 1181/10 March, 1768 A.D; *Muharram* A.H. 1183/1769-70 A.D. respectively. For *Dal-i-Jassa Singh*, *Akhbar,* dated 5 *Ramazan* A.H. 1183/21 January, 1770 A.D. For the Sardars of the Sikhs mentioned in their individual capacity and who are also described as chiefs of the misls later on in the 19th century sources, i.e., Khushal Singh Faizullapuria etc. *Sardar-i-Sikhan*, Gajpat Singh *Sardar-i-Sikhan*, Desu Singh *Sardar-i-Kaithal* vide *Akhbar*, 5 *Ramazan* A.H. 1183/21 January, 1170 A.D. 3 *Rajab* A.H. 1193/17 July, 1779 A.D. The Maratha Documents (in Marathi and Persian) only refer to the Sikhs or the Sikh Sardars, *Op.cit*. Nos. 13, 25. The contemporary English Records also refer simply either to the Sikhs or the Sikh Sardars or the chiefs/leaders of the Sikhs vide N.A.I. New Delhi, Foreign Department, Secret consultations/Proceedings 1776/1783. However, for the early 17th century, the term *misl* in the sense of a group has been traced to Saina Pat's *Sri Gur Sabha* (in Punjabi Gurumukhi script), ed. Ganda Singh, Punjabi University, Patiala, 1967, pp. 9, 124.

27. *Tarikh-i-Kunjpura*, *op.cit*. No.34, pp. 80-86 gives a detailed description of the various Sardars as the chiefs of the *misls* who operated in *chakla* Sirhind (*subah* Delhi) after the death of Ahmad Shah Abdali (1772 AD). It provides an insight into the internal organisation of the *misl* as well as the territorial and military relationship of the *misl* Sardare chiefs with the chief Sardar who was also one of the chiefs of the *misls* affiliated to him. As a case study, it narrates that after the death of Sardar Karwara Singh, Sardar Baghel Singh assumed the chiefship of the *misl*. It also runs into detailed description of the division of the villages of *qasba* Indri amongst his own co-partners as well as the Dalawalian *misl* and the *misl* of Rai Singh Bhangi. The Persian *Akhbar*, *op.cit*. No.1 are full of such instances. Also, *Tarikh-i-Kunjpura*, *op.cit*. No.34, pp. 87-94.

28. Of the numerous available *Akhbar*, only a few may be cited. *Akhbar,* dated 28 *Zulhijja*, A.H. 1176/11 July, 1763 A.D; 20 *Muharram*, A.H. 1177/13 August, 1762 A.D.; 29 *Shaban*, A.H. 1177/3 March, 1764 A.D.; 28

Zulhijja A.H 1177/28 June 1764 A.D.; 30 *Jamada* I, A.H. 1178/25 November, 1764 A.D.; 25 *Jamada* II, A.H. 1182/6 November, 1768 A.D.; *Shawwal*, A.H. 1182/1769 A.D. National Archives of India, New Delhi, Original Receipts Foreign Department Persian Branch *Akhbar* (henceforth N.A.I., *Akhbar*) No.160, OR, 10, p.3, 12 February, 1785; No.161 OR 10, pp. 8-10, 15 February, 1785; *Persian Documents*, Part-I: Text. ed. P. Saran, Bombay, 1966. (henceforth *Persian Documents,* ed. P. Saran, pp. 363-68.

29. N.A.I. *Akhbar*, *op.cit.*, 51 Persian Documents, ed. P. Saran, *op.cit*. 51.

30. Mufli Ali ud-din, *Ibrat Nama*, (Persian) Publication, Lahore, Pakistan.

31. *Dasam Granth*, 15/85 vide Maheem Singh, *Guru Gobind Singh aur un ki Hindi Kavita*, p. 100, tr. Grover. *Ibid*, 2 Sankhaya-7, Nihkalanki Avtar, 24 Avtar, p. 107, tr. Grover.

32. For details see Persian *Akhbarat*, N.A.I; Persian documents, Pt. I, Text (ed. P. Saran), Asia Publishing House, Bombay, 1966; *Persian Records of Maratha History* I, Delhi Affairs, New Letters, tr. J.N. Sarkar, Bombay, 1953; *Calender of Persian Correspondence*, N.A.I. vol. II, 1767/69, Calcutta, 1914, vol. III, 1770/72; also *op.cit.*, Nos. 18-19.

33. Mirza Muhammad Hasan with the poetical name (*takhlus*) of Qatil, Mirza, *Haft Tamasha*, British Museum, Rieu, ms. No. 476. Originally a Hindu from a khatri family, named Davali Singh, was converted to Islam at the age of eighteen. Apart from other books and a Divan, he wrote *Haft Tamasha* (Seven Chapters) and dealt at length with the creeds traditions and sects of the Hindus and of the Musalmans of India as well as curious facts relating to Indian *Faqirs*. He died in 1233 A.H./1817-18 A.D.

34. Denzil Ibbetson, Preface to the Report on the Census of 1881, dated 15th August, 1883 reproduced in *Punjab Castes*, Lahore, 1916, pp. iii-viii.

35. *Ibid.*, pp. 1-37, 102-31, 214-38.

36. Also for details, State Archives, Patiala, Letter No.957, dated 16.5.2000 *Samvat*/22.8.1943 from Sahib Deodhi Mualla to the Finance Minister, Patiala.

37. Exhibited in the Numismatic Collection of the Maharaja of Patiala, Maharaja's Palace, Patiala.

Chapter 7

Relationship between the Sovereign State (the Mughals and Afghans) and Punjab Hill Chiefs during the 17th and 18th Centuries*

(A Case Study of Chamba Chieftainship based on Bhuri Singh Museum, Chamba Documents)

Since the establishment of the Mughal rule in the Punjab in the course of the 16th century down to its annexation to British India (1849), the Punjab Hill States (*Zamindaran-i-Kohistan Punjab*) remained broadly under the sovereign rule of four powers, viz., the Mughals, the Duranis of Kabul, Maharaja Ranjit Singh of Punjab and finally, the English East India Company, which claimed sovereign and territorial rights over these territories. Some portions of the Hill states for an intregnum during the late 18th and the early 19th centuries remained under the suzeranity of two more powers, viz., the Sikh *Misls* (18th century) and the Gurkhas of Nepal till 1809 A.D. As such, these territories offer a very interesting study of the elements of continuity and change in the administrative and institutional set-up during this period. Though based on the Persian chronicles, *vansavalis* and the accounts of the foreign travellers, much work has been done on the political history of these regions. No adequate scientific analysis has been done in respect of relationship covering the economic aspects involved between the local chiefs and the sovereign power. During the last two decades, a few historians well equipped with methodology of research and working on the agrarian history covering 16th-18th

---

* Papers presented at Punjab History Conference, 16th Session, March, 1982, Punjabi University, Patiala.

centuries have analysed the economic and institutional aspects for many other portions of India. This has been possible because of the utilization of vast archival and epigraphic source material of various categories available at different places in India which had not been exploited earlier.

It is very fortunate for the students of history that the Bhuri Singh Museum at Chamba has preserved historical source material of various types covering the history of this region from the early medieval ages down to the 19th century. A fairly reliable catalogue of this Museum, compiled by J.P.H. Vogel, was published in 1909 A.D.[1] Thereafter, too, additional items have been collected by the Museum, which still remain uncatalogued. This is undeniably one of the richest repositories in India which throws immense light on the socio-economic and cultural life of the people of the hilly regions during the course of the centuries. Apart from the stone inscriptions, sculptures, metal inscriptions, wood carvings, wood work, embroideries, textiles, and paintings, there are large number of copper-plates and documents which cover the socio-economic and institutional aspects of this region. The present writer, having worked on this region, has collected photographs of all the epigraphic and archival documents of the museum. There are 36 copper plates dealing mostly with the land grants from around 10th century to the mid 19th century. One copper plate also covers the treaty between the two local chiefs (1788 A.D.). Apart from this, there are, in all, 128 documents of which 72 have been catalogued by Vogel whereas 56 *Tankari* documents were collected after the publication of the catalogue. The catalogued *Tankari* documents covering the later half of the 18th and early 19th century comprise *sanads*, letters agreements, title deeds, statements and treaties, etc. The uncatalogued *Tankari* documents cover more or less the same aspects. Apart from this, there are 28 Persian documents covering *viz. sanads, mazars* (declarations), *khatut* (letters), *hakum* (orders) and *parwanas* issued from time to time from around the middle of the 17th century to 1846 AD. In addition to this, there are two documents in Nagari, one in Gurumukhi, and one in English which cover the first half of the 19th century till 1846 A.D.

Though the *Tankari* documents are extremely useful for working out the internal socio-economic aspects, especially the land grants given to the Brahman families and the temples by the Chamba Raj, for the present, it has been considered advisable to confine the paper to only one aspect underlining the institutional and administrative relationship between the latter Raj and the Sovereign State. For the analysis of the topic under discussion, the present writer has mostly relied on the above mentioned Persian documents covering the 17th and the 18th centuries. It must be acknowledged that of these texts of six Persian documents along with English translation have already been published as an appendix to the catalogue of the Bhuri Singh Museum.[2] Of course, as a pioneering researcher, credit must be given to Vogel who incorporated this portion in the catalogue after having got the Persian texts translated into English by eminent Persian and Arabic scholars of the time.[3] All the same, it is evident to any expert working on administrative and agrarian history of the region that the translation is rather inept and extremely defective in respect of many a technical terms used in the documents. This was perhaps inevitable as the translators, even though literary experts, had the least idea about the territorial connotation and revenue terminology available to us today from the Persian archival sources in other parts of India. Credit may also be given to Hutchison and Vogel who have utilized the epigraphic and the Persian translated documents in their well-known work on the History of the Punjab Hill States[4] as well as other articles published earlier in the Journal of Panjab Historical Studies.[5] All the same, Hutchison and Vogel could hardly appreciate the technical institutional aspects outlined in the Persian documents due to inept translation as well as due to lack of understanding of the broad framework of the Mughal administration and institutions. They were equally inhibited by the limitation to the approach of the study of local history emphasising mostly the political and the military aspects and regional glorification. It is only in the recent years that the methodology of historical research on the local history, while underlining the integrating economic and institutional factors with other parts of the *subah* and country as a whole, has been developed so as to have a concerted approach to the analysis of the administrative and the economic history of India.

The earliest extant available Persian document, dated 1648 A.D., is a *mahazar* (declaration) issued by the Mughal imperial representative who had acted as an arbitrator relating to a boundary dispute between the *zamindaries* of Basohli and Chamba.[6] The imperial representative visited the territory on the spot and summoned both the chiefs, i.e. Raja Prithvi Singh of Chamba and Sangrampal of Basohli for investigation. The latter did not attend the Nawab (royal representative) who gave the verdict in favour of Raja Prithvi Singh of Chamba. The declaration clearly states that the disputed *pargana* of Bhalai had been for generations in the territorial jurisdiction and possession of Chamba territory (*mulk-i-Chamba*). It is equally interesting to note that the investigation was done through the testimony of the Quazis, *watandars* (*mutawatna*) and the zamindars. Both the Muslim and the Hindu witnesses gave evidence on oath according to their religious practice. The witnesses were not confined to the territories of Chamba and Basohli as they belonged to other adjoining hilly territories as well.

Of the 16 witnesses, there are chiefs of the adjoining and neighbouring areas; the *chaudharis*, the *qanungos*, and even a *wazir* of the neighbouring hilly regions coverable under the territorial *faujdari* and revenue jurisdiction of the Mughal *faujdar*. The Nawab, acting as arbitrator, further recommended that the settlement of the dispute thus effected may be confirmed by a royal *sanad*.

Another equally important Persian document, dated 1666 A.D., based on a petition by Raja Shatar Singh of Chamba, reiterates the earlier position and confirms the restoration of the disputed *pargana* Bhalai to *zamindari*.[7] It clearly mentions that the territory of Bhalai (*zamin wa* Bhalai), as inhabited, had been for generations in the *watan* of the above Raja and which had been forcefully occupied by Sangrampal (of Basohli). At the same time, *pargana* Bhadarwah previously given in *inam* (*jagir*) to Sangram (of Basholi) was transferred to Raja of Chamba in *jagir*. Thus, both the parganas Bhalai and Bhadarwah were transferred to Raja of Chamba. The document is extremely significant as, in accordance with the Mughal system, it makes a clear distinction between the *parganas* awarded in *watan* and *inam jagir*. Pargana Bhalai is confirmed as *watan jagir* whereas *pargana* Bhadarwah, being *inam jagir* and assignable at the discretion of the Mughal state, is transferred from Sangram, the *zamindar* of Basohli to Raja Shatar Singh, the *zamindar* of Chamba. The document also states that the Raja of Chamba should get it confirmed through regular *sanad* to be issued by the Mughal court.

The documents also show that apart from the *watan jagir*, the revenues of other *parganas* assigned in *jagir* were in lieu of the *tankhwah* of the zamindar with or without *mansab*. Interestingly, there are eight documents relating to *Pargana* Pathyar only situated on the border of *zamindaries* of Katoch (Kangra) and Chamba. The *Ain-i Akbari* puts Chari Chamba (Chamba) as a part of *Sarkar* of Rechna Doab[8] whereas Pathyar as well as Kangra are shown in *Sarkar* of Bari

Doab in the *Subah* of Lahore.[9] The *Ain* neither mentions the area nor the revenues of this *pargana* and is shown as one of the abandoned *parganas*. However, the earliest available document, dated 1744 A.D., puts the *jamadami* of this *pargana* at 3,80,000 (three lakh and eighty thousand) *dams*.[10] It states that this *pargana,* which since considerable past period belonged to the territorial *zamindari* jurisdiction of Chamba (*as qadium ul ayam taaluq chunan bud*), had been for some time taken in possession by the Katoch (of Kangra) who annexed the *zamindari* of that *pargana* to his territories. By the order of Zakariya Khan (the *subadar* of Punjab), *pargana* Pathyar is restored to the Raja of Chamba in perpetual *jagir* in lieu of his services to the Mughal State. The Raja of Chamba is mentioned as *Jagirdar-i-mustqil.* Incidentally, while mentioning the services of the Chamba family to the Mughal State, the document also refers to Udai Singh, elder brother of Raja Daler Singh of Chamba, who had been awarded the State *Mansab* along with *Jagir* comprising the territories (*zillah*) Dun and Nadaun. These *parganas* are mentioned being in *jagir* (*tankhwah jagir*) and are distinguished from the perpetual *jagir* of *pargana* Pathyar bestowed on Raja Daler Singh of Chamba. Two *sanadas,* dated 1746, issued by Mohammad Hayat Khan, further confirm the conferment of the *zamindari* of *pargana* Pathyar on Raja Daler Singh of Chamba in lieu of his services to Mughal state.[11] He is further enjoined to continue to render his services and payment of revenues to the Mughal state (*ba khatir Jama dar tasdim khidmat wa malguzari sar gharam bashad*). It is important to note that the *zamindar* of Pathyar is clearly mentioned as the *malguzar* and is instructed to continue the services of the collection and payment of the revenues to the *zamindar* of Chamba and not to the Katoch Chief who had illegally taken possession of the territory. Another *sanad,* dated 1747, reiterates the earlier position and confirms the revenues of *pargana* Pathyar amounting to 3,80,000 *dam* in the *tankhwah* of Raja Daler Singh of Chamba.[12] The *chaudharis, qanungos, muzarian* and *riaya* of the *parganas* are instructed to collect the revenues and pass on to the Chamba chief. A further Order, dated 1759, also accounts for the transfer of the *zamindari* of Pathyar to the Raja of Chamba.[13] It states that since the death of Rana of Pathyar, the *zamindari* for a long period had been transferred to the *zamindari* of Chamba and was at that time with Raja Umed Singh who may be retained in the same position. All the *zamindari* dues (*rasum-i-zamindari*) may be paid to the aforesaid Raja in accordance with the ancient practice. Another order, dated 1759, also states the same position and puts *pargana* Pathyar in the *jagir* and *zamindari* of Raja Umed Singh of Chamba.[14]

On the decline of the Mughal Empire in the later half of the 18th century, the territories of the Punjab, Multan and Kashmir came under the sovereign control of the Duranis of Kabul. The Persian chronicles and *Akhbarat* show that the Durani Kabul rulers appointed their own *subadars* in Lahore, Multan and Kashmir for the administration of these territories.[15] Even though the Durani rule was by no means stable in the Punjab, in principle, there is considerable continuity with the Mughal concept in respect of the sovereign rights and the revenues claimed by it. Two *sanads,* dated 1762 A.D., issued by Shah Wali Khan, Durani Wazir[16] and another by Ahmad Shah Durani[17] himself confirm the grant of *jagir* to Raja Umed Singh of Chambail (Chamba) on the same lines as previously done by the Mughal State. On the representation of Amolak Ram, Vakil of Raja Ranjit Dev of Jammu, a relation of the Chamba chieftain, the *pargana* of Pathyar with *Jama* of 3,80,000/- *dams* in accordance with the previous practice was conferred in *wajah* (*tankwah*) as perpetual *jagir* (*Jagir-i-harsala*). The Chamba chief is also mentioned as the superior *jagirdar* (*jagirdar-i-bazurg*) of the *pargana*.

Apart from this, there are two more Persian documents relating to the *parganas* of Palam, Barli (*Sarkar* Bari Doab, *subah* Lahore) and territory of Jundh which clearly bring out the institutional relationship between the Mughal State and the Chamba chief. A *sanad,* dated 1751, issued by Muina-ud-din Khan, states that the *parganas* of Palam and Barli had been in the *zamindari* of Raja Umed Singh (of Chamba).[18] In accordance with the past practice, the aforesaid *parganas* are confirmed as *wajah inam*. The *chaudharis, quanungos* of these *parganas* are instructed to hand over the customary revenues to the Raja. Another order, dated 1758 A.D., issued by Adina Beg Khan restores the territory (*zamin*) of Jundh alongwith 17 forts (*qilacha*) to Raja Umed Singh, son of Raja Ugar Singh.[19] It mentions that these territories belonged to the Raj (*zamindari*) of Chamba, but owing to the disloyalty of Raja Ugar Singh had been previously transferred to Medini Pal Balauria. Now that Raja Umed Singh had assured of his loyalty to the Mughal State, the aforesaid territories were being transferred to his administration (*aml*) as held previously (i.e. prior to the confiscation and transfer to Balauria). The document is extremely significant as it clearly brings out the right of the Mughal sovereign state to transfer even the hereditary *zamindari* territories of one Chief to another on ground of disloyalty and unfaithfulness. It also underlines the territorial administrative reshufflings affected by the Mughal State in the hilly regions by this time. It is evident that the administration of the Chamba and other hilly territories was under the jurisdiction of the *faujdar* of *chakla* Jammu. It seems that in the early 18th century, an administrative circle of *chakla* Jammu was formed[20] and the overall *faujdari* and revenue administrative control over the Hill Chiefs as the *thanadars* attached to the *chakla* and even the Kangra *faujdar* was vested with the *faujdar* of Jammu who also exercised the *diwani* powers.

As mentioned earlier in case of *pargana* Pathyar, the Duranis of Kabul claimed sovereign rights over the Hill Chiefs as successors of the Mughal State. A *sanad,* dated 1762 A.D., orders the transfer of the revenues of some of the areas of Chari on the border of Kangra territory to the *qiladar* of Kangra.[21] It states that these lands had been illegally taken possession of by Raja Umed Singh of Chambial (Chamba) and its revenues should be handed over to the deputed officials, Ibrahim Khan and Rahim Khan on behalf of Saif Ali Khan, the *qiladar* of Kangra. This order is exactly in line with the Mughal practice for the arbitration in respect of the border territorial disputes. It seems that the lands of Chari etc. under dispute formed a part of the *khalsa* administration.

Another *sanad*, dated 1777 A.D., issued by Timur Shah (of Kabul) seems to have been issued in response to an invitation extended by Raja Raj Singh of Chamba for visiting his territory.[22] The Raja of Chamba is mentioned as the faithful Chief for having rendered the services of uniting all the Hill Chiefs in allegience to the Durani kingdom. Later on, a *sanad* and a letter, both dated 1797, issued by Shah Zaman in lieu of faithfulness of Raja Jit Singh confers the *diwani* rights on Raja Jit Singh of Chamba along with Raja Sampuran Dev of Jammu.[23] As such, both Raja Jit Singh of Chamba and Raja Sampuran Dev of Jammu were given joint *diwani* rights for revenue administration over the hilly regions (in *chakla* Jammu). Another undated letter issued by the Durani king refers to march of the Durani king from Lahore to Kabul and orders Raja Jit Singh of Chamba not to give any shelter to the disaffected persons who had fled from there to the hilly regions.[24] It states that similar orders had been issued to other hill Rajas. This clearly shows that the Durani kings exercised full sovereign rights over the Punjab hill Rajas who could not give any shelter to the recalcitrants against the sovereign state.

As already noted, the *Ain-i-Akbari* does not record the area and the revenue of *pargana* Pathyar. As such, it seems that by the close of the 16th century the *pargana* was reckoned as *ghair-amli*. However, during the course of the 17th and early 18th centuries, its revenues were assessed and are put at constant figure of 3,80,000 *dams*. As recorded above, the revenues of this *pargana* during both the regimes, i.e., the Mughal and the Durani from 1744-1762 A.D. remained constant. It is clear that they were not based on annual returns. For want of evidence for the 17th century, it is difficult to ascertain whether the revenues of this *pargana* had been periodically fixed (*Jama muqarari istamrari*) for a long period or they had been perpetually fixed forming a part *ghair-amli* territory. However, the documents relating to *pargana* Pathyar make it absolutely clear that the *zamindari* pattern of the Chamba chieftainship was based on the hierarchical pattern of the landed intermediaries (*zamindars*) who acted as *malguzars* (revenue peers) to the Raja of Chamba who is regarded as superior (*bazurg*) zamindar-cum-*jagirdar* in respect of this *pargana*.

Similar heirarchical *zamindari* pattern within the Chamba Raj is confirmed by other documentary evidence. This Raja of Chamba stood as the highest landed intermediary in relation to the Chief of Bhadarwah. It has been observed that the *pargana* of Bhadarwah had been transfered by the Mughal State in the *zamindari* and *jagir* of Raja Chattar Singh of Chamba in 1666 A.D. Further, late 18th century *Tankari* documents[25] spell out the relationship between Raja Raj Singh of Chamba and Raja Fateh Pal of Bhadarwah. An undated agreement shows that during the ascendency of the Sikh *Misls*, the Raja Chamba exercised firm control over the Bhadharwah Chief. The latter undertook to be faithful to the former who would have rights to maintain troops in Bhadarwah. At the same time, the Bhadarwah Chief undertook not to enter into alliance with other chieftains without the consent of the Chamba Chief and further to pay Rs. 3,000/- yearly to the Chamba Chief. Another undated letter by Daya Pal of Bhadarwah to Raja Raj Singh of Chamba confirms the same position and further adds that the amount of tribute payable by Bhadarwah to the Sikhs would be paid through Chamba.

Even though the *Ain* mentions the area and revenues of Chari Chamba, for the other *parganas* above the area, revenues have not been recorded. In the absence of any documentary evidence, it is difficult to say whether during the 17th-18th centuries they were *amli* areas with measured lands and assessed revenues or they were regarded as *ghairamli*. In fact, in comparison to the other regions of north India, as analysed from the documentary evidence especially from State Archives, Bikaner, Chamba Persian documents, howsoever significant, remain fragmentary in character. With mere reliance on them, it is not possible to reconstruct full details of the *watan*, *zamindari* jurisdiction, *tankhawah jagir pargana* and unassigned areas in the *zamindari* territories of the Chamba chieftain during this period. All the same, they are highly significant in the sense that they clearly show that in principle, the Mughal *zamindari* pattern as analysed earlier was fully enforced on the Chamba Raj as well as on other chieftain (*zamindars*) of the Punjab Hill States.

References

1. J.P.H. Vogel, Catalogue of the Buri Singh Museum at Chamba (Chamba State, Punjab), (Calcutta 1909).
2. *Ibid*. Appendix III, Persian *sanads*, pp. 52-65.
3. *Ibid*. p. 52. The translators mentioned are Maulwi Nur Baksh (Chamba) Syed Ghulam Hussain Maulwi Hasan Din (Lahore) and Dr. J. Horovitz (Aligarh).
4. J. Hutchison and P. H. Vogel, *History of the Punjab Hill States* (Lahore, 1933).
5. *Journal of Panjab Historical Society*, Vols. IV-1, 1916; VI-2, 1917; VII-1; No.2 1918; No. VIII, I, 1920.
6. Documents No. C, 1-2, dated 19 *safar*, A.H. 1058/5 March, 1648 A.D., Buri Singh Museum (henceforth B.S.M.), Chamba.
7. Document No. C, 4, dated 22 *Ramzan*, 8th R.Y. Aurangzeb/18 March, 1666 A.D., B.S.M., Chamba.
8. *Ain-i-Akbari*, Vol.II, tr. Jarrett (Calcutta, 1949), p. 324.
9. *Ibid*., p. 323.
10. Document No. C, 6, dated 5 *Safar*, A.H. 1157/ 9 March, 1744 A.D., B.S.M., Chamba.
11. Documents No. C, 7-8, dated 11 *Muharram* 28 R.Y. Muhammad Shah/23 January, 1746 A.D.; 27 *Zulqadah* 29 R.Y. Muhammad Shah/30 November, 1746 A.D., B.S.M., Chamba.
12. Document No. C, 9, dated *Jamadi* II, 29 R.Y. Muhammad Shah/31 May, 1747 A.D., B.S.M., Chamba.
13. Document No. C, 12, dated 15 *Jamadi* I, 5 R.Y. Alamgir 11/14 January, 1759 A.D., B.S.M., Chamba.
14. Document No. C, 13, dated 2 *Jamadi* II, A.H. 1172/31 January, 1759 A.D., B.S.M., Chamba.

15. Some of the late 18th century documents throw considerable light in this respect. For details, see *Akbharat*, nos. 168, OR 330, dated 8 August 1793; 188, OR 62, 22 January, 1797; 190, OR 71, 24 January, 1797; 192, OR 75, 26 January, 1797; 193, OR 78, January, 1797;...OR 119, 7 February, 1797; 207, OR 385, 22 July, 1797; 209, OR 393, 27 July, 1797; 166, OR 525, October, 1788. *Akhbari* Oriental, National Archives of India, New Delhi.
16. Document No. C, 14, dated 7 *Shawwal*, A.H. 1175/24 May, 1762 A.D., B.S.M, Chamba.
17. Document No. C, 15, dated *Zulqadah*, A.H. 1175/May-June, 1762 A.D., B.S.M. Chamba.
18. Document No. C, 10, dated 5 *Jamadi* II 4th R.Y. Ahmad Shah A. H. 1164/ 20 April, 1751 AD., B.S.M., Chamba.
19. Document No. C, 11, dated 21 *Zulhijja* 5th R.Y. Alamgir II, A. H. 1171/26 August, 1758, B.S.M., Chamba.
20. A *chakla* as a distinct territorial revenue cum administrative circle in the Mughal administration in the *subah* of Punjab, introduced under Akbar though a reshuffling of the territorial division comprising a *chakla,* was effected during the reign of Shahjahan as well. The 17th century documents show that the *paragans* of the Hill Chieftains were usually covered by the *Sarkar* divisions of *subah* Lahore as described by the *Ain-i-Akbari*. However, the earliest document noticeable so far which mentions these *parganas* attached to *chakla* Jammu is dated 8th R.Y. Muhammad Shah A.H. 1138/1725-26 A.D. vide B.N. Goswami, J.S. Grewal, *The Mughals and the Jogis of Jakhbar*, Document No. XV, pp. 171-178, Shimla, 1967.
21. Document No. C, 16, dated *Rabi* I, A.H. 1176/September-October, 1762 A.D., B.S.M., Chamba.
22. Document No. C, 17, dated 18 *Rabi* II, A.H. 1191/29 May, 1777 A.D., B.S.M., Chamba.
23. Document No. C, 44, dated *Rajab*, A.H. 1211/January, 1797 (*sanad*). No. 45, dated *Rajab*, A.H. 1211/January, 1797 (letter), B.S.M., Chamba.
24. Document No. C, 46. The letter is undated, B.S.M., Chamba.
25. Documents No. C, 22 and C, 33, B.S.M., Chamba.

Chapter 8

Relationship between the Sirmur Chieftainship and the Mughal State based on the Sirmur Family Mughal Documents*

(second half of 17th and early 18th centuries)

The relationship between the Mughal State and the Punjab Hill chiefs (*zamindaran-i-kohistan-i-Punjab*) constitutes a significant area of study underlining the political and economic factors involved between the Sovereign power and the chiefs. The principles which governed the relations between the Mughal State and the chief zamindars as well as landed intermediaries (zamindars) of various categories in other portions of north India were equally operative in the hill regions of the Punjab. The recent researches based on the contemporary archival source material of the Mughal age point to the fact that after submission, even the *zamindaran-i-umda* enjoying the titles of Maharajas, Rajas, Marzbans, Raos, etc., with or without *mansab*, were regarded as the state servants and were governed by the *zamindari* and *jagir* patterns of the Mughal administration.[1] The view merely based on the study of the Persian chronicles or *vansavalis* of the chieftains so as to consider the latter semi-independent, autonomous is no longer tenable.

In comparison to Rajasthan, Gujarat, Bihar, Bengal and a few other regions of North India, very few chieftain families of the Punjab Hills have preserved the records from the 17th to mid-19th centuries. Even such available records do not constitute continuous series so as to

* Papers Presented at Punjab History Conference, 18th Session, December, 1983, Punjabi University, Patiala.

give a detailed picture of the political and agrarian relations with the Mughal State. Based on the family archives of the Chamba chiefs, the present writer has already analysed the institutional relationship between the Chamba chief and the Sovereign powers during the pre-British era.[2]

In the present paper, attempt has been made to analyse 21 Persian documents preserved in the family archives of the erstwhile Sirmur State (Himachal Pradesh) covering second half of the 17th and early 18th centuries. They depict the political phase, the institutional relationship between the chief and the Mughal State, inter-*zamindari* territorial disputes, conferment of *zamindari* rights as landed intermediaries as well as ties between the Sirmur chiefs and the Mughal Royal family. Many of the facts mentioned in the documents find equal support from the contemporary Persian chronicles. All the same, whereas the chronicles deal mostly with the political history, the documents in hand give a detailed description of many aspects on which the chronicles are either silent or make only a cursory reference. It goes without saying that only coordination of the documentary study and the description available from the chronicles can give an insight and proper perspective for the study of this region.

During the late 19th and early 20th centuries, many a writer, even members of the ruling families wrote the histories of their respective states, from the ancient times till date. For the pre- British era, they mostly relied on the local traditions, *vansavalis*, District Gazetteers and even on some Persian chronicles. However, a few of them utilised the documents of the Mughal age in personal possession of the chieftain families. All the same, their outlook remains insular, parochial and chauvinistic. On the pattern, in early twenties of this century, a scion of the ruling family wrote *Tarikh-i-Sirmur*.[3] He has, of course, given a detailed description of the geography, fauna and flora as well as socio-religious life of the people for the contemporary 20th century era. However, he had also the asset of the family archives. Of the vast number of documents available from the Mughal age down. to the British administration, he has even reproduced some of the documents.[4] All the same, his vision was circumscribed by lack of appreciation of the Mughal pattern of administration and the factors that governed the Mughal State in its agrarian relationship with the *zamindaran-i-umda* in various territories of north India.

Of the total number of 21 documents under study, there are 15 *farmans*, one *sanad* and six letters (*marsalas*). Of these, 4 *farmans* pertain to Shahjahan's reign, while 10 *farmans* were issued by Aurangzeb and one by Muhammad Muazam Shah Alam (entitled Bahadur Shah). Three *farmans* of Shahjahan's reign instruct the Sirmur chief to help in the envisaged plan of invasion and conquest of Garhwal. They also hold out a promise for the transfer of some of the territories in the jurisdiction of the Garhwal chief and bordering Sirmur as additional *zamindari* to the Sirmur chief. Later on, another *farman* issued by Aurangzeb gives instructions to the Sirmur zamindar for a campaign against the recalcitrant zamindar of Garhwal. Three *farmans* of Aurangzeb's reign give description about the movement of Suliman Shikoh, son of Dara Shikoh, during the war of succession to the Mughal throne, Suliman Shikoh's refuge in Garhwal and the instructions issued to the Sirmur chief for help in the planned apprehension of Suliman Shikoh. One *farman* of Shahjahan and later on four *farmans* issued by Aurangzeb from time to time, one issued by Muhammad Muazam Shah Alam (entitled Bahadur Shah) confer the *rajgi* and *zamindari* on the Sirmur chief conditional upon the rendering of the services and payment of *peshkash* to the Mughal State. They clearly confirm the fact that the Mughal State claimed sovereign political rights over the hill chiefs, who, after submission, were regarded as servants of the State and in lieu of the service rendered by them, they were entitled to their *zamindari*, certain categories of *jagir* and other perquisites (*haquq*). The *farmans* issued by Aurangzeb refer to the territorial disputes between the Sirmur and Srinagar and give instructions to the *Mughal faujdars* for the restoration of the territories to the Sirmur chief. Further, a *sanad* issued in Aurangzeb's reign dispossesses certain zamindars of the *zamindari* rights in their *mahals* in *sarkar* Saharanpur, *subah* Shahjahanabad, in the neighbourhood of Sirmur territories and confer the *zamindari* rights on the Sirmur chief. The above *farmans* and the *sanad* equally bring out the hierarchical pattern of landed intermediaries (zamindars) attached to the chiefs who acted as superior zamindars for payment of the revenues (*peshkash*) to the Mughal State. They equally emphasised the fact that the Mughal State as Sovereign Power had the right to reshuffle the superior *zamindari* rights on the part of the hill chieftains. They also underline the Mughal administrative set-up even on inter-*subah* basis for the suppression of the recalcitrance on the part of the local hill chiefs and the realisation of the revenues (*peshkash*) from them.

Six letters (*marsalas*) written by Jahan Ara (daughter of Shah Jahan), addressed to the Sirmur chiefs, acknowledge the receipt of various gifts as token of *peshkash*. They also refer to the fact that of the various items received from Sirmur, ice received during the summer season was an important item. In fact, the Mughal State had proper supply of ice by some of the hill chiefs and maintained regular establishment for the same.

The above documents may be summarised and analysed as under:-

Shah Jahan's *farman* dated 18th *Jamadi* II, 28th R.Y., 1064 Hijra/ 8 May, 1654, addressed to Raja Mandhata Parkash (1630-1654), gives description about the plan of Iraj khan, *faujdar* of Jammu and Kangra about the planned invasion and annexation of Srinagar and instructs the Sirmur chief to mobilise the support of the armed forces (*sawar* and *piyada*) of all the hill zamindars (*zamindaran-i-kohistan*).[5] It also holds out a promise that whatever territories were to be conquered from the *marzban* of Srinagar adjacent to Sirmur *zamindari* would be transferred to the latter in *watan*. The territories bordering Kumaon would be transferred to the latter chief and the territory of Dun would be annexed by the Mughal State. Another *farman* dated 24th *Muharram*, 28th R.Y., 1065 Hijra/4 December, 1654, communicated through Sād Ullah Khan, further mentions the campaign undertaken by Khalil Ullah Khan and requires the Sirmur chief to render full armed services to him.[6] It also reiterates that Dun outside the hills would be incorporated as *khalisa sharifs* whereas the adjacent territories to Sirmur would be transferred to him in *zamindari*. Another *farman* issued by Shah Jahan, dated 11th *Rabi* II, 28th R.Y., 1065 Hijra/18 February, 1655 communicated through Sād Ullah Khan and addressed to the Sirmur Raja Sobhag Parkash (1654-64) also refers to the campaign by Khalil Ullah Khan and holds out similar promises for the conferment of the *zamindari* from the territories of Garhwal on the Sirmur chief.[7] The 4th *farman* dated 22nd *Jamadi* I, 28th R.Y. , 1065 Hijra/30 March, 1655 addressed to Raja Sobhag Parkash, states that on the recommendation of Khalil Ullah Khan and in lieu of his services, the territory (*wilyat*) of Kotaha, bordering the territories of Sirmur, were conferred as *watan* and *altaghma* (*jagir*) on the zamindar of Sirmur. He should capture it from the *zamindari* of Kotaha territory and bring it under his occupation.[8]

Aurangzeb's three *farmans* dated 19th *Jamadi* I, 1069 Hijra/12 February, 1659, 16th *Shawal*, 1st R.Y., 1069 Hijra/9th July 1659,

16th *Muharram*, Ist R.Y., 16 October, 1659 addressed to Raja Sobhag Parkash, give details about the movements of Suliman Shikoh in Garhwal and the operational measures to be adopted for restricting his movements and ultimate arrest. The first of these *farmans* states that Shuja after passing from Allahabad was defeated by the Royal forces and later on having made his way as a wanderer towards Bengal was again defeated and that Muhammad Sultan Bahadur had been deputed to chase and arrest him. It also states that Suliman Shikoh had reached Srinagar and was in correspondence with Dara Shikoh. It enjoins upon the Raja to intercept correspondence and to take all appropriate steps for the arrest of Suliman Shikoh. The second *farman* also reiterates the position about Dara Shikoh and Suliman Shikoh. It regrets defiance and short-sightedness on the part of Raja of Srinagar. It further states that Raja Rajroop (of Jodhpur), along with a huge army comprising *amirs* and *mansabdars,* would be shortly leading an expedition against the Raja of Srinagar.[9] It enjoins upon the Sirmur chief to be ready along with his armed forces and to join the Royal forces after they reach Srinagar, for the punishment of Srinagar chief. The third *farman* reiterates the position. It further spells out that Raja Rajroop would enter the hills on 22nd of *Muharram* for the punishment of the zamindar of Srinagar. [10] It also adds that Motmad Rad Andaz Khan, along with heavy artillery, would also join the Royal forces for the devastation of the zamindar of Srinagar.

Aurangzeb's four *farmans* dated 5th *Shawal*, 32nd R.Y. (Shah Jahan), 1068 Hijra/6 July, 1658, 14th *Safar*, 10th R.Y./16 August, 1666; 20th *Rabi* I, 31st R.Y. 1109 Hijra/3rd February, 1687 and 2nd *Rabi* II, 46th R.Y./6 September, 1701 confirm the Raja of Sirmur in his position. The first of these *farmans* addressed by Aurangzeb to Raja Sobhag Parkash of Sirmur mentions the latter as obedient to Islam *(mutih-ul-Islam)* and informs him about the Royal enthronement. It directs the Raja to continue his submission, obedience and services to the monarch which would entitle him Royal favours. The second *farman* addressed to Bahari Singh, obedient to Islam, recognises him as the Raja of Sirmur after the death of his father, Sobhag Parkash and confers *khilat* along with the title of Budh Parkash (1664-84) and *rajgi* of *Wilayat-i-Sirmur*. It also enjoins upon him for the continuation of submission, obedience and rendering of services to the Mughal State. The third *farman* issued by Aurangzeb through Asad Khan to Jog Raj, obedient to Islam, accepts his request along with *peshkash* for his recognition as the Raja after the death of his father, Budh Parkash. It further confers on him the title of Mast Parkash along with the *rajgi* of *Wilayat-i-Sirmur*. It also directs him to continue his services on the lines mentioned in the earlier *farman* and also enjoins upon him to show complete obedience to the Mughal *faujdars*. The fourth *farman* issued by Aurangzeb to Hari Parkash, obedient to Islam, also accepts his request for his recognition of the Raja along with *peshkash* and *nazrana* etc., sent by him. It confers the *rajgi* and *zamindari* of Sirmur along with title on the Raja. On similar lines, as stated earlier, it enjoins the Raja for submission to the state as well as to the Mughal *faujdars* of the neighbouring territories. Similarly, the *farman* dated 29th *Rabi* II, 2nd R.Y./18 July, 1708 by Muhammad Muazam Shah Alam, son of Alamgir *Badshah* (entitled Bahadur Shah) to Bhim Parkash confers the title of *rajgi* and *zamindari* of Sirmur on him.

Aurangzeb's *farman* dated Ist *Safar*, 17th R.Y./18 May, 1673 informs Raja Budh Parkash, obedient to Islam, that the incompetent son of Suraj Chand, zamindar of Akbar Nagar alias Sohana, had been dispossessed of the *zamindari* which had been further conferred in *watan* on Fidai Khan Koka. It directs the Raja to march with his forces towards that *pargana* and also occupy the adjacent *parganas* of Muzafargarh and Jagatgarh. It states that Rustam Beg, along with his forces, had also been detailed to help him in the operational measures. It further states that the above mentioned recalcitrant zamindar should either be murdered or driven out of the *pargana* and that the management of the *pargana* should be handed over to Fidal Khan. A *sanad*, dated 5th *Zulhijja*, 3rd R.Y. of Aurangzeb's reign/14 August, 1660 states that as Ganga Ram and Bhupat etc., zamindars of Khala Kher of Sarkar Saharanpur, *subah* Shahjahanabad were being dispossessed of their *zamindaris* due to failure in the discharge of their duties; the above *zamindari* was conferred on Sobhag Parkash, Raja of Sirmur with effect from the *kharif* crop. He should look after the agricultural development and welfare of the *riaya* and equally remain obedient and continue to render service to the Mughal State. The *jagirdars, faujdars* and *karories* had also been given appropriate intimation to this effect.

Six letters written by Jahan Ara, daughter of Shah Jahan, dated 16th *Jamadi* II, 13th R.Y., (Aurangzeb)/7 April, 1670; 11th *Shawal*, 14th R.Y./21 February, 1671; 21st *Rabi* II, 18th R.Y./25 July, 1674; 7th *Jamadi* I, 21st R.Y./8 July, 1677; 21st *Ramazan*, 21st R.Y./6

November, 1678 and 25th *Muharram*, 43rd R.Y. (Aurangzeb)/2 August, 1698 to Raja Budh Parkash acknowledge the receipt of various gifts, the supply of ice from Sirmur and Garhwal and the boundary territorial disputes between the zamindars :of the above chieftainships.[11] The first letter acknowledges the receipt of a few animals and baskets of pomengranates along with a detail in a separate list as a token of *peshkash*. She also informs the Raja that she had not been able to make recommendations for him to the King who was then in Akbarabad. However, he should be well aware, that she would always pay attention to his affairs. The second letter also acknowledges the receipt of yellow myrobalans (*halila-i-zard*), wild pomegranates, jungle-fowls, pheasants and musk. It directs the Raja to send another pheasant.[12] It also states that out of kindness and graciousness, she (Jahan Ara) had bestowed *khillat* on him which he would receive shortly and that he should be rest assured of her kindness. The third letter also acknowledges the reciept of musk and *chanaur* as *peshkash*. It further mentions that the complaint lodged by the Raja about the misconduct of Sondha etc., his other *tahvildars* and that even though the zamindars of Sadhuara had first stood surety (*malzamni*) for the former for their presence, later on helped them to run away with all goods both in cash and kind. It further refers to request on the part of the Raja for issue of *farmans* to Ruh Alla Khan, the *faujdar* of Doab, Dilabar Khan, the *faujdar* of Sirhind, and Ali Akbar, the *faujdar* and *amin* of Sadhaura to take punitive measures against the above *tahvildars* and zamindars of above *pargana*. Jahan Ara states that the Raja had committed a mistake in having again entrusted them to the zamindars. Jahan Ara regrets that she, of her own, cannot interfere in the State affairs nor can she write to anybody else in this regard. She advises the Raja to approach the Royal Court to issue orders to all those (concerned affairs) to arrest and chain the above *tahvildars* and zamindars and send them to him. She further comments that Ruh Alla Khan would never do this. The fourth letter, while acknowledging the receipt of two boxes of ice, complains that the ice was dirty and not properly frozen. She wondered whether it was from the Royal *karkhanas*, as he had stated that this was sent by Sayid Shafi and Bhorai from the state ice-pit. The zamindars of Garhwal had also informed that they had sent this ice. Only God knows better as to who had sent it. As regards the territorial dispute with the zamindar of Garhwal, it states that she had communicated to His Majesty that the rightful owner should be restored his rights.His Majesty had already ordered the *bakhshis* to issue a *hosbul hukum* (command as desired by the Royal authority) to the effect that whosoever showed oppression and highhandedness would be punished. However, the zamindar of Garhwal had stated that he had not indulged in any aggression whatsoever and that his territorial boundary was traditional and hereditary and that he had reoccupied his legitimate territories of which he had been earlier forcibly dispossessed. "This is what he (zamindar of Garhwal) says while you have your own version." It informs the Raja that unless the king appoints an *amin* to make an enquiry into the matter, truth could not be revealed. Only after this, Royal forces would be deployed for this purpose. However, at present, the Royal forces were needed in Deccan and in Kabul and could not be spared for this reason. It also acknowledges the receipt of all the three boxes of ice. The fifth letter acknowledges the receipt of his communication (*arzdasht*) along with pods of musk and pomengranates. As the musk sent earlier has been of fine quality, he may send more of it. Hoowever, he may take full precaution in procuring the genuine (*asl*) quality and should not send any imitation. She assures him of her favours. The sixth letter also acknowledges the receipt of a communication (*arzdasht*) and gift of a falcon and honey. As the falcon was too young (*chuza*), she exchanged it for another one while honey was found to her liking. As regards the turbulance and hostililty on the part of the zamindar of Srinagar (Garhwal), "This is a recurring phenomenon between him and you as the former would never desist from such an unfortunate behaviour." It was good that he had brought it to the Royal notice. It also notes the complaint against that faulty inspection (*girdawari*) of ice by *daroga* Abul Rehman and the lower wages paid to the labourers at the time of snowfall. It further directs that the inspection (*girdawari*) of the icefall should be done properly and that the wages to the labour be paid as fixed earlier.

References

1. For details, see B.R. Grover, 'Nature of Land-Rights in Mughal India', *Indian Economic and Social History Review*, 1 (1963), pp. 1-23.
2. Grover, B. R., 'Relationship between the Sovereign State, the Mughals and Afghans and the Punjab Hill Chief during the 17th and 18th Centuries-a case study of Chamba chieftainship based on Bhuri Singh Museum, Chamba Documents', Proceeding *Punjab History Conference*, XVI Session, March 12-14, 1982, pp. 94-102; Relationship between the Lahore *Darbar* and Punjab Hill Chiefs during the first half of the 19th century till 1846', Proceedings *Punjab History Conference*, XVII Session, October 8-10, 1982, pp. 230-40.

3. *Kanwar* Ranzarwar Singh, *Tarikh-i-Sirmur*, 1912.
4. *Ibid.*, Appendix, pp. 1-50.
5. Also see, Nawab Sams-ud-Daula Shah Nawaz Khan, *Maathir-ul-Umara*. Persian text I, pp. 268-272, translated by H. Beveridge, Revised, Annotated and Completed by Beni Prasad (Patna, 1979), I, pp, .685-87.
6. *Ibid.*, pp. 775-82; tr. pp. 767-70.
7. *Ibid.*
8. *Ibid.*
9. *Ibid.*, II, pp. 277-81; tr. II, Part I, pp. 574-78.
10. *Ibid.*
11. Also see, H.A Rose, 'Persian letters from Jahan Ara, daughter of Shah Jahan, King of Delhi to Raja Budh Parkash of Sirmur', *Journal and Proceedings of the Asiatic Society of Bengal*, Vol. VII, No. 7, July 1911, pp. 449-58. Rose has merely provided the Persian text of the letters along with literal translation into English as well date wise abstracts of the letters in English. Rose has not given any background or commentary on the subject. The translation into English of many articles mentioned in the letters is rather inapt.
12. *Murgh-i-zarin*, Rose (*Ibid.*), has translated it as 'gloden-winged bird'. In fact, it is a pheasant with shining golden wings, greenish body colour and a crown (*kalghi*) on its head. It is known as *kulsa* in the local *pahari* dialect.

Chapter 9

An Analysis of the Contemporary Durrani Revenue Documents and Correspondence Pertaining to the Patiala Chieftainship (Zamindari) during the Later Half of the 18th Century*

I

Inherited from the erstwhile Patiala State, the Punjab State Archives, Patiala has preserved the revenue documents (in Persian) of the Durrani rule in *chakla* Sirhind (cis-Sutlej territories) relating to the periods of Raja Ala Singh and Raja Amar Singh. Mostly ignored by the historions hitherto,[1] these documents throw much light on the working of some of the aspects of the land revenue administration of the Durranis in the cis-Sutlej territories which had been formally ceded by the Mughal State to Ahmad Shah Durrani in 1757 A.D. The documents comprise three *taliqachas* (Orders), dated 1761 A.D., from the Durrani *Wazir-i-Mumalik* (Prime Minister) to the named revenue administrators of *chakla* Sirhind underlining the nature of *chaudurie-zamindari*, *faujdari* and *jagir* assignments to Ala Singh Jat in specified villages and *parganas*; two *sanad*s, dated 1764 A.D., issued by a Durrani official conferring the powers of *naib-faujdar/faujdar* on Ala Singh Jat in two *parganas* as well as entrusting him with the collection of the revenues therein on the payment of stipulated amount to the Durrani Government; and one document with two seals of the Durrani official, dated 1765 A.D., as a receipt given to Ala Singh for the mentioned amount of the revenues (*muamalat*) received from the latter. Apart from the above mentioned documents, there is Timur Shah's *Farman*, dated 5 August,

---

* Published in *Punjab Past and Present* Vol. XXIV-I, April, 1990. pp. 196-233.

1778 A.D., addressed to Maharaja Amar Singh and Timur Shah's *murasala* (communication), dated 5 August, 1778, addressed to Chauhar Singh Phul confirming them in their respective territorial possessions and the functions to be performed by them as per instructions.

In addition to the above collection of documents, there is a compilation comprising copies of seven *arzdashts* (Letters of obeisance), dated 1764-65 A.D., of which two were written by Raja Ala Singh and five by Raja Amar Singh to Shah Wali Khan, *wazir* of Ahmad Shah Abdali. Apart from the revenue and administrative matters, these *arzdashts* cover the contemporary political and military affairs.

The above documents are of great significance for the analysis of the agrarian pattern of *chakla* Sirhind under the Durrani rule. They equally underline the elements of continuity between the Mughal agrarian system and the Durrani set-up. The veracity of the contents of the above documents is as well corroborated by the contemporary Persian *Akhbarat* (News Letters) and other sources. These documents have been translated in extenso so as to dispel all doubts about the contemporary situation as well as to have an authentic analysis of the nature of the Durrani rule in these territories during the second half of the 18th century.

II

Translation

(i) A copy of *taliqacha* (Order), dated 22 *Shaban* A.H. 1174/29 March 1761 A.D., (bearing the seal of the *Qazi* dated A.H. 1162/ 1749-50 A.D.), issued by *Wazir-i-Azam* (Prime Minister, Nawab Shah Wali Khan) to Faiz Talab Khan Durrani, *subadar* and in charge of the revenues (*sahib-i-ikhtiyar-i-maliyat*) of *chakla* Sirhind states[2] that as Ala Singh Jat has been appointed in the category of the chief *wakils* holding *jagir* (*ba jagir-i-wukla-i-ali*), the latter may be considered as the chief *wakil* (*wukla-i-ali*). It has been recommended to the Royal Court (*Huzur*) that he (Ala Singh) should be given proper respect in this regard. It further enjoins Mirza Muhammad Taqi (*darogha*) and in charge revenue department, *chakla* Sirhind to recognise him with the above mentioned status and conduct the revenue matters relating to Ala Singh territories in cooperation with his representatives (*wakils*) Ram Singh and Kashmiri Mal. Keeping in view the above mentioned Order (*taliqacha*) and the chief *wakils* holding *jagir*, he (Muhammad Taqi) should prepare the total accounts (*tumar*) of the revenues (of the villages/*parganas* in the jurisdiction of Ala Singh) based upon actual assessment (*tashkhis*) and after having afforded rebate (*takhfit*) and other (customary) dues, etc, to Ala Singh. This may be done in cooperation with the *wakils* of the latter and the total accounts (*tumar*) should be duly attested and stamped by the *qazi*.

The revenue accounts relate to 726 villages (*qarya*) pertaining to the *jagir* assigned in the category of chief *wakils* (*jagir-i-wukla-i-ali*). The number of villages enumerated per *pargana* are: *pargana* Sanam inclusive of *qasba* 224: *pargana* Samana 266; *pargana Haveli* Sirhind 52; *pargana* Sanawar 89; *pargana qiryat* Rai Samun 4; *pargana* Jehat 8; *pargana* Sangan 17; *pargana* Gharam 6; *Pargana* Sanwar 37; *pargana* Mansurpur 23.

As such, 726 villages may be reckoned as his (Ala Singh's) *jagir* as the chief *wakil* (*jagir-i-wukla-i-ali*) and he (Faiz Talab Khan Durrani, the *subadar*) should not on any account make a claim over them for his own (revenue) jurisdiction as on the recommendation (already) made to the exhalted *Huzur* (the Royal Court), these *mahals* have been deleted from his administration and revenue management (*hakumat wa amaldari*) and assigned to Ala Singh. They (Faiz Talab Khan Durrani and Ala Singh) should regard each other's friend as a friend and each other's enemy as a foe. As such, Ala Singh is enjoined to act accordingly to this understanding and similarly he (Faiz Talab Khan Durrani) should not bear any enmity towards the former as there should be no animosity towards the chief *wakils* (*wukla-i-ali*) and the latter should make necessary earnest efforts for the implementation of the Royal Order.

(ii) A copy of *taliqacha* (Order, dated 22 *Shaban*, AH 1174/29 March, 1761 AD (bearing the seal of the *Qazi,* dated AH 1162/1749-50 AD) issued by *Wazir- i-Azam* (Shah Wali Khan, Prime Minister of Ahmad Shah Durrani) and addressed to Mirza Muhammad Taqi who should know[3] that Ala Sngh Jat holding the *jagir* as the chief *wakil* in the category of *jagir* of *wukla-i-ali* and having been vested with the powers of *darogha* and revenue administration (*zabt-i-maliya wa taujiat*) is hereby confirmed in his position. He (Muhammad Taqi), along with Ala Singh Jat, should undertake the assessment of the revenues (*maliya)* from season to season, i.e., crop to crop (*fasl ba fasl-kharif/rabi*) in these (*jagir*) *mahals* and the revenues thus fixed may be deposited in the treasury of *wukla-i-ali* (Ala Singh Jat) after the deduction of his own expenses (for assessment and settlement of the revenues). It is essential that he should extend full cooperation in this regard to Ala Singh Jat. The *chaudharies*, the *qanungos*, etc. and the residents of the territories should recognise the continued and absolute status of the afore-mentioned person, i.e., Ala Singh Jat, in the above mentioned directions (territories) and should extend complete willing cooperation (to him).

(iii) A copy of a *taliqacha* (order), dated 7 *Shaban* 4th R. Y. AH 1176/12 February, 1763 A.D., (bearing the seal of the *Qazi,* dated AH 1162/1749-50 A.D.) issued by the *Wazir-i-Azam* (Prime Minister, Nawab Shah Wali Khan) is addressed to Mirza Muhammad Taqi Ansari, *darogha* and revenue in charge (*darogha wa-zabit-i-maliyat*) pertaining to the *mahals* assigned in *jagir* to Ala Singh Jat, the chief *wakil* (*jagir-i-wukla-i-ali*).[4] He (Mirza Muhammad Taqi Ansari) should know that since the four *mahals,* i.e., the *parganas* of Sanam, Mansurpur, Gharam and Sanwar have been withdrawn from the jurisdiction of the *subadar* and in-charge finances, *chakla* Sirhind (*subadar sahib-i-Ikhtiyar maliyat*) and assigned in *jagir* to Ala Singh Jat (in the category of *jagir-wukla-i-ali*), the revenues as well as the cesses comprising the *taujis* of the *parganas* would be assessed by the latter in accordance with the prevalent practice (*dastur*) and varying settled schedules. Apart from it, (as) some portions (of the above *mahals*) which have been further detached from the *taalluqa* territories of Ala Singh Jat and are under the occupation of various zamindars, all such *mahals* have been put under the *faujdari* jurisdiction of Ala Singh Jat who has also been vested with the powers of *darogha* and revenue administration of the *mahals* (*darogha wa zabit-i-mahal*-Ala Singh *mushiarialah namuda bood*). The latter is enjoined to run the adminisration in a righteous manner so as to develop the *mahals*, look after the welfare of the *raaya*, to assess and collect the revenues (*maliyat*) as well as the cesses (*abwab ul jama*) in accordance with the established revenue administration in an efficient manner without any deficiency. The zamindars, the *chaudharies*, the *qanungos* and the *raaya* of the above mentioned four *mahals* are directed to recognize Ala Singh Jat as the *faujdar* of all the four *mahals* assigned as *jagir-i-wukla-i-ali* and willingly pay the revenues (*maliyat*) of these *mahals* every season, i.e., crop after crop, determined judiciously as per accounts to Ala Singh Jat to whom these *mahals* have been entrusted. They should continue to render the statement of the total assessed and realised revenues (*jama hasil*) to him in accordance with the established practice and recognise his above mentioned status.

Issued dated 7 *Sahr Shaban* 4th Regnal Year.

(iv) A Letter of Appointment (*sanad*) issued by Muhammad Ramazan, dated 2 *Safar* 5th RY. (AH 1178/1 August 1764 A.D.) bearing the latter's seal confirms the duties and functions (*khidmat*) of *naib faujdar* and *amin* (*nayabat faujdari* (*wa amanat*) of *parganas* Tohana and Jamalpur (*chakla* Sirhind) on Ala from *Kharif* 1166 *Fasli*/1759 A. D.[5] By virtue of this appointment, Ala Singh is also entitled to the established necessary perquisites as the (chief) *muqaddam* on behalf of the Government for the discharge of the official duties (in these territories). The *chaudharies, qanungos, muqaddams*, zamindars and the *raaya* are to recognise the aforementioned (Ala Singh Chaudhari) as the *amil* of these *mahals* and, as such, may render all revenue accounts (*malwajib*) to him.

(v) An Agreement (*qaul qarar*) bearing the seal of Muhammad Ramazan, dated 17th *Safar* 5th R.Y (AH 1178/16 August 1764 A.D.), executed with Ala Singh, states[6] that an amount of Rupees four thousand and one had been assessed as the revenues of the *mahals* of Tohana and Jamalpur with effect from the *kharif* crop 1166 *Fasli*/1759 A.D., with the consent of the aforementioned (Ala Singh). The latter should of his own deposit the assessed amount (with the state treasury) and he would be accordingly given acquittal against this (state) claim by way of written receipt.

(vi) A Receipt, dated 14 *Moharram*, 6th R Y. (AH 1179/3 July, 1765 A.D.), bearing the seals of Hasan Ali Khan and Musai Khan (dated AH 1170/1757 A.D.), for Rupees seven hundred and fifty only (is) issued to Sandhu Singh[7] in respect of the revenues (*muamalat*) realised by Ala Singh from the zamindars of village Hastpur, *pargana* Hansi for the year 1176 *Fasli*/1761 AD and deposited in the State Treasury through Mir Habiballah.

(vii) An undated document[8] gives a detailed statement of the revenues (*hisab-i-muamalat*) relating to Raja Ala Singh with effect from the *rabi fasl* of the 5th year (*Luyil*—the crockodile year, fifth in the Turkish cycle of twelve) to *rabi fasl* of the 8th year (*Quyil*—the sheep year, the 8th in the Turkish cycle of twelve) (*min ibtida-i-fasl-i-rabi Luyil linghayat fasl-i-rabi Quyil*) bearing the (attestation) seal of the said Raja in respect of three crops (*wajib seh faslha*).

Total amount: Rs. 3,46,800

(i) *Fasl-i-rabi* of 5th year (*Luyil*) =Rs. 85,800/-.

(ii) *Fasle-i-kharif* of the 5th year (*Luyil* and the arrears till 8th year (*Quyil*) =Rs. 61, 000/-

Total amount realised =Rs. 1,92,000/-

II. Hundis etc. =Rs. 1,52,000/-

(i) Rs. 72,000/- ii) Rs 40,000/- iii) Rs. 40,000/-

III. Remission on account of drought and damage as per *tumar* (*takhfif khushki wa paimali bamujab tumar*) =Rs. 40,000/-

Balance: =Rs. 154,800

(Other) clauses:

(i) Relating to *Inam* of the three crops. (*inam seh fasl*)

(ii) Clause which would be narrated by Ram Singh in his own letter (*khat*).

(iii) *Altma*: nil.

Attached page:

Perquisities of Raja Ala Singh fixed as per settlement =Rs. 4,001/

(viii) Timur Shah's *Farman* (original), dated 11 *Rajab* AH 1192/5 August, 1778 (bearing the Durrani *tughra* and seal of Timur Shah) addressed to *Raja-i-Rajgan*, Raja Amar Singh of Patiala,[9] the recipient of the royal favours (*Atwaf-i-Badshahi*) and exalted status (who) should know that since he has shown consistent and firm loyalty and has rendered services to Muhammad Husain (the royal representative), he is confirmed in his possession of *pargana* Tihara. As the *pargana* has always been in his possession as a part of his *taalluqa*, this is bestowed on him. Apart from it, news has reached (the Royal Court) that Hari Singh causes turbulence and rioting in these territories (*mulk*) and (as such), the latter should not be given possession (*dakhal wa tasaruf* in these territories) and should be sent (back) to his *watan,* i.e., Multan. Muhammad Husain, who has been sent (to Patiala), would explain to him (Raja Amar Singh) some of the matters (*muqadamat*). *Farmans* have also been sent to the other Rajas to the effect that they should remain obedient to him (Raja Amar Singh). The Rajas and the *Rajgan* should show cooperation to each other and exhibit (mutual) bond of friendship. He (Raja Amar Singh) should always consider himself as worthy of the royal favours and should be grateful in this regard.

Written on 11th (day) month of *Rajab* AH 1192/5 August, 1778 A.D.

(ix) A copy of *Farman* from Timur Shah (bearing the seal of Timur) (*Shah Badshah*), dated 11 *Rajab* AH 1192/5 August, 1778 A.D., addressed to Chauhar Singh (Jauhar Singh) Phul[10] confirms the latter in his past possessions (*taalluqa-i-qadim*) extending from *pargana* Tihara to the territories of Bahadur which have already been in his continuous possession. The latter is also authorised to continue the realisation of the cesses relating to *Pahul* (*rasum-i-pahul*) which he has been realising previously as well. He is further enjoined to owe obedience to the Raja of Patiala and also to place his services at the latter's disposal. It has also been brought to His Majesty's notice that Hari Singh creates disturbance and turbulance in his (own) territories. It is desired that he (Chauhar Singh), along with the support of the other Rajas, should stop him (Hari Singh) from such rioting so as not to cause suffering to the people. It further states that very shortly Muhammad Husain would be deputed towards these territories and with the help of the Raja of Patiala, he would see that Hari Singh's possessions are incorporated in the state territories (*dakhil-i-mulk-i Padshahi*). As the ancient *watan* (*watan-i-mamula qadimi*) of Hari Singh is situated towards Multan, he should go over there and the revenues of these territories (in possession of Hari Singh in the cis-Sutlej region) should be realised by the addressee (Chauhar Singh) with the support of the Raja of Patiala and these territories would remain in the royal possession. In any case, through the services of the Raja of Patiala, Hari Singh would be expelled towards his previous *talluqa* (i.e., towards Multan). In case the latter goes towards the *jangle* side (Lakhi *Jangle*), he (Chauhar Singh) should intervene (so as to drive Hari Singh away). However, he should, in accordance with the past practice, (*ain-i-qadim*), continue to owe obedience to the Raja of Patiala and consider himself to be worthy of the royal favours.

Written on 11 *Rajab* 1192 *Hijri almuqadas*/5 August, 1778 A.D.

III

Apart from the above mentioned documents there is also a manuscript,[11] comprising .copies of eight *arzdashts* (Letters of obeisance) supposed to have been written by Raja Ala Singh and Raja Amar Singh to Shah Wali Khan, the Durrani Prime-Minister. However, one *arzdasht* (No. 5 of the Manuscript-henceforth Ms.) supposed to have been written by Raja Amar Singh does not seem to be genuine. It is clear from its terminology and contendts that it was most probably written in the late 19th or early 20th century with a view to appease the *Dewan Khalsa* (*Dewan Shri Khalsa Jeo*) and was intermixed with the copies of the other above mentioned seven *arzdashts*, which, even though undated, are rather true copies of the originals, apparently, earlier in the possession of the Patiala Darbar. Of the seven *arzdashts* addressed by the above Rajas to the Durrani Prime-Minister (Shah Wali Khan), two were written by Raja Ala Singh and five by Raja Amar Singh during the most crucial years 1765-66 A.D. It is rather surprising that the scribe, who copied the *arzdashts* from the original, did not care to note the dates which are usually given at the end of each such an *arzdasht*. However, the internal evidence derived from the contents of each of the seven *arzdashts* does point towards their genuineness. The main facts as narrated in the correspondence are equally corroborated by some other sources and essentially pertain to the years 1765-66 A.D.

In the first *arzdasht* (No. 2 of the Ms.),[12] Raja Ala Singh most humbly acknowledges the receipt of the benign Order (*taliqacha*) from the Prime-Minister (Shah Wali Khan, *Wazir-i-Azam, Dastur Muazzam, Nawab Umadat ul Mulk* Asaf Ja.). He acknowledges the continued favour and kindness bestowed upon him (*gulam*-the royal servant) and expresses gratitude to the latter in most laudatory language for having planned to despatch three lakhs of "triumphant *sawars*" (troops) within three months for the help of his most humble servant (Ala Singh). At the end, he once again thanks the Prime-Minister (Shah Wali Khan) from the core of his heart and comments in a verse that he has no words to express his gratitude for this graciousness.

In the second detailed *arzdasht* (No. 3 of the Ms.),[13] Raja Ala Singh informs the Prime-Minister (Shah Wali Khan) that he has been entrusted with the duties of the management of the affairs of *chakla* (Sirhind) and that in accordance with the latter's orders, he has recruited proper troops for the purpose of administration. (As such), by God's grace, with the help of the staff and officials of the *mahals*, he has already accompolished the work of the assessment and realisation of the revenues, the habitation of Sirhind, the construction of the mausoleums (*rozas*) and improved the revenue administration. (However), after a month, suddenly the entire body of the ignoble Sikhs under the leadership of Hari Singh, Jai Singh, Tara Singh, Lakhna Singh and both the Jassa Singhs etc., along with two groups from the regions of *Majiha* and *Doaba*, larger in number than ants and locusts, entered the territories of the *chakla* (Sirhind). (At that time) he was encamping in the vicinity of Patiala. Amar Singh and Himat Singh were despatched towards the forts of Patiala and Handyala along with suitable troops so as to block the way of "all the assembled armies of the infidels destined to be vanquished (*Jama-i-maqhur*)." Assisted by proper forces, Hamir Singh, Bhola Singh, Bahadur Singh and Lakhan Singh were detailed to confront "the wretched assembled (Sikh) troops (*Jama-i-nukbat*)." Thousands of these 'outlaws' were butchered in this bloody battle and a large number of camels and horses were captured as booty. By the grace of God and supported by the good fortune of His Majesty (Ahmad Shah Durrani), with utmost efforts, he was able to chastise "the whole body of the vanquishable infidels (*Jama-i-maqhur*)." Supported by thousands of his brave soldiers and *sawars*, Hari Singh Nahangi killed (many) leaders of that group (*firqa*) such as Budh Singh, nephew of Jassa Singh, brother of Tara Singh and various other persons of known and unknown groups. After their suppression, the troops of "the vanquished infidels (*maqhuran*)" went helter skelter. Some fled towards *Doaba* while others to other different directions. Many of them took to wandering in Maler and Kot Rai. He (Ala Singh) detailed the leaders of his army along with seasoned troops to pursue the enemies and their atrocities were stopped. As such, these days, those "ill-fated men" were causing turbulence and rioting in Ambala and Shahabad and every day, there was confrontation with them.

(Ala Singh further informs that) whatever amount of the revenues (*maliyat*) of the *mahals* had been realised from the beginning (of the season), had been spent on the salaries of the soldiers. Besides, loans were (also) raised to make payments. May God Almighty bring him (the Durrani) in this country (Punjab-Sirhind) so that the host of enemies (the Sikhs) may be completely annihilated through his ominus sword and the ground made impious by these groups (the Sikhs) may be rendered as pious. His (Shah Wali Khan's/Ahmad Shah Durrani's) parting instructions relating to the matters of administration were being wholeheartedly and faithfully, acted upon. For meeting the losses due to the devastation of the territories and the heavy expenditure involved therein, he (Ala Singh) hopefully counts upon the royal magnanimity. Further position will be communicated through an *arzdasht*.

In his first *arzdasht* (No. 1 of the Ms.)[14] Raja Amar Singh after conveying his compliments to Nawab Sahib *Umdat ul-Mulk* Asaf Ja (Shah Wali Khan, the Durrani Prime Minister) states that his grand father Raja Ala Singh, in response to his (Durrani Prime-Minister's) *taliqacha* (Order), had already sent a reply through a messenger to his exalted Honour (Prime Minister) in which he expressed his gratitude for the latter's benefications and narrated detailed facts about the atrocities and calamity wrought by "the villainous multitude of the Sikh troops, i.e., the infidels destined to be vanquished (*nakbat mal jamai Sil han shakawat nishan*)." Thereafter, the very next day he (Raja Ala Singh) was taken ill and breathed his last on Friday, 4th *Rabi-ul-Awal* (22 August, 1765 A. D.) as a true and faithful servant of his Honour (the Durrani Prime Minister) and that his (Ala Singh's) devotion and (spirit of) submission were manifest from the letter that he wrote to the latter during his life-time. Raja Amar Singh reiterates that he too was imbibed with the same spirit of devotion and faithfulness and prays to the Almighty God for his (Durrani Prime Minister's) health and life.

(Raja Amar Singh further states) that "the vanquishable armies of the infidels (*maqhuran*-the Sikhs)," having been suppressed after various battles had calmed down (but) now these days again "their numerous wretched and wicked groups of troops (*amboh-i-groh nukbat pizhuh*)" intended to commit meanness and vagrancy. Since by God's grace, the addressee's (Nawab Shah Wali Khan's) sympathies were with him (Raja Amar Singh), those men would be soon subdued and put to shame. He (Raja Amar Singh) solely depends upon his help and feels confident that he (Shah Wali Khan) would always show kindness and bestow favours upon him. Further details would be known to him from the letter (*arz*) of Ghulam Muhammad Khan (the Reporter).

In his second *arzdasht* (No. 4 of the Ms.)[15] addressed to the Durrani Prime-Minister (Shah Wali Khan) and Raja Amar Singh states that the events (pertaining to the period) prior to the death of his grandfather, Raja Ala Singh, had (already) been reported to him. (However), ever since he (Raja Amar Singh) had been entrusted with the services (for the administration) of *chakla* Sirhind, through his grace, the condition of the taalluqas had considerably improved. Moreover, detailed information regarding the condition and state of affairs in these territories had been already communicated to him through the letter of Ghulam Muhammad Khan, the Reporter (*waqia-nawis*) of *chakla* Sirhind. He had also learnt through the official messenger (*harkara*) that the *taliqacha* (Order) addressed to him (Raja Amar Singh) had been lost in transit due to turbulence on the part of "the destined vanquishable infidels (*maqhuran*-the Sikhs)" and he was very sorry for its non-receipt. However, he respectfully submits that after the victorious Ahmad Shah's troops were withdrawn, "the contemptible and infidel armies (of the Sikhs) destined to be vanquished" have caused turmoil, devastated the territories (*mulk*), rendered the administration of *chakla* Sirhind chaotic and excepting the Capital (Delhi), they have pillaged the territories of Jawahar Singh Jat. During the (past) two years, he (Raja Amar Singh) had mobilised considerable army for the defence and management of the forts and *zamindaries* (*makanat*) and combated "the large gatherings of the infidel troops destined for destruction (*Jamhur-i-maqhur*)-the Sikhs." As such, whatever cash and kind had been confiscated during the life-time of his ancestor (grandfather) at the time of his (Shah Wali Khan's) campaign at Barnala (*wadah gallughara*) had (already) been spent in quelling rioting on the part of "the gathered infidel troops destined for destruction (*jama-i-maqhur* -the Sikhs)" and he has been put under considerable debt. Apart from this, his own younger brother Himmat Singh having been allured by the enemies had stood against him so as to cause turbulence. In these circumstances, he was obliged to draw his attention (to these facts) and seek his help. An understanding (*qaulnama*) bearing the Royal Seal for the protection and guardianship on hereditary basis had been issued in favour of his grandfather (Raja Ala Singh) and the *sanad* giving undertaking for the latter's welfare and financial interests on hereditary basis was in his possession. As he had rendered meritorious services with all humbleness, more than (even) that of his grandfather, he expected magnanimity and gracious kindness. May God afford him (Shah Wali Khan) a favourable time and opportunity so that the enemies (the Sikhs) may be annihilated by the victorious sword of Islam and the obedient ones (Raja Amar Singh) may pass their days in a fortunate and courageous manner with full faith in him. Further details will be known to him from the letters of Amir Beg and Kashmiri Mal.

It has already been observed that Raja Amar Singh's third *arzdasht*- i.e., No. 5 of the Ms.[16] does not seem to be genuine. As such, only a summary has been provided.

In this *arzdasht*, Raja Amar Singh offers his heartiest felicitations to Shah Wali Khan, the Durrani Prime-Minister on the latter's elevation by a grant of precious *khillat*, an elephant and a *khasa* horse from the King (Ahmad Shah Durrani). Thereafter, the Raja states that his family had been a true disciple of *Darbar-i-Guru* and *Sangat* for the last seven generations. Having been blessed by the Gurus, it had been recipient of special benefictations at Amritsar. Raja Amar Singh claims the association of his family with the fourth and the fifth Gurus. He further claims that his family earned distinction by defeating the Turks at Gurusar during the time of the sixth Guru and that after serving the threshold of the seventh Guru, it was deputed to manage the state of affairs of the *illaqa* (territory) of Malwa. The family further served the eighth Guru at Delhi and rendered service to the ninth Guru when the latter visited this part of the country (Malwa). The Raja further states that the tenth Guru (Guru Gobind Singh) visited this place and after blessing the family entrusted it with the service of the *illaqa* of Malwa. As such, the command of the Guru and Shah Wali Khan's benevolence account for the development of not only the Sikhs but even the state of animals and vegetation of this area. The Raja further points out that *Akal Purkh* (the Almighty God) has blessed the *Khalsa* (perhaps here the Durranis) with the kingdoms of Hindustan and Iran and would also show mercy to his family and that Shri Guru Gobind Singh would pay attention to the condition of the Sikhs of this *illaqa* and would do full justice by making it prosperous one. The Raja makes *ardas* (request) to *Khalsa Dewan* for the betterment of the Malwa. He equally attributes the elegance and prosperity to the Master and King of this country (here Ahmad Shah Durrani) and pleads for taking care of the Malwa and its Sikhs.

In his fourth *arzdasht* (No. 6 of the Ms.)[17] addressed to the Durrani Prime-Minister (Shah Wali Khan), Raja Amar Singh states that his previous letters *(araiz)* must have been pursued by the latter. At present, the position is that 'large number of wretched infidel troops destined to be vanquished *(groh-i-amboh-i-maqhuran shaqawat pizhuh*-the Sikhs)' have again created turbulance, have taken to vagrancy in the *mahals* of the *chakla* (Sirhind) and are indulging in pillage and plunder. He (Raja Amar Singh) further states that in addition to the permanent standing forces *(jamiat-i-qadim-fauj)*, he mustered auxiliary forces as far as he could. He had to incur enormous expenditure for the safety and preservation of his *zamindaries* (*makanat*) and the forts. Apart from the turmoil on the part of these "vanquishable armed infidels (*maqhuran*-the Sikhs)" these days, his own younger brother, Himmat Singh, having been seduced by the opponents on their side, has equally become hostile and turbulent. He (Raja Amar Singh) did his level best to persuade him, through reliable persons, to accept his share and to dissociate himself from the destruction of the villages. But being influenced by the jealous persons, he did not come around and participated in skirmishes. (As such), because of the aforementioned insurgence, the damage and devastation of the villages, he has been burdened with heavy expenditure and for the last three years, he has faced worries and great difficulties. Needless to stress that he has no other mainstay excepting his benefactor (Shah Wali Khan). He considers that his betterment and fortune, both physical and financial, lie in allegiance and servitude, to *Huzur-i-Ali* (Shah Wali Khan). (As such), he often seeks favours from the latter so that the victorious flag (the Durrani's) may fly over this territory (Punjab-Malwa) and his devoted servants (like Raja Amar Singh) may successfully live in peace and prosperity with full faith in him (Shah Wali Khan). This would as well enable in the mitigation of the evil disturbance on the part of the "impious group" (the Sikhs) by the sword of the fearless conquerors so as to render this territory a pious one. Further details are being communicated through the letters (*araiz*) of Honourable (*Alija*) Amir Beg and Kashmiri Mal.

In his fifth *arzdasht* (No. 7 of the Ms.)[18] addressed to the Durrani Prime-Minister (Shah Wali Khan), Raja Amar Singh states that in order to offer his obeisance he had traversed over three stages but returned (to Patiala) according to his (Shah Wali Khan's) instructions from the latter had hurriedly left due to an emergency. This return journey on his (Raja Amar Singh's) part took eight to nine days. Finding this an appropriate opportunity, Himmat Singh and Hamir Singh resorted to turbulance and pillages, occupied and attached two to three villages of the *taalluqa*. However, as soon as he (Raja Amar Singh) reached Patiala, he despatched the troops comprising both cavalry and infantry for confrontation with the enemies. By God's grace and with his (Shah Wali Khan's) constant kindness, there were continual skirmishes but the enemy forces having been defeated in every battle felt harassed and dispersed. (Consequently) ten to twelve villages of the enemy were annexed by him (Raja Amar Singh) and several more villages (of the enemy) were inclined to come under the jurisdiction of his *thanas*. By God's grace and his (Shah Wali Khan's) kindnesses, all the desired work will be accomplished. (As such) Himmat Singh who had committed mischief on the instigation of Hamir Singh and other opponents, would come to his senses shortly after having met with reverses. May God always bestow His gracious shadow of kindness upon him (Shah Wali Khan) so that the slaves (like Raja Amar Singh) may be blessed with prosperous material position by the former's kindness and favours. It may not be (considered as) impertinence on his part if he were to most humbly draw his (Shah Wali Khan's) kind attention for the issue of *parwanas* favourable to his (Raja Amar Singh's) family.

In his sixth *arzdahst* (No. 8 of the Ms.)[19] addressed to the Durrani Prime-Minister (Shah Wali Khan), Raja Amar Singh states that letters intimating the state of affairs had (already) been despatched to him and he must have pursued the marginal writings. Now the position is that "large number of contemptible infidel troops destined to be annihilated (*groh-i-amboh-i-maqabir nukbat pizhuh*-the Sikhs)" after having caused commotion and become mutinous and having destroyed the *mahals* and cities of *chakla* Sirhind are now rioting and roaming about in *Doaba*. They are (also) spreading mischief in the bordering *qasbas* and villages of *chakla* Sirhind by establishing *thanas* in his (Raja Amar Singh's) House (*Zamindari*) as well as through incursions and pillages. Apart from the turbulance of these "detested infidels destined for destruction (*maqhurran*)," these days, his brother, Himmat Singh being misguided by the mischief-mongers having caused disturbance and ruination of the homeland (*watan*) endeavours to establish his own hold (*taalluqa*). But as God's grace and his (Shah Wali Khan's) kindness are always with him (Raja Amar Singh), he (Himmat Singh) has always met with failure and the mischief-mongering opponents indulging in turbulance feel disillusioned and repentent. But he is not fully satisfied with the position. The enormous expenditure incurred on battles, the pay of the auxiliary forces (*sawar* and *piyada*) over and above the permanent troops (*jamiat-i-qadimi*) during the (last) three years as well as the devastation of the villages of the zamindari (*dehat-i-taalluq*) are beyond adequate description. As his (Shah Wali Khan's) generosity is as much a shelter for him as it was for his grandfather (Raja Ala Singh) and his betterment lies in absolute submission (*gulami*) to him (Shah Wali Khan), his eyes are keenly set on his (Shah Wali Khan's) expected visit. May God fulfill his ardent desire for his (Shah Wali Khan's) victorious visit in this direction so that the clouds of turbulance on the part of the enemies may be mitigated and their (Raja Amar Singh's and the Durrani's) objects may be accomplished in a victorious manner. He expects and would like to claim as much benevolence from him (Shah Wali Khan) as previously extended to the late Raja (Raja Ala Singh).

IV

Commentary

Hitherto, the historians have mostly highlighted the military and political aspects of the Durrani campaigns in North India during the course of 18th century.[20] Much has been written on the campaigns of Ahmad Shah Abdali *vis-a-vis* the Mughal State and the Marathas resulting in the third battle of Panipat (1761) as well as the Afghan-Sikh tussle for supermacy in the Punjab and the cis-Satlej (i.e. cis-Sutlej) territories (*subah* Delhi) during the second half of the 18th century. There is no denying the fact that many contemporary and later Persian sources, especially chronicles, a few Marathi and English sources have been tapped for the narrative details covering the politico-military aspects. However, it is much less realised that as a result of annexation of the *subahs* of Lahore, Multan, Kashmir (1752)[21] and *chakla* Sirhind (Sarhind), *subah* Delhi (1757)[22] to the Afghan Empire of Kabul extending from Afghanistan to Karnal (*chakla* Sirhind), the Durrani state set up its own administration both for the purposes of governance and realisation of the revenues of the territories. Undeniably, prior to the battle of Panipat (January, 1761), the Afghan rule in the *subah* of Lahore and cis-Sutlej territories experienced considerable instability. It was practically made extinct by the Maratha operations (February-April, 1758) which were supported mainly by Adina Beg, the *faujdar* of Jalandhar and partly by the Sikhs.[23] For about a year and a half (April, 1758-October, 1759), the Marathas virtually ruled over the Punjab and the cis-Sutlej territories. They appointed Khoja Mirza Khan as the *subadar* of Lahore whereas Adina Beg was continued as the *faujdar* of *sarkar* Jalandhar, Sahaba Patel was posted at Attock. However, after about a year because of the tyranny and highhandedness on the part of Khoja Mirza Khan, the latter was replaced by Dada Rao Shaisha Pandit as the *subadar* of Lahore.[24] They also appointed another *subedar* at Multan and *faujdar* at *chakla* Sirhind for the purposes of administration and collection of the revenues.[25] It is as well on record that for this period (April, 1758-October, 1759), they were able to realise the farmed out revenues from the Punjab and the cis-Sutlej territories.[26] Even though the battle of Panipat (January, 1761) gave a fatal blow to the Maratha Supermacy in Multan, Punjab and cis-Sutlej territories, the Durrani rule in the Punjab could not be easily consolidated due to severe opposition on the part of the Sikhs. As a matter of fact, the ultimate failure of the short but significant Maratha rule in Multan, Punjab and cis-Sutlej territories paved the way for the regional[27] forces leading to the rise of the power of the Sikh Sardars who were able to establish themselves on an institutionalised basis. Notwithstanding the repeated campaigns on the part of Ahmad Shah Abdali, there was a continual tug of war and during the interregnum of the campaigns, based on kinship and local territorial proximity, many a *groh* of the Sardars were able to carve out territorial jurisdictions in various parts of the Punjab over which they established superior *zamindari* rights. As such, they claimed share in the surplus produce from the traditional landed intermediaries and the local zamindars. Even though the contemporary Persian, Marathi and English sources do not use the term *misl*, the establishment of such an institution under a Sardar and *sardari* by a chief Sardar over and above the (*misl*) Sardars[28] fundamentally altered the character of armed struggle against the Durranis as well as the revenue administration of the agrarian set-up.

Based upon the hitherto unutilised contemporary archival source-material in coordination with the other Persian and Marathi sources of multifarious nature, it is worthwhile to examine the Durrani administrative pattern in detail in the Afghan territories of North India during the second half of the 18th century. Notwithstanding strong elements of continuity with the Mughal age, partly influenced by its own pattern of administration and partly due to pragmatic considerations based upon political and economic factors, some marked changes did take place in the evolution of the Afghan pattern of administration in its territories in North India.

As a case study, the above mentioned documents translated into English bring out some of the salient features of the Afghan pattern of administrative polity as well as agrarian infrastructure in the cis-Sutlej territories (*subah* Delhi). During the Mughal age, *chakla* Sirhind was put under the administrative and revenue charge of a *faujdar*.[29] Under the Durranis, this practice was continued for some time. However, the *taliqacha* (Order), issued by the Durrani Prime-Minister, dated 22 *Shaban* AH 1174/29 March, 1761 A.D., mentions Faiz Talab Khan Durrani as the *subadar* and in charge of revenue administration (*sahib-i-ikhtiyar-i-maliyat*) of *chakla* Sirhind.[30] The latter *chakla* had already been detached from the Mughal *subah* of Delhi and put under the direct Durrani administration. It seems in the context that under the Durranis, at times, the administration of the *chakla* was put under the charge of a *subadar* (Governor) who occupied quite distinct position from the Afghan *subadars* of Kashmir, Multan and Lahore. However, for many a year, the contemporary Mughal (*Akhbarat*) (News-Letters) as well as later sources usually mention *faujdar* as in charge of the administration of *chakla* Sirhind.[31] This may as well indicate that even though the *subahs* of Kashmir, Multan and Lahore were always put under the charge of *subadars*, *chakla* Sirhind could be governed by a *subadar* if the incumbent was rather senior but mostly by a *faujdar* on the traditional Mughal pattern. All the same, in 1761 A.D., the overall supervisory powers for the management of the revenues and administration of *chakla* Sirhind were vested with the Mughal *Amir-ul-Umra Bakshi-ul-Mulk* Najib Khan Bahadur (Najib-ud-daula) who acted as the *wakil* of the Durrani Government in this regard. After him, even *wakil-i-mutalik* Najaf Khan (d. 1782) as well as the Marathas as *wakil-i-mutlak* (Mahadaji Sindhia with effect from November, 1784) of the Mughal state continued to discharge this responsibility on behalf of the Durrani Government.

During the Mughal Age, Ala Singh Jat held the position of a *chaudhuri* and as a landed intermediary was reckoned as one of the chief *zamindars* responsible for the realisation of the revenues from the territories (villages/*parganas*) assigned in *zamindari* by the Mughal state.[32] He was equally responsible for the maintenance of law and order in these Mughal territories. In lieu of these services, he enjoyed revenue free *jagir* lands as well as *chaudhurie/zamindari* perquisites. After the occupation of the cis-Sutlej territories by the Durranis (1757), Ala Singh Jat accepted the Durrani sovereignty. As such, he was not only continued with the *status-quo* as the chief zamindar (*zamindar-i-kalan*) but was bestowed larger territories (villages/*mahals*) for the revenue administration for which he was responsible to the Durrani administration of *chakla* Sirhind.[33] He was also conferred the status of *rajgi* alongwith the functions of a *faujdar* of a few *parganas*.[34] As the *zamindari* system ran on hierarchical pattern, all the petty zamindars *chaudhuris* as well as the *qanungos* and the *ra'aya* in these territories were obliged to render him full services in the collection of the state revenues for which they were entitled to their respective revenue-free land grants, *inam* and perquisites, etc.[35] Of course, as *faujdar* on the Mughal pattern, he not only commanded jurisdiction over the other *zamindars*, the *chaudhuries*, the *qanungos* and *ra'aya* for the revenue administration but was equally responsible for the maintenance of law and order as well as for safeguarding the interests of the state (Durrani), both internally and externally.[36]

The *taliqachas* (Orders) of Shah Wali Khan, the Durrani Prime-Minister, dated 22 *Shaban* AH 1174/29 March, 1761 A.D., and 7 *Shaban* AH 1176/12 February, 1763 A.D., specifically mention Ala Singh Jat as a zamindar who held the *jagirs* in the category of *wukala-i-ali* (*jagir-i-wukala-i-Ali*,).[37] This clearly brings out the enhanced status of Ala Singh who was appointed as *wakil-i-ali* (chief representative) by the Durrani state. Even though under the Mughal Government, the chief zamindars (*zamindaran-i-umda*) did act on behalf of the state in the military, revenue and administrative matters, it is difficult to trace the designation of *wakil-i-ali* attached with any of them. Rather on the contrary, the chief zamindars (*zamindar-i-umda*) had their own *wakils* (representatives) attached with the Provincial or Central Mughal Headquarters. It seems in the context that after annexation, the Durrani Government recognized many a chief zamindar as its chief representative (*wukala-i-ali*) and clearly demarcated territories (villages/*mahals*) assigned in *jagir* to them under the category *jagir-i-wukala-i-ali*.[38] This distinguished their *jagir* lands from the *jagirs* of the other Durrani officials in the *zamindari* territories or the directly administered *khalisa* territories. This was quite parallel to the Mughal practice which equally demarcated the assignable territories in *jagir* to the *mansabdars* or zamindars (*jagir/paibaqi*) from the *khalisa* territories administered directly by the state.[39] It is also evident from the contents of the above mentioned *taliqachas* (Orders) that in the cis-Sutlej territories, Ala Singh Jat was one of the many zamindars who were granted *jagirs* as chief representatives (*wukala-i-ali*).[40] Of course, he had his own representatives (*wakils*) who acted as liasion officers with the Durrani administration.[41]

The Durrani pattern of revenue administration in *chakla* Sirhind shows that the villages/*mahals taalluqas* assigned in *jagir* to Ala Singh Jat as zamindar cum *wakil-i-ali* were detached from the direct administrative jurisdiction of the *chakla* authorities (*subadar/faujdar/darogha* etc.) and put under the revenue administration of Ala Singh as the *jagirdar*.[42] All the same, it is clear from the documents that before passing over the *jagir* territories to the *jagirdars*, the valuation of the revenues of the villages/*mahals* was made on the basis of actual assessment by the Durrani official (*darogha*) of *chakla* Sirhind.[43] For this purpose, Mirza Muhammad Taqi was entrusted with the job to be carried out in cooperation with the representatives (*wakils*) of the assigned, i.e., Ala Singh Jat and all the accounts were to be attested and stamped by the *qazi*. The expenses of the Durrani official for undertaking such revenue job were met and deducted from the revenues of the assigned *jagir*.[44]

It is rather significant to observe that by March, 1761 A.D., Ala Singh's *jagir* as the zamindar and *wakil-i-ali* comprised only 726 villages from the *parganas,* i.e., Sunam, Gharam, Sanwar and Mansurpur and that not a single *en block* (*darobast*) *pargana* was assigned to him.[45] It was only after about a couple of years, i.e., 12 February, 1763 A.D., that the revenues of four full-fledged *parganas,* i.e., Sanam, Mansurpur, Gharam and Sanwar were assigned *enblock* (*darobast*) in *jagir* to him with full control over the revenue administration of these *mahals*[46] Ala Singh was also vested with the *faujdari* jurisdiction of these four *parganas*.[47] As such, with enhanced status, Ala Singh was not merely a *chaudhuri* zamindar, chief Durrani representative (*wakil-i-ali*) but also the *faujdar* of these *parganas* from which stipulated revenues were also assigned to him in *jagir* in lieu of the services rendered to the Durrani state. There were, of course, various other petty *zamindaries* in these *parganas* which did not form a part of the *taalluqa,* i.e., personal *zamindari* jurisdiction of Ala Singh.[48] But in his capacity of the *faujdar*, *darogha* and *zabit-i-maliyat* (asessment officer), he possessed full revenue and administrative powers over all the petty zamindars, *chaudhuries, qanungos, thanadars* and other revenue officials of these territories.[49] Of course, as *jagirdar* vested with the powers of the *darogha* and *zabit* (administrator cum assessor), he was required to make assessment and collect the revenues (*maliyat* and *abwab-ul-jama*) in accordance with the local established practice.[50] This clearly shows that for purposes of revenue administration, the procedure of measurement of land, the methods of assessment and the magnitude of the revenues (*mal* and *abwab*) were the same under the Durrani administration as inherited from the Mughal age.

In addition to the assignment of *jagir* territories from the various above mentioned *parganas* as well as conferment of the *faujdari* powers of the four *parganas* (Sanani, Mansurpur, Gharam and Sanwar), by 1764 A.D., Ala Singh was given additional charge as the *naib* (deputy) *faujdar*, *amin* (assessment officer), cum *amil* (collector) of the *parganas* of Tohana and Jamalpur.[51] For the discharge of these duties, he was entitled to establish perquisites. It is also clear that Ala Singh had been discharging such functions in respect of these two *parganas* since 1759 A.D. (1166 *Fasli*).[52] However, they did not by any means form part of his personal *jagir* and he was required to deposit the revenues of these *parganas* in the Durrani state treasury (*chakla* Sirhind) after the deduction of his perquisites in lieu of the above mentioned duties performed by him.[53] Similarly, he acted as the zamindar cum collector of the revenues of some villages in *pargana* Hansi and deposited the same in the state treasury.[54]

As a matter of fact, from the above mentioned few documents, it is difficult to work out the total number of villages/*parganas* in the *taalluqa* (*zamindari*) jurisdiction of Ala Singh nor is it possible to determine the total revenues assigned to him in *jagir* in lieu of the services rendered by him as *darogha, faujdar, amin* and *amil* in many a *pargana* under his jurisdiction. However, significantly a revenue document of the above collection puts rupees three lakh, forty six thousand and eight hundred only (Rs. 3,46,800/-) as the total amount of the revenues (*muamalat*) realised by Ala Singh from his *zamindari* territories,[55] which he was obliged to pay to the Durrani Government after the deduction of his own perquisites. The statement of the revenue account (*hisab-i-muamalat*) covers the revenues of the *rabi* crop (*fasl-i-rabi*) and the *kharif* crop (*fasl-i-kharif*) or the 5th Year (*Luyil*) as well as the arrears till the 8th Year (*Quyil*). The statement also shows that during the process of assessment, a regular remission was afforded to the *ra'aya* on account of natural calamity or the other damages done to the crops.[56] This was equally in line with the Mughal practice.[57] In this regard, a regular remission of Rs. 40,000/- was given to the *ra'aya* on account of drought as well as destruction of the crops due to *paimali* (trampling of the crops by the horses/cattle/forces during the military operations).[58] Of the revenues realised by Ala Singh, payment was made to the Durrani Government both in cash and by *hundis*.[59] As regards remunerations for the services rendered as zamindar, Ala Singh was given *inam* (which could be made in cash or by way of land grant) in respect of all the three crops (*inam-i-seh fasl*) for which he collected the revenues on behalf of the Durrani state.[60] However, the amount of *inam* is not mentioned. But it is clearly stated that in lieu of his *zamindari* rights, Ala Singh was paid rupees four thousand and one only (Rs. 4,001/-), as perquisites as per settlement.[61] Here the term *maliyat* stands for the actual revenues payable by him to the Durrani state after the deduction of his own zamindari perquisites (*haquq*). This is well confirmed by the above document which puts the total amount of the realised revenues at Rs. 3,46,800/- for the two crops i.e., *kharif* and *rabi* along with the past arrears. In fact, the annual *peshkash/muamala* (revenues) was fixed periodically and in line with the Mughal practice, was subject to periodical revision.[62] As such, Ala Singh, as the chief zamindar (*Zamindar-i-kalan*) had to pay *peshkash/ muamala* (revenues) annually to the Durrani Government on periodically fixed basis.

This is well confirmed by the subsequent revenue settlements made with Ala Singh in respect of the *zamindari* territory held by him as landed intermediary and chieftain. After the great disaster (*Wadah Gahllughara*, 1762) and suppression of the Sikhs, Ala Singh was also arrested for having been in connivance with the former and was presented before Ahmad Shah Abdali at Lahore.[63] However, on the intervention of Shah Wali Khan (the *wazir*), who had a soft corner for Ala Singh, the latter was pardoned on the plea that he was a revenue paying chief zamindar (*zamindar-i-kalan malguzar*).[64] Ala Singh had, of course, to pay penalty of Rupees One lakh and twenty-five thousand (Rs. 1,25,000/-). Apart from it, having been reinstated in his *zamindari*, Ala Singh had to pay an amount of Rupees five lakhs (Rs 5,00,000/-) as *malia* which henceforth was fixed as an annual amount (*saliyana*) for payment.[65] Apparently, by 1762 A.D., Ala Singh held larger territorial possession of *zamindari* with enhanced revenues than held by him earlier. After the assassination of Zain Khan, the *faujdar* of Sirhind by the Sikhs in his next visit Ahmad Shah Abdali, on the recommendation of Shah Wali Khan (the *wazir*), entrusted the management of *chakla* Sirhind to Ala Singh (as *faujdar*) alongwith the bestowal of the title of *rajgi*.[66] In lieu of this, Ala Singh paid Rupees six lakhs, which apparently, included both *nazrana* and *malia*. The total amount of the revenues (*jama*) of the entire *chakla* was fixed at Rupees eighteen lakhs (Rs. 18,00,000) and Ala Singh was given *sanad* to this effect. This, of course, precluded the *jagir* territories like those of Muhammad Daler Khan, Maler Khan and a few other *taalluqdars* of the cis-Sutlej territories who paid the *nazrana/malia* (revenues) directly to the Durrani state.[68] However, after having acquired the *sanad* (for appointment as *faujdar*), Ala Singh fixed the respective amount (of *malia*) to be paid through the latter by the other zamindars, i.e., Hamir Singh, Gajpat Singh, Rai Kalan and Desu Singh through mutual settlement. At a later stage, after another campaign which Ahmad Shah Abdali was at Sirhind, Ala Singh paid a personal homage and a fresh settlement of the revenues of *chakla* Sirhind was effected whereby Ala Singh undertook to pay Rupees eight lakh (Rs 8,00,000/ -) annually as *muamala-i-muqarrari* whereas the other chief zamindars (of the cis-Sutlej territories), i.e., Hamir Singh, Desu Singh and Gajpat

Singh were assessed at Rupees two lakhs (Rs. 2,00,000/-) each annually and Rai Kalan Jagraon was required to pay Rupees four lakh (Rs. 4,00,000/-) annually.[69] Of course, the amount of the *muamala/muamalat* (revenues) was payable in instalments mutually settled by the Durrani administration and the zamindars. As already analysed, it could be paid both in cash and by way of *hundis*. At the same time, the periodically fixed (*muamala-i-muquarrari*) was always subject to revision based upon the actual seasonal assessment of the crops (*fasl ba fasl*) and the revenues realised (*hal-i-hasil*) after having taken into consideration the remissions afforded on account of calamities (*aft*) and the *zamindari* perquisites of Ala Singh and other zamindars mentioned above. Ahmed Shah Abdali received the respective stipulated amounts before he left for Kabul.[70]

Such institutionalised relationship for the payment of periodically fixed *muamala/peshkash* on the part of the Patilala Chiefs (as zamindars) to the Durrani state of Kabul continued during the periods of Maharaja Amar Singh and to a lesser degree even of Raja Sahib Singh all through 18th century. However, at the same time, there is no denying the fact that even during the period of Ahmad Shah Durrani, the Sikh Sardars after successful incursions realised dues in lieu of *karah prasad* (ceremonial sweet *suji* prasad distributed in the *Gurdwaras* at the end of the Prayer) from the Patiala chieftainship (zamindari),[71] the *faujdars* of *chakla* Sirhind under Durrani rule as well as the Mughal territories of Jamuna-Ganga *doab* (*chakla* Saharanpur).[72] Apart from it, they continually claimed and realised *nazrana muamala* from the territories under the regular Durrani or Mughal administration through negotiated settlement which was usually conceded by the latter administration.[73] At times, the *karah prasad,* if fixed as a substantial, could well serve the purpose of realisable *nazrana* or *muamala*. In the wake of the sack of Sirhind and the execution of Zain Khan, the *faujdar* of *chakla* Sirhind by the Sikhs (January-February, 1764), the chieftains of Malwa region, i.e., Chaudhuri Ala Singh, Gajpat Singh, Mohr Singh, Rai Ahmad Masie, the Afghans of Kotla and the zamindars (chiefs) of Kotkapura and Faridkot having made submission to the Sikhs undertook to pay *nazrana*.[74] Ala Singh paid an amount of Rupees twenty-five thousand on account of *karah prasad* and occupied *qasba* Sirhind along with a few villages.

In this context, it is essential to appreciate that the *muamala* exacted by the Sikh Sardars from a particular chieftainship/*zamindari* was by no means an exclusive claim over its revenue (*hal-i-hasil*) but formed only a part of the revenues (surplus produce) which otherwise would have gone to the Durrani or the Mughal State, as the case may be.[76] The amount of *muamala* was fixed by the Sikh Sardars taking into consideration the total realised revenues (*hal-i-hasil*) of the subjugated chieftainship/*zamindari* which was, otherwise, normally under the Durrani or Mughal administration.[77] The Sikh Sardars would realise the fixed *muamala* either as lumpsum or in instalments as settled through negotiations and agreement. Such incursions and claims by the Sikhs continued intermittently all through the later decades of the 18th century over the Durrani held cis-Sutlej territories,[78] Muslim *zamindaris* of *subah* Punjab[79] as well as over the territories of *subah* Multan.[80] Similar is the position with regard to many a region of the *Mughal subahs* of Delhi, Agra and Ajmer.[81] Paradoxically enough, in the medieval Indian polity, even though it was resented or at times opposed by the Durrani or the Mughal Governments, it was by no means considered absolutely incompatible with their own respective claims of sovereignty over these territories.

It is equally known from the other sources that Ala Singh also undertook *ijara* (farming of the revenues) from Zain Khan (the *faujdar*) for some of the *parganas* in *chakla* Sirhind,[82] which otherwise were not in his regular *zamindari* jurisdiction. Thus, as a *mustajir* (revenue-farmer), he was entitled to margin of stipulated share from the revenues collected and actually paid to the Durrani treasury at Sirhind.

The conferment of the titles of Raja to Ala Singh or *Raja-i-Rajgan* (Maharaja) to Amar Singh was by no means incompatible with the *zamindari* pattern of administration. This only meant recognition of the services rendered by the chiefs to the Durrani State and equally strengthened the institutional bond between them. As such, Timur Shah's *Farman,* dated 11 *Rajab* AH 1192/5 August, 1778,[83] recognises the services rendered by *Raja-i-Rajgan* Amar Singh to the Durrani royal representative Muhammad Hasan at Patiala and confirms him in possession of *pargana* Tihara which formed part of his *taalluqa* (*zamindari*). As Maharaja Amar Singh acted as the chief zamindar on behalf of the Durrani State, he was directed to oust turbulent Hari Singh (a Sardar of a *misl*) from the cis-Sutlej territories and send him to his *watan* around Multan. The *Farman* clearly shows that apart from the Patiala chief, the other Rajas in the cis-Sutlej territories equally owed allegiance to the Durrani sovereign. Moreover, in the hierarchical feudal pattern, Maharaja Amar Singh enjoyed a higher status and commanded obedience from some of the other chiefs. This is further confirmed by Timur Shah's *Farman* of even date addressed to Chauhar Singh[84] who, while being confirmed in his past possessions (*talluqa-i-qadim*) extending from *Pargana* Tihara to Bahadaur, was equally vested with rights to realise *pahul* cesses (*rasum-i-pahul*). As a zamindar, he is desired not only to owe continued obedience to the Patiala chief but is directed to drive away turbulent Hati Singh towards his *watan* (Multan) with the help of the other Rajas of the territories. The territories (in the cis-Sutlej region) in the possession of Hari Singh were seized by the Durrani State and incorporated into the state territories (*dakhil-i-mulk-i-padshahi*) and put under the royal possession (*khalisa*). As such, Chauhar Singh (zamindar) is further directed to help the royal representative Muhammad Hasan in the realisation of the revenues of these territories with the support of the Raja of Patiala (and pass on to the Durrani state treasury). Like the Mughals, the Durrani State equally claimed and exercised the right to decrease or increase or even confiscate the *zamindari* possessions. It was the duty of the chief zamindars to fight against any recalcitrant zamindar on behalf of the state. Here, in this case, Chauhar Singh (zamindar) is required to seek the support of the Patiala chief so as to chase even in the Lakhi *jangle* and drive him away to Multan.

It is clear from the above documents that all through the later half of the 18th century, the Durrani State claimed sovereignty and realised revenues from the cis-Sutlej territories which was characterised by *zamindari* pattern. The Patiala chieftain as the chief zamindar in lieu of his services and status enjoyed precedence in the hierarchical *zamindari* pattern in *chakla* Sirhind. There is no doubt that at times there was recalcitrance on the part of a few zamindars or Sardars but the Durrani State was able to suppress it through its landed administrative apparatus.[85] It is well confirmed by the Persian *Akhbarat* as well as by the numismatic evidence that even by the end of the 18th century, the Durrani currency was in vogue in Patiala during the chieftainship of Raja Sahib Singh.[86]

Apart from these documents, the above mentioned Letters (1765-66 A.D.), addressed by Raja Ala Singh and Raja Amar Singh to the Durrani Prime-Minister, Nawab Shah Wali Khan significantly show that there was regular correspondence between the Patiala chieftain and the Durrani Government. *Dak* (mail) was sent through special messengers (*harkaras*) though, of course, at times mail could be lost in transit due to turbulance *enroute*.[87] The Durrani Government at Kabul was apparently in correspondence with the other chiefs/zamindars in the cis-Sutlej territories (*subah* Dehli), Punjab, Multan and Kashmir and kept itself fully informed about the political developments and administrative problems in these regions all through the second half of the 18th century.

Ala Singh's letters show[88] that by 1765 A.D., as chief zamindar and *faujdar*, he had been entrusted with the administration as well as assessment and realisation of the revenues of *chakla* Sirhind. Even though he was able to realise revenues (*maliyat*) in these territories, the turbulance on the part of the Sikhs in the Punjab (especially in the Jalandhar *Doab* and *Majiha*) and incursions in the cis-Sutlej region for pillage and plunder rendered his financial position very hard. He states that he was obliged to spend all the realised revenues for administrative purposes, for raising more army, both regular and auxiliary, in order to meet the Sikh challenge. He had to raise loans from the local *sahukars* for this purpose. This position persists with his successor Raja Amar Singh. In such situation, it is difficult to visualise if annual instalments of *muamala peshkash* (revenue) could be regularly remitted by the Patiala chiefs to the Durrani Government at Kabul. On the contrary, due to heavy expenditure incurred for recruitment of army in connection with the continual tussle with the Sikhs, both beseach the Durrani Government for magnanimity and royal favour for issue of further *parwanas* (for additional grant of *zamindari* and *jagirs* etc.).[89] Raja Amar Singh claims to have rendered more meritorious services to the Durrani State that of his grandfather Raja Ala Singh, for having combated the Sikhs and makes persistent appeals for the enhancement of his territories (*zamindari, jagirs* and status through the issue of royal *parwanas*.[90]

It is rather significant to state that Letters written by Raja Ala Singh and Raja Amar Singh as faithful zamindars and representatives of Durrani State not only uphold the legitimacy of the Durrani sovereignty in the Punjab and the cis-Sutlej territories but are equally couched in traditional tone representing the royal authority. During the medieval age, in the official communications representing the Imperial Government, the adversaries were usually mentioned with contempt and the adjectives used for them were rather derogatory in character. Such a tenor of writing is equally reflected in the chronicles especially while narrating the campaigns against the people of the enemy territories or recalcitrant chiefs or tribes. Both Raja Ala Singh and Raja Amar Singh describe the large groups or troops of the Sikhs as 'contemptible' (*amboh-i-groh-i-nakbat pizhuh*) or 'large number of wretched infidel troops (Sikhs) destined to be vanquished (*groh-i-amboh-i-maqhurran shaqwat pizhu*) or 'vanquishable infidels' (*maqhurran, jama-i-maqhur* or *jamhur-i-maqhur*) or the 'wretched assembled troops' (*jama-i-nakbat*) or 'multitude of the Sikh troops-the infidels destined to be vanquished' (*ma'al jamai Sikhan shakwat nishan*) or the 'contemptible and infidel armies destined for utter destruction (*maqahir nakbat*) 'mean', 'vagrants', 'rioters' and 'impious group'.[91] In fact, both Raja Ala Singh and Raja Amar Singh consider such Durrani territories of the Punjab which were occupied by the recalcitrant Sikhs as having been defiled and rendered impious and could be made pious only after successful Durrani campaigns.[92]

The above correspondence on the part of Raja Ala Singh and Raja Amar Singh with the Durrani Prime-Minister as well as other contemporary documents reveal that while narrating the incursions of the Sikhs (*Sikhan*) or Singhs (*Singhan*) in their territories (*chakla* Sirhind), they used these terms (*Sikhan/Singhan*) with utter contempt and derogatory shiboleths. It is doubtful that they were using this language merely with a view to please their Durrani masters. It rather suggests that in the 18th century, the term Sikh or a group of Sikhs did not essentially connote persons belonging to a particular religious faith as both Raja Ala Singh and Raja Amar Singh were the followers of the Gurus and had been even baptized after performance of the ceremony of *Pahul*.[93] It seems in the context that the Sikhs or *Singhan* denoted those militant followers of the *Nanak Panth* and Guru Gobind Singh who had taken to arms against the Mughal state or the Durrani Government for the vindication of their religious rights and temporal power. As a matter of fact, ever since the creation of the *Khalsa* by Guru Gobind Singh (April, 1699), the militant groups of the Sikhs emerged as a vital force during the first half of the 18th century which undermined the traditional Mughal administrative institutions and polity in the Punjab and cis-Sutlej territories. They formed themselves into small *jathas* (armed bands), *grohs* (mobile warrior bands) and *dals* under the command of the Sardars, rather freedom fighters. The invasion of Nadir Shah (1739) and subsequent campaigns of Ahmad Shah Abdali (1748 onwards) not only gave a blow to the Mughal Empire but created a political vaccum which equally accelerated the phenomenal growth of the militant Sikhs who, during the second half of the 18th century, established institutionalised economic and territorial interests as well as chieftaincies based on hierarchical pattern. For the furtherance of their interests, both for defence and offence, many a Sardar would combine on an *ad hoc* basis under the command of one of the Chief Sardars which constituted the *Dal Khalsa*.[94] As such, in the contemporary terminology, the Sikhs/*Sikhan/ Singhan* who confronted the Mughal/Durrani states can be well distinguished from other denominational Hindu Sects who, even though claimed to be the followers of the Gurus and *Nanak Panth,* rather remained passive and usually pursued peaceful vocations.[95]

Even though the Persian *Akbarat* and other sources do provide a general and piecemeal information about the activities of the Sikhs in the Punjab and the cis-Sutlej territories, the above mentioned Letters of Raja Ala Singh and Raja Amar Singh offer most detailed description of some of the campaigns and incursions of the Sikhs in the cis-Sutlej and Haryana terriories (*subah* Delhi) during the crucial year following the defeat and disaster of the Sikh Sardars (*wadah ghallughara*) in the battle at Kup (1762) at the hands of Ahmad Shah Abdali.[96] They equally bring out the issues involved in the internecine conflict between Raja Amar Singh and his younger brother Himmat Singh over the Patiala *gaddi* and the partition of the *jagirs*. The detailed narration of the connivance of Himmat Singh with the Sikh Sardars of *Doaba* and *Majiha* for incursions in the *zamindari mahals* of the Patiala House and other territories of *chakla* Sirhind, even temporary occupation of some of the *mahals* by Himmat Singh and the Sikh Sardars as well as the battles fought by the contending parties is not available in any of the other contemporary sources.[97] As such, they considerably help in the reconstruction of the 18th century history of the Patiala Chieftainship, both internally and externally with regard to its relationship with the Sikh Sardars and the Durrani State at Kabul.

Written from the Imperial administrative angle, the ascribed motivation on the part of the Sikh Sardars for incursions in *chakla* Sirhind and other cis-Sutlej territories is turbulance, pillage, plunder and devastation of the royal Durrani territories. In fact, such a medieval terminology implies the temporary forcible occupation of the villages/ *mahals*/*zamindaries* wherein the Sikh Sardars equally illegally realised the revenues of Patiala chieftains and other Sirhind territories. The Letters refer to the atrocities and calamity wrought by the Sikh Sardars in chakla Sirhind, the Jat territories (of Bharatpur) and the regions around Delhi.[98] The Letters do not refer to any religious motivation on the part of the Sikhs. However, on the contrary, the contemplated annihilation of the Sikhs by the Durrani forces with the 'ominous sword of Islam' and the desired Durrani success is considered as 'the victory of Islam' over the turbulent Sikhs.[99] Notwithstanding such traditional medieval verbiage, the Letters do provide insight into the motivation of incursions by the Sikh Sardars in the territories of *chakla* Sirhind. A few statements in the Letters categorically mention the territorial acquisitions (and their revenues) as the main object of incursions on the part of the Sikh Sardars.[100] Both Raja Ala Singh and Raja Amar Singh claim to have combated the combined forces of many a Sikh Sardar and after having defeated them pushed them out of their territories.[101] However, during Amar Singh's period, the situation was rather critical because of the conflict between him and his younger brother Himmat Singh who also commanded the support of a few local zamindars. Himmat Singh, helped by Heimer Singh, was also in league with the Sikh Sardars (of the Punjab) in the furtherance of the latter's designs over the Sirhind territories.[102] The Sikh Sardars were able to establish their military posts (*thanas*) on the outskirts as well as in the territories of *chakla* Sirhind and even temporarily occupied some of the *mahals* and *zamindaries* therein (for the realisation of the revenues).[103] But they were eventually pushed back by Raja Amar Singh. In fact, the above Letters cover a period for only two years (1765-66 A.D.), along with background of the preceding years for the activities of the Sikhs in *chakla* Sirhind. It is known from other sources that there were brief phases, both earlier and later than these years, when the Sikhs (*Dal Khalsa*), especially under the supreme command of Sardar Jassa Singh Ahluwalia, were able to intermittently realise *muamala* (revenues) from the Patiala chieftain as well as the local Durrani administration at Sirhind.[104] They even imposed *rakhi* over many a village in the cis-Sutlej territories.[105] But in the last decades of the 18th century, the Durrani administration, supported by the Mughals or the Mughals-Maratha operations, exerted greater pressure over the local Sikh Sardars in the cis-Sutlej territories and was able to maintain its sovereign rights over *chakla* Sirhind till the end of the 18th century.[106] It is only the English East India Company which eventually ousted the Durrani influence and established its own protectorate over the chieftains of the cis-Sutlej territories by the early 19th century.[107] Of course, the Durranies were ousted root and branch from the *subahs* of Lahore, Multan and Kashmir by Maharaja Ranjit Singh from the closing years of the 18th century to second decade of the 19th century (1799-1819).[108]

References

1. The only administrator, scholar, who has briefly referred to two of these documents in a general manner (supra nos. 2 and 17) for the narration of political history of Patiala was Khalifa Sayyid Muhammad Hasan (Prime-Minister of Patiala State) in his work entitled *Tarikh-i-Patiala*, Safir Hind Press, Amritsar, 1878 (henceforth *Tarikh-i-Patiala*), pp. 56-57, 66. However, he did not appreciate the official status and differential territorial jurisdictions of Ala Singh as chief zamindar and as *jagirdar*. In fact, he has not analysed any of the documents for the purposes of the description of the Durrani administrative-cum-agrarian set-up in *chakla* Sirhind. Thereafter, Diwan Bahadur Sir Daya Kishan Kaul (Chief Secretary, Patiala State), in his paper on 'Care and Preservation of Old Records in Northern India' vide I.C.H.R., Vol. II, January, 1920 (Lahore Session), pp. 31-39, noted that in Patiala there were six documents which dated back to the time of Ahmad Shah Abdali and were still wrapped upon in the original narrow envelopes bearing the addresses only. He further remarked that, "They have been kept just as they were received, and there is absolutely no indication as to whether they were replied to or entered on a register: one is ignorant even of the exact date on which they came to hand." In fact, Kaul did not dwell on any of the contents contained in the documents. It can only be surmised that the documents referred to by Kaul are perhaps the same which are being analysed in this paper. Kaul also did not note the separate existence of the letters written by Raja Ala Singh and Maharaja Amar Singh to Ahmad Shah Abdali. Ganda Singh vide *Ahmad Shah Durrani, Father of Modern Afghanistan*, Bombay, 1959 (Bibliography, pp. 415-440) and Kirpal Singh vide *Maharaja Ala Singh of Patiala and His Times*, Amritsar, 1954, have not been referred to any of the documents under analysis.
2. Punjab State Archives, Patiala (henceforth P.S.A., Patiala), Foreign Ministry Case 2A/147 of 1174 A.H.; Sacred Documents pertaining to the reign of Shri 108 Maharaja Baba Ala Singh Surgbashi.

   It is regretted that the descriptive docketing of the documents as recorded by P.S.A., Patiala, is erroneous and misleading. Moreover, all the documents do not pertain to the year A.H. 1174/1761 A.D.

   Document (Doc.) No. 2A/147(B) of 1174 A.H., dated 22 *Shaban* A.H. 1174/29 March, 1761 A.D.
3. *Ibid.*, Doc. No. 2A/147 (A), dated 22 *Shaban* A.H. 1174/29 March 1761 A.D.
4. *Ibid.*, Doc. No. 2A(C), dated 7 *Shaban* A.H. 1174/12 February, 1763 A.D.
5. *Ibid.*, Doc. No. 2A/147(D), dated 2 *Safar* A.H. 1178/1 August, 1764 A.D.
6. *Ibid.*, Doc. No. 2A/147(F), dated 17 *Safar* A.H. 1178/16 August 1764 A.D.
7. *Ibid.*, Doc. No. 2A/147(E), dated 14 A *Moharram* A.H. 1179/3 July, 1765 A.D.
8. *Ibid.*, Doc. No. 2A/147(G), undated.

9. P.S.A., Patiala, *Farman* (original) No. D-143, dated 11 *Rajab* A.H. 1192/ 5 August, 1778 A.D., issued by Timur Shah to *Raja-a-Rajgan* Raja Patiala Amar Singh. The *Farman* bears the Durrani *tughra* and seal. File No. A 6 H, Case No. 149 comprises 15 pages inclusive of a copy of the above *Farman*. The file covers original notings (vide registers Nos. 149, 190, 32, dated 8 *Asoj Samvat* 1917/1860 A.D.), by Kishan Narain *sareshtadar* of the *Darbar* (of Patiala), which provide detailed information as to how the original *Farman* having been traced was acquired from Rahim Baksh and Hakim Khan Rajputs of village Goindwal on payment of Rupees twenty five (Rs. 25/-) as *inam*. The original *Farman* was kept in a sealed box in *Qila Mubarak* (where the archives of the State were preserved). It may be further observed that on fresh examination, the above *Farman* seems to be genuine in all respects.
10. *Ibid*., Doc. No. 3 A.H., Case No. 405 of 1192 AH; a copy of a *murasala* from Timur Shah Badshah to Chuhar Singh Phul, dated 11 *Rajab* A.H. 1192/5 August, 1778 A.D.
11. *Ibid*., No. 5 A.H. The manuscript (ms) comprises eight folios (fols. la-8b). The last letter by Raja Amar Singh (fols. 8a-b) is rather incomplete which shows that the entire ms. is rather incomplete and that originally, it may have covered even more letters. It may also be stated that even earlier, these letters were got translated into English by the Patiala *Darbar* and a verified version of the same, dated 1-12-1952, appended to the above ms. under the title 'Copies of letters from Raja Ala Singh and Maharaja Amar Singh to Shah Vali Khan of Kabul 1765-66 A.D., is also available in the file. However, the free-style translation, even though readable, is rather defective in many a respect. A few passages of some of the letters have been abridged in a manner so as to lose the original sense of the text. At the same time, the oriental technical Persian terms have been translated in a vague and ambiguous manner.
12. *Ibid*., fol. 2a.
13. *Ibid*. fols. 2a-3b.
14. *Ibid*., fols. la-2a.
15. *Ibid*., fols. 3b-5a.
16. *Ibid*., fols. 5a-6b.
17. *Ibid*., fols. 6b-7a.
18. *Ibid*., fols. 7a-8a.
19. *Ibid*., fols. 8a-8b.
20. Only works based on original sources may be cited. J.N. Sarkar, *Fall of the Mughal Empire*, Vol. II (1754-1771), Calcutta, 1934; H.R. Gupta, *History of the Sikhs* (1739-1799), Vol. 1, *Evolution of the Sikh Confederacies*, (1739-68), revised ed. Simla, 1952, Vol. II; *Cis-Sutlej Sikhs*, Lahore, 1944; *Marathas and Panipat*, Panjab University, Chandigarh, 1951; G.S. Sardesai,

New History of the Marathas, Vol. II, *The Expansion of the Maratha Power*, Bombay, 1948, pp. 353-461 ; Ganda Singh, *Ahmad Shah Durrani*, op. cit., No. 1; Kirpal Singh, *Maharaja Ala Singh of Patiala and His Times*, *op. cit.*, No. 1.

21. *Selections from the Peshwa Daftar*, ed. G.S. Sardesai, (henceforth S.P.D.), XXI, Letters Nos. 53 and 55 ; Saiyyad Ullah Shah Abadi, *Bagh-i-Sulaiman*, Research and Publications Division, J & K Srinagar, (written in A.H. 1194/ 1780-81 A.D.), Ms. No. 51, fols. 235a-239b.

22. *S.P.D.* II, p. 71. This is further confirmed by the fact that henceforth in the territories of *chakla* Sirhind, all the *sanads* relating to the land grants, fresh or renewed, in respect of *madad-i-maash* and *aimma* were issued under the seal of Ahmad Shah Durrani. For details, P.S.A., Patiala, copies of *Farmans/ Sanads* etc., vide Register D/1, fols. 20a, 22b-23b; Register D/3, fol. 8b ; Register D/5, fols. 51a-52b, 58b-59a, 64-b, 146a-b, 169a-b, 173a, 236a, 261b-262a.

23. Tahmas Khan Miskin, *Kitab-i-Qissa-i-Tahmas Miskin* (written in A.H. 1196/ 44 R.Y. Shah Alam/1780 A.D.), also popularly known as *Tazkira-i-Tahmas Miskin*, Ms. British Museum, Or m, 1918 No. Pers. 8807, fols. 83b-90a; *Tarikh-i-Alamgir Sani* (anonymous), Br. Mus, Persian Ms. Or 1749, fols. 150a-151b, 164b-165b, 178a-205a; S.P.D., Vol. 25, Letters Nos. 163, 178-79; Vol. 27, L. 220 ; Vol. 28, L. 218; Mofti Ali-ud-Din, *Ebratnameh* (*Ebratnameh wa Umadut-ul-Tawarikh*-completed in 1854 AD/1911 *Samvat*), ed. Muhammad Baqir, Lahore (Pakistan), 2 Vol., 1961 (henceforth Ali-ud-Din), pp. 218-23.

24. *Ibid.*

25. *Ibid.*

26. *Ibid.*

27. Asar Nayaz, *Tarikh-i-Kunjpura* (written in 1823 AD), ed. Muhammad Baqar, Lahore, 1973 (henceforth *Tarikh-i-Kunjpura*), pp. 80-86.

28. Rajasthan Archives Bikaner, *Akhbarat-i-Darbar-i-Mualla* (henceforth *Akhbar*). Of the numerous instances, only a few may be cited. *Akhbar,* dated 28 *Zulhijja*, A.H. 1176/11 July, 1763 A.D.; 20 *Muharram*, A.H. 1177/ 13 August, 1762 A.D.; 29 *Shaban*, AH 1177/3 March, 1764 A.D.; 28 *Zulhijja*, AH 1177/28 June, 1764 A.D.; 30 *Jumada* I, A.H. 1178/25 November, 1764 A.D.; 25 *Jumada* II, AH 1182/6 November, 1768 A.D. National Archives of India, New Delhi, Original Receipts, Foreign Deptt., Persian Branch *Akhbar* (henceforth N.A.I. *Akhbar*) No. 160, OR 10, p. 3, 12 February, 1785; No. 161, OR 10, pp. 8-10, 15 February, 1785, *Tarikh-i-Kunjpura*, pp. 87-94.

29. Although in the Mughal Age, the *faujdar* was in charge of the *sarkar* administration even when *chaklas* comprising numerous *parganas* were constituted (vide *Khulasatu-s-Siyaq*, Ms. Orient Qurat 243, Berlin, fols.

159a-b; Ms. Sulaiman Collection (74), Ms. 410/143, A.M.U. Aligarh, fol. 16a), the administrative charge of the *chakla* remained with the *faujdar* usually also vested with the functions of an *amin* and this office was always considered distinct and subordinate to *nazim/subadar* of a *subah*. *Sarkar/ Chakla* Sirhind formed a part of *subah* Delhi. It is well borne by all the contemporary sources that the position even for *chakla* Sirhind ramained the same during the first half of the 18th century prior to the Durrani campaigns or rather even till 1757 A.D., when it was ceded to the Durrani Empire. Some sources mention the *faujdar* as *hakim* of the *sarkar/chakla*. However, some later sources put him as the *chakladar* in respect of both Mughal/ Durrani periods. (vide *Tarikh-i-Kunjpura*, pp. 75-76); *Tarikh-i-Patiala*, pp. 46-47, 50-51). At the same time, a later source, Ali-ud-Din, p. 332 mentions Sadiq Beg as the *nazim* of Sirhind under Mohammad Shah Rangila (1718-48) which is a rather loose expansion. Many modern scholars too use the designation of Governor for the *faujdar/amin* of Sirhind which is rather inept.

30. *Op. cit.*, No. 2.

31. Only a few instances may be cited. *Akhbar,* dated 2 *Shawwal*, A.H. 1177/ 4 April, 1764 A.D.; 19 *Shaban* A.H. 1182/11 February, 1765 A.D.; 5 *Ramzan* AH 1183/21 January, 1770 AD. In fact, Abdus Samad Khan was the first *faujdar* appointed by the Durrani administration in *chakla* Sirhind vide *op.cit.*, No. 23. Ali-ud-Din, pp. 220, 234.

32. P.S.A., Patiala, Doc. No. D 142-a Mughal *Farman*, dated 21 *Ramzan*, AH 1137/3 June 1725 A.D., addressed by the Emperor Muhammad Shah to Ala, *zamindar (chaudhuri)* of Padur enjoins the latter to take up residence at Sirhind, stamp out dacoity and turbulance as well as to safeguard the (trade) route from Lahore to Delhi. The *Farman* also ensures the subordination of the other *jagirdars* and Rajas to him and in lieu of his services, also promises the confernment of the title of *rajgi* upon him. Also, *Tarikh-i-Patiala*, pp. 44-45, states that the *Farman* was conveyed to Ala Singh through Mir Mannu (son of Qamar-ud-Din Khan) and Samai Yar Khan. But Kirpal Singh vide *Life of Maharaja Ala Singh and His Times*, *op. cit.* No. 1, pp. 172-181 has contested the genuineness of the *Farman*. However, in view of the fact that the commercial caravans and even the royal convoys on the main Delhi-Kabul route passing through the disturbed territories of Sirhind were often plundered around 1721 A.D., and thereafter (vide Saiyid Muhammad Bilgrami, *Tabsirat-un-Nazirin* Ms., *Farisya Akhbar* No. 204. Aligarh Muslim University, Maulana Azad Library, Aligarh, fol. 82a) rather points out to the possibility of the issue of the *Farman* with the above mentioned contents. All the same, the *zamindari/chaudhurie* status of Ala Singh during the Mughal Age is well confirmed by the *kafiyats* (statements) based on the family revenue documents recorded around 1869-70 *Samvat*/ 1812-13 A.D., during the reign of Maharaja Sahib Singh of Patiala. (vide P.S.A., Patiala, Doc. No. A. 10. H-Farist *tafsil aulad Sardar Phul mai*

Kafiyat abadi mai mauza Phul, fols. 27b.). The *kafiyats* cover the geneology, ownership and *zamindari* rights in the inherited and self developed villages of the various *parganas* as well as respective *chaudhurie* shares held by the members/branches of the family since the late 17th century. The detailed list and *kafiyat* of *abadi* (settlement of villages etc.) traces the family history to Sardar Phul, the head of the family who initially developed land and acquired *chaudhurie/zamindari* rights. Apart from other descendant members of the branch families, Ala Singh, son of Sardar Rama and grandson of Sardar Phul inherited his own *zamindari/Chaudhurie* villages in a few *parganas* while he also further extended his territorial jurisdiction. (*Ibid.*, fols. 6a-7a, 14a-14b, 24a-27a); also Ali-ud-Din, p. 332.

33. *Op, cit.*, Nos. 2, 5-8; For Ala Singh's role as zamindar and for helping the Durrani administration in the realization of the revenues from different regions of the *chakla* Sirhind, also see *Akhbar,* dated 28 *Zulhijja* A.H. 1176/ 11 July, 1763 A.D.; 20 *Muharram* AH 1177/ 31 July, 1763 A.D.; 17 *Ramzan* A.H. 1178/ 10 March, 1765 A.D.
34. *Op. cit.*, Nos. 4, 5, 13; *Tarikh-i-Kunjpura*, p. 78.
35. *Op. cit.*, Nos. 4, 5.
36. *Ibid.*; also *op. cit.*, Nos. 12,13.
37. *Op. cit.*, Nos. 3 and 4.
38. *Op. cit.*, Nos. 2, 4, 9.
39. For details, B.R. Grover, 'Nature of Land Rights in Mughal India', Indian Economic and Social History Review, 1, 1963, pp. 1-23.
40. *Op. cit.*, Nos. 2, 3, 4.
41. *Op. cit.*, No. 2.
42. *Op. cit.*, Nos. 2, 3, 4.
43. *Ibid.*
44. *Op. cit.*, No. 3.
45. *Op. cit.*, No. 2.
46. *Op. cit.*, No. 4.
47. *Ibid.*
48. *Op. cit.*, Nos. 4, 5.
49. *Op. cit.*, No. 3, 4, 5.
50. *Ibid.*
51. *Op. cit.*, No. 4, 5.
52. *Op. cit.*, No. 6.
53. *Ibid.*
54. *Op. cit.*, No. 7.
55. *Op. cit.*, No.8.

56. *Ibid.*

57. *Khulasat-us Siyaq*, *op. cit.*, No. 29, fols. 151a-152b and fols. 10a-11b respectively.

58. *Op. cit.*, No. 8 ; also *Ibid.*

59. *Ibid.*

60. *Ibid.*

61. *Ibid.*

62. For details, B. R. Grover, 'Elements of Continuity and Change in Land Ownership and Rights from the Mughal Age to the Early British Administration in India, '*Proceedings of the Indian History Congress*, Presidential Address, Medieval Section, 37th Session, Calicut, 1976, pp. 143-178.

63. Ali-ud-Din, p. 230.

64. *Ibid.*

65. *Ibid.*

66. *Tarikh-i-Kunjpura*, p. 78. According to the same source, Nawab Najib-ud-Daula proposed the name of Sardar Jahan Khan (as *faujdar*) for the management of administration of *chakla* Sirhind. But this was resented by Shah Wail Khan (the *Wazir*) as the latter was rather on inimical terms with Sardar Jahan Khan. Ala Singh gave rupees six lakhs (Rs. 6,00,000/-) to Shah Wali Khan and was bestowed the title of *rajgi* along with a *sanad* for the management of *chakla* Sirhind (as *faujdar*) by His Majesty (*Huzur-i-Mualla*-Ahmad Shah Abdali). However, *Tarikh-i-Patiala*, p. 62 states that after Ala Singh took over the management of *chakla* Sirhind, he undertook to pay three and a half lakh (Rs. 3,50,000/-) as annual *malguzari* and was bestowed the *khillat* and the title of *rajgi* by Ahmad Shah Abdali. Out of the above amount, Ala Singh paid rupees two lakh and eighty thousand only in cash and thereafter managed to despatch the balance of rupees seventy thousand (Rs. 70,000/-) from Lahore by way of *hundis* to Kabul. This version varies from the above cited evidence known from *Tarikh-i-Kunjpura* which is much earlier source (1823 A.D.), equally based upon the Archives of the Kunjpura House.

67. *Ibid.*

68. *Ibid.*

69. *Ibid.*, p. 79. As the amount of the revenues (*muamala*) was payable in instalments and as already analysed vide Doc. op. cit., No. 8 that the periodically fixed *muamala* (*muamala-i-muqarrari*) was equally subject to revision based upon actual assessment (*tashkhis*) and exact amount of the revenues realised (*hal-i-hasil*) after deduction on account of calamity (*aft*) and *zamindari* perquisites of various types, it was difficult to determine the amounts of the revenues paid by Ala Singh to the Durrani

administration from one year to another. However, *Akhbar,* dated 17 *Ramazan* A.H. 1178/10 March, 1765 A.D., mentions that as per settlement made at that time, Ala Singh sent rupees forty thousand (Rs. 40,000/-)as *nazrana* to Shah (Ahmad Shah Abdali) and undertook to pay rupees three lakh (Rs. 3,00,000/-) as the revenues (*muamalat*). In this context, it is not clear whether the amount of *muamalat* was only for one season (*fasl-i-rabi*) or the whole past year (inclusive of *fasl-i-kharif*) or only an instalment thereof.

70. *Ibid*.

71. *Akhbar,* dated 2 *Shawal*, A.H. 1177/4 April, 1764 A.D.; 19 *Shaban* A.H. 1182/11 February, 1765 A.D.; 5 *Ramazan* A.H. 1183/21 January, 1770 A.D.; also Ali-ud-Din, p. 233.

72. *Akhbar,* dated 28 *Zulhijja*, A.H. 1177/28 June 1764 A.D.; Also *Persian Records of Maratha History,* I: *Delhi Affairs*: (1761-1788) News Letters. From Persian Collection, tr. J.N. Sarkar, Bombay, 1953 (henceforth *Persian Records of Maratha History*), A7-Delhi News Letter, dated 24th January 1770, pp. 19-20.

73. Of the numerous *Akhbar*, only a few may be cited. *Akhbar*, dated 28 *Zulhijja*, A.H. 1176/11 July, 1763 A.D.; 13 *Jumada* I, A.H. 1178/8 November, 1764 A.D.; 17 *Ramazan* A.H. 1178/10 March, 1765 A.D.; 4 *Zulhijja*, A.H. 1181/25 May, 1765 A.D.; 20 *Shawal*, A.H. 1181/10 March, 1768 A.D.; 20 *Zulqada*, A.H. 1182/20 March, 1769 A.D.; 5 *Safar*, A.H. 1183/10 June, 1769 A.D.; 5 *Ramazan*, 1183/21 January, 1770 A.D.; also *Persian Records of Maratha History*, A-10-(Delhi) News Letter to Peshwa, C. 20 May, 1770, p. 23.

74. Ali-ud-Din, *op. cit.*, p. 233.

75. *Ibid*; also *op. cit.*, No. 71.

76. *Op. cit.*, No. 73.

77. *Ibid*. Also National Archives of India (NAI), Sec. Proceedings, Vol. 23 September 1776 AD, pp. 776-777, 781, 783-785; For. Deptt. Sec. Progs., 23 June, 1783, Nos. 23, 42B.

78. For imposition of *rakhi* by the Sikh Sardars, see *Akhbar*, dated, *Jumada* 11, A. H. 1193/1779 National Archives of India, New Delhi, Original Receipts, Foreign Deptt., Persian Branch, *Akhbar* (henceforth NAI *Akhbar*), OR, 10, pp. 16-18; *Persian Documents*, ed. P. Saran), Bombay, 1966 (henceforth *Persian Documents*, ed. P. Saran), p. 370; *Persian Documents of Maratha History*, A56b-17 April, Second Sheet; 13, 6b-Letters to Nana Sahib Shrimat, C 28th February, 1783, p. 93 and 119 respectively; *Tarikh-i-Kunjpura*, pp. 93-94, 99-100, 106-107. For realisation of *karah prasad* by the Sikhs, NAI, *Akhbar*, dated,*Rajab* AH 1211/1795-96 A.D.; *Persian Documents*, ed. P. Saran, p. 401. For realisation of *nazrana/muamala* by the Sikhs, *op. cit.*, Nos. 73 and 76.

79. Of the numerous *Akhbar*, only a few may be cited. *Akhbar,* dated 10 *Muharram*, A.H. 1177/21 July, 1763 A.D.; 2 *Shawwal* A.H. 1177/4 April, 1764 A.D.; 28 *Zulqada* A.H. 1177/28 June 1764 A.D.; 21 *Rabi*/ I, A.H. 1183/25 July, 1769 A.D.; 17 *Rajab* A.H. 1206/11 March, 1792 A.D. For Zaman Shah's period (Date?), *Akhbarat-i-Wilayat Kabul wa Lahore* vide *Akhbarat-i-Mutfaraqa Darbar-i-Mualla* etc., SHR, Khalsa College, Amritsar, Accession No. 521, *Akhbar* No. 20/84, fol. 24a, *Roz Namcha Shah Alam Badshah* (from 31 R.Y. to 49 R.Y.) compiled on 1 June, 1810 AD by Mathan Lal from the material of Rai Tek Chand, the *akhbar-nawis* of the English E.I.Co., Khuda Baksh Oriental Public Library, Bankipur, Patna, Ms. No. 174, *Tarikh-i-Farsi Qalmi*, dated 16 *Shaban*, A.H. 1206, 35th R.Y./30 March, 1797 AD, fols. 68a-b.

80. Only a few instances may be cited. *Akhbar*, dated 2 *Shawwal* A.H. 1177/4 April, 1764 A.D.; 28 *Zulhijja* A.H. 1177/28 June 1764 A.D.; A.H. 1181/ 1767-68 A.D.; 11 *Rabi* I, A.H./1206/18 November, 1790 A.D.

81. Of the numerous instances, only a few may be cited. *Akhbar,* dated 5 *Ramazan* A.H. 1183/21 January 1770 A.D., *Persian Records of Maratha History*, A7-Delhi News Letter, 24th January, 1770, pp. 19-20; A10-(Delhi) News Letter to the Peshwa, C 20th May 1770, p. 23; B6b-Letter to Nana Sahib *Shrimant*, 28th Feb., 1783, p. 119. B8a-To the Peshwa, 28 *Jamada* I, Year 25 (1st May Records Series) ed. 1783), p. 124; Foreign Secret consultations 23 June, Nos. 26-27. Letters from James Browne to John Bristow, Resident at the Wazir's Court, dated 2 March, 1783 and 11 March, 1783 respectively; James Browne Correspondence (Indian K.D. Bhargava, NAI, Delhi, 1960, Letters Nos. 24, pp. 33-35; 28; 39; 41; 71-82; 55; 114-115; 60; 121-124; 126; 232-34; 127; 235-236; J.N. Sarkar, 'Delhi During the Anarchy, 1749-88 as told in Contemporary Records' with special reference to the Persian manuscript named by Sarkar as the 'Delhi Chronicle,' Indian Historical Records Commission, 1921, pp. 4-9; *Tarikh-i-Kunjpura*, pp. 84-115 ; also Sec. Proceedings vide *op. cit.*, No. 77.

82. *Tarikh-i-Kunjpura*, p. 76.

83. *Op. cit.*, No. 9.

84. *Op. cit.*, No. 10.

85. *Op.cit.*, Nos. 9 and 10.

86. NAI, *Akhbar,* dated 16 *Jumada* II AH 1211/17 December, 1796 A.D.; *Persian Documents*, ed. P. Saran, p. 398; Also Sayyid Imam-ud-Din Husaini, *Tarikh-i-Husain Shahi*, Khuda Baksh Oriental Public Library, Bankipur, Patna (written in 1798) states that even till then, i.e., 1798 A.D., the coin of Shah (Durrani) was current in the family of Amar Singh at Patiala and "whosoever succeeds to the throne issues the same coin in his country and considers himself as a subject of the Durrani Emperor." *Tarikh-i-Patiala*, pp. 75-76. The 18th century currency issued under the Durrani rule is still

available in the collection of the coins exhibited at Moti Bagh Palace, Patiala. Also Ganda Singh, *Ahmad Shah Abdali*, *op. cit.*, No. 1, pp. 371-72.

87. *Op. cit.*, No. 15.
88. *Op. cit.*, Nos. 12 and 13.
89. *Op. cit.*, Nos. 13, 14, 18.
90. *Op. cit.*, No. 15.
91. *Op. cit.*, Nos. 13-15, 17, 19.
92. *Op. cit.*, Nos. 13, 17. It is also known from the *Akhbarat* that Raja Ala Singh had been frequently writing to Ahmad Shah Abdali for undertaking further campaigns in the Punjab for the suppression of the Sikhs. *Akhbar,* dated 3 *Rabi* II A.H. 1177/11 October, 1763 A.D., states that Ala Singh had sent letters to Ahmad Shah Abdali requesting him to come to Lahore so that they might uproot the *thanas* established by the Sikhs in the Doaba (Jalandhar).
93. *Tarikh-i-Patiala*, pp. 58, 65; Ram Sukh Rao, *Sri Jassa Singh Binod* (Punjabi) P.S.A., Patiala, Ms. 772, fols. 241a-b; also Ram Sukh Rao, *Sri Fateh Singh Pratap Prabhakar*, ed. Joginder Kaur, Patiala, 1980, pp. 171, 211, 474.
94. Of the numerous available *Akhbar*, only a few may be cited. *Akhbar*, dated 28 *Zulhijja*, A.H. 1177/28 June, 1764 A.D.; 30 *Jumada* I, A.H. 1178/25 November, 1764 A.D.; 25 *Jumada* II, A.H. 1182/6 November, 1768 A.D.; NAI, *Akhbar* No. 160, OR, 10, pp. 3, 12 February, 1785 A.D.; *Persian Documents*, ed. P. Saran, pp. 363-68; *Persian Records of Maratha History*, A3b-10th December, 1766. Sheet 2, News about Sikh Sardars b.6; *Tarikh-i-Kunjpura*, pp. 87-94.
95. For the first half of the 18th century, numerous *Akhbar* mention the *Banjara* communities, the Kaiyasths, Gujars, Hindu *faqirs*, *sanyasis* and *bairagis* as the followers of *Nanak Panth*. See *Akhbar,* dated 10 *Ramazan*, AH 1123, 5th R.Y.B.S./11 October, 1711 A.D.; 12 *Rajab* A.H., 4th R.Y.F.S/3 July, 1715 A.D.; 16 *Jumada* I, A.H. 1122, 4th R.Y.B.S./2 July, 1710 A.D.; For the *Udaseen* as *Nanak Prasth* around the middle century, See *Tazkira Waqai Anand Ram Mukhlis*, (1746-48 A.D.), SHR, Khalsa College, Amritsar, Ms. Acc. No. 94, pp. 131-59. The *Nanak Shahi deras* and *maths* came to be established in various parts of North India. For philosophical aspects and popularity of *Udaseen*, see Sant Rein, *Udasi Bodh*, Ms. (1858 A.D.), fols. 1a-320b, History Deptt., G.N.D. University, Amritsar-a xerox copy of the original text available at *Dera* Sant Rein, village Bhudan, District Sangrur (Punjab); also Surjit Singh Hans, 'Early Sikh Tradition,' *Journal of Regional History*, History Department, GNDU, Vol. I, 1980, p. 185.
96. *Op. cit.*, Nos. 13-15, 17-19.
97. *Op. cit.*, No. 15, 17-19. *Tarikh-i-Patiala*, pp. 66-67 refers to the same letter addressed by Maharaja Amar Singh to Shah Wali Khan. However, a

kaifiyat (Date?) available at P.S.A., Patiala, No. A. 8. H mentions another incident, dated approximately 1829 *Samvat*/1772 A.D., when Kanwar Himmat Singh supported by Bhai Desu Singh and some forces of the Sikhs (*Singhan*) occupied the fort of Patiala when Maharaja Amar Singh had gone to the *jungle* side (for game). According to this *kaifiyat*, Maharaja Amar Singh supported by the other Rajas, the Phulkian Sardars, Raja Kirat Parkash (of Kangra) and the Afghans of Malerkotla beseiged the fort and after reconciliation with Himmat Singh reoccupied the city and fort of Patiala. In this settlement, Himmat Singh did not get anything excepting his own *Zamindari* (*makan*) as such returned to Dathoda (Dhoda). After about five to six months, he was taken ill and died. All the *jagir* and *zamindaries* (*makanat*) of Himmat Singh were occupied by Maharaja Amar Singh. The above *kaifiyat* was copied from the old documents and recorded on 22 *Poh* 1981/1924 A.D., under the caption *muqadma parcha-i-tarikh-i-halat-i-Patiala*.

98. *Op. cit.*, No. 15; of the numerous other sources, only a few may be cited. *Akhbar*, dated 28 *Zulhijja*, A.H. 1177/28 June, 1764 A.D.; *Tarikh-i-Kunjpura,* pp. 87-115; also *op. cit.*, No. 81.

99. *Op. cit.*, Nos. 15, 17, 19.

100. *Op. cit.*, Nos. 15, 17-19.

101. *Op. cit.*, Nos. 13-15, 17-19.

102. *Op. cit.*, Nos. 15, 17-19.

103. *Op. cit.*, Nos. 18-19.

104. *Op. cit.*, Nos. 73, 77-78, also *Akhbar,* dated 4 *Jumada* II, A.H. 1206/29 January, 1792 A.D.; 17 *Rajab* A.H. 1206/11 March, 1792 A.D. In fact, earlier Raja Ala Singh Jat was obliged to surrender 1/4th of the revenues of the *pargana* Issru and then the entire latter *pargana* as well as the *pargana* Kotla Maler to Sardar Jassa Singh Ahluwalia, the leader of the *Dal Khalsa*, Cf. *Tarikh-i-Patiala*, pp. 74-75.

105. *Op. cit.*, No. 78.

106. *Op. cit.*, Nos. 9-10; *Akhbar*, dated 3 *Rajab* A.H. 1193/17 July, 1779 A.D.; 5 *Shabban*, A.H. 1193/18 August, 1779 A.D.; 8 *Rabi* I, A.H. 1195/4 March, 1781 A.D.; NAI *Akhbar*, No. 101, OR 449, 5 September 1787 A.D., pp. 231-35; *Tarikh-i-Kunjpura*, pp. 87-90, 94-99, 101-115; also *op. cit.*, No. 86.

107. It was only after the British occupation of Delhi (11 September, 1803 A.D.), and the withdrawals of Marathas from the Jamuna-Ganges Doab and the Delhi-Agra region along the Jamuna in pursuance of the Anglo-Maratha Treaty of Surji-Arjan Gaon (30 December, 1803 A.D.), and the failure of Jaswant Rao Holkar's assault on Delhi (October 8, 1804 A.D.), and later futile negotiations for eliciting support from the Chiefs of the cis-Sutlej territories and Maharaja Ranjit Singh (of Punjab) that the English East India

Company penetrated into the cis-Sutlej territories for the establishment of its Protectorate. All this is confirmed by the NAI Pol. Progs. for these years. In fact, as late as 1804 A.D., Zaman Shah, the King of Kabul was in correspondence with Begum Samru (of Sardhana) for asserting his sovereignty vis a vis the English East India Company. Begum Samru received three letters from Kabul in this regard, which, she forwarded to Col. Ochterlony, the E. I. Co's Resident at Delhi: (Begum to Col. Ochterlony, dated 23.2.1804 vide Sec. Progs. 12.4.1804, No. 64). For details of Lord Lake's military operation and submission of the Chiefs in the cis-Sutlej territories as well as that of Jaswant Rao Holkar, see *Roz Namcha Shah Alam*, *op.cit.*. No. 79, dated 24 *Jamada* 11 A.H. 1220, 48 R.Y./20 September, 1805 A.D.; 16 *Rajab* A.H. 1220/48 R.Y./12 october, 1805 A.D.; 17 *Ramzan* A.H. 1220, 48 R.Y./10 December, 1805 A.D.; 27 *Shawal* A.H. 1220, 48 R.Y./19 January, 1806 A.D. (This *roz namcha* relates to Patiala), fols. 550a-552b, also P.S.A., Patiala, Doc. No. 144, Original Letter (in Persian) addressed by Mr. Seton, Resident, Delhi to Maharaja Sahib Singh about the protection of their territories by the British Government, as intimated to Maharaja Ranjit Singh of Lahore, dated 21 November, 1808 A.D.; also *Tarikh-i-Kunjpura*, pp. 112-115.

108. Zaman Shah led his last campaign to Lahore on 19 *Rajab*, A.H. 1213/19 September, 1798 A.D., but had to retreat towards Multan due to shortage of funds (Cf. *Roz Namcha Shah Alam* fols. 298b-299a). Notwithstanding the fact that the Sikhs were a great barrier to the fulfilment of the Durrani aims for the reoccupation of the territories of the Punjab and cis-Sutlej upto Karnal over which it claimed sovereignty (Cf. Sheikh Rahim Ali, *Tarikh-i-manazil-i-Kabul* written in A.H. 1211/1797 A.D., and recompiled by Abdul Qadir Khan in A.H. 1212/1798 A.D., Regional Archives Office, Allahabad (U.P.). Ms. No 12842, Question/Answer No. 22-henceforth *Turikh-i-Manazil-i-Kabul*, the English East India Company was also keeping strict watch over the Durrani designs (Cf. *Roz Namcha Shah Alam*, dated 14 *Rajab*, 41 R.Y./25 December, 1798 A.D., fols. 299a-b). By the end of the 18th century, the Durranis still realised *peshkash/nazrana* from many a Hindu chiefs of the Sub-Himalayan ranges (Chamba, Jammu etc.) as well as from the territories of *Chach*, Hazara and even at times from the *zamindaries* and *mahals* of the Gakkhars and Khataks of the regions between Jehlum and Sind and from many other Muslim Chiefs in West Punjab. (Cf. *Roz Namcha Shah Alam,* dated 16 *Shaban*, A.H. 1206, 35 R.Y./30 March, 1793; *Tarikh-i-Manazil-i-Kabul*, Questions/Answers, Nos. 4, 14, 21, 22; also B.R. Grover, 'Relationship between the Sovereign State (the Mughals and Afghans) and Punjab Hill Chiefs during the 17th and 18th Centuries, A case study of Chamba Chieftainship based on Bhuri Singh Museum, Chamba Documents, '*Nuskha-i-Insha-i-Majmua al Qawanin*', Punjab History Conference, 16th Session, March, 1982, Patiala, pp. 94-102 and 21st Session, March 1987, pp. 138-150 respectively. Apart from the Punjab, the Durranis

equally claimed revenues from the *Subah* of Multan, the Blochs and the territories West of (river) the Indus (Cf. *Roz Namcha Shah Alam,* dated 9 *Rajab*, A.H. 1213, R.Y. 41/19 December, 1798 A.D., fols. 298b-299a; 20 *Safar*, A.H. 1214, R.Y. 41/25 July, 1799, fols. 335b-336a; 8 *Zulqadda* A.H. 1214, R.Y. 42/3 April, 1800 A.D., fols. 369b-370a; also *Tarikh-i-Manazil-i Kabul*, Question/Answers Nos. 4, 13-14. After having occupied Lahore in 1799 A.D., Ranjit Singh realised that he could never consolidate his rule unless the Afghans were expunged from all the above territories. As such, he conquered Multan (January, 1818), Peshawar (November, 1818) and Kashmir (July, 1819). The real credit for stamping out the Afghan rule from the Indian territories goes only to Maharaja Ranjit Singh.

Chapter 10

The Importance of *Nuskha-i-Insha-i-Majma al Qawanin* of Ganesh Das Badehra (*Munshiat-i-Ganesh Das*) for the Late 18th and Early 19th Centuries History of the Punjab*

This paper reveals the importance of a Persian manuscript of 18th and early 19th centuries history of the Punjab by Ganesh Das Badehra. Although other works of Ganesh Das are well known, this manuscript delineates the functioning of land revenue system, especially of the regions to the west of Punjab before their final incorporation to his kingdom by Maharaja Ranjit Singh. It reveals the striking elements of continuity in the local administration from the Mughal age to the establishment of kingdom by the Maharaja in the Punjab even though on fragmented scale.

G. S. N.

Munshi Ganesh Das Badehra, Qanungo and resident of *qasba* Gujrat, Chanhat Doab, *Subah* Punjab, occupies a unique position as chronicler for the local history of Jammu *raj* and the regional history of the Punjab, more especially for the phases covering 18th and 19th centuries till the fall of the Sikh Kingdom and the establishment of the rule of the English East India Company. Ganesh Das Badehra has to his credit various works. Little known to the historians hitherto, his earliest attempt was the compilation entitled *Nuskha-i-Insha-i-Majma al Qawanin* accomplished in the early 19th century.[1] This was, of course, followed by *Raj Darshani,* popularly known as *Tawarikh-i-Jammu,* comprising briefly the history of the Rajas of Jammu (*Rajawali*) and completed in 1847 A.D. (11th *Bhadon,* 1904 *Bikrami Samvat/*

* Paper Presented at Punjab History Conference, 21st Session, March, 1987, Punjabi University, Patiala.

1283 A.H.).[2] A little later, Ganesh Das wrote a brief history of the Punjab in 1848 A.D. (1265 A.H.) covering the important dates and events upto 1847 and named it as *Chiragh-i-Punjab.*[3] At the same time, having made a judicious selection from a few histories of the Punjab, he compiled more comprehensive account of the Punjab history by 1849 A.D. (1906 *Bikrami-Samvat*/1265 A.H.) and named it *Risala-i-Sahib Nama,* popularly known as *Char Bagh-i-Punjab.* Of course, after some additions and alterations, the author ultimately completed this work by 1855 A.D.[4]

Though, in the *Raj Darshani,* Ganesh Das Badehra had briefly dealt with the career, activities and achievements of Maharaja Gulab Singh,[5] as a concluding part of the monograph, he expressed the desire that with more time at hand and if he remained alive, he would write a separate book on the latter Maharaja under the title *Gulab Nama* or else another courageous person might attempt to write on the life and career of the Maharaja.[6] It is, of course, well known that later on Diwan Kirpa Ram, the Chief Minister of Jammu and Kashmir State, compiled a book on Maharaja Gulab Singh in 1865 A.D. (*Bikrami Samvat* 1922) under the same title[7] as earlier planned by Ganesh Das. While giving an account of the Rajas of Jammu for the early medieval period and the achievements of Raja Arjun, Diwan Kirpa Ram does pay tribute to Lala Ganesh Das for his in-depth study based on investigation, lucidity and excellence of expression. He also acknowledges to have studied the account of Ganesh Das Badehra at an intimate level and having accepted the narration as given by the latter in this regard.[8] Thereafter, Diwan Kirpa Ram does not mention Ganesh Das Badehra at any stage and a few times, while referring to some of the events with which his own ancestors and late father were associated, he categorically claims himself to be the author of the *Risala* entitled *Gulab Nama.*[9] However, a critical examination of *Raj Darshani* and *Gulab Nama* would show that at innumerable places, he has completely adopted the narrative account especially relating to the administration, polity and agrarian set-up prevalent in the hilly and plain regions of the erstwhile Jammu *Raj* from the former while at other places he has simply summarised the facts in a pithy manner[10]. Except for a detailed treatment on the activities and territorial acquisitions by Maharaja Gulab Singh,[11] there is complete reliance on *Raj Darshani* without acknowledging and giving any credit to its author Ganesh Das Badehra. Notwithstanding all this, Ganesh Das Badehra's contribution to *Gulab Nama* is rather distinct. At present, it is difficult to say whether before his death any independent monograph entitled *Gulab Nama* was completed by him and passed on to the Jammu *Darbar,* which, as such, with minor alterations and personal references was adopted by Diwan Kirpa Ram. All this needs a further probe into this vital aspect of historiography of Jammu-Kashmir as well as Punjab.

Nuskha-i-Insha-i-Majma al Qawanin falls in the category of epistolary literature and, as such, after proper scrutiny and examination can be reckoned as one of the important sources for the reconstruction of the history of the period it deals with. In its preface, Ganesh Das Badehra states that ever since his school (*maktab*) days, he had wished to become a *munshi* and in order to accomplish his innate and fervent desire to compile one *Nuskha-i-Insha-i-Majma al Qawanin* based on originality of treatment so that it could serve as model writing (*imla*) for the studies of this younger brother, Ratan Lal and other seekers of knowledge.[12] It may be stated that by the time Ganesh Das Badehra wrote *Char Bagh-i-Punjab* (1849-55 A.D.), his younger brother Ratan Lal (the youngest amongst three brothers-Ganesh Das, Mahesh Das and Ratan Lal), was a grown up man who had acquired complete *marfat* (knowledge and insight in divine matters).[13] The latter was also known by the name of Ram Parkash *Saad param hans udasi.* Apart from the evidence available in *Nuskha-i-Insha-i-Majma al Qawanin,* the inclusion of his younger brother Ratan Lal in the family history, as recorded in *Char Bagh-i-Punjab,* confirms the authenticity and genuineness of the former manuscript. It is also significant to note that *Nuskha-Insha-i-Majma al Qawanin* under analysis bears two seals of Sahai Hira Nand, dated 1887.[14] It seems in the context that the date pertains to *Bikrami Samvat* which comes to around 1830 A.D., the period of Maharaja Ranjit Singh, the ruler of the Punjab. Sahai Hira Nand was in all probability some official or the custodian of the manuscript which apparently was compiled by Ganesh Das before 1830 A.D.

Nuskha-i-Insha-i-Majma al Qawanin is a brief treatise comprising in all 66 folios. It covers model letters, serving as an *imla,* to be written by a young school student to his parents, sister for various occasions, specimen official letters/orders viz. *ragam, nishans, parwanas* for zamindari/*chaudharie* functions and enjoyment of customary perquisites (*dastur*), bestowal of appointment for the posts of *amini* and *faujdari* of a *pargana* underlining the administrative and revenue functions, *dastkat* relating to the performance of duties by the tehsildar of a *pargana, karori* of a *chakla, faujdari* cum *diwani* appointments with jurisdiction over enumerated *mahals,* petitions (*ariaz*) and farmans dealing with the gift of land and jagir.[15] The manuscript also comprises copies of the *taliqachas* (inventories/ appendices) issued by the Durrani minister Kifayat Khan on 13th December, 1798 (5th *Rajab* 1213 A.H.) to the named local officials and zamindars relating to revenue matters and submission of *taujis* (revenue-registers) at the court.[16] A few *bai-namas* (sale-deeds), *chaknamas,* documents relating to *havelis* and land are also quoted.[17] Above all, in one of the statements, author also gives an account of his family's hereditary status as the *rais* with *qanungoi* jurisdictional shares in various *parganas.*[18]

Even though Ganesh Das Badehra's *Insha* compilation confines itself to the citation of the model official letters and copies of the official documents relating to a few particular regions of the West Punjab, namely *chakla* Gujrat (Chanhat Doab), Wazirabad, Sialkot and other *parganas* of Rachna Doab and *chakla* Hazara (Sindh-Sagar Doab), it is of great significance in so far as it sheds fresh light on the working of a few important aspects of the administration and land revenue system during the last quarter of the 18th century and early 19th century in these regions before their final incorporation to the Lahore *Darbar* by Maharaja Ranjit Singh in 1809 A.D. (1866 *Bikrami Samvat).* In this *Insha* compilation, there is not a single copy of a document which refers to the period of Maharaja Ranjit Singh. On the other hand, a couple of significant Durrani communications relate to Timur Shah's order (*raqm*), dated 21st January, 1779 (3 *Muharram,* 1193 A.H.) addressed to Chaudhari Ikhlas Khan and Wazir Kifayat Khan's order (*taliqa*), dated 13th December, 1798 (5 *Rajab,* 1213 A.H.) addressed to Wasakhi Mal and Bahadur Khan.[19] The Durrani Imperial authorities and many of the zamindars/*chaudharies* of particular localities addressed in these orders find equal mention later on in the local history of these *parganas/mahals* provided in *Char Bagh-i-Punjab.*[20] This further confirms the authenticity of these orders and the contents mentioned therein.

Even since Ahmad Shah Abdali had occupied Punjab and ceded it to the Afghan Empire, the latter claimed not only its sovereignty over it but also tried to establish its effective control for the realisation of the revenues, *peshkash, nazrana, malia* and *sair* etc. from the *riaya* through the chiefs (chiefs zamindars wherever prevelant), the landed intermediaries, i.e., zamindars, *chaudharies, qanungos* and *muqaddams,* etc.[21] It continued to realise *peshkash malia* intermittently from the hilly chiefs of the Punjab (*Kohistan-i-Punjab,* i.e., Jammu,

Chamba, Kangra and other hilly territories in the doabs of Chanhat and Sindh Sagar) by the end of the 18th century.[22] It equally established its rule over the *subahs* of Kashmir[23] and Multan[24] which were later on incorporated to the Lahore Darbar by Maharaja Ranjit Singh in the early 19th century. As regard the plain territories of the Punjab and the Sirhind territories of *Subah* Delhi (Malwa region), the position continued to fluctuate throughout the later half of the 18th century. The rise of the chiefs, i.e., the Sikh sardars, Muslim as well as Hindu zamindars in various regions led to the territorial fragmentation with more or less *de facto* rule over their respective jurisdictions. This equally accounts for the repeated Durrani campaigns till the end of the 18th century. It seems in the context that from around 1763 A.D., more especially after the death of Ahmad Shah Abdali in 1773 A.D., the Khalsa sardars as well as Muslim and Hindu zamindars chalked out their chiefships in the *subahs* of Punjab, Multan and Delhi. A few of the Sikh sardars even challenged the Durrani sovereignty over the hill chiefs so as to supplant their own overlordship for the realisation of *nazrana* and fixed tribute.[25] All the same, the position was not uniform throughout the territories over which the Durranis continued to claim suzerainty. It was of more assertive character in Multan and the West Punjab (doabs of Sindh-Sagar, Chanhat and Rachna along with a portion of Bari Doab around Lahore) being more amenable to immediate threats-campaigns from Kabul than East Punjab (especially Majha region of Bari Doab and Bet Jalandhar Doab). For want of the availability of *many* a contemporary revenue document, it is very difficult to determine the exact nature of the financial hold and the sovereignty claim that the Durranis continued to exercise in the last three decades of the 18th century over the Khalsa sardars, Muslim and Hindu chiefs of the various regions. All the same, the family archives of the Fatahabad-Kapurthala and the Patiala Chiefs (covering doabs of Bari, Bet Jalandhar in the Punjab and Malwa region of Sirhind, *Subah* Delhi) as well as the official communications emanating from Kabul in the reigns of Ahmed Shah Abdali, Timur Shah and Zaman Shah throw much light in this regard.[26] The farmans addressed to Sardar Jassa Singh Ahluwalia of Fatahabad confirm the latter's *qadim* (old) *maafi*-Jagirs and confer upon him the *Sardari* rights for the realization of *nazars* (*nazarat*-gifts in lieu of superior Zamindari rights) from many a jagirdar and Raja in the Bari and Bet Jalndhar doabs.[27] According to these farmans, some jagir and zamindari areas, i.e., Miranpur in *pargana,* Tihara across the River Sutlej are withdrawn from Sardar Jassa Singh in exchange for some jagirs in Bari Doab. The territories across the river Sutlej (in the South) stretching from *pargana* Tihara to Pak-pattan are included in the zamindari territorial jurisdiction of Raja Amar Singh Phul of Patiala. The above chiefs of Fatahabad, Patiala and Raja Abhay Chand Katoch (of Kangra) are enjoined to be obedient to the Durrani *Faujdar* at Sirhind.[28] This clearly shows that the Durranis continued to assert their sovereign power for the regulation of the zamindari territorial jurisdictions held by the chief zamindars (*Zamindaran-i-Umda,* sardars, rajas etc.). Apart from this, the family archives of the Patiala chiefs give an intensive insight into the zamindari and Jagir pattern, the assignment of Jagirs to the Durrani officers in lieu of their *tankhawah* (salary) and the revenues in the *pargana/mahals* of the Patiala Zamindari (Chieftainship) from the time of Raja Alah Singh onwards.[29] The nature and extent of claim by the Durrani Government of Kabul through its *faujdar* at Sirhind over the revenues of the Patiala Chiefship clearly brings out the sovereign character of the Durranis in the Malwa and Sirhind regions.

For an understanding of the nature of Durrani rule in the West Punjab, more of reliance has to be placed on the sporadic official Durrani communications.[30] *Akhbarat* (in Persian),[31] general statement contained in the chronicles of the 19th century and the *Insha* compilation entitled, *Nuskha-i-Insha-i-Majma al Qawanin* of Ganesh Das Badehra.

In *Char Bagh-i-Punjab,* Ganesh Das Badehra makes a categorical statement that out of his 27 years reign, Ahmad Shah Abdali ruled over Punjab for ten years.[32] Ganesh Das Badehra equally pays tribute to one of the administration in the Punjab, i.e., Shah Wali Wazir for his benevolent administration and comments that the *riaya* of the Punjab was indebted to the latter for his good treatment.[33] Timur Shah's campaign in 1788-89 A.D., (1845 *Bikrami Samvat*/1203 A.H.) remained confined to Multan when he ousted Diwan Singh Bhangi and installed Shiya Khan Sadawzari alias Suchi Khan Afghani as its subedar.[34] However, he did not carry any personal campaign against the Sikh or other chiefs in the Punjab. Ganesh Das Badehra comments that Timur Shah ruled for twenty years as a benevolent and noble King. Later on, Zaman Shah led a campaign in the Punjab in 1796 A.D. (1211 A.H.). Having ousted the Sikh chiefs who had hitherto been quite successful in their designs, he captured the seat of power at Lahore and realized *nazrana* and malia.[35] His son Prince Mahmud thrice caused turbulence in the Punjab. In 1795-96 A.D. (1210 A.H.), he created disturbance at

Hasan Abdal; in 1796-97 A.D. (1211 A.H.), he forcibly realised the dues *(mutalba)* and penalty from the city of Lahore; and in 1798-99 A.D. (1213 A.H.), he again forcibly captured and entered the city of Lahore.[36] The tenor in which Ganesh Das Badehra writes about the benevolent aspects of some of the administrators of Ahmad Shah Abdali and Timur Shah in the Punjab does suggest vital link with the *riaya* for administrative purposes and revenue matters. The hierarchical zamindari pattern and the establishment of the superior Sardari and Zamindari rights by many a chiefs, both Sikhs and Muslims, in the West Punjab does connote *de-facto* rule by the latter. But unlike East Punjab, for which categorical archival evidence is available, it is difficult to state the exact position of the landed intermediaries, the Muslim chiefs and the Sikh sardars as to their precise relationship with the Durrani Government for the payment of the revenues (*peshkash, malia, nazrana* etc.) to the latter during the last three decades of the 18th century. All the same, the fresh evidence in hand based on Ganesh Das Badehra's *Nuskha-i-Insha-i-Majma al Qawanin* does warrant a further probe in this regard.

In *Char Bagh-i-Punjab,* Ganesh Das Badehra has provided a detailed local, political and administrative history of *chakla* Gujrat since its inception.[37] Right from the late 16th century of the Mughal age, i.e., with effect from 1588-89 A.D. (997 A.H.) of Akbar's reign down to 1848 A.D., he has given a complete list of the administrators (*hukkam*) along with their respective tenures. For the 18th century administration in *chakla* Gujrat after the reign of Aurangzeb, he has covered the reigns of Bahadur Shah, Farrukh Saiyar, Mohammad Shah, the latter's son Ahmed Shah, Ahmad Shah Durrani, Sardar Gujar Singh, Sardar Sahib Singh, son of Sardar Gujar Singh before its annexation by Maharaja Ranjit Singh in 1809 A.D.[38] He states that Gujrat and other localities of Chanhat Doab were conquered by Sardar Charhat Singh and Sardar Gujar Singh Sandhu in 1763 A.D. and a few *parganas* were assigned in Jagir to some sardars.[39] Here, in this context, Sardar Gujar Singh and Sardar Sahib Singh are depicted as independent chiefs. Quite signigicantly, Badehra mentions a number of Hindu administrators (*hukkam*) of *chakla* Gujrat, which is as much true of the Mughal age as of the Durrani and the Sikh regimes. Apart from this, in comparison to the benevolent nature of Ahmad Shah Abdali's rule in the *qasbas* of Herat, Gujrat and Jalalpur, Badehra is highly critical of the 18th century Sikh rule which resulted in the desolation of the city (*Shahr*) of Gujrat.[40]

Earlier, in his *Insha* compilation, Ganesh Das Badehra had quoted an order (*raqm*) of Timur Shah, dated 21 January 1779 A.D. (3 *Muharram,* 1193 A.H.) and a copy of an order (*taliqa*), dated 13th January, 1798 (5th *Rajab,* 1213 A.H.-Zaman Shah's reign) addressed to the local zamindars/*chaudharies* relating to the administrative/ revenue matters and submission of the revenue ledgers (*taujis*).[41] This equally reveals direct communication between the Durrani government and the local landed intermediaries in *chakla* Gujrat and adjacent regions in Chanhat Doab. The copy of an order (*taliqa*), dated 13th January, 1798 A.D. pertaining to Zaman Shah's period corresponds to the years when the latter was in actual occupation of West Punjab. Though the Durranis continued to claim *de-jure* sovereignty over Punjab till the end of the 18th and opening years of the 19th century, in the absence of the archival sources, it is difficult to give a precise perception about the nature of control for the purposes of realisation of *peshkash*/revenue especially after the death of Ahmad Shah Abdali except for the period that the latter's successors or their subordinate commanders/administrators were in actual occupation of the regions in the West Punjab as known the chronicles and Persian *Akhbarat*. All the same, Ganesh Das Badehra's *Insha* compilation does give some direction in this regard.

Nuskha-i-Insha-i-Majma al Qawanin is equally significant for the information it provides regarding the personal family *qanungoi* jurisdiction of Ganesh Das Badehra[42] as well as the local machinery of revenue collection, especially in the doabs of Chanhat and Rachna. Even though the author, later on, gave a detailed account of his family history and the *qanungoi* territorial jurisdiction and their sub-divisions in the course of the centuries since the Lodhi and Mughal periods, in *Raj Darshani*[43] and *Char Bagh-i-Punjab,*[44] he is very precise on the actual position as it stood in the 18th century and early 19th century before the reign of Maharaja Ranjit Singh.

In one of the *wasiqas,* Ganesh Das Badehra (son of Shiv Dyal, son of Bhiwani Das), makes a precise statment that according to the ancient division, he held the *qanungoi* jurisdiction over complete *pargana* Sialkot (Rachna doab), one-third share in *pargana* Gujrat, one-half share in *pargana* Herat (previously one-tenth share) and complete *pargana* Shahjahanpur.[45] Apart from this, he held the status of a *rais* alongwith ancestral and hereditary land (here zamindari) in *qasba Khas* (i. e. Gujrat).[46] He further asserts that for the above position, i.e., *qanungoi* shares and status as *rais,* he had in his possession duly stamped *sanads* of the sultans and *hukams* (administrators) whereas some persons out of malice made their claims against it. He maintains that all those persons who belong to the categories of *ulema wa karam* (learned class), *qazat-i-azam* (chief *qazis*), *akbaran wa rusa* (chiefs), *chaudharies* and *qanungos* etc. of the territories (*mulk*) of Sialkot and Gujrat and know these facts should, in the name of God and in accordance with *dastur* (practice), accord their testimony to this statement so as to render it an authentic document to be produced before the higher authorities for reliance and rebuttal of false claimants.[47]

Taking the entire position in the round, it may be maintained that Ganesh Das Badehra had inter-doabs (Chanhat and Rachna) *qanungoi* jurisdiction over two complete *parganas* (Sialkot and Shahjahanpur) with one-half and one-third shares in the other two *parganas* (Herat and Gujrat respectively).[48] It is equally confirmed by *Raj Darshani* that for revenue administration, ever since the Mughal age, it was by no means incumbent to keep the territorial divisions of the two doabs completely independent of each other and that the territorial belt from Jammu-Sialkot (Rachna Doab) to Gujrat, Herat, Shahjahanpur, Bhimber, Khari and Kharyalai etc. (Chanhat-Doab) formed one administrative circle on a larger scale.[49]

Ganesh Das Badehra's *Insha* compilation also quotes model appointment letters and duties to be performed by the regional/local officers for the purposes of administration. For an appointment in the Rachna Doab, Sialkot alongwith three other *mahals* are put under the charge of a *faujdar* vested with *diwani* powers.[50] Similarly, at the *pargana* level, the combined *amini* and *faujdari* functions are vested with one person.[51] The office of the *Karori* is associated with the administration of the *chakla* (here comprising a few *parganas*).[52]

In the description given above, only a few significant aspects of the *Insha* compilation of Ganesh Das Badehra have been taken up for analysis. However, a close examination of *Nuskha-i-Insha i-Majma al Qawanin* reveals striking elements of continuity in the local revenue administration from the Mughal age to the Durrani phase as well as that of the Sikh (Khalsa) sardars and Muslim and Hindu zamindars who assumed the role of chiefs, even though on a fragmented scale, in the West Punjab before the establishment of the Kingdom by Maharaja Ranjit Singh.

References

1. *Nuskha-i-Insha-i-Majma al Qawanin* alias *Munshiat-i-Ganesh Das,* Manuscript (Ms), No. 358, Research and Publication Deparment, Government of Jammu and Kashmir, Srinagar (henceforth R & P Deptt., J & K, Srinagar).
2. *Raj Darshani almashhur Tawarikh-i-Jammu,* British Museum, 1634 (Photostat), R & P Deptt., J & K, Srinagar, fols. 4a; 313a. A copy of the same title available at J & K State Pratap Museum, Srinagar, is rather incomplete.
3. Ms. Sikh History Research Department, Khalsa College, Amritsar (henceforth SHR, Amritsar), also vide reference no. 4, p. XI.
4. *Char Bagh-i-Punjab* by Ganesh Das Wadehra (Persian text), ed. Kirpal Singh, Revised, Dewan Singh, Sikh History Research Department, Khalsa College, Amritsar, 1965, p. 2; Also Preface, pp. III-IV; Introductory Notes, pp. VI-X; For analysis, also see J. S. Grewal, *Ganesh Das's Char Bagh-i-Punjab, Miscellaneous Articles,* 1974, Article X, pp. 135-45. Also J. S. Grewal & Indu Banga, *Early Nineteenth Century Punjab* (From Ganesh Das's *Char Bagh-i-Punjab.* Translated and Edited), Amritsar, 1975, especially Introduction, pp. 13-33.

   In the present paper, only the above mentioned Persian text has been referred to.
5. *Ibid.,* reference no. (henceforth no.) 2, fols. 261a-313a.
6. *Ibid.,* fol. 313a.
7. Kirpa Ram, Diwan, *Gulab Nama,* compiled in 1865 A.D./1.22 Bikrami *Samvat* and published in 1876 A.D./1933 *Bikarmi Samvat,* Ranbir Printing Press, Jammu, pp. 8-12.
8. *Ibid.,* pp. 54-55.
9. *Ibid.,* pp. 76, 115, 135, 362, 365, 367-68.
10. Compare the passages in *Raj Darshani* with *Gulab Nama.* For example, fols. 95a-104a, 107a, 162a-163a, 110a-111a, 113b, 114a, 118b, 158b-159a, 221a-222a, 216b, 234b-285a, 236a, 288a-299b of *Raj Darshani* verses, pp. 60, 61-62, 73-78, 80, 73, 78-79, 82, 105-107 of *Gulab Nama* respectively. Also see comments by Sahibzada Hassan Shah in English Introduction to Pir Ghulsam Hasan Khuihami's *Tarikh-i-Hasan,* I, Srinagar, 1954, p. 17.
11. *Op. cit.,* No. 7, pp. 105-380.
12. *Op. cit.,* No. 1, fol. 1b.
13. *Op. cit.,* No. 4, p. 230.
14. *Op. cit.,* No. 1, fols. 62a, 66b.
15. *Ibid.,* fol. 4b-6a, 18b.
16. *Ibid.,* fol. 5a.

17. *Ibid.,* fols. 4b, 34a-35a.

18. *Ibid.,* fol. 37b.

19. *Ibid.,* fols. 4b-5a.

20. *Op. cit.,* No. 4, pp. 103, 171, 176, 247.

21. *Akhbarat-i-Mutfarka Darbar-i-Maullah Waghaira ba-ahad Alamgir Saniwa Shah Alam Ali Ghauhar, 1169 TA 1213 Hijri* (1756-1798 A.D.) SHR, Amritsar, no. 521. This is compilation of the *Akhbar Darbar-i-Maullah,* i.e. News Letters sent to the Mughal Court as well as other News Letters (*Akhbars*) received from important cities viz. Kabul, Lahore, Multan, Sialkot and other places relating to the period 1756 A.D. to 1798 A.D. For details, 20 *Muharram* 1177 A.H./31st July, 1763 A.D., no. 18/129, fol. 55b; 3 *Rabi* II, 1177 A.H./11th October 1763 A.D. No/18/124, fols. 59bb-60a; 29 *Shaban* 1177 A.H./3rd March, 1764; no. 18/11, fol. 64a; 28 *Zulhijja* 1177 A.H./28th June, 1764 A.D., 18/104, fols. 67b-68a; 17 Ramazan 1177 A.H./20th March, 1764 A.D., no. 18/87, fol. 75a; 17 *Ramazan* 1178 A.H./10th March, 1765 A.D., no. 18/88, fol. 75b; *Shawwal* 1182 A.H./ February-March, 1769, no. 20/927, fols 96b; 20 *Zulqada* 1182 A.H./28th March, 1769 A.D., no. 20/945, fols. 97a-97b. Also *Persian Records of Maratha History* I : Delhi Affairs (1761-1788) News Letters, Translated into English by Jadunath Sarkar, Bombay, 1953, pp. 10, 11, 16, 23; Tahmas Khan Miskin, *Tazkira-i-Tahmas Miskin,* a rotograph of the British Museum Ms. listed as *Tahmasap Nama,* M/1003, SHR, Amritsar (henceforth Miskin), fols. 21b-24b, 26a, 28b-29a, 39b-40a, 45a, 51b-52a, 58b-60a; *Tarikh-i-Ahmed* (1748-1754), Ms. Br. Museum, published 1266 A.H./1849 A.D., pp. 8-17. The author (annonymous) accompanied Ahmad Shah Durrani and has given an eye-witnessed account; *Tarikh-i-Hasan,* I, *op. cit.,* 10, pp. 641-642) quotes a tradition inherited from Munshi Abdul Karim to the effect that Sabir Shah named *Faqir-i-Diwana* was the author of *Tarikh-i-Ahmad* and belonged to Lahore. He was later on got executed by Shah Nawaz Khan, s/o Zakariya Khan, the *Subadar* of Lahore; Also, *op. cit.,* no. 4, pp. 92, 95-96.

22. For details, B.R. Grover, "Relationship between the Sovereign State (the Mughal and Afghans) and the Punjab Hill Chiefs during the 17th and 18th Centuries-A Case Study of Chamba Chieftainship based on Bhuri Singh Museum, Chamba-Documents," *Punjab History Conference,* XVII Session, Patiala, 1982, pp. 94-102; also *Akhbarat, op. cit.,* 21, dated 28 *Zulhijja* 1177 A.H./28th June 1764 A.D., no. 108/104, fol. 68b; 21 *Rabi* I, 1183 A.H./25July, 1769 A.D., no. 20/949; fol. 99a; Ghulam Ali Azad Bilgrami (1762-63), *Khazana-i-Amira,* Cawnpur, 1871, p. 100; *Persian Records of Maratha History,* I, *op. cit.,* No. 21, p. 10.

23. *Khazana-i-Amira, op. cit.,* no. 22, p. 114; Saiyadullah Shah Abadi, *Bagh-i-Sulaiman,* Ms. No. 51, R & P Deptt., J & K, Srinagar, fols. 4b-6b, 235a-247b; Bir Bal Kachru, *Majmauah-i-Twarikh (Tarikh-i-Kashmir),* Ms. no.

14, R & P Deptt. J & K, Srinagar, fols. 194b-202a, 206a-233a; *op. cit.*, no. 4, pp. 94, 100-101.

24. Miskin, *op. cit.*, 21, fols., 25a, 30a, 31b; *Akhbarat, op. cit.*, No. 21, no. 20/944, fol. 97a, dated 20 *Zulqada,* 1182 A.H./20th March, 1769 A.D., *op. cit.*, no. 4, pp. 92, 95-96.

25. *Op. cit.*, no. 22.

26. See nos. 27-29.

27. I am extremely obliged to Brigadier (Retd.) Sukhjit Singh, the Maharaja of Kapurthala for having given me an access to consult his family archives and permitted me to take the photo copies of the *farmans*. Some copies of the same (not very accurate) are also available at the Punjab State Archives, Patiala (henceforth PSA, Patiala), vide File No. 696, *Basta* no. 18. For details, Azizuddin alias Alamgir Sani, son of Muzaiddin Jahandar Shah Badshah Delhi's *farman*, dated 7 *Ramazan* 1171 A.H./4th R.Y./15th May, 1758 A.D. This was equally confirmed by the Durranis. Also Ahmad Shah Badshah *farman*, dated 23 *Ramazan* 1174 A.H./28 April, 1761 A.D.

28. *Ibid.*, Also Durrani *farman*, dated 11 *Rajab* 1192 A.H./5th August 1778 A.D.; also PSA, Patiala, File no. 695, *Basta* no. 18, pp. 11-12; Durrani *farman*, dated 20 *Shawwal* 1195 A.H./9th October, 1781 A.D.; PSA, Patiala, File no. 696, *Basta* no. 18, pp. 13-14. The contents of the above mentioned *farmans* are equally confirmed by the earlier Durrani *farman* addressed to Maharaja Amar Singh of Patiala vide *farman*, dated 11 *Rajab* 1192 A.H./ 5th August, 1778, A. 6 H., PSA, Patiala.

29. PSA, Patiala, Foreign Ministry Cases no. 2A 147 a-g, of 1174 A.H., copies of Orders (*taliqas/taliqachas*), from *Wazir-i-Mumalik* to Mirza Mohammad Naqi, dated 22 *Shaban* 1174 A.H./29th March, 1761 A.D.; from *Wazir-i-Mumalik* to Faiz Talab Khan Durrani, *Subadar* and *Sahib-i-Ikhtayar maliat-i-Chakla Sirhind,* dated 22 *Shaban* 1174 A.H./29th March, 1761 A.D.; from *Wazir-i-Mumalik* to Mirza Mohammad Naqi, dated 7 *Shaban* 4th Regnal Year (1176 A.H.)/12 February, 1763 A.D.; *Sanad* issued by Mohammad Ramazan, dated 2 *Safar* 5th R.Y. (1178 A.H.)/1st August, 1764 A.H. Receipt issued by Hussain Ali Khan and Musa Khan, dated 14 *Muharram* 6th R.Y. (1179 A.H.)/3rd July, 1765 A.D. regarding the revenues (*mamalat* to be paid to Alah Singh; *Sanad,* dated 17 *Safar* 5th R.Y. (1178 A.H./16th August, 1764 A.D. issued by Mohammad Ramazan to Raja Alah Singh, Detailed Statement of the revenues (*hisab-i-mumalat*) payable to Raja Alah Singh; 3A/H, Case No. 405 of 1192 A.H., a copy of communication (*murasla*) from Timur Shah Badshah to Chuhar Singh Phul, dated 11 *Rajab* 1192 A.H./5th Auguest 1178 A.D.; A.H. 5, copies of 8 letters (Persian) of Raja Alah Singh and Maharaja Amar Singh addressed to the Durranis (1765-1766 A.D.); *Halat-i-Riyasat-i-Patiala,* M/807, fols. 19a-92a.

30. *Calendar of Persian Correspondence,* 11 Vols. (1759-95 A.D.), Vols. I to VIII, Calcutta, 1911-1925, Vols. I to VIII, Calcutta, 1911-1925, Vols. IX to XI, New Delhi, 1949, 1969, National Archives of India, New Delhi. Specially, Vol II (1767-9), February 4, 1767, pp. 9-12; February 17, 1767, pp. 26-27; March 1, 1767, p. 39; April 5, 1767, p. 81; April 8, 1767, p. 84; April 12, 1767, pp. 86-87; April 15, 1767, pp. 89-90; Vol III (1770-72), March 29, 1771, p. 183; Vol V. (1776-80), April 24, 1780); p. 438; Original Receipts Foreign Dept., Persian Branch, covering the period 1795 to 1803 A.D., National Archives of India, New Delhi.
31. *Ibid.,* also P. Saran, *Persian Documents,* Part I, Text, Asia Publishing House, Bombay, 1966.
32. *Op. cit.,* no. 4, p. 101. However, for the administration of *chakla* Gujrat, pp. 202-203, the same source puts the period of Ahmad Shah Abdali's rule at 11 years and 6 months and even mentions the tenure of each of the 12 administrators of the *chakla.* The latter version seems to be more accurate.
33. *Ibid.*, pp. 101, 102.
34. *Ibid.*, p. 102.
35. *Ibid.*, p. 103.
36. *Ibid.*
37. *Ibid.*, pp. 200-211.
38. *Ibid.*, pp. 200-103.
39. *Ibid.*, pp. 129-133.
40. *Ibid.*, p. 206.
41. *Op. cit.,* No. 1, fols. 4b-5a.
42. *Ibid.*, fol. 37b.
43. *Op. cit.,* No. 2, fols. 182b-184a.
44. *Op. cit.,* No. 4, pp. 1, 81, 170, 175-176, 228-232, 247.
45. *Op. cit.,* No. 1, fols. 37b-38a.
46. *Ibid.*
47. *Ibid.*
48. *Ibid.*
49. *Op. cit.,* No. 2, fols. 220b-222b; *Op. cit.,* no. 7, pp. 79-80.
50. *Op. cit.,* No. 1, fol. 18b.
51. *Ibid.*, fol. 5b.
52. *Ibid.*, fol. 6b.

Chapter 11

Perspectives on Maharaja Ranjit Singh's Administration in Kashmir (1818-1839)*

Based on a Critical Analysis of Contemporary and Near Contemporary Sources

A

After the transfer of Kashmir to Maharaja Gulab Singh (1846) and more so with the annexation of the Punjab by the English East India Company in 1849, number of works of varying nature were produced by the English administrator-scholars as well as Indian historians on multi-facet aspects of the history of the *Khalsa* kingdom under Maharaja Ranjit Singh and his successors. Even though a few important works on Kashmir were written during the *Khalsa* regime itself, many works were published during the Dogra period by the English as well as Indian scholars-both Kashmiri and non-Kashmiri. However, with the changing methodology of the historical discipline as well as fresh approach based on the contemporary source material, numerous works on different aspects of the society and the Sikh polity, more so relating to the phase of Maharaja Ranjit Singh, have been produced during the last few decades. Notwithstanding all this, based on the analysis of the contemporary sources of multifarious nature, it is feasible to throw fresh light on the concept and nature of Maharaja Ranjit Singh's administration in Kashmir.

B

Kashmir has had a strong tradition of historical writing since early times. Its historiography has also been marked by distinct features by underlining its geographical aspects, the mythical origin and ethnic

---

* ~~*Papers presented at pending*~~

settlements in the Valley, the course of political development as well as cultural evolution in the course of the centuries. It is equally imbued with a sense of pride and regional patriotism. All the same, Kalhana in *Rajtarangini* (1150 AD) underscores the cultural, economic and, at times, even political ties with the other territories of India. He highlights the achievements of Lalitaditya (8th century) who claimed suzerainity over Tibet, North-Western portions of India as well as Northern India comprising Kanauj, Malwa, Gujarat and Sindh. Notwithstanding many a lacuna, Jonaraja, Srivara, Prajyabhatta and Suka Pandit carried on the tradition of *Rajtarangini* upto 1596 AD more or less on the same pattern. However, even before the establishment of the Mughal rule in Kashmir (1586 AD), historiography in Persian was equally developed. The historical works emphasise the spread of Islam in Kashmir during the course of the 14th century, cultural and religious ties with Central Asia, Persia as well as the territories of West Punjab and North Western regions of India. In the realm of polity, apart from internal aspects of Kashmir, Sayyid Ali, the chronicler of *Ratikh-i-Kashmir* (*Tarikh-i-Kashmir*) attributes to Sultan Shihab-ud-Din (1335-1373 AD) the subjugation of many a region of North India and the Punjab from the river Sutlej in the East to Ohind in the North-West. Many of these events, though not confirmed by the contemporary historical works of the Delhi Sultanate, are narrated with a sense of pride and local patriotism. In the socio-political spheres, like the Delhi Sultanate historiography, the religious tenor is rather significant whereby the Hindu-Muslim as well as the Shia-Sunni problems are emphasised. Thereafter, excepting the Mughal historiography to a considerable extent, the same traditions and events continue to be quoted in a similar manner by the chroniclers in Kashmir right till the early 20th century. To this was added a new factor whereby after the Mughal occupation of Kashmir (1586), the concept of the so-called 'alien' rule over Kashmir becomes more marked. With very few exceptions, the Kashmiri Persian chroniclers consider the Mughals, the Afghans, the Sikhs and the Dogras merely as conquerors and non-Kashmiri rulers, who ruled in an arbitrary manner fraught with social inhibitions and economic exploitation of the people of Kashmir.

In line with the above mentioned trends of historiography, Pir Ghulam Hasan Khuihami, the author of *Tarikh-i-Hasan* while narrating the establishment of the Sikh rule *(hakumat-Singhan)* in Kashmir and the appointment of Diwan Moti Ram as its first Governor in 1234 A.H./1819 A.D., comments, "...The Hindu community, after a lapse of 494 Solar years, emerged from the whirlpool of degradation and reached the shore of their cherished goal. The *Ahl-Islam* (Muslims) were confronted with days of misfortune and adversity, they having fallen from the heights of glory to the lowest ebb of distress and misfortune. Such is the way of the rough and oppressive world. Sometimes one's back is in the Saddle and sometimes the Saddle is on one's back."

Earlier, Mulla Hamid Shahabadi- a contemporary of Maharaja Ranjit Singh had written in a satirical manner with a similar bias on the state of affairs and administration in Kashmir during the Sikh rule. He writes :

کور سنگه حاکم و رنجیت چوں باشد سلطان
شکوه از جور مکن عالم کوڑا کوریست

When the *hakim* is *Kur* Singh (a man morally blind) and when the *Sultan* is Ranjit Singh (-Ranjit Singh, the one eyed), it is useless for one to decry tyranny and oppression, as it is a state of total dreariness."

He further comments :

بود ورد زبان اہل خراج
درم کا راج ملک کا تاراج

It was constantly on the lips of *ahl-i-kharaj* (here tax payers) that the *dhiram* (money) reigned and the country stood ravaged."

In another work dealing with the Anglo-Afghan war (wherein Ranjit Singh sided with the English in favour of Shah Shuja), he writes in a chauvinistic tone against the Sikh rulers.

ز کشمیر سردی نیامد پدید
بجز عارف جنگجو حمید
کہ او نیز تنہا نمودہ است جنگ
بصد کس ز سکہاں بچوب و سنگ

No bold person has emerged in Kashmir save, of course, Hamid, the wise and the war-like who alone has waged a war against hundreds of Sikhs and that too with sticks and stones."

In fact, the compostion of Hamid's *Akbar Nama* is guided by political motivation aimed against Ranjit Singh's rule in Kashmir and, as such, its study was banned under the Dogra rule. Notwithstanding the religious over-tones and the unscientific character in many a such historical writing, it has influenced even the modern scholarship.

C

Maharaja Ranjit Singh's conquest of Kashmir (April-July, 1819) was actuated by both political and economic considerations. From the political angle, it was an essential step for the security and preservation of the kingdom in the Punjab which he had carved from the Indian territories having formed a part of the Afghan Empire since the mid-18th century. There is no denying the fact that the political disturbances and civil wars within Afghanistan left the field clear to Ranjit Singh and helped him considerably in the establishment of his kingdom. Maharaja Ranjit Singh realised the fact that unless he expelled the Afghans root and branch from the remaining Indian possessions, his kingdom would never be safe. As necessary steps, the Afghans must be expelled from east of the Indus and thereafter with any favourable opportunity at hand, he would push his north-western frontier even beyond the Indus so as to obviate any recurrence of the Afghan incurssions which would jeopardise his kingdom. As such, finding opportune times, he annexed the Afghan Multan territories and beyond Indus the North-Western region with Peshwar as headquarters in 1818 AD. But Kashmir, the last Afghan strong hold, still loomed large before him.

Kashmir also offered considerable economic advantages. It was rich in production and resources. Notwithstanding difficult terraineous mountain routes, it was well connected not only with the Punjab but also in the North with Ladakh, Tibet, Tibet-China and other Central Asian regions. The commercial gains would be an assest to the economic stability of the Lahore *Darbar.* Saffron, Shawls, wool and, to some extent, even silk enjoyed both Indian and international markets. The forest produce, especially the medicinal herbs and timber were well in demand covering both Punjab and Sindh. The passage from Kashmir to Ladhakh and the feasibility of the latter's occupation would afford the mineral exploitation of iron which could be used for armaments and military establishment of the State.

Earlier, Maharaja Ranjit Singh had successfully suppressed the Sikh and Muslim Chief in the *Rachna. Chanhat* and *Sind-Sagar Doabs* and has also subjugated the hill Rajas of Jammu, Rajauri, Bhimker Kari Kariyali, Kotali and the *marzbans* of the Khewara (between Jhelum and Indus) who owed allegience to the Durrani suzerainity and formed the mountaineous belt around Kashmir. This was a necessary preliminary action before advancing further to Kashmir. However, Poonch still remained outside his territorial jurisdiction.

Maharaja Ranjit Singh's first campaign against Kashmir (1812 A.D.) was of a limited character to help Wazir Fatch Khan of Kabul in suppressing Ata Muhammad, the recalcitrant *nazim* of Kashmir as well as to liberate Shah Shuja-the Kabul King in exile from imprisonment at Shergarh. While he got nothing of the promised amount of Rupees nine lakhs and half, the share in the booty from Wazir Fateh khan, he picketed the precious diamond *Koh-i-Noor* for having liberated-Shah Shuja. The second expedition against Kashmir (1814 A.D.) proved abortive as Ranjit Singh personally remained upto Poonch and Tosa-Maidan pass. His further advance was rendered impossible by the suffering of his troops on account of rainy season, dampness and cold as well as the hostility on the part of Ruh-Ullah Khan, the Raja of Poonch secretly aided by the Raja of Rajauri and the strong hold of the Afghans at Tosa-Maidan.

His second wing under the command of Ram Dyal, son of Diwan Mohkam Chand, had to withdraw from the valley after a mere exchange of gifts with Azim Khan-the then *nazim* of Kashmir. With the third successful operation (April-July, 1819 A.D.), Kashmir was annexed to the *Khalsa* kingdom. The victorious entry of the army of the Singhs (*Singhan*) was connoted by the Chronogram.

بولو واہ گرو.جی کا خالصہ
بولو واہ گرو.جی کی فتح

Which comes to 1876 *Bikrami Samvat* /1819 AD.

By this time, Maharaja Ranjit Singh had completely ousted the Afghan power from its Indian strongholds. Even though much water flowed down the Indus before Ranjit Singh consolidated his position in the Peshawar region in 1838, Capt. Burns surmised that the power of the Sikhs and their supremacy depended on the existence of one man (i. e. Ranjit Singh) and that on the latter's death, the Afghans would seek to regain the possession of which they had been deprived east of the Indus. This clearly brings out the significance of the Afghan factor in Ranjit Singh's polity for the security and preservation of the *Khalsa* kingdom of which he was the founder.

D

The contemporary sources of Maharaja Ranjit Singh's reign in Kashmir, though not many, are of varying nature written with particular ends in view. For the administration in Kashmir, primary importance may be attached to the *Khalsa Darbar* Records which, barring a few years, cover the entire period of Ranjit Singh and even beyond till Bikrami Samvat 1902/1841 AD. These records pertain to revenues realised from Kashmir regarding different categories viz. *nazrana, maliat, rasum* (customary cesses) on , *malia, Sair-i-dagh Shawl. Ijara-i-dagh* Shawl, *Muwajib Qilajat, Zakhirajat* and, at times, total income of the *subah*. For some years, *tahvil* and *jama-kharch* are also mentioned.

The private Bhandari Collection, covering correspondence of multifarious nature, throws considerable light on the conquest of Kashmir and some aspects of the working of its administration. Apart from this, there are original *Sanads* issued by the Lahore *Darbar* to the Dogra family in respect of *Jagir* grants not only in the Jammu territories but also in the regions which at that time constituted part of *Subah* Kashmir. *Akhbar Ludhiana* (from 1834 AD onwards) throw light on the subject to some extent. Above all, the available archaeological and numismatic evidence as well as the works of art and craft, especially the *pashmina* shawls of different qualities still preserved at Sri Pratap Singh State Muesum, Srinagar, further spell out a few aspects of the social life of the times.

Dasturul-aml-i-Kashmir, compiled by Munshi Mir Ahmad, son of Nur Mohammad Jalalabadi in 1835 A.D., during the *nazamat* of Colonel Mehan Singh (1834-41 A.D.), is the most unique and one of the rarest manuscripts available in any of the archival repositories of India. After the severe famine in Kashmir (1832-33 A.D.),Col. Mehan Singh as *nazim* was enjoined upon to undertake measures for the amelioration of the condition of the people and their rehabitilation. After the accomplishment of this task to a considerable extent and with a view to stablise the economy of Kashmir, he got compiled the

Dasturulaml (Manual of Regulations) with the assistance of his *sahibkar* (Collector of Revenues) Pandit Ganesh and the Chief Qazi, Qazi Mohammad Afzal as well as the experts and experienced officers of the Departments. It covers in a most comprehensive manner the geography and topography of different regions of Kashmir, the routes to different directions, detailed aspects of the rural and urban economy, description of the administrative units along with their villages, the agrarian system, the classification of land, the land revenue alongwith various cesses (both in kind and cash), the crafts and industries and the taxes imposed upon them, horticulture, the *mahsul* realised on items of import and export, the officials and the mode of their remunerations, weights and measures, different kinds of *Jagir* and *dharamarth* grants, and above all, trade and commerce. In a way, the *Dasturumal* does not merely describe the administrative pattern under Col. Mehan Singh but codifies the customary practices, rules and regulations prevalent in Kashmir since the Mughal age. A comparison of this Dasturulaml with the earlier *Dasturulaml* entitled *Gulshan Dastur,* written during the Mughal age in 1132 A.H/1721-22 A.D., brings out striking elements of continuity in many an aspect of the administration.

Birbal Kachru, having been associated as an official in the Shawl Department under Col. Mehan Singh, compiled *Majmaut Tawarikh* (alias *Khulasatul-Tawarikh*) having taken nearly eleven years for its completion in 1262 AH/1846 AD. Well-versed with the connotation of the technical terminology, he has lucidly narrated the agrarian aspects of administration under the Mughals, Afghans and the Khalsa regime in Kashmir. He has also provided a detailed account of the arts and crafts, especially the shawl industry with which he was intimately connected. He has been quite analytical about the growth of this industry during the *Khalsa* rule-a rare feature not easibly traceable in the chroniclers of the later Dogra phase. He has also offered his own assessment about Maharaja Ranjit Singh's administration in Kashmir. He has equally emphasised the commercial intercourse with Central Asia for the period. A student of economic history has to be fully equipped with the connotation of the technical terminologies relating to different aspects of topography and administration before proper evaluation of the facts involved.

Maulvi Mohammad Nizamamud-Din's *Waqiat-i-Nizamiya* (1824 AD)-a supplement to Mohammad Azam'z *Waqiat-i-Kashmir* "(written in 1747 AD)" mostly covers the political and religious aspects of Kashmir.

As already observed, Mulla Hamid Shahabadi's (a contemporary of the *Khalsa* period) works were too politically motivated and marked by religious obsession and chauvinism so as to present any balanced portrayal of the aspects covered. Diwan Mehdi Mirza's *Dewan-i-Mujrim,* a poetical work-runs on similar lines and is highly critical of the *khalsa* regime in Kashmir. He makes no exception of the *subadari* tenure of Col. Mehan Singh, who is otherwise highly spoken of by practically all the chroniclers for his benevolent administration.

Baha ud-Din Khwushnawis's *Labbul Tawarikh,* though written a little later than Ranjit Singh's period during the *Khalsa* phase (1262 AH/1846 A.D.), and at times mere reproduction from Birbal Kachru's *Majmaut Tawarikh,* has dealt in a critical manner about some of the socio-economic aspects, more especially the Shia-Sunni problems and the sectarian riots during Ranjit Singh's period.

Of the non-Kashmiri sources, Diwan Amar Nath Kashmiri Dehlvi's *Zafarnama-i-Ranjit Singh* (1836-7) is significant as the author had official information of the events gathered from the Lahore Darbar. Sohan Lal Suri's *Umdat--ut-Tawarikh* throws considerable fresh light on the conquest and administration of Kashmir under Ranjit Singh. As the author was a diarist at the Lahore *Darbar,* he had an easy access to the official records of the period. Ganeshi Lal's *Kashmir Nama,* also known as *Siyasat-i-Kashmir* (1846), also affords considerable insight into the administrative and economic aspects of Kashmir Ghulam Muhayy-ud-Din, alias Bute Shah's *Tawarikh-i-Punjab* (1848 A.D.), is extremely useful for many an event connected with Kashmir. Mufti Ali-ud-Din, the author of *Ibratnama wa Umdat-ul-Tawarikh* (1854 A.D.), considers his own work far superior to those of the above mentioned accounts of Diwan Amar Nath Kashmiri Dehlvi, Sohan Lal Suri and Bute Shah. He considers that Sohan Lal Suri being a co-religionist (of Ranjit Singh) often showed partiality and Diwan Amar Nath's work has merely a brief description of events whereas Bute Shah's work was rather obscure due to style of writing with long sentences undermining the understanding of the same. Apart from narrating inter connected events with the Punjab, Mufti Ali-ud-Din has given a separate account of Kashmir. Both in *Raj Darshani* (1847 A.D.), popularly known as *Tawarikh-i-Jammu* and *Char-Bagh-i Punjab* (1849-55 A.D.), Ganesh Das Badehra (a Zamindar cum *rais* and hereditary *qanungo* of numerous parganas in the *Rachnao* and *Chanhat Doabs* under the Lahore *Darbar*) has given adequate treatment of the Jammu-Kashmir links in historical perspective. Being a revenue official, he has appreciably covered the ethnic settlements and the territorial conflicts amongst the chieftains in the upper and the lower ranges of the mountaineous regions from Jammu to Muzaffarabad-belt around Kashmir valley. He is equally clear about the administrative circles in these regions during the 18th and 19th centuries until the establishment of the Dogra rule in Jammu and Kashmir.

The contemporary English sources for Kashmir under Maharaja Ranjit Singh, comprising the Foreign/Political Consultation Files, Foreign/Political Procedings Volumes, Foreign/Secret Consultation Files, though extremely useful and informative in many a respect, are by no means complete. Barring a few for the earlier phase, they mostly cover the thirtees of the 19th century for Ranjit Singh's period. The recorded correspondence and the Minutes were based upon the intelligence reports gathered by the English officers and other commissioned for the job. At this phase, the English East India Company was basically interested in gathering information on the political situation in the territories of the Sikh kingdom and even its other bordering states and, above all, in the avenues for the furtherance of the English trade in Punjab, Sindh, Afghanistan, Kashmir, Tibet and Central Asia. The English had also a vested commercial interest to manufacture its own shawls from the *pasham* imported from Tibet, China and other regions of Central Asia, and thereby to supplant the Kashmiri shawls in the Indian markets and abroad. Moreover, the intelligence received about the state of affairs in Kashmir was piece-meal and, at times, unauthentic. However, later on, with the eatablishment of the Dogra rule in Kashmir, the information gathered is more document oriented and reliable.

The travelogues of the period, especially of William Moorcraft, Victor Jacquemont, Godfrey Thomas Vigne, Rev. Joseph Wolff, and Baron Charles Hugel, who visited Kashmir in 1819-25, 1831, 1832 and 1835 respectively, provide detailed information on the fauna and flora, topography, routes, various aspects of the Kashmiri society covering customs and manners, art and architecture, crafts and cottage industry, especially the production of wool shawls, rural and urban economy, agrarian position and trade and commerce. Though each one of the travellers was specialist in one branch of science or another and had a particular mission for visit to Kashmir, it is really suprising that he proposed to understand all the aspects of the socio-economic structure and comments upon them in his own convincing manner. William Moor Craft was a British surgeon and was entrusted by the

English East India Company to explore the possibility of importing the breed of Turkistan's horses for domestication in India and more especially for establishing commercial intercourse with the Trans Himalayan regions. Jacquemont, a French naturalist, had been deputed by the Museum of National History, Paris, to investigate and collect information on the natural aspects of India with a view to promote the progress of science. Joseph Wolff was a clergyman and his purpose was the spread of evangilism in Kashmir. G.T. Vigne was deputed by the English East India Company for the study of minerology and botanical aspects and to analyse the commercial prospects in the territories adjoining the mountain course of Indus and the Himalayas North of the Punjab. Baron Charles Hugel, a German national, was deputed to gather information on the greatness and powers of the English East India Company. William Moor Croft came to Kashmir practically at the fag end of the Afghan rule and the *Khalsa* administration was still in the formative stage. Nor such information is supplied by Joseph Wolff. As a matter of fact, the European travellers made observations according to their personal tastes and predelictions and sometimes in contradiction with each other. In essence, they have left a very dismal picture of socio-economic life of the people governed by the tyrannical Sikh regime. Though the importance of the travelogues is undeniable, these sources cannot be accepted at their face value. Apart from their specialised discipline for gathering information on the physical features and natural products of Kashmir, they made general observations on superficial study and for historical portion based on mere hearsay. Like the 17th century European travellers in India, with their pre-conceived notions, they failed to understand the Indian concept fo proprietary rights in land, the institutional character of the *jagirdari* system of the administration and the agrarian pattern governing the rural society. However, before the acceptance or rejection of their testimony, their observations and the official intelligence reports of the English officers referred to above, need critical examination by cross checking with the other indigenous sources, both official and non-official.

E

For nearly a decade before Maharaja Ranjit Singh took over, Kashmir had been marked by political disturbances which were by no means conducive to the normal economic life. Even though Ranjit Singh gave political stability, unfortunately, his regime was visited by natural calamities which resulted in considerable loss to life and property. The spread of Cholera (1827 A.D.), the earthquake (1828 A.D.), followed after a few years by severe famine (1832-33 A.D.), completely shook the socio-economic order of the Kashmiri society. The calamities wipped off nearly two third to three fourth of the population in the valley and brought about an economic crisis. The shortage of manpower affected the agrarian economy as well as the *shawl* and small scale cottage industries which had been the main stay of the society. It led to not only the dwindling of the state revenues but to the diacotomy of administrative pressure for maximising the agricultural and industrial production for stabilising the economy in the abnormal circumstances. This equally accounts for anxiety on the part of the Lahore *Darbar* and frequent change in the *nazamat* (governship) of Kashmir prior to the posting of Col. Mehan Singh. The *nazims* Diwan Kirpa Ram, Bhamman Singh Ardali and Kanwar Sher Singh were virtually dismissed on grounds of administrative inefficiency. Numberous other officials were removed either due to misappropriation or malpractice. Due to difficult means of communication with the interlocked valley of Kashmir, Maharaja Ranjit Singh kept vigilance over the administration and issued instructions to the effect that if the Chief *Sardars* (*nazims* etc.) being posted to Kashmir worked for the welfare and habitation of the people to their satisfaction, would be duly rewarded with fresh assignments as he considered the mission of welfare of the *riaya* as a trust bestowed on him by the Almighty. When in 1833-the famine year Jamadar Khushal Singh brought huge sum of money from Kashmir, Ranjit Singh was simply shocked and displeased. He immediately sent thousands of wheat loaded mules to Kashmir for disturbution to the people at the mosqunes and temples. He deputed four companies of soldiers to distribute flour, blankets and money to the Kashmiri immigrant families. He also wrote sympathetic letters to the *kardars* of Raja Gulab Singh and Hari Singh as well as to the chiefs namely Sher Baz Khan of Poonch, Rahim Khan of Rajouri, Namdar Khan of Thakkar to the effect that he had abolished all taxes upon the grains and merchandise goods to be imported in *Subah* Kashmir.

All this speaks for Ranjit Singh's concept and concern for administration in Kashmir. But the difficulty arose due to lack of easy communucation. The *nazims,* the *sahibkars* and their subordinate staff had to be entrusted with discretionary powers for enforcement of law and order as well as the collection of the revenues but the responsibility was not always aptly discharged.

The *Subah* of Kashmir under Ranjit Singh remained with traditional boundaries touching Tibet in the north-east, river Kishan Gang in the West and the territories of the Ghakars in South-West. Apart from 39 *parganas,* covered the territories of Kishtwar (annexed in 1821 comprising 9 parganas), Pirpanchal, inhabited by the *kahas* tribe on the snowy range and allied hills, Bhimbar, Makhowal, Rajouri, Poonch and Muzaffarbad inhabited by the *Gakkars.*

Ranjit Singh followed the traditional polity of dividing the territories of *Subah* into two main categories, i.e., the territories which ramained with the vassal chiefs and those which fell under his direct administration. Of the first category, not all the erstwhile chiefs were given autonomous status simply on the payment of annual fixed *peshkash* to the State. Depending on the geographical situation and political expediency, differential treatment was meted to them. Most of them were left with a few villages in perpetual *Jagir* and the rest of their territories were subjected to revenue payment and were further assigned in *Jagir* to the State officials. Even the conferrment of the heredilary *Jagir* to the vassal Chiefs was conditional upon obedience and service to the State. In case of recalcitrance, their *Jagirs* could be confiscated and if reinstated after submission, they could be obliged to offer their near relations as hostages with the State as a guarantee for their good behaviour.

As at the time of the conquest of Kashmir (1819 A.D.), Ruh Ullah Khan, the Poonch Chief, had sided with the Afghans against the *khalsa* forces, he was expelled from his State. The head of a collateral branch of the family Sher Raza Khan was granted a small *Jagir* in Poonch. Later on, the territories of Poonch were assigned in perpetual *Jagir* to Raja Dhian Singh. Similary, after conquest (1821 A.D.), Kishtwar was annexed to *Khalsa* kingdom and its Chief Raja Tegh Singh was allowed to retain some portions of his territories in *Jagir* on the condition of service of Raja Gulab Singh at Jammu. The Bhimbar and Rajouri Chiefs had already submitted in 1810 A.D., and 1812 A.D. The Bhimber Chief, Sultan Khan, having remained in confinement for seven years, was reinstated in 1819 A.D., for having tendered services to the *Khalsa Darbar* in the campaign against Kashmir and was awarded *Jagir.* Raja Rahimullah Khan of Rajori for similar services was granted perpetual *inam Jagir* comprising the revenues of five villages viz. Akbar, Babgam, Bawalpora (*pargana* Shawara), Saibooj and Kanopora (*pargana* Manchahoma) worth Rupees eleven thousand only. Raja Muzafar Khan of Uri was assigned in *Jagir* 28 villages in *pargana*

Manchahoma. Sultan Zabardast Khan, Raja Mauezud Din Khan and Raja Mansur Khan were assigned the revenues of only eleven, eight and six villages respectively in *Jagir* in *pargana* Patauttara. Similarly, Raja Attaullah Khan of Doputta, Raja Rehmatullah Khan of Kuthari, Raja Najaf Khan of Khouri and the Chiefs of Chikar, Buttair and Ghoona were assigned Jagirs on the same pattern. As the hill chiefs had been intermittently recalcitrant all through the Afghan phase as well, the Chiefs of Baramullah and Muzaffarbad were required to furnish hostages. As a matter of fact, the *khalsa* administration in its relationship with the vassal chiefs was of far more penetarating nature than the previous regimes and was successful in restricting their *Jagir* grants in their repective territories.

Even though the revenues of the villages not under the personal *Jagirs* of the vassal chiefs were assigned to the State officials, the *mahals* of the other territories of the *Subah* had further two fold broad division, i.e., the *parganas* or villages whose revenues were assigned in *Jagir* to the State officials or *dharam arth* and the *parganas* which formed a part of the *khalsa* administration wherein the revenues were realised directly by the State officials. Such a pattern was traditional in character inherited since the Mughal age.

The overall reponsibility for administration and collection of the revenues was vested with the *Nazim* (governor) and *Sahibkar* (collector of revenues). There was also the chief Qazi who discharged judicial functions under the jurisdiction of the *subadar.* The appointment of the *subadar, sahibkar,* the chief *Qazi* and the assignment of *Jagirs* to the vassal chiefs and all other high military cum civil officers from within the *Subah* or outside was made by the Lahore *Darbar.* During the *khalsa* regime in Kashmir (1819-1846 A.D.), there were in all ten regular *subadars,* i.e., Diwan Moti Ram (1819-20 A.D.), Sardar Hari Singh Nalwa (1820-21 A.D.), Diwan Moti Ram (second term, 1821-25 A.D.), Diwan Kirpa Ram (1825-27 A.D.), Diwan Chuni Lal (1827-30 A.D.), Bhamman Singh Ardli (1830-31 A.D.), Kanwar Sher Singh (1831-34 A.D.), Col. Mehan Singh (1834-41 A.D.), Sheikh Ghulam Muhiyuddin (1841-46 A.D.), and Sheikh Imamuddin (1846 A.D.). Of these, eight *subadars* acted under Ranjit Singh, two under his successors while Col. Mehan Singh served under both the phases. The distinguished *sahibkars* vested with *diwani* powers who served under the *nazims* were Pandit Bir Dhar, Mirza Pandit Dhar, Pandit Sehag Ram Dhar, Kwaja Munawar Shah, Gurmukhi Singh, Shiekh Ghulam Muhiyuddin, Pandit Ganesh, Desha Singh and Munshi Tilok Chand.

It is not intended to run into detail about the local administration except to make some general observations based on the contemporary sources. For administrative and revenue purposes, Kashmir was divided into 39 *parganas* or *mahals* which were further divided into *zilas* and villages (*mauzas*). The number of *zilas* in a *pargana* and villages in a *zila* varied from one *pargana* to another. A small *pargana* like Achan comprised only 10 villages whereas larger *parganas* like Nagam, Bangil and Divasar had 276, 188 and 178 villages respectively. As per list provided by the *Dasturulaml-i-Kashmir* in respect of each village and every pargana, the total number of villages comes to 3451 in the valley of Kashmir. The officials associated with the pargana administration were *amil, kardar, tehsildar, thanadar, qanungo, sazawal, shiqdar, tahvildar, patwari* and *muqaddam*. The first three nomenclatures, i.e., the *amil, kardar* and *tehsildar* did not essentially constitute distinct offices with earmarked units and could be each other's substitute. It seems in the context that these could as well be associated with the office of the *qanungo* and in general parlance could be even the latter's substitute. The main functionaries of the *pargana* administration were the *thanadars* and the *qanungos* and during the governorship of Col. Mehan Singh, the former were specially enjoined to keep a strict watch over the malpractices of the latter. However, the *qanungo* continued to remain directly responsible to the *sahibkar.* Assisted by the *patwaries, muqaddams* and other subordinate officials connected with the villages, his main duties were the maintainance of all records relating to the receipt of revenues, expenditure and various items regarding the agrarian system. He was the main stay of the *pargana* administration. Apart from the realisation of the revenues, he was equally reponsible for the protection of the life and property of the people and, as such, was even vested with quasi judicial powers for the punishment of the culprits. He had also to make full efforts for the extension of the culturable land of the villages. Ordinarily, there was one *qanungo* in a *pargana* but depending upon the size of its *pargana* and its revenues, the number may be more. According to *Dasturulaml-i-Kashmir,* there were two *qanungos* in *pargana* Anantnag and four in *pargana* Divasar. As regards remunerations, both the *qanungo* and the *muqaddam* were given land grants and were equally entitled to *dastur* (customary share) from the produce of the peasants. The other members of the subordinate staff got only a share from the produce. As such, the *qanungos, shiqdars* and *sazawals* received 1½ *seer* and 3 *paus* of grain per *kharwar* whereas the *muqaddam* and the patwari were entitled to 1½ *seer* per *kharwar* of grain from the produce. The Kashmiri Pandits and the local Muslims constituted the subordinate staff in the *pargana*.

Notwithstanding some modifications in respect of the magnitute of the State share and appropriation of the surplus produce, the agrarian system in Kashmir, as established by the Mughals, continued to prevail throughtout the Afghan period. For the cultivation of varying nature of crops and assessment of revenues thereupon, Kashmir had its own indigenous classification of cultivable land, i.e., *abi* (irrigated), *sambu* (flooded), *nambal* (swampy), *lalmi khushk* and unirrigated) and *karewas* (capable of producing saffron). In the *abi* land, there were two categories, *abi Shali* which grew rice and *abi sagzar* which grew vegetables, tobacco, poppy, chillies and fennel. The *sambu* or the flooded lands near the river banks and lakes grew rice, oil seeds and maize. The *nambal* further divided into *nambal shali* and *nambal sagzar* grew rice and vegetables etc. However, *nambal-banjar* grew only reeds and grass. The *lalmi* or unirrigated land grew crops like wheat, barly, millet, mashang, rape and linseed. The *kharewas* was a special class of land for the production of saffron as well as covered the floating gardens in the lakes. The *kharif* crops comprised rice, pulses (*mung, moth, urd* and *mash*), cotton, chillies, maiz, kangni, *kotto,* china and Jute whereas the rabi harvest covered wheat, barley, peas and tobacco.

Kashmir had also its own method and varying units for measurement for the cultivable and the residential land (*purnis*) as well as floating gardens. The *Dasturnlaml-i Kashmir,* while explaining the methods of measurement, aligns the units and method of assessment of the floating gardens identical with the measurement of the habitations. However, for cultivable land, different units and method of assessment of crops are prescribed. For the latter, though 20 biswas constituted a *bigha*. Due to variation in the measurement units, the area of one Kashmiri bigha was equal to 4 *bighas* in the Punjab, the area in which a particular crop could be grown and its measurement of land was reckoned by the quantity or measure of seed (*tukham*) required for it. The nature of classified land, the quantity of seed in terms of *kharwar* required for its cultivation was counted as *kharwar.* Thereafter, the *Jinsi* crops were divided between the State and the peasant according to the *ghallabakshi* system. However, the cash crops grown on the *abi sagzar* were assessed according to the *Zabti* system. As regards State demand, the State claimed ½ of the gross produce both in kind and cash in terms of *kharwar.* For the *rabi* crops, of the peasant's share nearly 16% was claimed in cash on yearly rates fixed per *kharwar* for each crop. Similarly, ½ share was taken from the *singhara* (waternuts) produce and honey production. Fixed amount per tree was charged on the walnut, almond and fruit bearing trees and herbs like charas and *bhang*. Apart from it, extra share under the name of *tarki* comprising *rasum* and *abwab* (cesses) of miscellaneous nature amounting to nearly ¼th of the produce was charged. Thus with the land revenue along with the *rasum* for the remunerations of the subordinate revenue staff and other cesses of varying nature, the peasant proprietor *(khud kashta) riaya* was left with 25% of the gross produce and the *paikashtkar* who paid comparatively less assessment rates and *tarki* charges with a little more than that. Even by supplementing from vegetables, fruits, milk and waternuts, the ordinary cultivating family lived on mere subsistence.

The contemporary evidence shows the stratification of landholding and cattle wealth. There were *khudkashta* riaya (peasant proprietors), *muzarian* (occupancy tenants) and *paikashtkars* (outside cultivators settled in the village). The *khudkashta* riaya had usually large holdings and apart from itself cultivation also got their lands cultivated by the tenants on sharing basis. The *Sirkishti* land was owned by the *khudkashta riaya* whereas *paikishti* land was held by the *paikashtkars*. The *paikashtkars,* originally from the outside villages, were initially assessed on lighter rates and paid less share on the additional *tarki* charges. In due course of time, they may as well acquire occupancy rights in land. Like many a part of North India, the existence of the *paikashtkars* in Kashmir shows a gap between the manland ratio wherein there was still considerable scope in the reclamation of the available vast tracts of culturable land. As the *khudkastha riaya* (peasant proprietor) was the owner of the land, it had the right to mortgage or sell it. As distinguished from the safforn land wherein the varying rates per *futto* (1/12th of a Kashmiri *bigha*) of the three categories of land were quite high, the agricultural land in the developed villages had since long acquired saleable value. Though varying in number from one region to another, the transections were quite common. This is equally confirmed by the State income on account of *cabala* (sale) cess on land. The quantification of the available data in *Dasturulaml-i-Kashmir* with regard to the *khudkashta* and other holdings as well as the sale transactions of agricultural land in different regions of Kashmir would be a very fruitful exercise for the detailed determination of the stratification of the rural society in the precolonial society and economic history of Kashmir.

Maharaja Ranjit Singh's administration in Kashmir was quite responsive to meet the challenge thrown by the famine in 1832-33. The famine was by no means confined to Kashmir only as by 1833, it had ravaged the territories of the Punjab as well. Col. Mehan Singh appointed as *nazim,* especially for the betterment of the administration and amelioration of the condition of the suffering people, took positive and bold steps in this direction. His capable *sahibkar* Pandit Ganesh had personally brought with him twenty thousand maunds of cereals and also imported large quantities of cereals from Rajauri, Muzaffarabad,Karna and Kishtwar at higher rate of Rs. 16/- per *maund* and distributed at much lower rate of Rs. 3/- per *maund.* The administration also imported cattle, fowls, seed grains and poultry to replenish the stock and distribution to the agricultruists in the villages. Col. Mehan Singh also reduced the incidence of cesses imposed on the land revenue. The additional imposition of one *trak* per *kharwar* which had continued since the governorship of Sukh Jiwan in the 18th century Afghan rule on account of advancement of one Lakh *kharwars* as seeds and *taqavi* was abolished. Remission was also given to the revenue farmers at the rate of 6 *manotas* (9 Kashmiri *seers*) for the losses incurred by them. The escheated Jagirs were restored. One lakh *kharwar* of cereals were distributed to the Brahmins and *faqirs.* As a result of some administrative reshuffling, the charge of the sifted grain was taken from the *kardars* and entrusted to the *tahvildars.* Twenty *thanadars* with respective regional jurisdictions were appointed to supervise the work of the subordinate officials and enforcement of law and order. To safeguard the interest of the *riaya,* stamped standardised weights and measures were introduced. The marriage cess (*zar-i-nikah*), which had been prevalent since the Afghan rule, was abolished. The gulban tribe, which had often caused disturbances since the Afghan period and indulged in plunder of the produce of the peasantry, was crushed. Due to floods, a number of river bridges at Bijabiharva, Pampore and Mirakadal, Srinagar had been damaged. Similarly, numerous river *bunds* had been broken since the Afghan period. These were all not only repaired but regular funds were earmarked for their future maintenance. The administration kept a keen watch on the price movement and unauthorised storage of grain for profiteering purpose was not permitted. By 1835 AD, the price of *shali* (rice) was fixed at Rupee one (Hari Singhi) per *kharwar.* Col. Mehan Singh toured the valley personally to supervise the relief measures and the working of the administrative machinery. Within a couple of years, normal life was restored and the *riaya* was quite well off. Many people who had fled outside Kashmir because of the famine conditions returned to their native places.

Though varying figures are available from different sources, it is estimated that earlier under the *nazamat* of Diwan Kirpa Ram, the *Jama* (revenues) of Kashmir as in 1886 *Bikrami Samvat* stood at Rupees Twenty two lakhs forty four thousand three hundred and ninety (Rs. 224,4390/-) in *naqd* (cash payment) and twelve lakhs ninety thousand four hundred and thirty five (Rs. 12,90,435/-) *kharwars* as *Jinsi hissa Sarkar* (State share realised in kind). After the deduction of the amount assigned in cash in respect in *Jagirs* and *dharamarth* and incidental expenses of the office of the *kardar* dealing with the cash *Jama* (revenues) of *parganas/mahals,* the *malia* (revenues) of Kashmir covering both cash and *Jins* came to Rs. 34,56,825/-. As the shawl weavers were obliged to pay Rs. 3/- per *kharwar* of *shali* (instead of Rs. 1/- fixed otherwise), an additional sum of Rupees six lakhs could be added to the above mentioned amount. However, according to a contemporary source, the annual revenues during the *nazamat* of Col. Mehan Singh amounted to Rs. 20, 68, 691/- only. Later on during the *nazamat* tenure of Ghulam Mohiyuddin (1841-46 AD), the price of *shali* ranged between Annas-13/- to Rs. 1/- per kharwar and as such after the deduction of the expenditure relating to *ijara* (revenue farming), *jagirs* and *kardari* establishments, the total *Jama* (revenues) of Kashmir in *naqd* and *Jins* came to Rs. 23,20,507/-. Apparently, in comparison to Ranjit Singh's earlier phase of administration, the revenues of Kashmir declined considerably by the end of the Sikh rule in 1846 when the Dogras took over. The above mentioned figures also clearly exhibit that there was a drastic fall in the revenues after the occurrence of calamities like earthquake, cholera and severe famine which devastated and ravaged the whole of Kashmir. For want of census records of those days, it is difficult to determine the exact number of the loss of human and cattle life. However, the graphic picture drawn by the contemporary chroniclers about the loss of human life is simply horrible. The estimates provided by the contemporary travellers and the English intelligence reports in this regard also differ. Based on their observations, it may well be considered that the population of Kashmir, which was around eight lakhs in the earlier phase of the *khalsa* rule, fell to about 2 lakhs or even less by 1833 A.D., as a result of the calamities. This is, of course, true that during the *Khalsa* phase, a number of families left Kashmir for good on political ground as well as due to calamities. But this was only a marginal factor. Such a phenomenon was much more pronounced during the Afghan period which was marked by political instability and religious persecution.

It is also known from *Dasturulaml-i-Kashmir* that during Col. Mehan Singh's tenure of governorship, the total agricultural produce in the post-famine period was twenty seven lakhs fifty eight thousand two hundred and fifty five (27,58,255/-) *kharwars* (in terms of *shali*) which was much less than during the earlier phase of the *Khalsa* rule. The decline in the agricultural production cannot be essentially ascribed to arbitrary taxation and administrative coersion leading to desertion of culturable land. The data provided by *Dasturulaml-i-Kashmir* is a clear testimony in this regard. There is no denying the fact that the prevalence of the *ijara* (farming) in the land revenue system was a great drawback in the machinery responsible for the collection of the revenues. Sometimes, the *sahibkars* themselves were given *ijara* for the total revenues of Kashmir. Many an official, especially the *qanungos* were given *ijara* of their respective jurisdictions. Same was true of the Afghan administration. There was also corruption in the revenue department especially at the lower rungs of the set-up—a feature which had prevailed throughout the medieval age in the rural society.

It required the State to keep a strict watch on the working of the *ijara* system as per regulations and local practice or else it would work against the interests of the agruculturists and the artisans. The Lahore *Darbar* was fully conscious of the fact. The chronicles quote various instances when stern action was taken by the State against the *ijaradars* and officials for extortion and indulgence in malpractice. The *begar* practice, which had persisted in Kashmir all through the centuries, was not only a social bane but adversly affected the life of the agriculturists. However, the shawl weavers were exempted from this cess.

The wool industry in Kashmir had flourished from the ancient times and since the medieval age, it had witnessed various ups and down trends due to political and economic factors. The shawl industry with various new designs evolved during the course of centuries became very popular during the Mughal age. With an intimate commercial intercourse, for manufacturing purpose, the *poisham* (wool) of the domesticated goat and *Asli Tus* (Finer wool of the wild goat) were imported from Chanthan, Yarkand, Khutan, Tibet, Chinese Turkistan and other parts of Central Asia. The manufacturing processes, i.e., the picking the coarse hair at home by women and then weaving with the handlooms in the *karkhanas*/workshops as well as the *sadabaf* in different sizes and colours with primitive indigenous technology were fully developed in Kashmir. The quality of shawl depended upon the fineness of the thread, harmony of colour and perfection of workmanship. However, the best shawls were manufactured in Srinagar and its neighbourhood. Shahabad and Anant Nag came next to it. The finished goods were well in demand within India and abroad. Having seen its hey days during the Mughal age, the shawl industry had shown some declining trend during the Afghan period due to continual political disturbances and maladministration. This was despite the fact that the Durranis were quite conscious of its export value and cherished fervent desire to keep up its quality in manufacture. Much before the conquest of Kashmir (1819), many a Kashmiri families had migrated from Kashmir due to political instability and famine (1806-7 A.D.), and settled at different places in the Punjab. The shawl manufacturers concentrated at Amritsar, Nurpur, Ludhiana and Lahore which became the centres for this industry. They were supplemented by the fresh exodus during Ranjit Singh's own reign in Kashmir on account of spread of epidemic (1827 A.D.), and famine (1832-33 A.D.). In the long run, it added a further dimension to the economic pattern and social life in the Punjab. Amritsar imported considerable quantity of *pasham* for *shawl* manufacture. All the same, the Amritsari *shawls* and those manufactured at other centres in the Punjab could not compete with the Kashmir craftmanship. The Kashmiri labour was trained for generations and the climatic condition, the ready availability of wool and other materials could not be easily made available outside Kashmir. As such, Ranjit Singh's administration greatly emphasised the development of the industry within Kashmir. It is estimated that within a few years of the annexation of Kashmir, the number of the shawl manufacturing *karkhanas* increased from two to three times of the position inherited from the Afghan phase. The private enterprise with the establishment of the workshops comprising handlooms was the main basis of this industry. The State imposed duties on the import of raw *pasham* as well as cesses as *shawl dagh, sair* and transit export duties on the manufactured goods. The income was included in the *naqdi mahal* (cash department) set up for the shawls.

The travelogues portary miserable plight of the shawl weavers on account of low wages-2 to 6 annas per day and long hours of work and unhygenic conditions. According to them, many of the weavers 'chopped' off their fingers to avoid being forced to work on the handlooms. Though such observations have influenced many a modern writer, it seems difficult to believe that large scale manufacture of the *shawls* in the workshops owned even by the private enterprise could possibly get the production done under the whip. As a matter of fact, the shawl industry under the *khalsa* regime prospered considerably. But the deterring factor to even greater development of the industry was the rivalry of the English trade in this regard which was already apparent during the reign of Maharaja Ranjit Singh. The English East India Company had already started importing raw wool from Ladakh and Tibet via Rampur and Luhri (in the then Punjab Hill States acquired after the Anglo-Gorkha war in 1815 AD) for export to England for the production of finished goods to be re-exported to the international as well as Indian markets. Through its officials commissioned for the job and intelligence, it had done its best to acquire the technical know how which was conveyed to England but the experiment was not a complete success. The English East Indian Company had even planned to manufacture cheap immitation shawls for capturing the outside and Indian markets, even at Srinagar itself supposed to have a population of about 20,000 people. At home, the English were already proficient in the production of the woolen goods. Even though the English manufacture of the wool shawls from the Indian raw material was still in initial stages, apparently for political reasons, Maharaja Ranjit Singh's administration did not stretch the rivalry beyond a limit. However, it did have an impact on the growth of the industry in Kashmir. The English were considerably successful in their designs only after the establishment of the Dogra rule in Kashmir (1846) and thereafter the *shwal* industry in Kashmir declined.

The silk industry, too, had occupied an important postition in the Kashmir economy since ancient times. However, it received a set back during the Afghan phase as a large number of mulberry trees had been cut off. Under the *khalsa* administration, with fresh stimulus, this industry made considerable progress and involved a sizeable portion of the population comprising rural and commercial sectors. A good variety of mulberry trees were grown in the Kothar division which produced the best quality of silk at that time. The production of good cocoons improved the nerve and strength of the silk thread. As such, the Kashmiri silk found market in the other territories of India and even in the European countries. The large quantity of silk production, about 2/3rd, was exported only to the Punjab. By 1846, being an import trade article, it fetched Rs. One lakh (Rs. 1,00,000/-) as *mahsul* (income from excise duty) to the State. However, even though the technical know how of the sericulture was known to the local people, the seeds for the mulberry trees, as done earlier even during the Mughal age, continued to be imported from outside, especially from Gilgit and Tibet.

Known for its specialised items, Kashmir exported shawls, safforn, woolen cloth, silk cloth, tobacco, inkstands, paper bedmusk water, black zarrah, ghee, apples, charas and kuth. It imported shawl wool from Tibet, tea, salt, sugar, molasses, spices, medicines and groceries, indigo, iron and steel, brass and copper plates, cloth including silk cloth, chintez, coconuts and fruits, colours for painting, quick silver, arsenic and snuff. The State charged *sair* (duties) both on export and import which amounted to about Rupees one lakh and forty thousand by the end of the *khalsa* regime in Kashmir.

The *khalsa* administration also struck coins in Kashmir. The *Nanak shahi* coin, the principal coin of the kingdom was minted in 1876 *Bikrami samvat* / 1819 AD, the very first year of the annexation. The coin preserved at the Pratap Singh State Museum, Srinagar, bears the words "Zarb Khita-i-Kashmir" on the reverse and the well known inscription on the obverse:

> "Deg Tegh Fateh,
>
> O-Nusrat
>
> Baidarang
>
> Yaft uz Nanak
>
> Guru Gobind Singh"

Note: In fact these coins (Nanak Shahi) were struck continously every year from July 1819 AD, Sambat 1876 to 1846 AD, Sambat 1903.

Later on Sardar Hari Singh Nalwa, the *nazim* of Kashmir, also issued *Rupaya Hari Singhi* of mixed silver and alloy at six mashas each with similar inscription on the obverse. It is known from the statistical Report of John Lawrence (1846) on the mints at Lahore and Amritsar, that *Nanak Shahi* coins were also struck in Kashmir in 1894 *Bikarami samvat*/1837 AD (during the *nazamat* of Col. Mehan Singh). The erstwhile *Zaman Shahi* coins also remained in currency at prescribed discount.

In line with the Mughal practice of granting revenue free lands or making cash payment to individuals or institutions of various religious communities covered under various nomenclatures, *i.e., madad-i-maash, aimma, muafi* and *waqf* for philanthrophist charitable and educational purposes, Ranjit Singh had set up in his kingdom the Department of *Dharamarth* which maintained regular records under different heads of *dharamarth*. A similar *dharamarth* department was established in Kashmir too.Under this category, land grants, assignation of revenues of the villages in kind or cash were made to revenues of the villages in kind or cash were made to religious persons, i.e., *Imams, khadims* (attendants), *mujawars* (holy persons), *faqirs,* Pandits as well as institutional establishments of the mosques, *khankas,* temples, *tiraths* and *dharamsalas*. Such grants were made to all the religious communities and their sects-the beneficiaries being the Sunni and the Shias (Muslims) as well as the Hindus. Apart from it, stipulated amount was diverted from the *naqdi mahals* of *Jawahar bazar shawl dagh* and *singhara* to the *dharamarth* for futher assignation to *maskins, faqirs,* brahamins, *pujaris,* sadhus and *Jotshis* involving payment on monthly or annual basis. The *Dasturulaml* compiled under the patronage of Col. Mehan Singh provides a detailed list of the *naqdi* (cash) and *Jinsi* (kind) *dharamarth* beneficiaries and also spells out the culturable areas of both irrigated and unirrigated land granted for this purpose. It even provides separate lists for the Shias and the Sunni beneficiaries. Apart from various such recipients, it states that the *khadaman* (attendants) and *wazkhwadan* of the holy shrine of Shah Hamdan received annually from the *dharamarth* Rupees forty seven (Rs. 47/-) in cash and eighty nine *kharwars* in kind (*Jinsi*). Khwaja Mohammed Shah Naqshbandi was assigned villages in *dharamarth*.

The *khalsa* administration was quite liberal in the *dharamarth* grants and, as such, it appropriated revenues amounting to appoximately Rupees two lakhs for this purpose. The fact of liberal grant running over three thousand in number is well conceded by the English Report and settlement officers of the Dogra period who had inherited the old records in this regard.

Even though all such grants were regarded hereditary in nature, ever since the Mughal age, the State had always exercised its right for enhancement or curtailment or even escheat depending on the need and behaviour of individual or institutional beneficiaries. These grants were required to be renewed by every succeeding monarch or new regime.Usually, they were renewed though depending on the situation, a part could also be withheld. Though practically all the grants prevalent in the Afghan period were renewed by the newly established *khalsa* regime, it has been maintained that a portion of the old grant of Jama Masjid of Srinagar was reduced.

The concept of secularism in India in the modern sense is a recent development since the late 19th and 20th centuries. In the medieval polity, religious tolerance, equity in taxation and co-existence of different religious communities may constitute the hallmark of a liberal State. But the State may deviate partially in one respect or another, it may still consider itself to be broad minded and tolerant. Notwithstanding the socio-political background of the Durrani regime in the Punjab, Ranjit Singh established a liberal and just State, though of course to some extent, within the limitations imposed by the contemporary social atmosphere. He stopped the practice of cow slaughter (*gaukushi*) and as a symbol of ascendency of the *khalsa,* he forbade public calls for prayers *(azan)* at certain significant mosques in some cities. In Kashmir, the Afghan polity had given weightage to the Hindu Pandits for employment even in the higher posts of financial and some administrative departments. But this was by no means taken to be incompatible with the imposition of *jizya* upon the Hindus in general and their persecution by some Afghan *subadars*. Even the Shia Muslims were persecuted. But the Hindu Pandit community remained quite sensitive over the cow slaughter practice and took it an offence to their religious sentiments. When Sukh Jiwan became the governor of Kashmir, as a backlash measure, he stopped the practice of cow slaughter and imposed ban on *bangh-i-namaz* (public call for prayers) at the mosques. After nearly six and a half decades, similar action was taken by Diwan Moti Ram, the very first *subadar* of the *khalsa* regime. According to some sources of the Dogra period, not only cow-slaughter was banned on pain of death penalty and *bang-i-namaz* (at mosques) declared forbidden, restrictions were imposed on the Jama Masid, the new mosque (Palhar), and various other mosques were escheated to the State property. It was only later on that the *Subadar* Sheikh Ghulam Mohiyuddin (1841-46, of course, within the *khalsa* regime but after the death of Ranjit Singh) removed the earlier restrictions and spent considerable amount on the repair of Jama Masjid and, as in the past, provided for flowing water in the courtyard. However, Bir Bal Kachru, the contemporary chronicler of the Sikh regime, makes a general statement that after the conquest of Kashmir by Ranjit Singh, prayers continued to be offered by the *ahl-i-sunnat* (Suni Muslims) at different mosques.

Basing judgement on the later sources of the Dogra period and the travelogues with regard to the taxation and religious policy of Maharaja Ranjit Singh in Kashmir, a recent writer stresses the fact that "The Sikh Governors posted in Kashmir unleashed a reign of terror and if one Muslim was killed by a Sikh, the compensation allowed to his family was two rupees and four if a Hindu. The Sikh soldier was given a free hand to kill the local Muslims." Such a trend in historical writing needs no comment. Even though it is conceded that because of certain social inhibitions of the age, Maharaja Ranjit Singh's rule was not completely secular in the modern sense of the word, it was liberal enough to foster peaceful co-existence amongst different religious communities. The Shia Muslim community had often been the target of repression and intermittent persecution during the Afghan rule. In Ranjit Singh's period, there was only one unfortunate communal Shia-Sunni riot during the governorship of Bhamman Singh Ardli (1830-31 AD) which was crushed with an iron hand by the administration. With all its limitations, Maharaja Ranjit Singh gave a stable government to Kashmir which it had not known since the times of the great Mughals.

Chapter 12

Political and Social Situation of Punjab After Ranjit Singh Era*

Mr. Chairman, Ladies and Gentlemen,

I am extremely indebted to the Punjabi Academy, Delhi, for the honour done to me for having invited me to deliver Maharaja Ranjit Singh Memorial Lecture on 'Political and Social Situation of Punjab after Ranjit Singh Era'. More than anybody else, I am fully aware of my own limitations as an historian in comparision to the previous scholars who delivered these Memorial Lectures in the past. Apparently, it is only my long standing association with the Punjabi Academy and the affection shown to me by its organisers that I have been conferred this honour and privilege to speak on this occasion.

The Punjab under Maharaja Ranjit Singh and his successors (1799-1849 AD) has attracted the largest attention on the part of the British and the Indian historians. This is essentially due to the fact that the British took over the territories of the *Dar-ul-Sultanat* of Lahore from the Sikh rule and were tempted to write the past history of the Sikh community. A number of Indian writers produced works both in Persian and the vernacular languages. In fact, during the Sikh regime itself, a number of historical accounts in the Persian language were prepared both by the Hindu and Muslim historians. The students of the Punjab history are fortunate to have inherited all these sources to which can be added the original archival source-material comprising the *Khalsa Darbar Records,* the correspondence of various categories (in Persian) under the *Bhandari Collection* available at State Archives, Patiala, as well as the English reports of multifarious nature. A few good works on Ranjit Singh, his successors and the circumstances leading to the

---

* Maharaja Ranjit Singh Memorial Lecture organised by Punjabi Academy, Delhi, 9th October, 1992

annexation of the Punjab by the East India Company have been attempted. All the same, with rare exception, not much analytical work has been done so as to cover various socio-economic and cultural aspects of the people of the Punjab under the Sikh rule.

As we have to construct a fairly accurate and dependable picture of the political situation and socio-economic life of the people of Punjab in the pre-colonial period, it is imperative to adopt an objective approach and disciplined methodology of historical reserach. Our methodology is essentially related to our purpose of research for discerning the historical and evolutionary analysis. A scholar has to deliberately adopt the method of following a historical process step-by-step, which according to the annalistic method is blended with the mode of fitting the facts within a well-defined frame of institutions. For proper appreciation of the pre-colonial history of the people of India, one has to understand the social and political scenario of a particular phase under analysis, essentially based upon the then contemporary source-material and connotations. We have to be extremely cautious against the free use of the European terminology in the Indian context. Moreover, during the colonial period in India, many socio-religious movements and political developments took place in the later half of the 19th and 20th centuries, which attempted to make their base with historical orientation, howsoever flimsy or with vested political interests, it might be. All the same, these movements influenced the minds of the people at large. To all this, Punjab was no exception. All this is happening even today in free India. The gullible mind is very much prone to such misconceived past historical analysis, more especially, on the socio-religious matters. This, infact, poses a serious challenge to a disciplined historian.

A regional variation is an important factor in the socio-economic and political analysis of the Indian society. Social and political ideas as well as their institutional set-up has to be worked out. Apart from the trends of the historiography in the medieval times, emphasis has, as well, to be laid on the historical languages, literature, speculative ideas, thought, art, architecture, music, science, technology and medicine. Notwithstanding the continuation of work on the traditional line of political history, a seemy beginning has as well been made in the social history of pre-colonial Punjab. All the same, we are to concentrate more on the rural society, the agrarian set-up, the role of caste and landed intermediaries, the condition of the peasantry, the concept of the village community, rural trade, handicrafts and industries in the rural and the urban society. Even though we have ample of source-material in English, Persian and regional languages (i.e. Punjabi and Urdu) supplemented by numasmatic and epigraphic sources, we have mostly carried on the tradition from the British times to bank mostly on the Persian chronicles and English sources, which is an extremely inadequate methodology. Unless we exploit the full range of source-material available to us, we can never reconstruct a proper perspective of the social development of the people during the pre-colonial Punjab. We have to study both at the regional and the all India level. The varying and the unifying factors of the Indian culture have to be clearly underlined.

The identity, concept, personality and territorial jurisdiction of the Punjab is of vital importance. The Mughal sources (16th to 18th centuries) identify Punjab with the territorial boundaries of *Darul Saltanat* Lahore or *subah* Lahore or *subah* Punjab or *wilayat-i-Punjab.* The territorial boundaries extended from the river Sutlej in the east to river Indus (Sind) in the north west and comprised five *doabs* or *sarkars* viz, Bet Jalandhar, Bari, Rechna, Chenhat and Sind Sagar. Apart from this, some hilly regions to the north or Bet Jalandhar not covered in the doabs entitled as *Berun-i-Panjnand* also formed part of the *subah.* The earmarked mountaineous regions (*parganas*) to the north of the *doabs* formed the respective *doabs* or *sarkars.* The Bari *Doab* with headquarters at Lahore formed the core of the Punjab. By the end of the 17th century, five *parganas* of *subah* Multan were also transferred to *subah* Punjab. However, the *doabs* viz., Bari, Rechna, and Sind Sagar along with *mahals* beyond the five rivers of the Multan territories continued to form part of *subah* Multan.

The territories between the river Jamuna and Sutlej and the trans-Sutlej territories formed parts of the *sarkars* of Delhi, Hissar Firozah and Sirhind of *subah* Delhi. Notwithstanding the fact that during the course of the 18th century, many a Sikh *zamindari, misl* and chieftainship were established in the above mentioned territories, they continued to be well within the jurisdiction of *subah* Delhi. At the close of the 18th century and nearly four decades of the 19th century, the Kingdom of Lahore established by Maharaja Ranjit Singh (1799-1839 AD) covered all the territories of the erstwhile Mughal *subahs* of Punjab, Kashmir, Multan, some of the trans-Indus *ilaqas* of *subah* Kabul viz., Peshawar, Kohat, Bannu and a few tribal regions. Except for the two *subahs* of Kashmir and Multan, all other territories were divided into more or less distinct primary administrative divisions.

On the eastern side, the cis-Sutlej chieftainship viz., the chiefs of Malwa and Sirhind being under the British protection remained outside the territorial boundaries of the kingdom of Lahore. The Lahore Darbar covered the traditional territories of the Punjab, the *subahs* of Multan and Kashmir as well a few *ilaqas* of Afghanistan. All the same, the concept of Punjab remained the same as before. However, notwithstanding the rigid territorial division for administrative purpose, the impact of the Punjabi culture in the other territories of the kingdom, more especially in Multan and North Western region as well as outside the state territorial jurisdiction in the cis-Sutlej region is undeniable.

As a matter of fact, the real change in the territorial concept and the traditional boundaries of the Punjab came only after its incorporation in the British Empire. After the First Anglo-Sikh War, the British occupied Lahore in February, 1846. In accordance with the Treaty signed in March, 1846, the Lahore Darbar ceded to the English East India Company all the territories in the *doab* between the Beas and the Sutlej as well as the hill territories between the Beas and the Indus including Kashmir and Hazara. After the Second Anglo-Sikh War, all other territories of the Lahore Kingdom were annexed to the British Empire (30-31 March, 1849) and were incorporated in the newly formed province of the Punjab. At the same time, the administration of the cis-Sutlej states as well as districts comprising Thanesar, Ambala, Ludhiana and Ferozpur were merged with the Punjab in 1849. In 1858, the Delhi division of the North Western provinces comprising the six districts of Delhi, Gurgaon, Panipat, Rohtak, Hissar and Sirsa was also merged with the Punjab. Later on in 1901, the districts of Peshawar, Hazara, Bannu and its Marwat tehsils as well as the trans-Indus part of Dehra Ismail Khan excepting the *ilaqa* of Vehoa were separated from the Punjab so as to form a new North Western Frontier Province. With the transfer of the British Indian capital from Calcutta to Delhi, the Delhi *tehsil* alongwith the Mahrauli *thana* of Ballabgarh was separated from the Punjab and formed into the Delhi Provinces. Thus, it is very clear that the Punjab, as it stood on the eve of the partition of India in 1947, has been formed by the British Indian government purely due to administrative expediency for the stability of its colonial rule in India.

By the end of the 18th century, the Durranis still realised *peshkash/ nazrana* from many a Hindu chiefs of the Sub-Himalayan ranges (Chamba, Jammu etc.) as well as from the territories of Chach, Hazara and even at times from the *zamindaries* and *mahals* of the Gakkhars and Khataks of the regions between Jehlum and Sind and from many other Muslim Chiefs in West Punjab. After having occupied Lahore in 1799 AD, Ranjit Singh realised that he could never consolidate his rule unless the Afghans were expunged from all the above territories. As such, he conquered Multan (January, 1818), Peshawar (November, 1818) and Kashmir (July, 1819). The real credit for stamping out the Afghan rule from the Indian territories goes only to Maharaja Ranjit Singh. This was possible only because he had secured his eastern frontier by signing the well-known Anglo-Sikh Treaty with the English East-India Company (1809) by which he had accepted river Sutlej as the eastern boundary of his kingdom. This could be well safeguarded by a powerful military machinery as well as a stable civil administration. All criticism against Maharaja Ranjit Singh that by singing this Treaty, he exhibited weakness against the English is rather unrealistic, for he would not have been able to face challenge on the two fronts, i.e., East and West. Rather, this enabled him to build a strong kingdom at Lahore, with all potentialities for expansion even towards North in the Himalayas.

In the Himalayan frontier policy, the most important contribution made by the Lahore Darbar under Maharaja Ranjit Singh and his successors is the conquest and annexation of Ladakh and Balistan, then also known as Iskardu or Skardu. These territories became an integral part of the territorial boundaries of the Lahore kingdom. As explained later, after the Jammu territories and Kashmir were passed on to Raja Gulab Singh (1846), the Dogra ruler, these territories formed a part of his dominions. After India became free in 1947 from the colonial rule of the British Empire, they equally form an integral part of India. One can well imagine the socio-economic and strategic importance of these Himalayan territories for the defence of modern India in the relam of Sino-Indian relations. Such is the legacy and gift of Raja Gulab Singh under the Lahore Darbar to the present day India.

Briefly speaking, it was Maharaja Ranjit Singh, who after his conquest of Kashmir (1819), having realised the economic and strategic importance of Ladakh, imposed his suzerainty over the Gyalpo of Ladakh (1820) and obliged the latter to pay regular tribute to the Lahore Darbar through the *nazim* of Kashmir. On the evasion of the payment of tribute in 1834 AD, Raja Gulab Singh, the Dogra *Jagirdar* and feudatory chief of the Lahore Darbar deputed General Zorawar Singh, the Governor of Kishtwar to invade Ladakh (1835). After a successful military operation, General Zorawar Singh signed a peace treaty with the Gyalpo (July, 1835) and exacted *nazrana* from the latter on behalf of Maharaja Ranjit Singh. Thereafter, on account of revolt on the part of the Gyalpo, after another expedition by General Zorawar Singh, Ladakh was annexed to the Lahore Darbar (1839). Similarly, after another expedition in November, 1839, Zorawar Singh annexed Balistan (1839-40). As such, both Leh and Skardu became part of the Lahore Kingdom. Even though Zorawar Singh temporarily conquered even West Tibet (1841), this was a short lived gain as in the struggle that ensued, Zorawar Singh was killed (November, 1841) and the war ended with a Peace Treaty (September-October, 1842) between the Lahore Darbar and the Lhasa officials on behalf of China. This Treaty put an end to the war between the Chiefs of Raja Gulab Singh and the Viceroy of Lhasa (on behalf of China) and clearly stipulated the political subjugation of Ladakh to the Lahore Darbar and reaffirmed the previous boundaries. It equally restored trade relations between Leh and Lhasa.

The concept of secularism in India in the modern sense is a recent development since the late 19th and 20th centuries. In the medieval polity, religious tolerance, equity in taxation and co-existence of different religious communities may constitute the hallmark of a liberal state. But the State may deviate partially in one respect or another, it may still consider itself to be broad minded and tolerant. Notwithstading the socio-political background of the Durrani regime in the Punjab, Ranjit Singh established a liberal and just state, though of course to some extent, within the limitations imposed by the contemporary social atmosphere. He stopped the practice of cow-slaughter (*gau kushi*) and as a symbol of ascendency of the *khalsa,* he forbade public calls for prayers (*azan*) at certain significant mosques in some cities. Even though it is conceded that because of certain social inhibitions of the age, Maharaja Ranjit Singh's rule in Kashmir was not completely secular in the modern sense of the word, it was liberal enough to foster peaceful co-existence amongst different religious communities. The Shia Muslim community had often been the target of repression and intermittent persecution during the Afghan rule and even earlier during the later Mughal times in the 18th century. In the Ranjit Singh's period, there was only one unfortunate communal Shia-Sunni riot during the governorship of Bhamman Singh Ardli (1830-31 AD) which was crushed with an iron hand by the administration. With all its limitations, Maharaja Ranjit Singh gave a stable government to his kingdom which it had not known since the times of the Great Mughals. In all these respects, the broad-minded State policy was continued by his successors.

In line with the Mughal practice of granting revenue free lands or making cash payment to individuals or institutions of various religious communities covered under various nomenclatures, i.e., *madad-i-maash, aimma, muafi* and *waqf* for philanthrophic, charitable and educational purposes, Ranjit Singh had set up in his kingdom the Department of *Dharamarth* which maintained regular records under different heads of *dharamarth*. Under this category, land grants, assignation of revenues of the villages in kind or cash were made to religious persons, i.e., Imams, *khadims* (attendants), *mujawars* (holy persons), *faqirs,* pandits as well as institutional establishment of the mosques, *khankas,* temples, *tiraths* and *dharamsalas*. Such grants were made to all the religious communities and their sects – the beneficiaries being the Sunni and the Shias (Muslims) as well as the Hindus, more especially the Udasis of the Nanak Panth. The *khalsa* administration was quite liberal in the *dharamarth* grants. Even the grants prevalent in the Afghan period, with rare exception, were renewed by the Khalsa Darbar.

It would not serve any purpose to give any detailed account of the political events of Punjab till 1849 AD. In fact, the decade after Ranjit Singh's death (27th June 1839) is characterised by the succession of three monarchs on the throne, i.e., Khark Singh (1839), Sher Singh (January, 1841) and Dalip Singh (1843). The successions were never free from top level intrigues on the part of the nobility at the Lahore Court. Maharaja Khark Singh's promising Prince Nao Nihal Singh, the heir apparent to throne was killed on the same date his father died. Now the throne was contested by Maharani Chand Kaur, widow of Maharaja Khark Singh, supported by the Sandhanwalia Sardars and Prince Sher Singh, supported by the Prime-Minister, Raja Dhian Singh. On Sher Singh's accession, the jagirs of the Sandhanwalia Sardars were confiscated and they crossed over to the Malwa. On the latter's return to Lahore and through their intrigues, both Maharaja Sher Singh and Raja Dhian Singh were treachrously killed. After Hira Singh, son of Raja Dhian Singh assumed office as Prime-Minister, the Sandhanwalia Sardar Attar Singh was killed (May, 1844) during the fight with the former. Raja Hira Singh, the Prime Minister, was also assassinated (21st December, 1844) and his *jagirs* were confiscated by the new Prime-Minister, Sardar Jawahar Singh, a younger brother of Maharani Jind Kaur, the widow of Maharaja Ranjit Singh. Above all, after Maharaja Sher Singh's death (1843), there was violence on the part of the Khalsa army, which also assumed the role the 'king Maker'. In the choatic conditions, the Khalsa army attacked the veteran generals of Ranjit Singh's times, Court and Ventura, who were obliged to leave Lahore and return to their native places.

The decade after Ranjit Singh's death was also marked by two Anglo-Sikh wars, which ultimately sealed the fate of the Lahore kingdom. Even though the experiment of the Khalsa Communal Republican order was a complete failure and the role of the Khalsa army was disastrous in consequences, the arrears of pay of the army soldiers was accentuated by a serious financial problem, which was equally related with the crisis of the *Jagirdari* System. Historians have validly raised the question of the responsibility of the two Anglo-Sikh wars. Undeniably, Lord Hardinge, the Governor General of India, right from the day of the assumption of office in July, 1844 had expressed his conviction that in the existing circumstances, the Sikhs had become incapable of maintaining a stable Government and that Punjab could not act as a buffer state between the British Empire and Muslim states beyond Indus, the role of the Khalsa Chiefs as well as Rani Jindan, who were more interested in their lives and *jagirs* rather than the interests of the Khalsa Darbar, was really deplorable. The contemporary English official records as well as those of the Lahore Darbar show that the Khalsa chiefs, viz. Lal Singh and Tej Singh were in league with the English and even provided advance military intelligence to them for the destruction of the Khalsa army. The role of Raja Gulab Singh for being in league with the English for his personal political ends and acquisition of *Jagirs* is not above board.

Once the strong hand that governs the affairs is removed, the emergence of the political intrigues is but natural in a medieval phenomenon and monarchical set-up. Even though the main pattern of administration remains the same, in the absense of a strong monarch, the lack of proper governace is bound to land the state in a financial crisis, personal motives, intrigues at the court and threat of the rule of the army versus civilian authorities. What happened in the Punjab after 1839 is no exception but the tradegy is that the kingdom of Lahore was extinguished as a result of all such mechanisations, after the two Anglo-Sikh wars (1845-46; 1848-49). Maharaja Ranjit Singh had secured the eastern frontier by signing the Treaty of Amritsar (1809) with the English East India Company and had of his own stamped out the Afghan element from the Punjab polity. The wheel had undergone a full circle and now the Afghan polity was dependent on the Lahore Court as is clear from the case of Shah Shuja seeking help from Ranjit Singh and the later Tripartite Treaty resulting in the Anglo-Afghan war (1839). In any case, the Afghan element could not reappear even after Ranjit Singh's death. But it was the eastern frontier problem., which had remained secure till Ranjit Singh's death and a little later, which ultimately mitigated the Lahore kingdom. The prying British eyes, after the occupation of nearly the whole of India, would not spare Punjab unless it was able to withstand the threat effectively. Once the strong hand of Ranjit Singh was removed, it was but natural that finding the weakness of the Lahore Government characterised by intrigues, internal dissensions, break down of proper law and order machinery and confusion within, the English would exploit the situation and embark upon an aggressive policy in a single stroke or in a phased manner. Governed by their political policy and financial resources, the English opted for aggression in a phased manner and ultimately engulfed the Lahore Kingdom in 1849.

The loss of Kashmir and a few other territories of Punjab as a result of the first Anglo-Sikh War (1846) was a severe blow to the Lahore Darbar. Though during the Sikh regime (*Sarkar khalsa*), the Dogra brothers held vast *jagirs,* even hereditary and perpetual in the hilly territories stretching from Jammu to North Western regions as well as in the plains of the Punjab, the position underwent a revolutionary change after the first Anglo-Sikh war. According to the Treaty (9 March, 1846), the Lahore *Darbar* perpetually ceded the territories lying to the south of river Sutlej, i.e., Ludhiana and Ferozpur as well as the territories lying between river Sutlej and Beas inclusive of the hilly regions to the English East India Company. At the same time, in lieu of the total war indemnty of Rupees one and a half crore, the Lahore Government paid Rupees fifty lakhs in cash and for the balance amount of rupees one crore, it perpetually ceded all rights (*haquq*) over the hilly territories stretching from river Beas to Sind Sagar inclusive of Kashmir (*diyar-i-Kashmir*) and Hazara. It was also stipulated (vide clause no. 12) that in consideration of friendship and loyalty shown by Raja Gulab Singh, *Rais-i-Jammu* towards the English Government during his tenure with the Lahore Government, all hill territories which had been in his possession (as *jagir*) since the time of Maharaja Kharak Singh would be conceded to him with *status quo*. At the same time, in consideration of his good conduct, the British Government would recognise his permanent status in these territories and admit him to the privileges of a separate treaty. As such, according to Treaty of Amritsar (16 March, 1846), the English Government bestowed (*ata named*) the territories of Kashmir, Hazara along with the hilly regions lying between the west of river Beas to the east of river Sindh as well as the territories to the west of the river Ravi comprising Chamba, excepting Lahul as already stipulated in clause 4 of the Treaty of 9 March, 1846 on Maharaja Gulab Singh in heredity (*nasalan bad nasal wa batan bad batan*) and in perpetuity (*barai doam*) to his descendants. Further, in lieu of the bestowal (*ata shudan*) of these territories, Maharaja Gulab Singh would pay the amount of *Nanak Shahi* Rupees seventy five lakhs to the British Government, out of which fifty lakhs would be paid at the time of the ratification of the treaty and the balance amount of Rupees twenty five lakhs to be paid within six months of the ratification of the treaty. At the same time, the Maharaja undertook to pay annual *nazrana* (tribute) comprising one horse, twelve perfect shwal goats of excellent breed, six male and six female, as well as three pairs of *shwals* (*do shala*).

After signing of the treaty of Amritsar (16 March, 1846), due to vehement opposition and insistance on the part of the Chamba Chief, the territories of Chamba to the west of river Ravi were withdrawn from the jurisdiction of Raja Gulab-Singh. In exchange, Bhadarwah was ceded by Chamba Chief to the latter. In the other territories of the newly founded *riyasat,* the Maharaja met with open revolt on the part of the recalcitrant chiefs and zamindars of Muzaffarbad and Hazara. Having suffered an armed reverse and being unable to administer the territories of Hazara and Balkot, he earnestly requested the British Government for exchange of these territories with some portions in the plains near river Jehlum of the Lahore kingdom. Consequently as a result of the British mediation and a Treaty signed by him with the Lahore Darbar (25 May, 1847), the Maharaja received the territories of Munawar, Sijanpore and Pathankot in exchange for Hazara and Balkot. But after some time he was obliged to surrender Sijanpore and Pathankot to the English administration and retained only a part of Munawar and territories of Kathua and Suchetgarh.

In fact, the transfer of the territories of Jammu and Kashmir by the British administration to Raja Gulab Singh was actuated by political considerations. At that stage of its position in India, the British Government thought that direct occupation of these territories would be rather disadvantageous as it would bring it in collusion with many a powerful chief and create new distant and conflicting interests with races of people with whom it had no intercourse so far. It would require large military establishment and resources for the management of vast distant borders from the base provinces of its operation. From the financial viewpoint, excepting Kashmir, the other territories were comparatively unproductive and hardly able to meet the expenses for occupation and management. On the contrary, the newly created state (*rajgi*) of Raja Gulab Singh in the territories detached from the Lahore kingdom would lower the latter's pride and prestige in the eyes of other Asiatic countries. Moreover, the creation of a strong and friendly state under a Rajput family in the northern region of the Lahore kingdom would be advantageous from the strategic military viewpoint as in case of need it would threaten or attack in the most vulnerable territories of the Lahore *Darbar.* Financially too, it would be beneficial to the British Government as it would be able to realise at least a substantial amount as indemnification for the expenses of campaign against the Lahore kingdom which otherwise the latter was unable to pay. Apart from this, excepting Kashmir and Hazara, Raja Gulab Singh and his family had already been in possession of the greater part of the territories bestowed on the Raja. Above all, the treaty signed with Raja Gulab Singh (16 March, 1846) offered best possible interference in the latter's affairs consistent with the maintenance of permanent position of the British Government over Jammu and Kashmir.

As regards the socio-economic structure in the pre-colonial Punjab, on the basis of the source material of the various categories mentioned above, it can be well established that there was an integrated pattern of commercial life. In the developed regions, the concept of village self-sufficiency can no longer be maintained. The regional sources point towards the interdependence of groups of adjacent villages on the local *mandis* both for commercial crops and non-agricultural products. Within a *pargana* or a larger territory, a few commercial centres served as links between the villages and the *qasbas*. The *qasba,* apart from serving as the administrative headquarters of the *pargana,* was also the main commercial centre of the rural areas.

However, it is hard to lay a strict line of demarcation between the rural and the urban areas in the then Punjab society; a qasba with its jurisdiction over *tappahs, mandis* and villages was more a part of the rural society than an urban centre. The names of the peddling castes with specialisation in certain merchandise commodities as well as the pastoral and animal breeding tribes are available for the Punjab. The internal trade, the local agricultural and industrial products, the export commodities, the river-system for transportation, the inland road transportation, organisation of the *banjara* communities, the commercial organisation with *Hundi* system, the revenues from the commercial items, the commercial organisation in the urban centres, the inter-provincial and foreign trade and the role of the trading castes can be well constructed from the above sources. A clear picture of the inland trade routes and external routes connecting with the other provinces and the neighbouring West and Central Asian countries can be well drawn. Because of the turbulent conditions of the 18th century, a change had occurred in the commercial set-up which equally affected the trade routes. But with stable Government in Punjab during the first half of the 19th century, many a discarded trade route were resumed.

The composition of an agricultural population and the nature of land tenures may vary from one group of villages to another or at times from one village to another. Under the Sikh rule in Punjab, the rights of the revenue paying land owning *zamindari, riaya,* the ordinary peasant proprirtor *riaya,* the *muzarian* settled in the villages whether belonging to the same clan or different cultivating clans and castes, were confirmed and acquired an element of stability. All the same, a comparison of the clans and castes with Zamindari rights in the 17th century Punjab and 18th-19th centuries pre-colonial Punjab would show that tremendous changes had occurred in the *Zamindari* title to the ownership of the land in the villages. Thus, the social picture on an ethnic plane in the agrarian society is by no means static. The practice of communal *vesh* traceable in many villages in the western Punjab during the second half of the 19th century involved periodical redistribution of the land amongst verious branches of the clan on inter-village basis or the redistribution and readjustment of the land within a single village or periodical exchange of certain ancestral land within a single family. The ethnology and economic study of these tribes suggests how the joint family proprietary notions of the medieval age descended from the communal rights of the tribes. It is not intended to suggest that this communal order of land ownership had existed in these villages all through, for this region had been the scene of political vicisstitudes and clannish domination in the 18th century which may have brought about this practice into existence. In other regions of Punjab there were no communal lands owned by the village community. In matters relating to the agricultural life, their revenue administration and social behaviour, a village society in pre-colonial Punjab was never a complete socio-economic entity. It was essentially an integral part of larger territorial and clannish settlement. The obligation of the maintenance of the irrigation and channels drawn from lakes, canals, streams and river beds was basically a territorial and clannish concept being the joint responsibility of the Zamindars and the *riaya,* even though it ultimately devolved on the village agricultural *riaya.* During the 18th-19th centuries in many a region of the Punjab, the nature of *pattidari* and *bhaichara* land tenures are traceable.

Based on the chronicles and the contemporary documents, it can be well maintained that in the Punjab, the Lahore Darbar was keenly interested in the extension of the irrigation facilities to the cultivators for the development of agricultural economy. Though the chronicles attach importance to a few canals like those in East Punjab, i. e., West Jamna, the Lahore, i. e., Upper Bari, the Delhi canal entitled Nahr-i-Bihisht, scattered regional contemporary sources point towards the existence of many a perennial small canals in either parched areas or at places where even constant water was available from the streams, and the *nalas.* A number of such canals were constructed both by the Lahore Government and the Zamindars for stepping up the agricultural and horticultural production. Though the British Government improved and extended the perennial irrigation system in the Punjab, it has yet to be established whether the apparent addition to the irrigated area by the large scale Government canals was a net addition to the effectively irrigated acreages. This is because of the fact that the new canals often replaced the older inundation canals and the problem of water logging and salinity resulted from the neglect of proper drainage system. The problem has also to be viewed against the demographic factor.

The British rule in the Punjab, more or less, adopted the proprietary concept and rights of the agricultural classes as enforced by Bird and Thompson in the North-Western Provinces. However, the North-Western and South-Western portions of the Punjab as well as the hilly tracts of Kangra were equally influenced by the traditional practices. Ordinarily, the communal *zamindari* lands, and when further split into *zamindari* possessions, were held in severalty for payment of land revenue on separate individual family holdings rather than on joint basis. In the communal *zamindari* estates, the occupancy tenants owned individual responsibility for the payment of the revenue and *malikana* on their respective holdings. In some village communities, there were owners (*malik kabaza*) of certain fields with complete proprietary title (*malkiyat makbuza*) who did not belong to the village brotherhood and did not share the joint rights, profits, and responsibilities of the members of the village communities. The division of the proprietary right of the superior (*ala malik*), the inferior (*adna malik*) and title holders was on the same pattern as in vogue in North-Western Provinces. In line with the practice of the North-Western Provinces, the settlement was invariably decided in favour of the inferior proprietors and the share of the allowance of the superior proprietors was fixed in accordance with the regulations. The occupany tenancy was also framed on the same lines except that in the *bhaichara* villages of certain regions based on the traditional practice, the occupancy tenants (*muzarian maurusi*) who possessed rights of mutation in holding, mortgage and sale as well as right of grazing their cattle on the waste land but without claim to share the profits of the *shamlat,* were confirmed with ownership rights within certain limits. In some cases, they were recorded even as inferior proprietors (*adna maliks*). On the other hand, in certain regions, under certain circumstances, they were liable to enhancement of the revenue rates.

Ordinarily, the medieval chronicles that deal mostly with the political history and aspects of the social life of the people have to be gleaned from their accounts. However, Mufti Ali-ud-din, a resident of Lahore in his *Ibrat Nama* (1854) has dealt with the social life of the common people during the reign of Maharaja Ranjit Singh and thereafter in a comprehensive manner. According to him, the society comprised three major groups of people, i.e., the Muslims, the Hindus and the Sikhs. The Muslims formed nearly two-third of the entire population. They were soft spoken, courteous and brave with great fondness for sports like horse-riding and fighting. They were very much averse to riding in a palanquin which was considered rather womanish. They were equally fond of keeping guns, swords, spears, daggers and *nachakhs*. They also exhibited fondness for recreations and enjoying picnics in the gardens. Even though they did not neglect education, there was lot of economic backwardness, social segregation and stagnation. The author does not blame the Sikh Government for their economic weakness as it did not make any discrimination against the Muslims on account of their faith. He rather ascribes it to their own extreme laziness and lack of initiative for accumulation of capital. Ordinarily, they did not take to trade and business as their vocation. They equally lacked originality in arts and crafts. Despite education, they showed fanatic attachment to the laws of Shariat. Even though the Quran accorded fairly equitable treatment to women, the Muslims never gave up their claims for the plurality of wives in spite of lack of financial resources. They were fond of back-biting, and were rather treacherous. It was their fanaticism which was responsible for their hatred of the Sikhs and utter disregard of the *faqirs* and saints of other denominations and sects. Their fanaticism was equally matched by the Akalis and the Nihangs among the Sikhs. They would never eat food cooked by a Sikh. All such traits were responsible for their segregation from the general social life and their economic backwardness.

Mufti Ali-ud-Din equally hits at the social drawback of the Hindus. According to him, the caste system had divided them into watertight compartments which had affected the ranks of the Brahmanas themselves. The subdivisions even amongst the Brahmanas relegated a section of their community unto that of Shudras. However, such subdivisions amongst the Brahmanas were not hereditary in character. The Brahmanas were not free from ordinary social vices of sex and greed. Fraudulent practices,treachery and falsehold were common on their part. They mostly showed aversion to army service. As distinct from the Brahmanas, the Khatris were mostly businessmen. They were a prosperous community but they showed no sense of morality in business. They were equally averse to military service. Despite economic prosperity, they were not very hospitable. In matters of dress, food, manners and etiquettes, they did not observe any formality. Accumulation of capital was their main business. Their children were married at a very tender age of 6 to 10. The other two groups of the Vaishyas and the Shudras mostly continued their normal traditional ways of life. There was considerable flexibility and many of them rose to higher positions in life.

As regards the Sikhs, the author comments, they generally shook off the rituals that the Brahmanas fostered on the other Hindu society. They mostly took to agriculture and invariably joined army. Many Sikhs belonged to the Zamindari class. They were highly sensitive for the Zamindari class. They were highly sensitive for the protection of the honour of their womenfolk. They did not observe the practice of preparing a *chauka* before eating meals. Meat was their staple diet but they would never eat meat of any animal slaughtered by a Muslim. They did not observe any formality in the matter of dress and social intercourse. Instead of saying 'Ram Ram' like the other Hindus, they would utter *Waheguru ji ki Fateh*. In the morning hours, they would recite only the Guru's Bani, i.e., *Japji* and the *Sukhmani*. The main section of the Sikhs was that of the cultivators. A large number of those who embraced Sikhism called themselves *Singh Guruji Ka* and were engaged in the trade. They were, by and large, very fond of wearing arms. Those who could well afford liked riding horses and elephants. The Sikhs made extensive use of Gurumukhi and read and wrote in that script. In social life, they indulged in wine and sex. The sections known as the Akalis and Nihangs were extremely fanatic.

The above description is only a gist of the description about the common people of the Punjab as provided by Mufti Ali-ud-din's *Ibrat Nama*. This work written in Persian, even though published in Pakistan, has not been translated into English or any of the regional languages in India or Pakistan. Similarly, Rae Kali Rai and Lala Tulsi Ram's work, *Kitab-i-Sair-i-Punjab* gives a fairly comprehensive account of the religious beliefs and practices, food habits, dress, amusements and recreation, fairs and festivals and above all, the customs and traditions of the common people, more especially in the rural areas of the Punjab during the mid-19th century. Despite all its drawbacks for the historical portion, it is a highly significant source of information for the period under review. Its importance can be well realised from the fact that the later English works, i.e., Ibbetson's *A Glossary of Tribes and Castes of Punjab,* Griffin and Messey's *Chiefs and Families of Note* and Richard Temples's *Legends of the Punjab* and various other works are based upon it to a great extent. One can equally glean significant passages on the social life from Ganesh Dass Badhera's *Chahar Bagh-i-Punjab.* The *Vars* and the *Kissas* speak of the habits and social outlook of certain sections of the people in a significant manner.

It is significant to observe that even though Persian was the court language of the Lahore Darbar, the common people of all religious faiths, the Muslims, the Hindus and the Sikhs spoke Punjabi which was written both in Arabic and Gurumukhi scripts. All the same, in 1882 A.D., Urdu was introduced by the British Government as an official vernacular language, more or less, against the wishes of many a section of the Punjab society.

At the end, it may be reiterated emphatically that right from the 16th century down to at least the mid-19th century, the Nanak *Panth* was regarded as an integral part of the Hindu society. Even though distinct from the other Hindu faiths, viz., the Brahmanical order, Vaishnavism, Shivaism, other *bhagti* cults and the socio-religious orders like the Jains, Jogis (*faqirs,* i.e., Kanphattas and Augars, etc.), it remained within the Hindu socio-religious structure. As a matter of fact, right from the 8th century onwards, the Muslim writers used the term Hindus (*Hanud*) in India in contrast to the followers of Islam (*Musalmin*). In the early medieval age, even though Buddhism was well established in Sindh, Multan and other parts of the west Punjab, despite social tension between the Buddhist and the Brahmans, the Arab accounts insist on covering both as a part of the Hindu society. From 13th century onwards, the Persian sources maintain this concept of the Hindus and Muslims and consider all religious sects in Hindustan which were outside the Islamic religion and its people (*Musalmin*) as the Hindu people (*Hanud*), though, of course, both were divided into various clannish social groups (*firqas*). It is clear from the hymns of Guru Nanak and the writings of Guru Gobind Singh that when they appeal for social cohesion and composite human culture, they only mention the Hindus and the Muslims as the two main religious classes in Hindustan and regard their own socio-religious order as a part of the larger Hindu society with multifarious sects. It is evident from the 18th century documents that gradually the term *Khalsaji* or the *Panth* comprised all the Sikhs (*Singhan*) divided for political purposes unto various ethnic, trible and clannish groups (*qabial* or *qabalian* or *qabilas*) under the Sardars (*Sardaran-i-Khalsa*) with their respective *dals* and territorial *zamindari* and *taaulqadari* jurisdictions (*makanat*) all over the Punjab, cis-Sutlej territories and other regions of *subah* Delhi. As before, the distinction between the *firqas* of *ahl-i-Islam* and the Hindu *aqwam* (*qaums*) is maintained and the Sikh *aqwam* (*qaums*) are considered as a part of the latter. At the close of the 18th and the early 19th century, Mirza Qatil, a converted Sikh-Muslim in *Halft Tamasha* while giving an account of the creeds, traditions and sects of the Hindus, and of the Musalmans of India regarded "the Sikh disciples of Peshwa Nanak Shah Punjab as part of the Hindus of the Punjab". This concept is maintained both by the Hindu and Muslim writers in the reigns of Maharaja Ranjit Singh and his successors. It is only after the annexation of the Punjab that the British administrators, while writing their memoranda and reports in the English language, gave connotations to the existing technical aspects of the socio-religious orders so as to make Sikhism as distinct from Hinduism.

Prior to the annexation of Punjab (1849), both the English Governor-Generals of India, Lord Hardinge and Lord Dalhousie while considering the viability of the annexation of Punjab, in their correspondence and respective Minutes had considered the Lahore Government as a Hindu Government. When after the first Anglo-Sikh war, Lord Hardinge advocated the non-annexation of Punjab, his main argument was that this being the last Hindu state in India could well serve as a buffer between "the Sutledge and the Khyber", i.e., between the English and the Muslim states of Afghanistan and Iran etc. Both Hardinage and Dalhousie considered the 'Lahore Court', 'Khalsa State', 'Hindu Government', and the Lahore Government' as co-terminous and identical. Even as late as 1881-83 when the Report on the Census (1881) was compiled as the first experiment in the Punjab, the English administrator responsible for carrying out the census conceded the fact that it was based on "the initial experience", "infinite diversity of the material to be dealt with" and their own, i.e., the English, "infinite ignorance of that material" as well as "ignorance of the customs and the beliefs of the people". It was meant not only for the guidance of the British Indian officials but it also aimed to feed "European Science" about "the social and religious phenomena" of the Punjab. All the same, in many a region of the people of various castes and clans professing the same religious faith, some got themselves recorded as Hindus while others as Sikhs. As a matter of fact, it is only in the late 19th and 20th century that in the changed political circumstances, the Sikhs have come to be viewed as a separate religious entity as distinct from the Hindu Society.

Chapter 13

Relationship between the Lahore Darbar and Punjab Hill Chiefs during the first half of the 19th Century till 1846*

The importance of the epigraphic and documentary source material available at Bhuri Singh Museum, Chamba (Himachal Pradesh) for analysing the socio-economic aspects of the hilly regions of the Punjab during the medieval and the pre-British era has already been highlighted by the present writer.[1]

Based on the above source material, the institutional relationship covering the agrarian aspects involved between the Punjab hill chiefs (*Zamindaran-i-Kahistan-Punjab*) and the Mughal State as well as the Durranis of Kabul during the 17th and 18th centuries has also been analysed.[2] It may be reiterated that both in the *Rechna* and *Bari Doabs,* the *zamindari* pattern of the chieftainship was based on the hierarchical pattern of the landed intermediaries (zamindars) who acted as *malguzars* (revenue payers) to the superior zamindars who, in their own turn, paid the revenues (*peshkash*) to the sovereign states. This is well-borne by the above mentioned documentary evidence. It fact, this is equally true of the hilly regions of the other *Doabs* attached to the *Dar-ul-sultanate* of Lahore. During the 18th century, the hilly regions of the *Rechna* and *Bari Doabs,* i.e., the central and the eastern groups were managed by the *faujdars* of the *chaklas* of Jammu and Kangra. Notwithstanding this broad territorial division of the *chakla* administration for the purposes of the revenue collection, the superior rights of the chief zamindars over their subordinate chiefs always cut across the *chakla* demarcations. It may also be reiterated that during the second half of the 18th century, the Mughal sovereign rights over

* Papers Presented at Punjab History Conference, 17th Session, October 8-10, 1982, Punjabi University, Patiala.

these territories had practically vanished and the Durrani rule of Kabul had stepped in. Apart from the occupation of the Kashmir and Multan, the Durranis claimed political sovereignty and realized *peshkash* (revenues) more or less on the Mughal pattern and principles. It also seems that during the last three decades of the 18th century, even though the Durranis continued to claim political sovereignty, their effective administrative control for the realization of the revenues over the Punjab hill chiefs was either intermittent or minimal. The Sikh Ramgarhia *misl* under Jassa Singh and later on the Kanhiya *misl* under Jai Singh claimed revenues from many a hill chief and established their effective administrative control for their realization. The Durranis continued to claim only *de jure* political rights. This phase was equally marked by territorial reshufflings in the superior *zamindari* rights on the part of the hill chieftains both in the Jammu and the Kangra divisions.[3] During the first decade of the 19th century till 1809, the Gurkhas of Nepal were able to establish their sovereign territorial rights over some parts of the eastern hill regions (later on covered by Simla Hill States). The Gurkha incursions equally affected the Kangra region but were effectively checkmated with the support of the Sikh power under Maharaja Ranjit Singh in 1809 A.D. Thus, from 1809-1846 A.D., the Lahore *Darbar* under Ranjit Singh and his successors exercised sovereign political rights and claimed revenues from the Hill chiefs through well organised administrative set up. It is equally decernable from the contemporary evidence that the State under Ranjit Singh claimed sovereign rights over the hill chiefs as having been inherited from the Sikh Ramgarhia and Kanhaya *misls* since the seventies of the 18th century. This is notwithstanding the fact that for a short period, the Kangra ruler had also established his *de facto* rights over some of these chieftains.[4] In fact, the Lahore *Darbar* claimed both *de jure* and *de facto* rights as successor to the Durrani rule.

For the first half of the 19th century, there are as many as 24 documents in Persian, Tankri, Nagari, Gurumukhi and English available at Bhuri Singh Museum Chamba (Himachal Pradesh), which throw considerable light on the mutual relations amongst the chiefs, their *zamindari* and territorial problems as well as relations between the Lahore *Darbar* and these chiefs. They cover *sanads,* treaties, agreements, statements, Royal Orders (Ranjit Singh's), *jagir* assisnments, and letters addressed by the Lahore rulers to the chiefs and amongst the chiefs themselves. A few documents in Persian specifically spell out the nature of claim which the Lahore *Darbar* asserted over the revenues of some of these hilly regions. It may be well maintained that for proper analysis and perspective, it is equally essential to coordinate the other primary sources of the Sikh period available in Persian, Punjabi and English.

The letter *(dharam patra),* dated 27 *Jeth Vikrami* 1878/13 June 1821, addressed by Maharaja Ranjit Singh to Raja Charhat Singh of Chamba (1808-1844 A.D.)[5] confirms the annexation of *taaluqa* Rihlu to the Sikh State. Its revenues were to be attached to the latter. As the *dharam patra* is extremely significant underlining relationship between the Lahore *Darbar* and the Chamba Chieftain, it has been reproduced in *extenso* as follows :

On submission of the *qala* Rihlu along with the *taaluqa* as per old boundaries of Raja Charhat Singh, Raja of Chamba *wala* and on the establishment of the *thana* of the *sarkar* at the said *qala* and the *taaluqa,* the *Hazur* has approved the arrangement and on account of these efforts and manifestation of loyalty and obedience, the following have been awarded to the said Raja according to the *dharam patra* issued to Wazir Nathu.

(a) In return for a few villages of *taaluqa* Rihlu, the *sarkar* has granted the *Raj* of Bhadrawah to Raja Charhat Singh. He may remain in possession of it without any fear on the condition of helping the *Hazur* in the reduction of the entire hilly region to submission and obedience. The hill chiefs should also report for personal attendance before the *Hazur* (i. e. Lahore *Darbar*) with whole-hearted devotion. He (i.e. the Raja of Chamba) should also present fine quality of apples from his gardens to the *Hazur-o-Nur* (Maharaja Ranjit Singh).

(b) A yearly *jagir* valued at Rs. 3,000/- (Rupees three thousand) only has been fixed in the *wajah* of Mian Pahar Chand of Bhadrawah as a *madad-i-maash*. This is to be paid by the Raja of Chambal (Chamba) to the Bhadrawah (chieftain) every year.

(c) *Muamala* and *nazrana,* as assessed previously (*mushaqsa sabiqa*) with details given below are exampled in the *wajan* of Raja Chambal (*muaf-wa-bakshida bashad*).

(i) *Nazrana* as assessed previously (*nazrana mushaqsa sabiqa*);

(ii) *Muamala* relating to Torai, etc. having been fixed previously in Kangra, (*muamala ba dastur*) Kangra;

(iii) *Rusum* relating to the *musahiban* and Desa Singh etc, excepting the dues (*takalif*) of the *thanedari* of Sardar Desa Singh Majitha, etc.

(d) The Raja was exempted from the payment of the yearly assessed *nazrana*. Whatever the (amount) of *nazrana* and *rusumat* as previously fixed, the Maharaja (Ranjit Singh) would not claim.

(e) The Raja of Bhadrawah and Wazir would owe complete submission obedience and faithfulness and would obey the *sarkar* and do whole-hearted service (*naukari*) in the entire hilly region and would also offer personal attendance on the conditions stated above,

(f) Wazir Nathu and his sons are to present themselves at evey place before *Hazur* (i. e. the Lahore *Darbar*) for the satisfaction of the latter. The aforesaid Raja would continue to be the chieftain of Chamba with the understanding and consent of the *Hazur.*

(g) An amount of Rs. 1,000/- (Rupees one thousand) only in *taaluqa* Dewar (in Rihulu) for the acquistion of *basmati* rice (*baranj-i-basmati*) is hereby bestowed in *wajah* (*tankhwah*) on the Raja of Chamba, who is authorised to collect it every year.

(h) Two horses *kothia* and two pairs of fine breed of falcons (*baz*) worthy of excursion/hunting (purposes) for the *Sarkar* are to be sent every year at the time of Dussehra festival.

And as such by the grace of *Sri Akal Puruk Jiu,* these few lines contained in the clauses of the *dharam patra* have been issued to the said Raja.

Dated this day of 27th of *Jeth* 1878 *samwat,* this *parwangi* of *Hazur* is conditional on the terms laid down herein provided there is no deviation from the submission, obedience and service (*naukari*) conditions, this *ihadnama* (agreement) would be treated as binding and final.

It may be maintained that in accordance with the Mughal practice, after conquest, the Lahore *Darbar* considered the revenues of the hill chieftainships as the revenues of the Sikh State itself. After submission, the hill chiefs were regarded as the servants of the State and in lieu of the service being rendered by them, they were only entitled to certain categories of *jagirs* and other perquisites (*haquq*). Depending on the political situation, the family status, the geographical and strategic position of the chieftainship and, above all, the terms and conditions of submission, their revenues might be taken as fixed or might be assessed from time to time. It was by itself an evolutionary process and only when the sovereign State was firmly in saddle, the revenues could be revised from one period to another.

As a matter of fact, in line with the Mughal tradition, the Lahore *Darbar* too fixed the revenues periodically.[6] The State may or may not concede the right to the chieftain to make payment of revenues on periodically fixed rather than on annual return. The revenues of the *zamindaries* of the territories were both in the *amli* and *ghair amli* liable to be revised for a reasonable span of period. At every settlement the Sovereign State had the discretion to retain the previously fixed revenues for that year and for the future as well or to enhance it in accordance with the revenue returns of the territories of the chieftainship. The State may retain fixed revenues in respect of some villages or *parganas* while for others, the revenues may be revised. Any retention of the fixed revenues was conditional upon continuous loyalty and service to the State. The extent of special concession was essentially governed by the political relationship between the sovereign State and the chieftain. By and large, in the initial stages, after the conquest of a chieftainship, the revenues may ramain fixed for some period but they were revised when the State had consolidated its position. This also was enforced by the Sovereign State on the chieftains both in the planes and in the hilly regions. The chronicles and the records of the Sikh period clearly bear out for the hill chieftains as well for the periodical revision of revenues (*nazrana*) after undertaking of campaigns by the Lahore *Darbar.*[7] As for the other hill chieftains, the revenues (*nazrana*) of the Rajas of Jammu, Mandi Suket and Chamba were also revised periodically.[8] For instance, in 1807, the Raja of Chamba paid Rs. 30,000/- as *nazrana.*[9] But later on, in 1816, the *vakil* of the Raja personally presented the Maharaja Ranjit Singh at Adinanagar *hundis* worth Rs. 40,000/- in lieu of partial *nazrana* while for the remaining amount (unspecified), surety (*zamni*) was stood by Lala Ramanand, the *saraf* and *ilatichigir* the *faqir.*[10] The position underwent further change in June 1821 as already analysed in the above mentioned document.[11] The documents also make it clear that in these hilly regions, the traditional *zamindari* pattern was still based on the hierarchical pattern of the landed intermediaries (zamindars) who acted as the subordinate chiefs of the superior zamindar-cum-*jagirdar* who dealt directly with the Sovereign State for the payment of revenues and discharge of other obligations.

The documents relating to the Mughal period and the Durrani Rule during the course of the 17th and the 18th centuries show the payment of the revenues as *peshkash* to the Sovereign State.[12] In contrast to these, documents of the Sikh period are much more detailed bringing out various aspects of the nature of the revenues being claimed by the Sovereign State. It is rather significant to note that the chronicles of the Sikh period ordinarily do not refer to the *peshkash* and use other general terms denoting the revenues to be paid by these chiefs. For instance, Sohan Lal Suri in *Umdat-ul-Tawarikh* ordinarily refers to the fixed dues (*mabaligh-i-mutaiyana/mubaligh/mahuda*) or else he refers to the *nazrana* realisable from the Rajas of the hilly regions.[13] Here *nazrano* denotes all the categories of the revenues and does not imply merely the realisation of 'tribute' or fixed token gift etc. At times, Sohan Lal Suri uses the term *muamala* and in the same passage by referring to the realisation from the chieftains of Kangra, Nurpur, Kulu, Chamba, Jasrota and Haripur puts *nazrana* and *muamala* more or less synonymous.[14] Here, too, though the two terms *nazrana* and *muamala* in matters of details were distinct from each other, they are used as general terms for the revenues on the whole. Similar description is available from the other contemporary chronicles as well.[15]

Another contemporary chronicle, Ram Sukh Rao's *Sri Fateh Singh Partap Prabhakar,* while describing the revenues to be realised from the chieftains of Kotlehr (Kotal Hari, Kangra, Mandi, Kulu, Nur Mahal and Rajauri, etc. refers to the revenues as *muamala* and *baj (baju)* as well as *lawazmat* (*lawajme*).[16] Of course, he makes distinction between land revenue proper (*muamala*) and *baj* (*bajmi*), i.e., other miscellaneous cesses.[17] As a matter of fact, while going through the chronicle or a regional biographical history, one has to read between the lines of the text and not to be carried away by the general term used by the author *nazrana* or *muamala,* which by no means stood for mere 'tribute' to be paid by the hill chiefs. What the Mughal documents put the *peshkash* standing for the revenues *malwajbi was haquq-i-dewani,*[18] the chronicles of Sikh period ordinarily refer to *nazrana* or *muamala* in the same sense.[19] All the same, the two terms *muamala* and *nazrana* from the technical point of view were distinct revenue terms. It is only the documentary study which absolutely makes it clear for the Sikh period as well. Such fine distinction between various categories of revenues is confirmed by the *Khalas Darbar Records* wherein the amount of the revenues comprise both *nazrana* and *muamala* (*muamala-i-qadim*, i.e., having been in vogue previously *hasb mahmul*).[20]

In line with the Mughal tradition,the Sikh Sovereign State not only claimed the revenues of the territories of the princely chiefs as that of the Lahore *Darbar,* it fully exercised its discretion with regard to alienation and even regulation for succession to *gaddi* of chieftainship. The relations between the Lahore *Darbar* and the princely chiefs cannot be characterised as simply between the paramountcy and Indian States as in vogue during the succeeding British period of Indian occupation. The limitations imposed by the Lahore *Darbar* upon the *zamindaries* of the princely chiefs was of far more penetrating nature than visualised hitherto and institutionally speaking with rare exceptions, such chieftainships can hardly be termed as States whether semi-independent or subordinate paying merely what has been considered to be 'tribute' comprising particular amount. Most of them enjoyed only limited 'autonomy' confined to internal administration of the chieftainship. The case of the Bhadrawah chieftainship referred to in the above documents is a clear illustration of relationship between the Sovereign State and chieftainship. During the reign of Aurangzeb (1666 A.D.), the *pargana* Bhadrawah previously given in *inam jagir* to Sangrampal of Basohli was transferred to the Raja of Chamba. This was further confirmed through regular *sanad* issued by the Mughal State. As such, in the hierachical *zamindari* pattern, the Raja of Chamba stood as the highest landed intermediary in relation to the chief of Bhadrawah. This is further confirmed by an agreement (Tankari) of the late 18th century which spells out relationship between Raja Raj Singh of Chamba (1764-94 and Raja Fateh Pal (1770-1790 A.D.) of Bhadrawah. The latter was to pay Rs. 3,000/- yearly to the Chamba chief who continued to exercise firm control over the former even during the ascendancy of the Sikh *misls*.[21] The above mentioned letter *(dharam patra*) of Ranjit Singh, dated June 1821, finally transferred the chieftainship of Bhadrawah to the Chamba chief while Mian Pahar Chand of Bhadrawah was only assigned maintenance grant (*madad-i-maash*) of Rs. 3,000/- per year in lieu of the services rendered by him. Thus, the age-old line of succession of the Bhadrawah chieftainship became extinct at the hands of the Sikh State.

Another *sanad* (in Persian), dated 1st *Har,* 1881 *Vikrami* (12 June 1824 A.D.), grants the *waziri* or *taaluqa* Bhadarwah in *wajah* to Wazir Nathu in perpetuity (*naslan bad naslan*).[22] In 1833, Zorawar Singh, the brother of Raja Bhadarwah and was then spoken as *chota* Raja. Two subsequent letters (in Persian), dated September 1843 and 21st December 1844, addressed by the Lahore *Darbar* to Raja Sri Singhji of Chamba (1844-70) confirmed the chieftainship of Chamba and Bhadarwah on the Raja.[23] The second letter referred to above States that in case the Raja liked, he could give Bhadarwah to the sons of

Zorawar Singh and if he so pleased, he might not do so. He should look to his interests only. This letter was issued after Pandit Jhalla had visited the Royal court.[24]

Two *parwanas* (in Persian) relating to Nurpur chieftainship clearly bring out the fact that the Lahore *Darbar* claimed the total revenues of the chieftainship and maintained its claim to assign the revenues to the State servants at its discretion. It equally asserted its right to determine the extent of *jagir* of the chieftainship at its discretion. In 1815, Raja Bir Singh (1789-1846) was called along with other chiefs to present himself at Sialkot. But he did not attend the court. He was again offered a *jagir* of Rs. 12,000/- per annum which, too, was not accepted by him. A *parwana* (in Persian), dated 3rd *Har* 1884 *Vikrami* (12 June 1827 A.D.), addressed by the Lahore *Darbar* to Lehna Singh, Chaūdhari Koricha and *kardars* (*kardaran*) of Nurpur assigns *jagir* to Inder Singh, son of Wazir Nathu being in service.[25] It further informs the *kardars* that the *nazrana* of Rs. 400/- being demanded by them had already been remitted by a previous *parwana*. It enjoins upon the assignees not to collect *lajma,* etc. It specifically instructs them not to levy charges like *karobekar, nazar* and *chut* (exemption) etc. Another order (*parwana*) of Maharaja Ranjit Singh (in Persian), dated 1st *Pos,* 1891 *samwat* (17 December 1834 A.D.) issued to Lehna Singh, confirms the grant of village Sarthi in *qasba* Nurpur with effect from *Rabi samwat* 1892 in the *wajah* of Lehna Singh, grandson of Wazir Nathu, valued at Rs. 3,000/- in lieu of service.[26] The order enjoins upon the grantee to render personal service along with the *sawars,* to remain obedient and in occupation of the *muamala* from the above villages on account of service (*naukari*) and to continue to render other services to the *sarkar.* Similarly, the revenues of the other territories of Nurpur must have been realised by the Sikh State by assigning in (*tankhwah*) *jagir* to other State servants or directly, if declared as *khalisa* region.

Two undated letters (in Persian), addressed by the Lahore *Darbar* to Raja Charhat Singh of Chamba refer to the disturbed conditions in Pangi and Padar and inform that Nathu Wazir had been sent to settle down the conditions for the purposes of law and order.[27]

Apart from the above,there are three uncatalogued documents (in Tankari) which involve correspondence amongst Raja Gulab Singh of Jammu, Raja Charhat Singh of Chamba and Raja Bir Singh of Nurpur. The letter, dated 1st of *Bhadon Sastra* 3/1827 A.D., addressed by Gulab Singh of Jammu to Raja Charhat Singh assures that he would help him in connection with Raja Bir Singh of Nurpur[28] (who had been imprisoned by Ranjit Singh in the Govindgarh fort at Amritsar). Another letter, dated 12th *Sawan, Sastra* 10/1834 A.D., addressed by Raja Charhat Singh to Raja Bir Singh of Nurpur promises him of pecuniary help.[29] Thirdly,in a letter dated 12th *Sawan, Sastra* 10/1834 Raja Bir Singh of Nurpur promises to always accept the sincere advice of Raja of Chamba.[30]

Another undated letter (in Persian), addressed to Raja Sri Singh, informs him regarding the approach of the English forces towards Chamba which intended to encamp at Chari. The letter also assures the Raja that *parwanas* had already been issued both by the *Sarkar-i-wala* (i.e., the Lahore *Darbar*) and *Sahiban-i-alishan* (i.e., English East India Company) for his (Raja's) satisfaction.[31] This was evidently written after the Anglo-Sikh war in 1845 A.D. Two subsequent letters (in Persian) also relate to beginning period of the English East India Company. A letter dated 29th *Phagun* 1902 *Vikrami* 1846 A.D., notifies Raja Sri Singh that Chamba had been transferred to the English *sarkar* and that he should present himself before it,[32] Another significant letter (in Persian) issued by Henry Lawrence, dated 16th March 1846 A.D., (issued at Amritsar), addressed to Raja Sri Singh of Chamba informs that the *ilaqa* of Chamba had been transferred from the English *sarkar* and conferred on Maharaja Gulab Singh (of Jammu).[33] It enjoins the Raja that on the basis of this order, he should present himself before the *ahalkars* (*ahalkakaran*) of the Maharaja (of Jammu) for the payment of the *muamala* previously fixed. He is further instructed not to indulge in any recalcitrance in the neighbourhood and that he would continue to enjoy his ancient perquisites (*haquq-i-qadima*) and that he would be held guilty for any evasion in the payment of the *muamala* to the Maharaja (i.e., of Jammu).

The above position emerged as a consequence of the Anglo-Sikh Treaty of Lahore (19th March 1886) according to which the Sikh State had ceded to the Hon'ble East India Company, in perpetual sovereignty as equivalent to one crore of rupees, all forts, territories, rights and interests in the hilly countries, which were situated between two rivers Beas and Indus, including the provinces of Kashmir and Hazara.[34] However, fortunately for Chamba, this treaty was later on modified by the Anglo-Sikh Treaty[35] of Amritsar (16th March 1848) and the special arrangement made by the English East India Company with Maharaja Gulab Singh of Jammu in 1847. Through the mediation of Colonel Lawrence and consequent on the arrangement made by the English East India Company with Maharaja Gulab Singh, the latter relinquished all claim on Chamba on both sides of the river Ravi and in lieu thereof the Raja of Chamba surrendered all claim on Bhadrawah to Jammu and the Lakhanpur *taaluqa* was also conferred on the latter.[36] A *sanad* dated 6th April, 1848, issued by the English East India Company, conferred the territory of Chamba upon Raja Sri Singh, providing that, failing heirs-male of his own body, the succession would devolve on his elder surviving brother.[37] Thus, in 1848, Chamba became directly under the English East India Company.

References

1. B.R. Grover, "Relationship between the Sovereign State (the Mughals and Afghans) and the Punjab Hill Chiefs during the 17th and 18th centuries. A case study of Chamba Chieftainship based on Bhuri Singh Museum, Chamba Documents", *Punjab History Conference*, XVII Session, March 12-14, 1982, pp. 94-102. This was for the first time introduced at the 41st Session of the *Indian History Congress*, Bombay, 1980.
2. *Ibid.*
3. For details, see Bhuri Singh Museum, Chamba Documents (henceforth B.S.M.) (Persian), c-20, c-44, c-45; catalogued Docs. (Tankari) c-18, dated 1st *Magh Vikrami* 1834/1778 A.D.; c-21, c-24, dated 30th *Jeth Vikram samvat* 1837/1780 A.D.; c-25, dated 15th *Bhadon, Sastra* 57/1781 A.D.; c-28, dated 7th *Kartik, Sastra* 58/1782 A.D.; c-31, dated 18th *Bhadon, Sastra* 59/1783 A.D., c-39, dated 2nd *Sawan*, *Sastra*/1786 A.D.; c-40, dated 1st *Kartik*, *Sastra* 65/1789 A.D.; c-43, dated 5th *Sawan, Sastra* 71/ 1796 A.D.; c-51, dated 13th *Bhadon*/1801, A.D.; c-52, dated 2nd *Bhadon, Sastra* 77/1802 A.D.
4. *Ibid.*, Doc., c-54, dated 17th *Maghair, Sastra* 1709/1803 A.D.; uncatalogued (Tankri) document No. 77.35, dated *Baisakh pravishte* 5, *samwat* 1851; Document (Nagari) No. c-57. The letter addressed by Amar Singh Thapa and Ranjit Singh (Gurkhas) to Raja Jit Singh of Chamba. Also, Ram Sukh Rao,. *Sri Fateh Singh Partap Prabhakar,* (*A History of the Early Nineteenth Century, Punjab*), ed. Joginder Kaur, Patiala (henceforth Ram Sukh Rao), pp. 66-253.
5. B.S.M., Chamba, Document c-59. It bears a seal in Gurumukhi, J. Hutchison and J.P.H. Vogel, *History of the Panjab Hill States,* Lahore, 1933 (henceforth Hutchison), inaccurately mentions it as *sanad* which, in fact, is a *dharma patra.*
6. For details of the Mughal System, B.R. Grover, "Elements of Continuity and Change in the Land Ownership and Rights from the Mughal Age to the Early British Administration in India", Presidental Address Medieval India Section, *Proceedings of the Indian History Congress*, 37th Session, Calicut, pp. 143-178.

7. For details, Sohan Lal Suri, *Umdat-ul-Tawarikh* (henceforth *Umdat*) Persian text, Lahore, 1887, II, pp. 23, 86-89, 92-93, 102-103, 128-129, 132-133, 155, 164, 167, 174, 192-193, 243-244, 253.
8. *Ibid.,* also pp. 287-288, 306; also Diwan Amar Nath, *Zafarnama-i-Ranjit Singh* (ed. Sita Ram Kohli), Lahore, 1928, pp. 12, 58, 141.
9. *Umdat,* II, pp. 69, 128-129, 192-193, 277.
10. *Ibid.*
11. See fn. 5.
12. See details, fns 2 and 6.
13. *Umdat,* II, pp. 23-24, 92-93, 102-103, 164, 174.
14. *Ibid.,* pp. 128, 132-133, 192-193.
15. See fn. 8.
16. Ram Sukh Rao, pp. 339-342.
17. *Ibid.,* Joginder Kaur, in Introduction of the text pp. 25-31, has used the English term 'tribute' and has not been able to appreciate the corect position in respect of the realisation of *nazrana, muamala, baj,* etc. from the hill chiefs by Ranjit Singh nor is her understanding of the Mughal practice of realisation of *peshkash/muamala* correct.

    Muamala stood for land revenue and this term was current under the Marathas in many a portion of North India. At the same time, the term *muamala* connoting the land revenue being realised both in cash and kind during the *rabi* season was in vogue in the plains of the Panjab during the late 18th century under the Sikh Chiefs. *Nazrana* is also realised simultaneously. (For details, see National Archives of India, New Delhi, *Farsi Akhbarat wa murasalat* (Persian), *Akhbar* Raja Saheb Singh Bahadur, dated 1st *Rajab* 1211 A.H./21 December, 1796, Patiala). Under the Mughals, it was generally covered under heading *mal-o-jihat.* (For details, *Ain-i-Akbari,* British Museum, Add. 7652, fol. 147a). While giving details about Ranjit Singh's campaigns in Muzaffargarh and Bhawalpur, Ram Sukh Rao (vide fn. 16) clearly mentions the realisation of *muamala* from the village Tut by Budha Singh, the *thanadar* of Fateh Abad as based on *kan* (i.e., appraisement method of assessment), pp. 380-81. *Baj* related to cess, especially on articles of trade and commodities collected in the markets or tha highway. Under the Mughals, it was covered under the heading *Sair Jihat* (For details, *Akbar Nama,* British Museum. Add. 26, 207, fol. 124a; *Insha-i-Allami,* Ms. Orient. Oct. 1140, Berlin, fols. 47a-48a).
18. See details vide fns. 1 and 6.
19. See fns 7 and 8.
20. Punjab State Archives, Patiala, *Khalsa Durbar Records,* Bundle 3, Vol. IV, 109 and 189. Indu Banga, *Agrarian System of the Sikhs,* New Delhi, 1978,

pp. 39-62, usually uses the term tribute for *nazarana* as done by Hutchison. However, based on the study of the above records, though after some speculation about the connotation of the term *muamala-i-qadim* does ultimately concede the "possibility that the term *muamala* refers to the amount of revenue taken up the suzerain from a vassal in addition to the stipulated annual tribute" (pp. 18-40). In general, it is a correct statement if here 'tribute' simply stands for *nazarana.* In fact, as during the Mughal Age, the term *peshkash* in revenue terminology in relation to the chieftains comprised *nazarana, muamala* and other customary dues etc., Under the Sikh rule, as often put by the chroniclers, the annual *nazarana* (if at all translated as 'tribute') in general terminology comprised *nazarana, muamala* and other customary dues etc.

21. B.S.M., Chamba, Doc. c-22.
22. *Ibid.,* Doc. c-60. It bears the seal of Maharaja Ranjit Singh in Gurumukhi.
23. *Ibid.,* Doc. c-69.
24. *Ibid.*
25. *Ibid.,* Doc. c-61.
26. *Ibid.,* Doc. c-65.
27. *Ibid.,* Doc. c-66 and c-67.
28. *Ibid.,* Doc. c-62.
29. *Ibid.,* Doc. c-63.
30. *Ibid.,* Doc. c-64.
31. *Ibid.,* Doc. c-72.
32. *Ibid.,* Doc. c-71. This was issued by Dhuleep, i.e., Dalip Singh in Gurumukhi.
33. *Ibid.,* Doc. c-70.
34. Aitchison, C. V., *A Collection of Treaties, Engagements and Sanads,* Calcutta, 1892-93 (henceforth Aitchison). Also Hutchison, II, Article IV, Appendix I, p. i.
35. *Ibid.,* Hutchison Appendices II and III, pp. iii and iv.
36. *Ibid.*
37. Aitchison, II, No. cxxix.

Chapter 14

A Note on the Sikh Revenue System, State Demand and Methods of Assessment*

A fixed share in the produce was charged from the cultivators except in the case of crops like sugar-cane, cotton and tobacco on which money was charged. This was prevalent both in the Punjab and cis-Sutlej states.

Kankut was the most preferred method of assessment; also *Batai*.

State Demand: — Varied from 1/3rd to 2/5th of the crop but for the land with good advantages, 1/2 was taken. The rates in the cis-Sutlej were lower on the whole. The demand was increased by *Abwab*.

Cash assessments were occasionally introduced, the most famous being the very equitable one introduced by Mr. Rup Lal in the two plain districts of Jullunder Doab (1832-39 AD).

The revenues of villages and even of large tracts were sometimes leased at fixed sums to revenue farmers, and there were many large jagirs. Farmers and Jagirdars were left to make their own arrangements with the cultivators.

Diwan Sawan Mal's Revenue System

Diwan Sawan Mal, the greatest of the Sikh Governors, was a revenue farmer on a very large scale, paying into the Lahore treasury nearly 22 lakhs per annum from Multan, Muzaffargarh, and Dera Ghazi Khan, and parts of Montgomery, Jhang, and Dera Ismail Khan.

In Multan, Sawan Mal levied a fixed cash assessment on each up-land well. For wells and 'jhalars' in the riverain tracts leases, fixed cash demands were sometimes given, but the finest crops like cane, indigo, etc. paid special rates. A normal well area was fixed according to the circumstances of each locality, and any cultivation in excess of that limit was charged a fixed money rate per bigha. In some places, the demand varied according to the number of oxen employed on the well and was remitted when the well was deserted. For flooded lands, a moderate share was taken in kind and occasionally cash rates were charged. The share of the state was pitched especially low in the case of new cultivation. Diwan Sawan Mal's system seems to have been inherited from the past.

The Sikh policy of extention of cultivation

Colonisation was done of extensive waste lands of the older zamindaries and employment was given to industrious cultivators of lower castes, thereby increasing cultivable land.

Conception of property and Zamindari villages

The Sikhs did not ignore property in land. There were authenticated deeds of sale and other transfers during the Sikh regime.

Refer to *Sir Richard Temple's Report (1851)* on the first regular Settlement of Jullunder. It quotes the documents of the Sikh rule.

The occupant cultivator claimed the proprietory right. The *muqaddam* and the zamindars only got their *malikana* rights. Under Misr. Rup Lal in Ranjit Singh's rule, the assessment was done directly on the cultivators who were engaged for payment. The zamindars simply enjoyed their perquisites. They were responsible for collections and extension of waste lands, etc.

Malba was shared in relation to *hals* (ploughs). In joint Zamindari villages (*bhaichara* estates), the shares were ancestral. In case, desertion land went to the nearest kin, it would be restored on his return. Amidst all the alterations of cultivation and dispossession, the shares in the common land and in the common liabilities remained the same. The revenue responsibility coincided with actual possession and this was a corollary to *Batai* System. But joint profits and losses were shared in another way. The owner of 1/3rd might only cultivate 1/4th and pay revenue accordingly but he would get 1/3rd of the common stock and bear 1/3rd of the village expenses.

Right of pre-emption

Strangers were jealously excluded from cultivating communities, and what is known as the right of pre-emption was closely watched. Transfers among the members of the community by gift, bequest, mortgages, or sale were not infrequent. The distinction between peasant-proprietor and an occupancy tenant was not a broad one.

Zamindari villages were of various types (Classified by the British as *Khalis* (landlord), *mushtarika* (communal); *pattidari* (mukammil-perfect), na *mukammil, i.e.,* imperfect; *bhaichara, mukammil* and *na mukammil*). In the cis-Sutlej areas, the Superior Zamindar was known as Biswadar and the inferior as Zamindar.

Malik Kabiz—Owners of land not belonging to the Zamindari brotherhood; *malkiyat makbuza*—in the districts of Gujrat, Rawalpindi, Jehlum, Attock, Hazara—Proprietary rights on the part of a person with a well or developed means of irrigation. The *malik* or *waris* descended from the original founder of the village, and the cultivators, where father or grand-father had settled in, were on a common level. *Malikana* dues were not unknown.

Muqaddam—generally a *malik;* where assessments were in cash, the leading men or *maliks* in different communities who were already recognized as *muqaddams* took up the engagements; some influential families were given as much as 1/4th. *Zamindar* or *muqaddam* (as *ala malik*) peasant proprietor (adna malik) occupancy tenants were also recognised by the British.

Simla Hill States—Kangra

The Raja was recognised as the landlord—and the cultivators as *warsis*: A *warsi* had a permanent title in his holding. A good Raja never evicted any one but there was no safeguard against a bad Raja. Practice shows that for generations, the *warsis* have continued.

In Kangra, some members of the ruling family who were the jagirdars also enjoyed *taaluqdari* rights.

South-West Punjab

There were levelling effects of the Sikh rule in Jhelum and Rawalpindi. All the same, there was existence of (a) *zamindars* (b) *muqaddams, riaya* and *chakladars*.

The zamindars with *Haq-i-Zamindari-Haq-i-muqaddami*—when the number of the outsiders became quite large, he would cease to collect such dues from his own clansmen.

Chakdars were peasant proprietors with self-developed lands and means of irrigation.

Zamindar dues—*zamindari, haq-i-muqaddami* and *malikana* were at *adh serman, i.e.,* ½ seer against a maund, *satan pawan,* or seven-quarters of a rupee, *i.e.*, Rs. 1-12.

Chakdar's rate from a tenant in Indus was known as *lich* and *chenab* as *kasur* at *solh satari, i.e.,* 1/17th of the gross produce which might vary from region to region. At some places, *hak-i-kasur* of the *Chakdar* was at 5%, for example, Mianwali District.

Adlapi

The *Adlapi* tenure in South-West Punjab – A man who sinks a well in land which does not belong to him with the owner's permission becomes proprietor of half of the land which it commands. He cultivates half of the land, as in Dera Ghazi Khan and such a tenant who sank well in Jhang and cleared jungle was known as *tardaddar* – hereditary tenure that he would take half and give half to the proprietor.

North-Western Punjab and Hazara

Includes the districts Attock, Jhelum, Rawalpindi, Hazara – *i.e.* between rivers Indus and Jehlum and Jehlum and Chenab. Here zamindars were as *taaluqdars; muqaddams* as *malikan* or *warisan, riaya, malikan qabiz.*

Zamindars and *muqaddans* with rights to receive a percentage on the land revenue as an acknowledgment of ancient claims were also found in many villages.

Pathan Tenures

There were Pathan tribes in the country to the east of Suleiman Hills.

There was partition of the tract by the invading Pathan tribes – The lot of each main sub-division was sometimes called a *Tappa* and described as its *daftar* and the cultivators as *daftaris.* The lot was divided into *Vands* – Here the *maliks* or leading men and even the Khan got no more than any one else in his division but the latter sometimes received lands as *seri* or a free gift from the tribe.

Communal Concept

There was Vesh or periodical redistribution. In Peshawar, Marwats – in Pathan tracts there was exchange of *Tappas* (getting rarer), exchange of villages; and exchange of holdings, known as *Khula* in Marwat. In Gurgaon district, known as *Panapalat,* exchange of whole *Panas* or sub division of estates were confined to some villages in Rewari.

In the Whole of Punjab

(a) Occupancy tenants entitled to hold lands at fixed rates could not be ejected so long as they paid the rents. They could not alienate lands without the consent of proprietors. They had hereditary rights but could not sink well or plant an orchard, known variously as *chapparaband, khudkasht, kadimi, maurusi, haqdar* etc. All *khudh kashta* ryots belonged to this catagory.

(b) *Paikashtkars*—residing in other villages with no rights.

(c) There were some tenants at will.

Revenue Assignments

Under Ranjit Singh, more than 1/3rd of the revenues were assigned to private individuals. It was the natural result of the process by which his power had built up over the 'misls' and the convenience under the old system of (a) administration of assigning the revenues to state servants in lieu of their salaries.

(b) Military tenures—The members of various 'misls' subordinated on the condition of furnishing contingents of horsemen to reinforce the regular army in time of war. It was the same relationship with the Rajput Rajas of the Hills. The Muslim chiefs of West Punjab too were left with some of their territories as their *jagirs* (in line with *watan jagir* of Mughal times, e.g. the Rajas of Mandi and Suket functioned as *Jagirdars*. Sikh Sardars between Beas and Sutlej were reduced to subjection and held their territories on the condition of furnishing horsemen in times of war. Other *jagirdars* of the cis-Sutlej states received their jagirs as rewards for services to the Lahore Darbar.

(c) *Inams*—Jagirs were given to *maliks* or *muqaddams* or *Chaudharis* (in line with the Mughal practice).

(d) Religious and charitable grants were given to Hindu *dharmsalas* and Muslim *takias* and *fakirs, i.e.,* to holy men.

I. *Service grants* were of the following kind:

(a) Military; (b) Civil; (c) Feudal; (d) Household.

II. Pensions—Grants were also given.

III. Religious-Endowments; Charitable grants to holy men.

***Inams of Biloch tumandars* in Dera Ghazi Khan**

Greater part of the revenues were assigned to Biloch tribes who discharged administrative and magisterial functions. They enjoyed the position of *mustajirs, i.e.,* they collected in kind from their tribes the shares of the produce, varying from 1/7th to 1/3rd, which was taken prior to the British rule and they paid into the treasury the cash land revenue assessed upon the villages of their tribes.

Assignments in the Delhi territory were: *altamgha, aima, madad-i maash, tayul,* etc.

Concept of Village Community

In the Central and East Punjab, the villages were still built on traditional lines, the houses of the members of the brotherhood and their descendants being erected close to each other. Such villages were divided into separate parts which were themselves sometimes again sub-divided. In the South-East of the province, the proprietary body (*i.e.,* zamindars etc.) of each village or sub-division of a village claimed to be kinsfolk, their rights in the common land being measured by ancestral shares. Further to the North-West, the communities were often much less homogenous, and whatever may have been the original form of land holding. Under the Sikhs, the land in each man's possession had come to be recognised as the measure of his liabilities and also of his right in any property or profits. In the South-Western districts, while regular village communities were frequently found in the fertile lands fringing the rivers, all trace of these disappeared where the cultivation was dependent on scattered wells beyond the influence of the river. Here, the well was the true unit of property but where the proprietors of several wells were sufficiently close together to be conveniently included within one village boundary, the opportunity was taken to group them into village communities by the British. There were different regions with different qualities of soil and means of irrigation (bearing indigenous, technical names, *i.e., dhur, khadir, nurmotah or mugdah*). *Bhoor* of various categories, *Banjar* lands etc. were with different rates of assessment per bigha of land in cash or kind.

Kankut; Batai and Zabti

The *kharif* and *rabi* crops were frequently assessed by *kankut* either as to extent in bighas or in maunds.

Batai was based on actual measurement or division of produce but the *zabti* crops were always based on and paid for on measurement.

In Ambala, there were *kankut, zabti* or cash payment for sugar cane and cotton crops. Assessment of sugar cane was on each *'Koloo'* or presser. Assessment on a presser working for 24 hours—Rs. 1/8. There were some extra collections by the Zamindars known as *Sewaee Jumma.*

(i) *Kathe i.e.,* saddle taken from the cultivator.

Chapter 15

The Three Battles of Panipat – Their Legacy to Indian History and Culture*

The geographical features of the territories of Sirhind-Kurukshetra-Karnal-Panipat-Delhi have conditioned to a great extent their political destiny, demographic and social structure, economy, language, literature, arts, religions and indeed, the entire culture. Situated in longitude about 114^{0}38 and latitude about 28^{0}15, Panipat-Delhi form a part of the geographical sub-region of the Western part of the Indo-Gangetic plains covering present day Haryana and some parts of Western Uttar Pradesh. Before the territorial changes were effected by the British Government during the course of the 19th century for their addministrative convenience, under the Mughal Government, these territories inclusive of the cis-Sutlej region as well as some Western portions of present day Uttar Pradesh across river Jamuna formed part of *Subah* Delhi which was, as conceded by Abul Fazl in the *Ain-i-Akbari,* conceptually and culturally co-territorial with the boundaries of Haryana. Bounded by the sub-Himalayan ranges in the extreme North at some distance, the Punjab plains extending from Indus to Sutlej in the west, the main Indo-Gangetic plains in the East and the Aravali range and Rajashthan in the South, these territories have always enjoyed a unique strategic position. Foreign invaders from the North-West had to cross Panipat-Delhi before they could proceed towards either the Gangetic plains or Rajasthan. All through the medieval period, the rulers of Delhi and the people of these territories had offered stiff resistance to foreign aggression. This equally explains the settlement and intermingling of many a tribe and people in this region. Commercially, too, Panipat-Delhi always fell on the main trade routes of North and Western parts of India. Above all, the geographical features, flora and fauna have moulded the cultural traits of the people

* Paper Presented at Panipat Seminar at Panipat, 19-20 August, 1997.

of these territories, which have always formed an integral part of larger geographical-cum-cultural region of Haryana.

Apart from the *Mahabharata* war during the ancient period, for the medieval age, the decisive battles of Taraori (1191-1192 A.D.), between Prithviraj Chauhan, the ruler of Ajmer-Delhi and Shahabuddin Muhammed Ghuri which led to the establishment of the Turkish rule in India, the battle of Tarawari (24th December, 1759) lost by the Maratha Chief Dattaji against the Durranis as well as the desecration and destruction of the most sacred Hindu temple of Kurukshetra/ Thanesar at the hands of the foreign invaders, i.e., Mahmud of Ghazni (1014), Amir Timur (1898) and the Mughal Emperor Aurangzeb (1658-1707) fall in the same belt of the Haryana region.

Apparently, it looks rather paradoxical that the Government of Haryana should commemorate the three battles of Panipat (1526, 1556 and 1761 A.D.), which were all lost by the then Indian rulers. But they are hard facts with far reaching effects which cannot be erased from Indian history. In the first battle of Panipat (20th April, 1526 A.D.), the Afghan ruler Ibrahim Lodhi was defeated by Zahiruddin Muhammad Babar resulting in the establishment of the Mughal ruling dynasty in Hindustan. In the second battle (5 November, 1556 A.D.), Himu, the Hindu Minister of Mohammad Adil Shah, the last sur ruler of Delhi was defeated by Bairum Khan, the regent of young ruler Akbar which led to the perpetuation of the Mughal rule in India. The third battle of Panipat (14 January, 1761 A.D.), led to the defeat and disaster of the Marathas, the *defacto* rulers of Delhi on behalf of the *dejure* Mughal monarchs. This resulted in the signal victory of Ahmed Shah Abdali, the alien Afghan ruler of Kabul and the consequent continued cession of the territories of Karnal-Sirhind (*sarkar* Sirhind, *subah* Delhi) as well as the *subahs* of Multan and Punjab to the Durrani ruler of Afghanistan. The Durrani claim over the revenues of these territories lasted till the end of the 18th and early 19th century when the Durrani sovereignty in Multan, Punjab and Kashmir was over-thrown by Maharaja Ranjit Singh and in the cis-Sutlej territories by the English East India Company.

It is equally pertinent to note that Afghan ruler, Sher Shah Suri, who had defeated and driven out Babar's son Humayun out of India, during his short rule (1539-1545) had the unfulfilled desire to build two commemorative monuments on the battle-field of Panipat, one to the Afghan ruler, Ibrahim Lodhi and the other to the celebration of his own victory over the Chaghatai Sultans of the Mughal army. Earlier, in order to commemorate his own victory at Panipat, Babur had built a victory tower comprising the heads of the slain Afghan soldiers and also built a still standing mosque about a mile to the north-east of the town of Panipat (Vide Appendix No. I). During the early 20th century, based on the study of historical records and topographical survey, it was surmised that later on at the third battle of Panipat (1761), the Marathas occupied, more or less, the same ground where Babur had entrenched his army and the British Government erected a monument to mark the scene of Ahmed Shah Abdali's victory. That this was close to Babur's entrenchment at the battle field is borne out by Saiyed Gulam Ali in *Nigar Nama-i-Hind*. However, to commemorate the three battles of Panipat, the Haryana Government has built a war memorial (1982) at *Kala Amb,* about 6 km. from Panipat where the third battle of Panipat (1761) is supposed to have taken place. Now it is proposed to construct a suitable War Museum at this complex. It may, however, be observed that based on the study of historical records, it is feasible to identity and earmark the wide areas and places of battle-field chosen by the Marathas and Ahmad Shah Abdali at and around Panipat, but it is difficult to identify the place where the Maratha General Sadashivrao Bhau fell at the battle-field.

II. (i) As the War Memorial Museum is proposed to be built at Panipat, the very site of the decisive battles fought in the 16th and 18th centuries, it is essential to give a brief history of Panipat, its commercial and strategic importance during the medieval age, its geographical and topographical features, its environment and closeness to river Jamuna, the main *ghats* on the river Jamuna connecting Panipat-Sonepat with the territories across the river (at present in Uttar Pradesh), the Grand Trunk Road (Sher Shah Suri/Mughal Road) and the main canal *(Shah Nahr)* for supply of water to the armed camps, the routes connecting Panipat with Delhi, Saharanpur and Meerut as well as on the East with other places of *Subah* Delhi. In fact, a sketchmap depicting all these aspects may be prepared. For the 16th-18th centuries, all this information can be gathered from the Persian chronicles, the travelogues, 18th century archival documents available at the National Archives, New Delhi, the map of the Canal available at Hyderabad Archives and the late 19th and early 20th century Settlement Reports/District Gazatteers. For the first battle of Panipat, *Babur Nama* is quite informative in this respect (vide Appendix No. II). The relevant pages from the above mentioned sources can be photographed for exhibition in the museum. The cultural aspects of Panipat in the light of history may be presented.

(ii) For the theme in hand, the most important aspect of the museum is the historical source-material which may comprise historical data of varying nature. It may cover archival documents, manuscripts, travelogues, paintings, decorative art comprising costumes, arms-different weapons used in the wars, arms paintings and illustrations as well as numismatics, i.e., coinage etc. As spelt out further, considerable source-material is available for the three battles of Panipat in different archival departments and libraries in India and abroad. It may be difficult at this stage to acquire original documents but to start with photocopies of the relevant portions of the above mentioned sources can be gathered and exhibited in the Museum in a scientific manner.

(iii) For the study of the art of warfare, arms and costumes of the armies of Babur and Ibrahim Lodhi, apart from *Babur Nama,* Zainuddin Khawf's, *Waqiat-i-Baburi,* Khwand Amir's *Habibus Siyar* and later Mughal and Afghan sources as spelt out in Appendix No. III, it is rather essential to cover some of the important central Asian sources dealing with the Timuride and Chagtai traditions. In this respect, the presumed Turki memoirs *(Malfuqat)* and counsels *(Tuzukat)* of Amir Timur as well as Sharafuddin Ali Yazdi's *Zafarnama* (1424-25 A.D.), and some of the Iranian sources dealing with Babur's activities in Central Asia over the Samarkand issue vis a vis the Uzbeks are quite significant.

(iv) The impact of the Central Asian and Ottoman Turkish on art of warfare, on Babur's array of army and the techniques adopted at the battle of Panipat is well confirmed by *Babur Nama*. While the town of Panipat with its suburbs was on the right side of the army, Babur arranged about seven hundred carts joined together with ropes of raw-hide instead of chains and between every two carts, 5 or 6 mantelets were fixed behind which match-lockmen took position. Such carts and match,lockmen were positioned in the front whereas the left and the western sides were covered with ditches and branches. At some distance, cavalry was posted. This arrangement was put under the charge of Ustad Ali-quli who, it seems, had observed the battle of Chaldrian (August, 1514 A.D.), near Tabriz between the Ottomans and the Safvids. Similarly, apart from the arrangement of the army into divisions, i.e., Advance, Centre, both Right and Left,Babur adopted the Central Asian *tulghama* system, i.e., the turning parties at the point of the right wing and left wing and put them under seasoned commanders. Besides the empolyment of the archers, Babur used gun powder muskets and artillery which caused havoc in the army of Ibrahim Lodhi. (For details, see Annexures No. IV & V a). The matter of arming, the mail (battle dress) and the cavalry mounting was also influenced by the Central Asian System. Before the actual battle, Babur even resorted to night-attack *(shabghon)* to checkmate the enemy advance. Ibrahim Lodhi's army arrangement was mostly traditional with divisons into wings, i.e., Front, Right and left with reliance on swordsmen, archers, cavalry and elephant force.

IV. There is no illustrated Turki text of *Babur Nama* available in any library in the world. However, there are four copies of illustrated *Babur Namas* in Persian, earlier translated by Abdur Rahim *Khan-i-Khanan,* which are available at the British Museum (U. K.), Albert Museum, London, State Museum of Eastern Cultures, Moscow, and National Museum, New Delhi. The *Babur Nama* manuscript of National Museum, New Delhi, though belonging to the late 16th century, is somewhat incomplete at the end. All the same, it has two monochrome illustrations depicting scenes of the battle of Panipat. In one illustration, the battle of Panipat is depicted and in another, the rival armies of Ibrahim Lodhi and Babur are engaged in hand-to-hand fight (Nos. 259 and 260) vide M. S. Randhawa, *Paintings of Babur Nama,* National Museum, New Delhi, 1983, pp. 85, 124-125). The features of the Mail and armaments of different categories as well as the mounted cavalry and hooded elephants, the swords, spears in hand to hand fight are clearly discernable. It is not out of place to mention that the details of the Mughal guns, armaments, artillery, cavalry, elephants and infantry, etc. as evolved till Akbar's reign, are available in Abdul Fazl's *Ain-i-Akbari*.

V. For the Museum on the first battle of Panipat, it is rather imperative to prepare a brief life sketch of Babur before and after 1526 A.D. It should narrate the reasons which inspired Babur to invade India. While Babur conquered Hindustan in 1526 A.D., in his fifth expedition, his own brief career alongwith the first four expeditions may as well be narrated for the sake of background (vide-Appendices V & V a). Moreover, the brief sketches of the generals of Babur, who fought the battle of Panipat, may be prepared. Similarly, the biographies of Ibrahim Lodhi and other Afghan nobles involved in the Mughal-Afghan politics leading finally to the battle of Panipat may be attempted. These can be easily work out from the Afghan sources narrated in Appendix No. III.

VI. The details about the second battle of Panipat (5 November, 1556 AD) between Himu, the commander-in-Chief of the Surs and

Bairam Khan, the brief history of the Sur dynasty along with various other aspects of the Afghan regime under the Surs, the dominant position of Himu *baqal* of Rewari and his final defeat at Panipat can be worked out for exhibiting in the Museum from the Afghan Sources narrated in Appendix No. III. Of course, the mail and weaponry of the Mughals vis a vis the Afghan is not very much different than what has been described in the preceeding paras. Of the secondary works, recently a monograph on Himu under the title *Hemchandra Bikermaditya*, authored by late Dr. M. L. Bhargava, was published. Apart from the main contemporary Afghan and Mughal sources utilised, the author claimed to have used some unpublished archival documents pertaining to Himu and the Sur dynasty. All this can be well utilised for the proposed Museum.

VII. In the annals of Indian history, the third battle of Panipat (14 January, 1761) between the Marathas and Ahmad Shah Abdali has been of crucial importance. Huge source-material (Persian, Marathi, Punjabi and English) dealing with multifarious aspects is available. In contrast to the earlier 16th century battles of Panipat, contemporary Persian documentary evidence comprising the Daily News Bulletins *(Akhbarat-i-Darbar-i-Maula),* correspondence between various personalities involved in the politics (1759-1761) and the actual battle, the various Indian chiefs (Hindu, Sikh and Muslim) as well as the contemporary correspondence in Marathi is available at different Archives and Libraries in India (Amritsar, Patiala, New Delhi, Bikaner, Rampur, Lucknow, Sita Mau, Calcutta and Pune) and abroad (U.K). A few monograph on the subject have already been published by eminent Indian historians along with comprehensive bibliographies. A few distinguished historians who deserve special mention are Sardesai, G. S. *(New History of the Marathas),* Vol II, Bombay, 1948, *Selections from the Peshwa Daftar,* Government of Bombay); Sarkar J. N. *(Fall of the Mughal Empire,* Vols. I and II, 1934; and Research Papers published on Ahmed Shah Abdali in '*Islamic Culture*', 1932 and 1933); Srivastava A. L. *(The Maratha-Afghan Diplomatic Tussel on the eve of Panipat,* Sardesai Commemoration Volume, Bombay 1938); Ganda Singh *(Ahmed Shah Abdali,* 1958) and Hari Ram Gupta *(Marathas and Panipat,* Chandigarh, 1961). Of the provincial histories, Maulana Hakim Muhammad Najamual 'Gani's *Tarik-i-Awadh,* Vol. II, 1909-1910, Rampur) with comprehensive bibliography is quite useful. Apart from the sources used by the above mentioned scholars, the present writer B. R. Grover, *(Jassa Singh Ahaluwalia and the 18th Century Punjab*

Polity, New Delhi, 1990 and 'An Analysis of the Contemporary Durrani Revenue Documents and Correspondence pertaining to the Patiala chieftainship *(Zamindari)* during the later half of the 18th century', *Punjab Past and Present,* Patiala, 1990, pp. 196-233) has utilised the hitherto unpublished and unutilised Persian documents relating to the correspondecne between the Kapurthala and Patiala Chiefs and the Durranis, available at the Punjab State Archives, Patiala, National Archives of India New Delhi, and Regional State Archives, Allahabad (U.P.).

The proposed Museum can acquire the photo-copies of the relevant portions of the various above mentioned source materials from the different libraries. However, the particular aspects to be covered are the factors which led to the third battle of Panipat (1761), Shah Waliullah's correspondence with Ahmed Shah Abdali and the formation of the Islamic alliance, i.e., Najibul Daula, the Rohilla chief, Shujauddaula, the Nawab of Awadh under the leadership of Ahmad Shah Abdali vis-a-vis The Marathas (vide Appendix No. VI), the Durrani blockade which disabled the Marathas to get ration supplies from the outside regions for the camp; the formation of the respective Durrani-Maratha armies at Panipat; the qualities of generalship of Ahmad Shah Abdali vis-a-vis Sadashivrao Bhau, the Maratha General and, above all, the consequences which flowed from the Maratha debacle leading to the domination of the Durrani rule in Karnal-Sirhind, cis-Sutlej areas, West Punjab, Multan and Kashmir which lasted till the end of the 18th century/ early 19th century. All research-oriented published material on the above mentioned aspects can be well exhibited in a section of the proposed Museum.

The main lesson to be learnt from the battles of Panipat is that the people of India must keep united as a nation and should take full security measures against any apprehended aggression. It is also proposed that for all the material required for building the War Museum at Panipat, all such Museums like Red Fort, Delhi, State Museum Hyderabad, Salar Gang Museum, Hyderabad and National Museum, New Delhi, may be checked and studied.

Appendix No. I

When after his victory of Panipat, Babur had already become the *padshah* of Hindustan, probably to commemorate his victory, Babur built a grand mosque, popularly known as Baburi Masjid at Panipat. The construction of the mosque was started in A.H. 934 (27th September 1527 to 15th September, 1528) and completed in A.H. 935 (15th September, 1528 to 5th September, 1529 A.D.). Apparently, the construction of the mosque was started at least a year and a half after the battle of Panipat (20 April, 1526). There are three inscriptions on the mosque (vide Maulvi Ashraf Hussain" article, "Inscriptions of Emperor Babur" Epigraphica Indica—An Arabic and Persian Supplement, 1965, pp. 50-51). The first inscription is dated A. H. 934/ 1527-28 and gives the name of the scribe as Malik Salih. The second inscription (in Persian), dated A.H. 935/1528-29 A.D., states that the mosque, the wall and *Chahar-bagh* were completed in A.H. 935/1528-29 by the orders of Shah Babar by one Pahalwal Muhammad, son of Hasan. The third inscription installed above the *mihrab,* which is fragmentory and damaged, simply states that the mosque was constructed by Zahiruddin Muhammad Babar *Gazi Badshah*. Apparently, the inscription was installed only in 1527-28 AD as Babur had assumed the title of *Gazi Badshah* only after the victory at the battle of Kanwa (25th *Jumada* II, A.H. 933/ 29th March, 1527 A.D.), over Rana Sanga of Mewar.

Appendix No. II

As the topic is of crucial importance, it is essential to briefly appraise the historical source in this regard.The most important primary source of information is Babur himself, who in his History, i.e., *Babur Nama,* has given details about his conquest and plundering activities in the country of Kabul (modern Afghanistan), North-Western territories of Hindustan, Punjab and the neighbourhood of Delhi before and after the battle of Panipat (1526).

Zahirud-din Muhammad Babur (Babur-14th February, 1483-26th December, 1530) who after having defeated Ibrahim Lodhi, the ruler of Delhi Sultanate, at the battle of Panipat (7th *Rajab,* A.H. 932/20th April, 1526) became the first Mughal monarch *(padshah)* of Hindustan, wrote his date-wise daily dairy from the 12th year of his age (June, 1494) when he became the ruler of the territory of Farghana (Central Asia) to 1529-30 A.D. (died on 26th December, 1530 A.D.). Of course, as spelt out further, there are numerous lacunae in the events *(waqai)* narrated in the diary/memoirs. Babur wrote his diary narrating the daily events and his activities in the Turki (Chagatay Turkish) text. However, Babur does not call it a mere diary. He claimed to have written his own 'History' comprising the events *(waqai)* of his life-career. Zainuddin of Khawaf, Babur's Courtier who summarised Babur's diary/'History' in the Persian language calls his work as *Waqiat-i-Baburi* (The Events of the life of Babur) or *Tabaqat-i-Baburi*. This work, in fact, is a record of a few months of Babur's campaign (1525-26) and description of Hindustan. On Akbar's command given in AH 995/1587 A.D., Babur's own daughter, Gulbadan Begum, also wrote about the lives and reigns of Babur and Humayun for being used by Abul Fazl in *Akbar Nama* (1593). In her well-known work entitled *Humayun Nama* (written in Persian), she calls the book written by her father comprising the events of his own life *(waqai)* as *Waqia Nama (Waqia Nama-i-Hazrat Badshah Baba am)*. This, it can be briefly put as *Waqia-Nama-i- Babur.* The modern writers have preferred to call Babur's work as his Memoirs/ Autobiography *(Tuzuk),* i.e., *Tuzk-i-Baburi*.

The Turki (Chagatay Turkish) text of Babur's work was translated into Persian language under the title *Waqiat-i-Baburi* (1589) by Abdur Rahim *Khan-i-Khanan* by Akbar's order for the use of this book by Abul Fazl in his well-known work, *Akbar Nama* (1595). Abdur Rahim's *Waqiat-i-Baburi,* as it has reached us today is, in fact, as Mrs. Beveridge correctly remarks a "shrunken amount" of the pure Turki text or "maximum of the dwindled text" of the original translated version. Later on, Mulla Muhammad Qasim Hindu Shah in *Tarikh-i-Firishta* (early 17th century) followed the title given by Abdur Rahim *Khan-i-Khanan* and calls it as *Waqiat-i-Baburi/Risala-i-Waqiat-i-Baburi*.

Appendix No. III

Apart from the aforementioned two significant eye-witness accounts, there are a few contemporary as well as early 17th century Afghan historical chronicles which throw light on the subject. Rizqullah Mustaqi's (1492-1581 A.D.), *Waqiat-i-Mushtaqi,* almpst a contemporary account, Abdul Haqq Delhevi's *Tarikh-i-Haqqi* (AH. 1005/1596-97 A.D.), based on personal eyewitness observation and hearsay; Ahmad Yadgeir's *Tarikh-i-Salatin-i-Afghana* (a little later than AH. 1001-2/ 1592-94 A.D.), Niamatullah's *Makhzan-i-Afghana* (AH, 1018-1021/ 1609-1612 A.D.); Abdullah's *Tarikh-i-Daudi* (written in early Jahangir's reign) while dealing with the Lodhi period narrate many an anccdote and, at times, while describing Babur's campaigns against Hindustan do mention about his plundering activities as well as the Afghan military system. In this respect, Ahmed Yadgar's *Tarikh-i-Salatin-in-Afghana* is quite significant as it not only dialates on the intrigues on the part of Daulat Khan (Governor of Punjab) and his son Dilwar Khan with Babur against Ibrahim Lodhi, the ruler of Delhi, but also narrates plunder and rapine on Babur's part in the Punjab and the territories of Dipalpur/Multan in 1520 and 1525-26 A.D.

In addition to the above Afghan sources, the Mughal sources, i.e., Zainuddin Khwafi (died in A.H. 940/ 1533-34), a courtier and *sadr* of Babur, poetically called Wafai's *Tarikh-i-Baburi/Tabaqat-i-Baburi* covering the period from 1st *Safar* AH. 932/1525 A.D. when Babur left Kabul on his fifth and last expedition against Hindustan till 15th Juma I AH. 933/ 1526 A.D., (copied form the author's copy in AH. 998/1589 A.D.), Khwand Amir's *Habibus Siyar* (AH. 927/1521-AH. 935/1528-29), Mirza Haider Dughlat's, (cousin of Babur, died AH. 958/1551 A.D.), *Tarikh-i-Rashidi* (A.H. 952/1546 A.D.); Gulbadan Begum's (daughter of Babur) *Humayun Nama; Tarikh-i-Akbari/Tarikh-i-Arif Qandhari* (A.H. 987/1579 A.D.); Alaudaula's *Nafais ul Maasar* (AH. 973/1565 A.D., Yahya bin Abdul Latiful Husayin ul Qazwini's *Lubb-ut-Tawarikh* (1551 A.D.—covering the reigns of Babur and Humayun only); Abul Fazl's *Akbar Nama* (1595 A.D.), and Muhammad

Kasim Hindu Shah Firishta's *Tarikh-i Firishta/Gulshan-i Ibrahim* (early 17th century, died around 1612 or 1623 A.D.), and an early 18th century work titled *Muntakhab al Lubab* (A.H. 1144/1731 A.D.), by Khwafi Khan do fill up some of the gaps in the activities of Babur especially during the years of the campaigns against Hindustan not covered in the *Babur Nama*.

Appendix No. IV

There is no denying the fact that having passed through a multitude of vicissitudes, losing and winning a battle all through his life, Babur had become quite a seasoned soldier in the art of warfare. The adoption of the gunpower and artillery from the Ottoman-Turkish Empire as well as the Central Asian *tulughama* system (i.e. flanking wings in the array of the army for pincer movement) in both the decisive battles in India (Panipat in April, 1526 A.D., and Kanwa in March, 1527 A.D.), were the major factors for his victory against Ibrahim Lodhi and Rana Sanga of Mewar which led to the establishment of his rule in India. In his Memoirs, Babur has given details about the array of his own troops and the drawbacks in the arrangement of the armies of his adversaries, i.e. Ibrahim Lodhi and Rana Sanga. All the same, after the battle of Panipat, Babur boasts that he conquered the realm of Hindustan with total army of 12,000 men as against Ibrahim Lodhi's army of 1,00,000 men and 1,000 elephants. However, the Afghan sources put Ibrahim Lodh's army at lesser number with only 500 elephants. That with vast resources at his command, as commented by Babur, Ibrahim Lodhi could have mobilised an army of 5 lakhs, is a hypothetical premise.

In fact, in order to show his superiority as a general, Babur has deliberately underestimated the strength of his own army as against the estimated much larger army of Ibrahim Lodhi. According to his own earlier statement, having crossed the river Indus (on 29th December, 1525 A.D.), he entered the plains of Hindustan with an army of 12, 000 men. Thereafter, by the beginning of April 1526 A.D., *enroute* from Indus to Punjab and the vicinity of Delhi, he had suppressed many local chiefs and big Zamindars and on the latter's submission, in accordance with medieval practice, must have enlisted their militias in his army. The Afghan sources also throw light on this subject. Ahmed Yadgar, the author of *Tarikh-i-Salatin-i-Afghana* (AH. 1001-2/1592-94 A.D.), comments that after his agreement with Daulat Khan, Babur ordered fresh troops to be enlisted, and by the time he reached Lahore, he was surrounded by numerous army, and the Punjab fell into the hands of the Chaghatai nobles. In fact, many other chiefs and Zamindars would have joined Babur's own army at the various places mentioned by him before reaching Panipat. Babur states that after the capture of Milwat (Malot) on 2nd-3rd January, 1526 A.D., Ismail Khan, son of Ali Khan, i.e., grandson of Daulat Khan (Governor of Punjab), along with others chiefs joined him with their armies. Similarly, thereafter, the local chiefs and Zamindars of Kahlur (Bilaspur), Ropar, Karnal, Sirhind, Samana, Hissar-Firoza, Ambala etc. after suppression joined the Mughal forces. According to the statement of Ahmad Yadgar, the author of *Tarikh-i-Salatin-i-Afghans,* at the battle of Panipat (20th April, 1526), the regular Mughal army was no less than 24,000 strong while that of Sultan Ibrahim numbered 50,000 men and 2,000 war elephants. Clearly, Babur's army was much larger than just 12,000 men who had come with him from Kabul and crossed the river Indus in December, 1525 A.D. Still, in order to show his own superiority as a general in the art of warfare, Babur has deliberately undermined the factual position.

Appendix No. IVa

Babur-Nama

(Memoirs of Babur)

Translated from the original Turki Text of Zahiru'd-din Muhammad Babur Padshah Ghazi by Annette Susannah Beveridge

(t. Preparations for battle.)[1]

While we were merching on in array of right, left and centre, the army was numbered;[2] it did not count up to what had been estimated.

At our next camp it was ordered that every man in the army should collect carts, each one according to his circumstances. Seven hundred carts *(arāba)* were brought[3] in. The order given to Ustād 'Ali-qulī was that these carts should be joined together in Ottoman[4] fashion, but using ropes of raw hide instead of chains, and that between every two carts, 5 or 6 mantelets should be fixed, behind which the matchlockmen were to stand to fire. To allow of collecting all appliances, we delayed 5 or 6 days in that camp. When everything was ready, all the begs with such braves as had experience in military affairs were summoned to a General Council where opinion found decision at this :-Pānī-pat[5] is there with its crowded houses and suburbs. It would be on one side of us; our other sides must be protected by carts and mantelets behind which our foot and matchlockmen would stand. With so much settled we marched forward, halted one night on the way, and reached Pānī-pat on Thursday the last day (29th) of the second Jumāda (April 12th).

(u. The opposed forces.)

On our right was the town of Pānī-pat with its suburbs; in front of us were the carts and mantelets we had prepared; on our left and elsewhere were ditch and branch. At distances of Fol. 264*b*. an arrow's flight[6] sally-places were left for from 100 to 200 horsemen.

Some in the army were very anxious and full of fear. Nothing recommends anxiety and fear. For why? Because what God has fixed in eternity cannot be changed. But though this is so, it was no reproach to be afraid and anxious. For why? Because those thus anxious and afraid were there with a two or three months' journey between them and their homes; our affair was with a foreign tribe and people; none knew their tongue, nor did they know ours :-

A wandering band, with mind awander;

In the grip of a tribe, a tribe unfamiliar.[7]

People estimated the army opposing us at 100,000 men; Ibrāhīm's elephants and those of his amīrs were said to be about 1000. In his hands was the treasure of two forbears.[8] In Hindūstān, when work such as this has to be done, it is customary to pay out money to hired retainers who are known as *b : d-hindī.*[9] If it had occurred to Ibrāhim to do this, he might have had another *lak* or two of troops. God brought it right ! Ibrāhim could neither content his braves, nor share out his treasure. How should he content his braves, when he was ruled by avarice and had a craving insatiable to pile coin on coin? He was an unproved brave[10]; he provided nothing for his military operations, he perfected nothing, nor stand, nor move, nor fight.

In the interval at Pānī-pat during which the army was preparing defence on our every side with cart, ditch and branch, Darwīsh-i-Muḥammad *Sārbān* had once said to me, "With such precautions taken, how is it possible for him to come?" Said I, " Are you likening him to the Aūzbeg khāns and sulṭāns?

In what of movement under arms or of planned operations is he to be compared with them?" God brought it right ! Things fell out just as I said !

> *(Author's note on the Aūzbeg chiefs).* When I reached Ḥiṣār in the year I left Samarkand (918 AH.-1512 A.D.), and all the Aūzbeg khāns and sulṭāns gathered and came against us, we brought the families and the goods of the Mughūls and soldiers into the Ḥiṣār suburbs and fortified by closing the lanes. As those khāns and sulṭāns were experienced in equipment, in planned operations, and in resoulte resistance, they saw from our fortification of Ḥiṣār that we were determined on life or death within it, saw they could not count on taking it by assault and, therefore, retired at once from near Nūndāk of Chaghāniān.

(v. Preliminary encounters)

During the 7 or 8 days we lay in Pānī-pat, our men used to go, a few together, close up to Ibrāhim's camp, rain arrows down on his massed troops, cut off and bring in heads. Still he made no move; nor did his troops sally out. At length, we acted on the advice of several

Hindūstānī well-wishers and sent out 4 or 5000 men to deliver a night-attack on his camp, the leaders of it being Mahdī Khwāja, Muḥammad Sl. Mīrzā, 'Ādil Sulṭān, Khusrau, Shāh Mīr Ḥusain, Sl. Junaid *Barlās,* 'Abdu'l-'azīz the Master of the Horse, Muḥ. 'Alī *Jang-jang,* Qūtlūq-qadam, Treasurer Walī, Khalīfa's Muḥibb-i-'alī, Pay-master Muḥammad, Jān Beg and Qarā-qūzī. It being dark, they were not able to act together well, and, having scatterd, could effect nothing on arrival. They stayed near Ibrāhīm's camp till dawn, when the nagarets sounded and troops of his came out in array with elephants. Though our men did not do their work, they got off safe and sound; not a man of them was killed, though they were in touch with such a mass of foes. One arrow pierced Muḥ. 'Alī *Jang-jang's* leg; though the wound was not mortal, he was good-for-nothing on the day of battle.

On hearing of this affair, I sent off Humāyūn and his troops to go 2 or 3 miles to meet them, and followed him myself with the rest of the army in battle-array. The party of the night-attack joined him and came back with him. The enemy making no further advance, we returned to camp and dismounted. That night a false alarm fell on the camp; for some 20 minutes (one *garī*) there were uproar and call-to-arms; the disturbance died down after a time.

(w. Battle of Pānī-pat.[11]*)*

(April 20th) On Friday the 8th of Rajab,[12] news came, when it was light enough to distinguish one thing from another *(farṣ-waqtī)* that the enemy was advancing in fighting-array. We at once put on mail,[13] armed and mounted.[14] Our right was Humāyūn, Khwāja Kalān, Sulṭān Muḥammad *Dūldāī,* Hindū Beg, Treasurer Walī and Pīr-qulī *Sīstānī;* our left was Muḥammad Sl. Mīrzā, Mahdī Khwāja, 'Ādil Sulṭān, Shāh Mīr Ḥusain, Sl. Junaid *Barlās,* Qūtlūq-qadam, Jān Beg, Pay-master Muḥammad, and Shah Ḥusain (of) Yāragī *Mughūl Ghānchī (?).*[15] The right hand of the centre[16] was Chīn-tīmūr Sulṭān, Sulaimān Mīrzā,[17] Muḥammadī Kūkūldāsh, Shāh Manṣūr *Barlās,* Yūnas-i-'alī, Darwīsh-i-muhammad *Sārbān* and 'Abdu'l-lāh the librarian. The left of the centre was Khalīfa, Khwāja Mīr-i-mīrān, Secretary Aḥmadī, Tardī Beg (brother) of Qūj Beg, Khalīfa's Muḥibb-i-'alī and Mīrzā Beg Tarkhān. The advance was Khusrau Kūkūldāsh and Muḥ. 'Alī *Jang-jang.* 'Abdu'l-'azīz the Master of the Horse was posted as the reserve. For the turning-party (*tūlghuma*) at the point of the right wing,[18] we fixed on Red Walī and Malik Qāsim (brother) of Bābā *Qashqa,* with their Mughūls; for the turning-party at the point of the left wing, we arrayed Qarā-qūzī, Abū'l-muḥammad the lance-player, Shaikh Jamāl *Bārīn's* Shaikh 'Alī

Mahndī (?) and Tīngrī-bīrdī *Bashaghī (?) Mughūl;* these two parties, directly the enemy got near, were to turn his rear, one from the right, the other from the left.

When the dark mass of the enemy first came in sight, he seemed to incline towards our right; 'Abdu'l-'azīz, who was the right-reserve, was sent therefore to reinforce the right. From the time that Sl. Ibrāhīm's blackness first appeared, he moved swiftly, straight for us, without a check, until he saw the dark mass of our men, when his pulled up and, observing our formation and array,[19] made as if asking, "To stand or not? To advance or not?" They could not stand; nor could they make their former swift advance.

Our orders were for the turning-parties to wheel from right and left to the enemy's rear, to discharge arrows and to engage in the fight; and for the right and left (wings) to advance and join battle with him. The turning-parties wheeled round and began to rain arrows down. Mahdī Khwāja was the first of the left to engage; he was faced by a troop having an elephant with it; his men's flights of arrows forced it to retire. To reinforce the left I sent Secretary Aḥmadī and also Qūj Beg's Tardī Beg and Khalīfa's Muhibb-i-'alī. On the right also there was some stubborn fighting. Orders were given for Muḥammadī Kūkūldāsh, Shāh Manṣūr *Barlās,* Yūnas-i-'alī and 'Abdu'l-lāh to' engage those facing them in front of the centre. From that same position Ustād 'Alī-qulī made good discharge of *firingī* shots.[20]

References

1. *fars-waqtī,* when there is light enough to distinguish one object from another.
2. *dīm kūrūldī* (Index *s. n. dīm).* Here, the L. & E. *Memoirs* inserts an explanatory passage in Persian about the *dīm.* It will have been in one of the *Wāqi'at-i-bāburī MSS.* Erskine used; it is in Muḥ, *Shīrāzī's* lithograph copy of the Udaipūr Codes (p. 173). It is not in the Turkī text or in all the MSS. of the Persian translation. Manifestly, it was entered at a time when Babūr's term *dīm kūrūldī* requires explanation in Hindustan. The writer of it himself does not make details clear; he says only, "It is manifest that people declare (the number) after counting the mounted army in the way agreed upon amongst them, with a whip or a bow held in the hand." This explanation suggests that in the march-past the troops were measured off as so many bow-or whip-length (Index *s.n. dīm.*).
3. These *arāba* may have been the baggage-carts of the army and also carts procured on the spot. Erskine omits *(Memoirs* p. 304) the words which show how many carts were collected and from whom. Doubtless, it would be through not having these circumstances in his mind that he took the

arāba for gun-carriages. His incomplete translation, again, led Stanley Lane-Poole to write an interesting note in his *Bābur* (p. 161) to support Erskine against de Courteille (with whose rendering mine agrees) by quoting the circumstance that Humāyūn had 700 guns at Qanauj in 1540 A.D. It must be said in opposition to his support of Erskine's "gun-carriages" that there is no textual or circumstantial warrant for supposing Bābur to have had guns, even if made in parts, in such number as to demand 700 gun-carriages for their transport. What guns Bābur had at Pānī-pat will have been brought from his Kābul base; if he had acquired any, say from Lāhore, he would hardly omit to mention such an important reinforcement of his armament; if he had brought many guns on carts from Kābul, he must have met with transit-difficulties harassing enough to chronicle, while he was making that long journey from Kābul to Pānī-pat, over passes, through skirt-hills and many fords. The elephants he had in Bīgrām may have been his transport for what guns he had; he does not mention his number at *Pānī-pat;* he makes his victory a bow-man's success; he can be read as indicating that he had two guns only.

4. These Ottoman (text, *Rūmī,* Roman) defences Ustād 'Alī-qulī may have seen at the battle of Chāldirān fought some 40 leagues from Tābrīz between Sl. Salīm *Rūmī* and Shāh Isma'īl *Safawī* on Rajab 1st 920 A.H. (Aug. 22nd 1514 A.D.) Of this battle, Khwān-amīr gives a long account, dwelling on the effective use made in it of chained carts and palisades (*Habību's-siyar* iii, part 4, p. 78; *Akbar-nāma* trs. i, 241).
5. Is this the village of the Pānī Afghāns ?
6. Index *s. n.* arrow.
7. *Pareshān jam'ī u jam'ī pareshān;*

   Giriftār qaumī u qaumī 'ajā'ib.

   These two lines do not translate easily without the context of their original place of occurrence. I have not found their source.
8. *i. e.* of his father and grandfather, Sikandar and Buhlūl.
9. As to the form of this word the authoritative MSS. of the Turki text agree and with them also numerous good ones of the Persian translation. I have made careful examination of the word because it is replaced or explained here and there MSS. by *s : hb : ndī,* the origin of which is said to be obscure. The sense of *b : d-hindī* and of *s : hb : ndī* is the same, *i.e.* irregular levy. The word, as Bābur wrote, it must have been understood by earlier Indian scribes of both the Turkī and Persian texts of the *Bābur-nāma.* Some light on its correctness may be thought given by Hobson Jobson (Crooke's ed., p. 136) *s. n.* Byde or Bede Horse, where the word Byde is said to be an equivalent of *pindārī, lūtī,* and *qāzzāq,* raider, plunderer, so that Bābur's word *b : d-hindī* may mean *qāzzāq* of Hind. Wherever I have referred to the word in many MSS., it is pointed to read *b : d,* and not *p : d,* thus affording no warrant for understanding *pad,* foot, foot-man,

infantry, and also negativing the spelling *bīd, i.e.,* with a long vowel as in *Byde.*

It may be noted here that Muḥ *Shīrāzī* (p. 174) substituted *s : hb : ndī* for Bābur's word and that this led our friend the late William Irvine to attribute mistake to de Courteille who follows the Turkī text *(Army of the Mughūls,* p. 66 and *Mémoirs* ii, 163.

10. *bī tajarba yīgīt aīdī* of which the sense may be that Bābur ranked Ibrāhim, a solider, with a brave who has not yet proved himself deserving of the rank of beg. It cannot mean that he was a youth *(yīgīt)* without experience of battle.

11. Well-known are the three decisive historical battles fought near the town of Pānī-pat, *viz.* those of Bābur and Ibrāhim in 1526, of Akbar and Himū in 1556, and of Aḥmad *Abdālī* with the Mahratta Confederacy in 1761. The following lesser particulars about the battle-field are not so frequently mentioned :— *(i)* that the scene of Bābur's victory was long held to be haunted, Badāyūnī himself, passing it at dawn some 62 years later, heard with dismay the din of conflict and the shouts of the combatants; *(ii)* that Bābur built a (perhaps commemorative) mosque one mile to the n. e. of the town; *(iii)* that one of the unaccomplished desires of Sher Shāh *Sūr,* the conqueror of Bābur's son Humāyūn, was to raise two monuments on the battle-field of Pānī-pat, one to Ibrāhīm, the other to those Chaghatāī sulṭāns whose martyrdom he himself had brought about; *(iv)* that in 1910 A.D., the British Government placed a monument to mark to scene of Shāh *Abdālī's* victory of 1761 A.D. This monument would appear, from Sayyid Ghulam-i-'ali's *Nigār-nāma-i-hind,* to stand close to the scene of Bābur's victory also, since the Mahrattas were entrenched as he was outside the town of Pānī-pat. (Cf. E. & D. viii, 401).

12. This is important date is omitted from the L. & E. *Memoirs.*

13. This wording will cover armour of man and horse.

14. *ātlāndūk,* Pers. trs.*sūwār shudīm.* Some later oriental writers locate Bābur's battle at two or more miles from the town of Pānī-pat, and Babūr's word *ātlānduk* might imply that his cavalry rode forth and arrayed outside his defences, but his narrative allows of his delivering attack, through the wide sally-ports, after arraying behind the carts and mantelets which checked his adversary's swift advance. The Mahrattas, who may have occupied the same ground as Bābur, fortified themselves more strongly than he did, as having powerful artillery against them. Aḥmad Shāh *Abdalī's* defence against them was an ordinary ditch and *abbattis,* [Bābur;s ditch and branch,] mostly of *dhāk* trees (*Butea frondosa*), a local product Bābur also is likely to have used.

15. The preceding three words seem to distinguish this Shāh Ḥusain from several others of his name and may imply that he was the son of *Yāragī Mughūl Ghānchī* (Index and I.O. 217 f. 184*b* l. 7).

16. For Bābur's terms *vide* f. 209*b*.
17. This is Mīrzā Khān's son, *i.e.*, Wais *Mīrān-shāhī's*.
18. A dispute for this right-hand post of honour is recorded on f. 100*b*, as also in accounts of Culloden.
19. *tartīb u yāsāl,* which may include,as Erskine took it to do, the carts and mantelets; of these however, Ibrāhīm can hardly have failed to hear before he rode out of camp.
20. f. 217*b* and note; Irvine's *Army of the Indian Mughuls,* p. 133. Here, Erskine notes (*Mems.,* p. 306) "The size of these artillery at this time is very uncertain. The word *firingī* is now (1826 AD.) used in the Deccan for a swivel. At the present day, *zarb-zan* in common usage is a small species of swivel. Both words in Bābur's time appear to have been used for field-cannon." (For an account of guns, intermediate in date between Bābur and Erskine, *see* the *Āyīn-i-akbarī*. Cf. f. 264 n. on the carts (*arāba*)).

Appendix No. V

Zahiruddin Mohammad Babur, the first ruler of the Mughal dynasty in India is a very controversial personality in the medieval historiography. He hailed from small territorial state of Farghana with capital at Andijan situated in Central Asia in the region of Trans-Oxiana (Mawaraun-nahr-covered by modern Uzbekistan and part of Tajikistan) i. e. to the west of Kashghar and east of Samarkand. Babur claimed his family in the lineage of Timur Beg/Amir Timur/Tomarlane (1335-1405 A.D.), and through his father Umar Shaikh Mirza, he inherited the chieftainship of Farghana and became its ruler in AH. 899/June, 1494 A.D., at the age of twelve. As Babur claimed other territories of the Timur family, he had an incessant conflict with the Uzbeks and their chief Shaibani Khan over Samarkand. But after he was ultimately defeated and ousted from Samarkand (1500-1501 A.D.), Babur bacame virtually a destitute and homeless. Most of the empire of Timur came under the domination of the Uzbek Khanate and the Safavid Empire (of Iran) which were powerful enough to defend their respective territories. The only alternative with Babur was to try his fortune at the expense of the weak dynasties of Kabul and North-Western portions of Hindustan which too had once formed a part of the Timuride empire. As such, staking his Timuride claim, Babur invaded and captured Kabul replacing the Arghun dynasty in October, 1504 A.D.

There is a gap in the *Babur-Nama* for a prolonged period, i.e., w.e.f. 25th January, 1520 A.D., to 17th October, 1525 A.D. However, Babur claims that his December, 1525-April, 1526 A.D., campaign in which he won the battle of Panipat (20th April, 1526 A.D.), was his fifth and last expedition against Hindustan.

As recorded by Babur himself, he had set his mind on the conquest of Hindustan ever since he occupied Kabul in October, 1504 A.D. Thereafter, he made two moves against Hindustan in 1505 A.D., and 1507-08 A.D. but never crossed river Sindh and returned to Kabul.

According to Babur's concept, the North-West boundary of Hindustan started with Behra (in Sindh Sagar *Doab*) which, infact, at that time was the North-Western territorial boundary of the Lodhi kingdom as well. It was only in his 1519 A.D. campaign that Babur crossed river Sindh for the first time and occupied Behra, Kushab and Chinaut etc., i.e., the Chanhat Doab region of the Punjab. Later on, there is a gap in the *Babur Nama* w. e. f. 25th January, 1520 A.D., to 17th October, 1525 A.D. As such, apparently the next three campaigns of Babur in Hindustan fall during this gap period. As analysed from the internal evidence of the *slokas* (hymns) of Gur Nanak Dev recorded in the *Adi-Granth* (1604 A.D.), as well as *Akbar Nama* and few early 17th century Mughal sources, it is evident that Babur led these campaigns against Hindustan in the years 1520, 1521 and 1524 A.D.

Index